# 1 MONTH OF
# FREE
# READING

## at

## www.ForgottenBooks.com

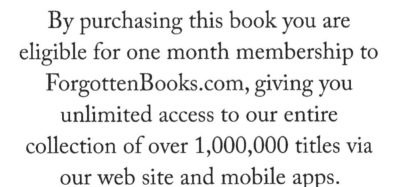

By purchasing this book you are
eligible for one month membership to
ForgottenBooks.com, giving you
unlimited access to our entire
collection of over 1,000,000 titles via
our web site and mobile apps.

To claim your free month visit:

www.forgottenbooks.com/free477998

ISBN 978-0-484-38725-5
PIBN 10477998

# "RAILWAY FREIGHT RATES AND POOLING."

# HEARINGS

BEFORE THE

/ S. Co ress,

# COMMITTEE ON INTERSTATE COMMERCE,

## UNITED STATES SENATE,

HAVING UNDER CONSIDERATION THE BILLS (S. 3521) "TO ENLARGE THE JURISDICTION
AND POWERS OF THE INTERSTATE COMMERCE COMMISSION," INTRODUCED
IN THE SENATE FEBRUARY 4, 1902, BY MR. ELKINS; AND (S. 3575)
"TO AMEND AN ACT ENTITLED 'AN ACT TO REGULATE
COMMERCE,' APPROVED FEBRUARY 4, 1887, AND ALL
ACTS AMENDATORY THEREOF," INTRODUCED
FEBRUARY 5, 1902, BY MR. NELSON.

## VOLUME I.

WASHINGTON:
GOVERNMENT PRINTING OFFICE.
1902.

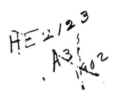

57th CONGRESS.

# INTERSTATE COMMERCE COMMITTEE.

## SENATE OF THE UNITED STATES.

STEPHEN B. ELKINS, of West Virginia.
SHELBY M. CULLOM, of Illinois.
NELSON W. ALDRICH, of Rhode Island.
JOHN KEAN, of New Jersey.
JONATHAN P. DOLLIVER, of Iowa.
JOSEPH B. FORAKER, of Ohio.
MOSES E. CLAPP, of Minnesota.
JOSEPH H. MILLARD, of Nebraska.
BENJAMIN R. TILLMAN, of South Carolina.
ANSELM J. McLAURIN, of Mississippi.
EDWARD W. CARMACK, of Tennessee.
MURPHY J. FOSTER, of Louisiana.
THOMAS M. PATTERSON, of Colorado.

II

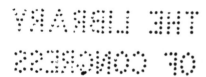

# TABLE OF CONTENTS.

———

*2. 0*

[S. 3521, Fifty-seventh Congress, first session.]

A BILL To enlarge the jurisdiction and powers of the Interstate Commerce Commission.

1    *Be it enacted by the Senate and House of Representatives of the United States of*
2 *America in Congress assembled,* That any definite order made by the Interstate
3 Commerce Commission after hearing and determination had on any petition
4 hereafter presented pursuant to section thirteen of an act entitled "An act to
5 regulate commerce," approved February fourth, eighteen hundred and eighty-
6 seven, declaring any existing rate or rates in said petition complained of, for the
7 carriage of any given article or articles, person or persons, or any regulation or
8 practice affecting such rates, to be unjustly discriminative or unreasonable,
9 and declaring what rate, regulation, or practice affecting such rate for the
10 future, in substitution, would be just and reasonable, shall become operative
11 and be observed by the party or parties against whom the same shall be
12 made, within thirty days after notice; or in case of proceeding for review as
13 hereinafter provided, then within forty days after notice; but the same may
14 at any time be modified, suspended, or revoked by the Commission, but shall
15 in no case continue in force and be obeyed beyond the period of one year
16 from the day the same becomes originally operative and is observed. If
17 such substituted rate shall be a joint one, and the carriers parties to that rate
18 shall be unable to agree upon the apportionment thereof among themselves
19 within ten days after any such order shall become operative, then the Com-
20 mission may declare as part of its order what would be a just and reason-
21 able proportion of such rate to be received by each carrier. Such order
22 as to its justness, reasonableness, and lawfulness, whether in respect to the rate,
23 regulation of practice complained of, or that prescribed in substitution therefor,
24 or the apportionment of a joint rate, or otherwise, shall be reviewable by any
25 circuit court of the United States for any district through which any portion of
26 the road of the carrier shall run, to which a petition filed on its equity side shall
27 be first presented by any party interested. Pending such review the said order
28 shall be suspended unless upon application to and hearing by said court it shall
29 be otherwise ordered; said court and the Supreme Court in case of appeal may,
30 at any time, upon application and notice, suspend or revoke the said order. The
31 several circuit courts of the United States are hereby invested with full jurisdic-
32 tion and powers in the premises, including the issuance and pursuit of the neces-
33 sary process to secure appearance of the parties. The court shall also direct
34 notice to the Commission of the filing of said petition; whereupon it shall be the
35 duty of the Commission, within ten days after the receipt thereof, to cause to be filed

1 in said court, duly certified, a complete copy of its entire record, including peti-
2 tions, answers, testimony, report, and opinion of the Commission, order, and all
3 other papers whatsoever in connection therewith.  The court shall thereupon
4 proceed to hear the same either upon the petition, record, and testimony returned
5 by the Commission; or, in its discretion, may, upon the application of either
6 party, and in such manner as it shall direct, cause additional testimony to be
7 taken; and thereupon if said court shall be of the opinion that said order was
8 made under some error of law, or is, upon the facts, unjust or unreasonable, it
9 shall suspend or revoke the same by appropriate decree; otherwise said order
10 shall be affirmed.  Any party to the cause may appeal to the Supreme Court of
11 the United States within thirty days of the rendition of any final decree of said
12 court, which court shall proceed to hear and determine the same in due course
13 without regard to whether the one year hereinbefore limited for the continu-
14 ance of said order shall have expired or not.
15    Sec. 2.  That it shall be lawful for any two or more common  carriers  to
16 arrange between and among themselves for the establishment or maintenance of
17 rates.  It shall also be lawful for such carriers to agree, by contract in writing,
18 filed with the Interstate Commerce Commission, upon the division of their
19 traffic or earnings, or both; and upon the complaint by petition or any party
20 interested that any such contract so filed unjustly and unlawfully affects any
21 person or persons, community or communities, it shall be the duty of the Com-
22 mission to promptly investigate the matters so complained of in such manner
23 and by such means as it shall deem proper, and make report in writing with
24 respect thereto, which report shall include the findings of fact upon which the
25 conclusions of the Commission are based, and be entered of record.  If such
26 findings sustain in any material particular the allegations of said petition, then it
27 shall be the duty of said Commission to make an order either annulling said
28 contract after thirty days' notice, or directing that the said contract and the
29 practices thereunder, in the respects found to be unjust and unlawful, shall be
30 changed in the manner prescribed in the order.  Should such requirements of
31 the Commission as to changes be not observed by the carriers, and written
32 acceptance thereof be not filed with the Commission within thirty days after
33 notice, then said contract filed as aforesaid shall be annulled.  Any such order
34 shall be subject to all the provisions of section one of this act with respect to
35 definitive orders made upon petitions presented pursuant to section thirteen of
36 an act entitled "An act to regulate commerce," approved February fourth,
37 eighteen hundred and eighty-seven.
38    Sec. 3.  That if any party bound thereby shall refuse or neglect to obey or per-
39 form any order of the Commission mentioned in section one or secton two of this
40 act at any time while the same is in force as provided by said section, obedience
41 and performance thereof shall be summarily enforced by writ of injunction or
42 other proper process, mandatory or otherwise, which shall be issued by any cir-
43 cuit court of the United States upon petition of said Commission, accompanied by a
44 certified copy of the order alleged to be violated, and evidence of the violation
45 alleged; and in addition thereto the offending party shall be subject to a penalty

1 of ten thousand dollars, which, together with costs of suit, shall be recoverable
2 by said Commission by action of debt in any circuit court of the United States,
3 and when so recovered shall be for the use of the United States. Where, how-
4 ever, any order made by the Commission shall involve the rate on traffic passing
5 in part over the line or lines of any railroad company operating in any foreign
6 country, and passing in part over lines of railroad companies operating within
7 the United States, or shall involve the usages of such foreign road with respect
8 to such traffic, then in case such order shall not be observed it shall be lawful
9 for the Commission, or the court having jurisdiction, in addition to the other
10 remedies herein provided, to enforce the order against the traffic so passing in
11 part through a foreign country and in part through the United States, by suspen-
12 sion of the movement thereof within the United States, save upon the condition
13 that the terms of the order shall be complied with.
14 Sec. 4. That anything done or omitted to be done by a corporation common
15 carrier, subject to the act to regulate commerce, which, if done or omitted by
16 any lessee, trustee, receiver, officer, agent, or representative of such corporation,
17 would constitute a misdemeanor under said act, shall be held to be a misde-
18 meanor by such corporation, and upon conviction thereof it shall be subject to
19 like penalties as are prescribed in said act with reference to individuals, except
20 as such penalties are herein changed. The willful failure upon the part of any
21 carrier subject to said act to file and publish the tariffs of rates and charges as
22 required by said act, or strictly to observe such tariffs until changed according
23 to law, shall be a misdemeanor, and upon conviction thereof the individual or
24 corporation offending shall be subject to a fine not less than one thousand dol-
25 lars nor more than twenty thousand dollars for each offense; and the willful
26 complicity upon the part of any person owning or interested in the traffic to
27 which any other rate shall be given than those prescribed in said tariffs shall
28 likewise constitute a misdemeanor, and, upon conviction, shall subject the
29 offender to the like penalties last hereinbefore prescribed with reference to the
30 carrier. In all convictions occurring after the passage of this act, for offenses
31 under said act to regulate commerce (whether committed before or after the
32 passage of this act), or for offenses under this section, no penalty shall be
33 imposed on the convicted party other than the fine prescribed by law, imprison-
34 ment wherever now prescribed as part of the penalty being hereby abolished.
35 Sec. 5. That in any proceeding for the enforcement of the provisions of the
36 statutes relating to interstate commerce, whether such proceedings be instituted
37 before the Interstate Commerce Commission or be commenced originally in any
38 circuit court of the United States, it shall be lawful to include as parties all per-
39 sons, in addition to the carrier interested in or affected by the rate, regulation,
40 or practice under consideration, and inquiries, investigations, orders, and decrees
41 may be made with reference to and against such additional parties in the same
42 manner, to the same extent and subject to the same provisions, as is or shall be
43 authorized by law with respect to carriers.
44 Sec. 6. That whenever the Interstate Commerce Commission shall have reason-
45 able ground for belief that any common carrier is engaged in the carriage of

1 passenger or freight traffic between given points at less than the published rates
2 on file, it shall be authorized to present a petition to the circuit court of the
3 United States having jurisdiction of the parties, alleging such practice; where-
4 upon it shall be the duty of the court to summarily inquire into the circum-
5 stances, and, upon being satisfied of the truth of the allegation, to enforce an
6 observance of the published tariffs by proper orders and process, which said
7 orders and process may be enforceable as well against the parties interested in      ·
8 the traffic as against the carrier.
9     Sec. 7. That all acts and parts of acts in conflict with the provisions of this
10 act are hereby repealed, but such repeal shall not affect causes now pending nor
11 rights which have already accrued, but such causes shall be prosecuted to a con-
12 clusion and such rights enforced in a manner heretofore provided by law.
13    Sec. 8. That this act shall take effect from its passage.

# THE ELKINS BILL WITH PROPOSED AMENDMENTS PENDING BEFORE THE COMMITTEE.

[S. 3521, Fifty-seventh Congress, first session. (Committee print.)]

[Proposed amendments printed in italics. Omit the words in brackets.]

A BILL To enlarge the jurisdiction and powers of the Interstate Commerce Commission.

1    *Be it enacted by the Senate and House of Representatives of the United States of*
2    *America in Congress assembled,* That any definite order made by the Interstate
3    Commerce Commission after hearing and determination had on any petition here-
4    after presented pursuant to section thirteen of an act entitled "An act to regulate
5    commerce," approved February fourth, eighteen hundred and eighty-seven,
6    declaring any existing rate or rates in said petition complained of, for the carriage
7    of any given article or articles, person or persons, or any regulation or practice
8    affecting such rates *facilities afforded in connection therewith,* to be unjustly discrimi-
9    native or unreasonable, and declaring what rate *or rates,* regulation, or practice
10   affecting such rate *or rates* for the future, in substitution, would be just and rea-
11   sonable, shall become operative and be observed by the party or parties against
12   whom the same shall be made within thirty days after notice, or in case of
13.  proceeding for review as hereinafter provided, then within forty days after
14   notice; but the same may at any time be modified, suspended, or revoked by
15.  the Commission, but shall in no case continue in force [and be obeyed] beyond
16   the period of one year from the day the same becomes originally operative and
17.  is observed[. If such substitute rate shall be a joint one, and the carriers
18   parties to that rate shall be unable to agree upon the apportionment thereof
19.  among themselves within ten days after any such order shall become operative,
20   then the Commission may declare as part of its order what would be a just and
21   reasonable proportion of such rate to be received by each carrier.] *Provided,*
22   *however, That if any carrier shall thereafter see fit to increase the rate or rates (or change*
23   *the regulation or practice) established by such order, it shall file thirty days' previous*
24   *notice thereof with the Commission in the manner provided by law. When the rate*
25   *substituted by the Commission as hereinbefore provided is a joint rate, and the carriers*
26   *parties thereto fail to agree upon the apportionment thereof among themselves within*
27   *twenty days after notice of such order, the Commission may issue a supplemental order*
28   *declaring the portion of such joint rate to be received by each carrier party thereto,*
29   *which order shall be observed by such carriers. When the order of the Commission*
30   *prescribes the just relation of rates, to or from common points on the lines of the several*
31   *carriers parties to the proceeding, and such carriers fail to notify the Commission within*
32   *twenty days after notice of such order that they have agreed among themselves as to the*

1 *changes to be made to effect compliance therewith, the Commission may issue a supple-*
2 *mental order prescribing the rates to be charged, to or from such common points, by*
3 *either or all the parties to the proceeding, which order shall be observed by the carriers*
4 *concerned.* [Such] *Every* order as to its justness, reasonableness, and lawful-
5 ness, whether in respect to the rate *or rates,* regulation [of] *or* practice com-
6 plained of, or that prescribed in substitution therefor, or the apportionment of a
7 joint rate *or the relation of rates,* or otherwise, shall be reviewable by any circuit
8 court of the United States for any district through which any portion of the road
9 of the carrier shall run, to which a petition filed on its equity side shall be first
10 presented by any party interested. [Pending such review the said order shall
11 be suspended unless upon application to and hearing by said court it shall be
12 otherwise ordered; said court and the Supreme Court in case of appeal may, at
13 any time, upon application and notice, suspend or revoke the said order. The sev-
14 eral circuit courts of the United States are hereby invested with full jurisdiction
15 and powers in the premises, including the issuance and pursuit of the necessary
16 process to secure appearance of the parties. The court shall also direct notice to
17 the Commission of the filing of said petition; whereupon it shall be the duty of
18 the Commission, within ten days after the receipt thereof, to cause to be filed in
19 said court, duly certified, a complete copy of its entire record, including peti-
20 tions, answers, testimony, report, and opinion of the Commission, order, and all
21 other papers whatsoever in connection therewith.] *It shall be the duty of the*
22 *Commission, within ten days after notice, to cause to be filed in any court to which such*
23 *petition shall have been presented a duly certified copy of its entire record in connection*
24 *with the order to be reviewed, including petition, answers, testimony, report and*
25 *opinion of the Commission, order, and all other papers whatsoever in connection there-*
26 *with.* The court shall thereupon proceed to hear the same either upon the peti-
27 tion, record, and testimony returned by the Commission; or, in its discretion,
28 may, upon the application of either party, and in such manner as it shall direct,
29 cause additional testimony to be taken; and thereupon if *after hearing* said court
30 shall be of the opinion that said order was made under some error of law, or is,
31 upon the facts, unjust or unreasonable, it shall suspend or revoke the same by
32 appropriate decree; otherwise said order shall be affirmed. *Pending such review,*
33 *however, the court may, upon application and hearing, suspend said order.* Any party
34 to the cause may [appeal to the Supreme Court of the United States] within
35 thirty days of the rendition of any final decree of said court *appeal to the Supreme*
36 *Court of the United States,* which court shall proceed to hear and determine [the
37 same in due course without regard to whether the one year hereinbefore limited
38 for the continuance of said order shall have expired or not.] *such appeal. The*
39 *said several courts of the United States shall be and are vested with full jurisdiction and*
40 *all necessary powers in the premises. The case in both the circuit court and the Supreme*
41 *Court shall have precedence over all except criminal cases. But such appeal shall not*
42 *operate to stay or supersede the order of the circuit court, or the execution of any writ*
43 *or process thereon.*
44 *The defense in all such proceedings for review shall be undertaken by the United*
45 *States district attorney for the district wherein the action is brought, under the direction*

1 *of the Attorney-General of the United States, and the costs and expenses of such defense*
2 *shall be paid out of the appropriation for the expenses of the courts of the United States.*
3 *The Commission may, with the consent of the Attorney-General, employ special counsel*
4 *in any proceeding under this Act, paying the expense of such employment out of its own*
5 *appropriation.*

6 SEC. 2. That it shall be lawful for any two or more common carriers to arrange
7 between and among themselves for the establishment or maintenance of *just and*
8 *reasonable* rates. It shall also be lawful for such carriers to [agree, by] *make*
9 [contract] *contracts* in writing *to be* filed with the Interstate Commerce Com-
10 mission, [upon] *for* the 'division of their traffic or earnings, or both *thereof;* and
11 [upon] *for the formation of traffic associations;* [the complaint by petition or any
12 party interested that any such contract so filed unjustly and unlawfully affects'
13 any person or persons, community or communities, it shall be the duty of the
14 Commission to promptly investigate the matters so complained of in such manner
15 and by such means as it shall deem proper, and make report in writing with
16 respect thereto, which report shall include the findings of fact upon which the-
17 conclusions of the Commission are based, and be entered of record. If such
18 findings sustain in any material particular the allegations of said petition, then
19 it shall be the duty of said Commission to make an order either annulling said
20 contract after thirty days' notice, or directing that the said contract and the-
21 practices thereunder, in the respects found to be unjust and unlawful, shall be
22 changed in the manner prescribed in the order. Should such requirements of the
23 Commission as to changes be not observed by the carriers, and written acceptance
24 thereof be not filed with the Commission within thirty days after notice, then said
25 contract filed as aforesaid shall be annulled. Any such order shall be subject
26 to all the provisions of section one of this act with respect to definitive orders
27 made upon petitions presented pursuant to section thirteen of an act entitled "An
28 act to regulate commerce," approved February fourth, eighteen hundred and
29 eighty-seven,] *and said Commission shall have the right to examine by its duly*
30 *authorized agents, and may require to be filed with it from time to time copies of the*
31 *proceedings taken or decisions promulgated or other papers received or issued under, or*
32 *pursuant to, or in the execution of any such contracts in writing. After any such con-*
33 *tract in writing shall have gone into operation, the Commission may, either upon its*
34 *own motion or upon complaint of any party interested, inquire into the actual effect*
35 *thereof, and if it shall be of opinion that such contract results in unreasonable rates,*
36 *unjust discrimination, inadequate service, or is in any respect in contravention of said*
37 *act to regulate commerce it may enter an order annulling said contract on a date*
38 *named, which shall not be less than ten days from notice of said order, and thereupon*
39 *said contract shall cease and determine, or it may enter an order directing that said*
40 *contract and the practices thereunder shall be changed in the manner prescribed in*
41 *such order; and if all parties to such contract shall within fifteen days after notice of*
42 *such order file with the Commission written acceptances of such order, said contract shall*
43 *be held to be re-formed and thereafter be maintained accordingly; otherwise said con-*
44 *tract shall cease and determine.*

1   Sec. 3. That if any party bound thereby shall refuse or neglect to obey or per-
2 form any order of the Commission mentioned in section one or section two of
3 this act at any time while the same is in force as provided by said section, obedi-
4 ence and performance thereof shall be summarily enforced by writ of injunction
5 or other proper process, mandatory or otherwise, which shall be issued by any
6 circuit court of the United States upon petition of said Commission, accompanied
7 by a certified copy of the order alleged to be violated, and evidence of the violation
8 alleged; and in addition thereto the offending party shall be subject to a penalty
9 of [ten] *not less than five* thousand dollars *for each day of the continuance thereof,*
10 which, together with costs of suit, shall be recoverable by said Commission
11 by action of debt in any circuit court of the United States, and when so recov-
12 ered shall be for the use of the United States. Where, however, any order made
13 by the Commission shall involve the rate on traffic passing in part over the line
14 or lines of any railroad company operating in any foreign country, and passing in
15 part over lines of railroad companies operating within the United States, or shall
16 involve the usages of such foreign road with respect to such traffic, then in
17 case such an order shall not be observed it shall be lawful for the Commission,
18 or the court having jurisdiction, in addition to the other remedies herein pro-
19 vided, to enforce the order against the traffic so passing in part through a foreign
20 country and in part through the United States, by suspension of the movement
21 thereof within the United States, save upon the condition that the terms of the
22 order shall be complied with.
23   Sec. 4. That anything done or omitted to be done by a corporation common
24 carrier, subject to the act to regulate commerce, which, if done or omitted by
25 any lessee, trustee, receiver, officer, agent, or representative of such corporation,
26 would constitute a misdemeanor under said act, shall be held to be a misdemeanor
27 by such corporation, and upon conviction thereof it shall be subject to like pen-
28 alties as are prescribed in said act with reference to individuals, except as such
29 penalties are herein changed. The willful failure upon the part of any carrier
30 subject to said act to file and publish the tariffs of rates and charges as required
31 by said act, or strictly to observe such tariffs until changed according to law, *or*
32 *any departure therefrom by such carrier by means of the payment of a rebate or other-*
33 *wise,* shall be a misdemeanor, and upon conviction thereof the individual or cor-
34 poration offending shall be subject to a fine not less than one thousand dollars
35 nor more than twenty thousand dollars for each offense; and the willful com-
36 plicity upon the part of any person owning or interested in the traffic to which
37 any other rate *or rates* shall be given than those prescribed in said tariffs shall
38 likewise constitute a misdemeanor, and, upon conviction, shall subject the
39 offender to the like penalties last hereinbefore prescribed with reference to the
40 carrier. In all convictions occurring after the passage of this act, for offenses
41 under said act to regulate commerce (whether committed before or after the
42 passage of this act), or for offenses under this section, no penalty shall be imposed
43 on the convicted party other than the fine prescribed by law, imprisonment
44 wherever now prescribed as part of the penalty being hereby abolished.

1    SEC. 5. That in any proceeding for the enforcement of the provisions of the
2    statutes relating to interstate commerce, whether such proceedings be instituted
3    before the Interstate Commerce Commission or be commenced originally in any
4    circuit court of the United States, it shall be lawful to include as parties all per-
5    sons, in addition to the carrier interested in or affected by the rate, regulation,
6    or practice under consideration, and inquiries, investigations, orders, and decrees
7    may be made with reference to and against such additional parties in the same
8    manner, to the same extent and subject to the same provisions, as is or shall
9    be authorized by law with respect to carriers.

10    SEC. 6. That whenever the Interstate Commerce Commission shall have rea-
11    sonable ground for belief that any common carrier is engaged in the carriage of
12    passenger or freight traffic between given points at less than the published rates
13    on file, *or is rendering any additional service in any way beyond what is specified in*
14    *its published tariffs*, it shall be authorized to present a petition to the circuit
15    court of the United States having jurisdiction of the parties, alleging such prac-
16    tice, whereupon it shall be the duty of the court to summarily inquire into the
17    circumstances, and, upon being satisfied of the truth of the allegation, to enforce
18    an observance of the published tariffs by proper orders and process, which said
19    orders and process may be enforceable as well against the parties interested in
20    the traffic as against the carrier.

21    SEC. 7. That all acts and parts of acts in conflict with the provisions of this
22    act are hereby repealed, but such repeal shall not affect causes now pending
23    nor rights which have already accrued, but such causes shall be prosecuted to a
24    conclusion and such rights enforced in a manner heretofore provided by law.
25    *And all existing laws relative to testimony in cases or proceedings under or connected*
26    *with the act to regulate commerce shall also apply to any case or proceeding authorized*
27    *by this act.*

28    SEC. 8. That this act shall take effect from its passage.

[S. 3575, Fifty-seventh Congress, first session.]

A BILL to amend an act entitled "An act to regulate commerce," approved February fourth, eighteen hundred and eighty-seven, and all acts amendatory thereof.

1   *Be it enacted by the Senate and House of Representatives of the United States of*
2   *America in Congress assembled,* That section ten of an act entitled "An act to
3   regulate commerce," as amended March second, eighteen hundred and eighty-
4   nine, be amended so as to read as follows:
5   "Sec. 10. Every carrier, every lessee, trustee, receiver, officer, agent, or rep-
6   resentative of a carrier who shall transport or offer to transport traffic subject
7   to this act at any other rate or upon any other terms and conditions than are
8   duly published in accordance with the provisions of the act, or who by the pay-
9   ment of any rebate, or by any other device, departs from such published rate
10  in the transportation of such traffic, or who transports such traffic without having
11  first published a tariff applicable to the same, agreeably to the provisions of the
12  act, and any person who procures, or solicits to be done, or assists, aids, or abets
13  in the doing of any one of the aforesaid acts, shall be deemed guilty of a misde-
14  meanor and shall, upon conviction thereof, be subject to a fine of not less than
15  five thousand dollars nor more than twenty thousand dollars for each such offense.
16  "Any person, whether an employee or a principal, or a member of a firm or
17  company, or an employee, agent, or officer of a corporation, for any of whom as
18  consignor or consignee any carrier subject to the provisions of this act shall
19  transport property, who shall knowingly, by false description, false weight, or
20  false representation of the contents of any package, or by any other fraudulent
21  means, obtain or attempt to obtain the transportation of property, with or with-
22  out the collusion of the carrier or any of its employees, agents, or representa-
23  tives, for a less compensation than that prescribed by the published tariffs or
24  schedules of rates in force at the time shall be deemed guilty of a misdemeanor
25  and shall, upon conviction thereof, be subject to a fine of not less than one thou-
26  sand dollars nor more than five thousand dollars for each such offense.
27  "Every carrier, every lessee, trustee, receiver, officer, agent, or representative
28  of a carrier who knowingly violates any provision of this act, or fails to perform
29  any requirement thereof, for which no penalty is otherwise expressly provided,
30  shall be deemed guilty of a misdemeanor, and upon conviction thereof shall be
31  subject to a fine of not less than one thousand dollars nor more than five thou-
32  sand dollars for each such offense. Every corporation which shall be guilty of

1  any act or omission which if done by an individual would be a misdemeanor
2  under the provisions of this act shall be deemed guilty of such misdemeanor
3  and shall be subject to the same penalty which is provided against the individual.
4    "Every violation of this act shall be prosecuted in any court of the United
5  States having jurisdiction of crimes within the district in which such viola-
6  tion was committed; and whenever the offense is begun in one jurisdiction
7  and completed in another, it may be dealt with, inquired of, tried, determined,
8  and punished in either jurisdiction in the same manner as if the offense had
9  been actually and wholly committed therein.
10   "In construing and enforcing the provisions of this section, the act, omission,
11  or failure of any officer, agent, or other person acting for or employed by any
12  common carrier shall, in every case, be also deemed to be the act, omission, or
13  failure of such carrier as well as that of the person.
14   "All offenses heretofore committed shall be prosecuted and punished as pro-
15  vided for by the laws existing at the time such offenses were committed, for
16  which purpose all acts or parts thereof inconsistent with this act are continued
17  in force."
18   Sec. 2. That section fifteen of said act is hereby amended by adding the fol-
19  lowing words thereto:
20   "If the Commission, after full hearing had upon any petition hereafter pre-
21  sented, determines that the defendant or defendants are in violation of any of
22  the provisions of the act, in respect to any rate, relation of rates, whether
23  between localities or commodities, classification of freight, or other practice, it
24  shall be its duty to determine what rate, relation of rates, classification, or other
25  practice should be observed for the future in order to correct the wrong found
26  to exist, and it shall order said defendants to observe the same.  In case of
27  ordering a change in the relation of rates, if it shall become necessary, in order
28  to establish or maintain a just relation thereof, to prescribe the rate or rates to
29  be observed by either or all of the parties concerned therein, it shall be its duty
30  so to do; and when a rate involved in any case is a joint rate, it shall further
31  determine the proportions in which the rate shall be shared by the several
32  carriers, if they fail to agree among themselves in respect thereto.  In either of
33  these cases, if the several defendants shall not have notified the Commission
34  within ten days from the service of the order that they have come to an agree-
35  ment in respect to the relative rates in question, or in respect to the division of
36  the joint rate prescribed, the Commission shall thereupon fix the rates or
37  proportions to be observed for the future, in the case in question, as above
38  provided.
39   "Any such order shall be termed a 'definitive order,' and shall specify the
40  time when the same is to take effect, which shall in no case be less than twenty
41  days after service of said order upon defendant.  Any defendant may review
42  said order by filing, within twenty days from the service thereof, with the cir-
43  cuit court of the United States for that district in which its principal office is
44  situated, a bill in equity for that purpose, and where there are several defend-

1   ants, that court shall have jurisdiction in which such petition is first filed.   The
2   United States shall be made the defendant in such proceeding and the Commis-
3   sion shall be forthwith notified of the pendency thereof.   Within fifteen days
4   from receiving such notice the Commission shall file in such court a complete
5   certified copy of the entire record in such case, and the court shall thereupon
6   proceed to hear the same upon such record; but it may also, in case either party
7   desires to submit further testimony, and such testimony could not reasonably
8   have been produced before the Commission, instruct the Commission to take
9   and certify up such testimony.   If upon hearing the court shall be of the opinion
10  that the order of the Commission is not a lawful, just, and reasonable one, it
11  shall vacate the order; otherwise, it shall dismiss the proceedings in review.   In
12  either case the court shall file with its decision a statement of the reasons upon
13  which such decision is based, a copy of which shall be certified forthwith to the
14  Commission.   If the order of the Commission is vacated and no appeal is taken,
15  the Commission may reopen the case for further hearing and order, or it may
16  make a new order without further hearing; but such subsequent order shall be
17  subject to the same right of review as above provided.
18      "The filing of a petition to review an order shall of itself suspend the effect
19  of such order for thirty days, and the court before which the same is pending
20  may also, if upon an inspection of the record it plainly appears that the order
21  proceeds upon some error of law, or is unjust and unreasonable upon the facts, ·
22  and not otherwise, suspend the operation of the order during the pendency of
23  the proceedings in review, or until further order of the court.
24      "Either party may, within thirty days, appeal from the judgment or decree
25  of the circuit court to the Supreme Court of the United States; but such appeal
26  shall not operate to stay or supersede the order of the circuit court.
27      "The defense in all such proceedings for review shall be undertaken by the
28  United States district attorney for the district wherein the action is brought,
29  under the direction of the Attorney-General of the United States, and the costs
30  and expenses of such defense shall be paid out of the appropriation for the
31  expenses of the courts of the United States.
32      "The Commission may, with the consent of the Attorney-General, employ
33  special counsel in any proceeding under this act, paying the expenses of such
34  employment out of its own appropriation."
35      SEC. 3. That section sixteen of said act as amended March second, eighteen
36  hundred and eighty-nine, is hereby amended by striking out all of the first para-
37  graph down to and including the words "and the costs and expenses of such
38  prosecution shall be paid out of the appropriation for the expenses of the courts
39  of the United States," and inserting in lieu thereof the following:
40      " A definitive order which has become operative by its terms and has not been
41  suspended or vacated in the manner specified in the preceding section shall be
42  obligatory upon and observed by the defendant carrier or carriers against whom
43  it is made: *Provided,* That when a carrier has actually observed said order for

1 the space of two years it shall no longer be binding upon said carrier: *And pro-*
2 *vided further,* That the Commission may at any time rescind or modify such
3 order.

4     "If, however, the carrier, after the expiration of that period, shall make any
5 change from the rate or other practice directed by the Commission, any party
6 interested may file with the Commission his objection to such change within
7 sixty days, and the Commission may thereupon order the carrier to restore and
8 maintain the rate or practice required by the original order pending its investi-
9 gation as to the lawfulness or reasonableness of such change. The order of the
10 Commission directing a restoration of the rate originally required shall not be
11 subject to review, but its final order, issued pursuant to such investigation, shall
12 be subject to the same right of review as is provided in the preceding section of
13 this act.

14     "If a carrier neglects or refuses to obey an order which is obligatory upon it
15 as above, the circuit court of the United States for any district through which
16 any portion of the road of such carrier runs shall, upon petition of the complain-
17 ant in the original suit, or of the Commission, or of any party interested, enforce
18 obedience to such order by mandamus, injunction, or other summary process of
19 said court, and the circuit courts of the United States are hereby invested with
20 the necessary powers thereto. Every carrier, or the receiver, lessee, trustee, offi-
21 cer, or agent of such carrier, neglecting or refusing to obey such order shall also
22 be subject to a penalty of ten thousand dollars for each and every day which
23 he or it is in default, said penalty to be recovered for the use of the United
24 States in an appropriate suit brought in the name of the United States in the
25 circuit court for any district through which any portion of the road of the car-
26 rier runs.

27     "Any circuit court of the United States for a district through which any por-
28 tion of the road of a carrier runs shall, upon petition of the Commission or of
29 any party interested, enjoin such carrier or its receivers, lessees, trustees, officers,
30 or agents from giving, and a shipper from receiving, with respect to interstate
31 transportation of persons or property subject to the provisions of this act, any
32 concession from the lawfully published rate, or from accepting persons or prop-
33 erty for such transportation if a rate has not been lawfully published; and by
34 'concession' is meant the giving of any rebate or drawback, the rendering of
35 any additional service, or the practicing of any device or contrivance by which
36 a less compensation than that prescribed by the published tariffs is ultimately
37 received, or by which a greater service in any respect than that stated in
38 such tariffs is rendered. And in proceedings of this nature said court shall
39 have power to compel the attendance of witnesses, both upon the part of the
40 carrier and of the shipper, who shall be required to answer on all subjects relat-
41 ing directly or indirectly to the matter in controversy, and to compel the pro-
42 duction of all books and papers, both of the carrier and of the shipper, which
43 relate directly or indirectly to such transaction; but all persons so required to
44 testify shall have the same immunity from prosecution and punishment as is

1 provided in an act approved February eleventh, eighteen hundred and ninety-
2 three, entitled 'An act in relation to testimony before the Interstate Com-
3 merce Commission, and in cases or proceedings under or connected with an
4 act entitled, "An act to regulate commerce," approved February fourth,
5 eighteen hundred and eighty-seven, and amendments thereto.' "

6    Sec. 4. That all acts and parts of acts in conflict with the provisions of this
7 act are hereby repealed, but such repeal shall not affect causes now pending nor
8 rights which have already accrued, and such causes shall be prosecuted to a
9 conclusion and such rights enforced in the manner heretofore provided by law.

10    Sec. 5. That this act shall take effect from its passage.

# HEARINGS.

# FREIGHT RATES ON LUMBER.

UNITED STATES SENATE COMMITTEE
ON INTERSTATE COMMERCE,
*February 7, 1902.*

A committee (composed of Messrs. E. M. Adams, E. R. Burkholder, E. S. Miner, J. E. Evans, and Harry A. Gorsuch) representing the Missouri, Kansas and Oklahoma Association of Lumber Dealers, appeared before the Committee on Interstate Commerce.

The CHAIRMAN (Mr. Elkins, of West Virginia). This meeting has been called for the purpose of hearing the gentlemen present, who represent the lumber interests of Kansas and the West, and who desire, as I understand, some amendment of the interstate-commerce law. Gentlemen, we have just an hour in which to hear you, and you can parcel out the time among yourselves.

## STATEMENT OF E. M. ADAMS.

Mr. E. M. ADAMS (of Mound City, Kans.). Mr. Chairman and gentlemen of the committee, this committee represents the Missouri, Kansas and Oklahoma Lumber Dealers' Association; also that association represents the Southern manufacturers' interests, and behind that are the great interests of the people, and they are really the most interested of all parties concerned—more so than even the association we particularly represent, because they receive the ultimate benefits of anything that may be done by Congress in the way of strengthening the interstate-commerce law, which is, after all, what we are here for.

We in the West, Mr. Chairman, have suffered a great many grievances, among which are the excessive and unjust rates of freight charged by the railroads, and unjust discrimination in rates. We had intended to give you some facts and figures, having a prepared statement of that kind, but unfortunately that is not at this moment in our hands. Perhaps I ought to apologize, but the fact is that Mr. Burkholder, a member of our committee, who has possession of that statement, was detained so that he has not been able to arrive here from New York in time for this hearing. Consequently, while we are without data, yet we can briefly state our points. It might seem an unusual, almost an improper, thing if I should state to you the full extent of the discriminations practiced against us by the railroads; it is certainly astonishing. We appealed to the railroad authorities in regard to it, asked them to reduce the discriminations; in fact, to reduce the rates that they had advanced arbitrarily about a year ago. The committee of railroad freight agents, to whom we made representations, stated to us that they did not consider that they had had their share

3

of the Republican prosperity, of which we had boasted, and as a consequence the rates were arbitrarily advanced.

The CHAIRMAN. By what railroads?

Mr. ADAMS. By all the railroads that carry lumber in our section,
west of the Mississippi River; perhaps our secretary can give you
their names.

Mr. GORSUCH. The Iron Mountain, the Santa Fe, the Rock Island,
the Union Pacific, the Cotton Belt, the Kansas City Southern, the
'Frisco—in fact, every road that runs into Kansas City; there are 23
distinct lines.

The CHAIRMAN. You may proceed, Mr. Adams.

Mr. ADAMS. We complain that these roads arbitrarily advanced
their rates from 1 to 5 cents per hundred.

Senator FORAKER. Did you state when that advance was made?

Mr. ADAMS. A little over a year ago. Perhaps our secretary can
give you the exact date.

Senator FORAKER. That is not important.

Mr. ADAMS. We made a showing of facts and figures, that on general
averages the rate on lumber per ton per mile was a great deal more
than the average rate on all other commodities per ton per mile; that
lumber, being a nonperishable commodity, should have a low rate; it
is always used as ballast in freight matters, and whenever there is anything to be thrown out of a freight train on account of overloading, or
for any other cause, a car of lumber is side tracked; so that, in addition to the discrimination against us in rates, they also discriminate
against us in the matter of carrying our lumber promptly and quickly
to its destination. The railroads in our section, west of the Mississippi River, carry an unusually large share of the lumber, and it pays,
too, large a share of the whole sum paid for freights. That is the claim
we make.

Senator CULLOM. Allow me to ask where this lumber comes from.

Mr. ADAMS. Mostly from Arkansas, Texas, and Louisiana, going
north.

Senator CULLOM. Not from the North?

Mr. ADAMS. Going north.

The CHAIRMAN. Going where?

Mr. ADAMS. Going to all points through Oklahoma, Kansas, Nebraska, Illinois, Indiana, Missouri, and to Chicago.

The CHAIRMAN. You do not have any export lumber?

Mr. ADAMS. No.

The CHAIRMAN. Your complaint is as to freight rates in those States?

Mr. ADAMS. Yes, sir.

The CHAIRMAN. You say they advanced the rates how much?

Mr. ADAMS. From 1 to 5 cents a hundred.

Senator KEAN. Did the price of lumber advance also?

Mr. ADAMS. The price of lumber advanced also very largely, which
made it very hard on the consumers. It is really in the interest of
the consumers—the general public—that we are here now.

Senator CLAPP. This bill that Senator Nelson introduced he told me
was introduced at the request of the lumbermen. Was it upon your
request?

Mr. ADAMS. It was not at the request of this committee as a committee. I will say, however, that, as I understand that bill, it largely
corrects the difficulties of which we are complaining.

Senator CLAPP. Are there any northwestern lumbermen here, as far as you know?

Mr. ADAMS. I do not know of any other lumbermen's association that is represented here except our own.

The CHAIRMAN. No; they were heard the other day by the Committee on Commerce. The basis of their complaint was largely the export trade to Europe.

Senator CLAPP. But Senator Nelson told me he prepared and introduced his bill at the request of some lumbermen, and I think there were some northwestern lumbermen in it.

The CHAIRMAN. Mr. Adams, you say that they advanced the rate from 1 to 5 cents per hundred. What is the ordinary rate, say, from Little Rock, Ark., to St. Louis or Chicago, on a carload?

Mr. ADAMS. It is 23 cents a hundred to St. Louis from all points.

The CHAIRMAN. How much is that a carload?

Mr. ADAMS. A carload is usually about 40,000 pounds.

Senator FORAKER. What did you say was the rate from all points to St. Louis?

Mr. ADAMS. I said it was 23 cents per hundred. I was wrong about that; it is 25 cents to Kansas City, and only 15 cents to St. Louis.

The CHAIRMAN. What is that per carload?

Mr. ADAMS. A carload is about 40,000 pounds.

The CHAIRMAN. How many feet to the hundred?

Mr. ADAMS. About 16,000 feet of lumber in an average carload; about 16 tons to the carload.

The CHAIRMAN. What would be the through rate per carload from Arkansas? Would that be $60?

Mr. ADAMS. I pay on a carload from $80 to $90 per car, and from that up to over $100.

The CHAIRMAN. You are a shipper or consumer?

Mr. ADAMS. I am a retailer.

The CHAIRMAN. You are not a shipper?

Mr. ADAMS. No. There are no shippers present.

The CHAIRMAN. You are consumers?

Mr. ADAMS. We are retailers who sell directly.

The CHAIRMAN. I had received the impression that you were shippers, and were complaining of excessive rates from the shippers' standpoint.

Mr. ADAMS. No, sir; though at the same time we are representing them, in a way, simply because their interests and ours run on the same lines.

The CHAIRMAN. Do you have any complaint to make on behalf of the people who sell the lumber, or on behalf of the mill men, the manufacturers?

Mr. ADAMS. No; although they are interested just as much as we are so far as rates are concerned.

Senator FORAKER. What is your business?

Mr. ADAMS. Retailer of lumber.

Senator FORAKER. Where are you located?

Mr. ADAMS. At Mound City, Kans.

The CHAIRMAN. I interrupted you, Mr. Adams; proceed.

Mr. ADAMS. Now, gentlemen, in order to make it impressive and to particularize in regard to the difficulties we have suffered in rates, I will say that a year ago we appointed a committee to meet the General Traffic Association and try to arrange rates, but utterly failed to do so. We told them that if they gave us no relief we should be obliged to proceed to extreme measures in that respect, and in carrying out that idea a committee was appointed, with authority to draw upon the treasurer for any necessary expenses, to procure the best counsel that we were able to obtain in Kansas, and we employed the ex-chief justice of the supreme court of Kansas, a former justice, and also the attorney-general of the State of Kansas. After looking the interstate-commerce law over thoroughly they informed us that the remedy we had anticipated taking—going before the Interstate Commerce Commission—would fail us; that the best remedy, in their judgment, that we could find—and, of course, we deferred to their judgment, because it was the best we could buy—that in their judgment there was more chance for relief under the old common law in the courts of the justices of the peace of the State than we had under the interstate-commerce law in going before the Interstate Commerce Commission, because they said there was not vitality enough in the interstate-commerce law to enable us to obtain the relief we sought unless we should be very long lived, and some of us have not a great while to stay, I am sorry to say.

Therefore we proceeded to have prepared a large number of suits to be brought before justices' courts in the State of Kansas in order to relieve us from this difficulty. We did not actually commence any suits, but we prepared a large number of cases based upon excessive charges to individuals. At first we declined to pay those charges, but in order to make a foundation for a suit we paid under protest, tendering the exact amount of money we were willing to pay as a just and equitable rate, and took two receipts, one for the first lot of freight and the other for the excess. Then we went before the justices' courts to recover our money. That has been our method. The Traffic Association found that we were putting them to a large amount of trouble; that, although they might win out hereafter, they had a large number of suits to defend. We told them that we intended to call for juries in each case—juries of our own citizens; that we were sure of a verdict, and that that verdict would be carried into effect, so that they would have to fight against an adverse verdict in each case in every county in the State of Kansas. The result of that action is what I want to call your attention to.

When they realized the difficulties they were going to have to contend with from this course of action they proposed a compromise with our committee. which was finally accepted, although it did not come up to what we thought was right. We told them, however, that it would be only temporary. Yet I may say that these terms, effected on this compromise, accepted and adopted by our committee, have saved the western half of the State of Kansas over $75,000 a year on freights. I take that to be a conclusive admission on the part of the railroads that they were wrong; they never would have yielded that amount if they had not been wrong and known it themselves. In fact, some of their agents told us privately that they knew those rates were excessive, and that if they had the power they would be willing to grant what we asked, on the ground taken in our complaints, but that if they should undertake to do so it would cost them their positions. That is what the general freight agent of one of the greatest railroad systems in the United States stated to us.

Now, gentlemen, it is these difficulties we complain of. In the first place, excessive rates are charged arbitrarily, and in the next place there is discrimination.

The Interstate Commerce Commission have informed us that on our bare statement of the facts and figures to them we had a good case, a strong case, and they advised us to proceed before them; but, as I said before, our term of life as individuals is limited.

Senator FORAKER. What is the difficulty about getting a hearing before the Interstate Commerce Commission?

Mr. ADAMS. There is no difficulty whatever.

Senator FORAKER. Unless I have been wrongly informed, you can have a hearing there very expeditiously?

Mr. ADAMS. At once. In fact, they invited us to bring our case before them; but they say the remedy is not perfect. I wish I had here the facts and figures that I handed to our Mr. Burkholder, but he has been detained.

Senator FORAKER. I am only trying to get at your idea, not for any controversial purposes, but simply to suggest.

Mr. ADAMS. Allow me to state one case in which I think I am entirely accurate, and I know if I am wrong the secretary can correct me.

As one instance, I wish to cite a certain rate of freight on lumber, 300 miles for 29 cents per hundred, on practically the same line, with a little deviation (another branch of the same line), when the rate to Chicago, 1,100 miles, was 24 cents per hundred; 300 miles for 29 cents; 1,100 miles over practically the same line for 24 cents. We claim that that is an unjust and unreasonable discrimination. It does not give people the same opportunities to engage in the same kind of business and in the same way at equal rates with others.

Senator CULLOM. You say you got relief by going into the courts of the State, and they finally compromised?

Mr. ADAMS. We think we forced them to make that concession; and it was a great concession.

Senator CULLOM. If you can scare them, as you seem to have done in that case, why can you not keep on doing the same thing?

Mr. ADAMS. I do not know. But, gentlemen, you are here for the purpose of legislation; and we look to you to give us a better remedy.

Senator CULLOM. We want to see whether we need to legislate. That is the main thing.

Senator FORAKER. As I understand the interstate-commerce law, the action of the railroads, of which you complain here, is just what is positively prohibited by that law.

Mr. ADAMS. It is.

Senator FORAKER. There is no question about that, is there?

Mr. ADAMS. No; no question.

Senator FORAKER. And there is no question but that the Interstate Commerce Commissioners are empowered to correct that violation of law?

Mr. ADAMS. That is correct.

Senator FORAKER. They can do it summarily—a great deal more expeditiously than the Congress of the United States can act.

Senator CULLOM. I wish to ask whether the Interstate Commerce Commissioners advised you to proceed before justices of the peace, or whether they advised you to come before them and make your case?

Mr. ADAMS. Our employed attorneys advised us to go to the justices' courts.

Mr. EVANS. May I correct you, Mr. Adams?

Mr. ADAMS. Yes.

Mr. EVANS. In regard to bringing these suits before justices, we were advised that every individual who had a case for $20 or less could bring such a suit before a justice of the peace; that while that would involve the necessity of every party aggrieved bringing his individual claim before a justice (which would be very burdensome to individuals), yet at the same time we would succeed. They also advised us that we would not succeed before the Interstate Commerce Commission because of its lack of power to enforce its orders or decisions.

Senator FORAKER. If the Interstate Commerce Commission is empowered to adjudicate your complaint, what do you want with anything more?

Mr. ADAMS. I think I can explain that point.

Senator FORAKER. That is what I want to know—whether it is because they have not power to enforce their judgments, and you want additional legislation on that point.

Mr. ADAMS. Our point is just this: We would have to bring each individual case before the Commission. For instance, in order to have judgment for an overcharge or discrimination against me, I should have to bring a case for each act of discrimination; that case would be adjudicated and an order issued. That order could be appealed to the courts, from one court to another, until it was taken to the Supreme Court of the United States, and the very next case would have to take the same course. It does not give us any relief for the future.

Senator CULLOM. I take it that this is the point that the gentleman wishes to make—and it is the real point of the case—that if the Commission should render a verdict (if you choose to call it a verdict) or make an order, under the present decisions of the Supreme Court as to the power of the Commission, that would not be effective until it is passed upon or approved by the courts of the country.

Mr. ADAMS. That is it exactly.

Senator CULLOM. What they want is power to make an order which shall stand as a determination of the case until it is set aside by the courts?

Mr. ADAMS. That is it. We want that made immediately effective until set aside by the courts. Another thing, Senator: We want it forbidden that the railroads shall charge excessive rates on that same line, if you please, and under the same circumstances or under similar circumstances in the future. We want that decision to cover future transactions.

Senator CULLOM. The court says that under the present law that can not be done.

Mr. ADAMS. No, sir. We think that is a lameness of the present law. We think it is weak; that it lacks vitality, virility, if you please. As we understand it, those are the particular points wherein the present law is weak, though I will say that we did not come here prepared, and I doubt whether it is within our province as a matter of propriety to formulate legislation for you.

The CHAIRMAN. You can suggest.

Mr. ADAMS. We can make suggestions, of course; but our intention was to tell you the difficulties we labor under, how the whole of the great West is complaining of it among the people, where the real interest is. We look to you to find a remedy, to find the best way out. That is the purpose of this committee coming here.

Senator CULLOM. What you state is the complaint of your people that you are discriminated against and overcharged in freight rates?

Mr. ADAMS. Yes, sir.

Senator CULLOM. As matters of fact?

Mr. ADAMS. Yes, sir. If we can say anything that will throw new light on the circumstances connected with this problem, or in regard to the difficulties that we run against, and that will aid in securing new remedial legislation, we shall be only too glad that we have come. I do not know that there is anything further I care to say. Mr. Evans, would you like to make any additional statement?

## STATEMENT OF J. E. EVANS.

Mr. J. E. EVANS (of Emporia, Kans., a retail dealer in lumber, and a vice-president and director of the Missouri, Kansas and Oklahoma Association of Lumber Dealers). The rate on lumber from any point in the southwest—Arkansas, Louisiana, or Texas—to Kansas City is 23 cents a hundred; it was 22, but now it is 23. Understand, the rate to Topeka and other points closer to the shipping point is 26 cents; at Emporia, which is still closer, the rate is 28 cents; Chicago gets her yellow pine from the same points at 24; Indiana at 38; and Cottonwood Falls, only 30 miles west of Emporia, gets the rate of 30 cents.

Mr. ADAMS. I might state, in this connection, that not only are localities discriminated against, but certain States are discriminated against. It is the habit of the railroads to make a blanket rate, covering a large section of country. At important points I get lumber from Texas, Indian Territory, Louisiana, and Arkansas, all at the same rate. Any yellow-pine lumber from the South comes to me at 23 cents per hundred, no matter where it comes from.

Senator CULLOM. Do you complain of that?

Mr. ADAMS. Oh, no; but the State of Kansas pays a relatively higher rate of freight than Missouri, Illinois, or even Nebraska.

Mr. EVANS. There is no doubt about that.

Senator FORAKER. The gist of the whole matter, then, is that you contend that there are discriminations in violation of the interstate-commerce law, and that the Interstate Commerce Commissioners are not empowered by the statute, as it now stands, to give you the remedy you desire, viz, to prevent these discriminations?

Mr. ADAMS. That is it.

Senator FORAKER. You want such an amendment to the interstate-commerce law as may give them that authority?

Mr. ADAMS. That is it exactly.

Senator FORAKER. So as to save you from the necessity of going into the courts to work out your remedy?

Mr. ADAMS. Yes, sir.

The CHAIRMAN. Does any other gentleman wish to be heard? [A pause.] If not, you gentlemen can now be excused while the committee holds a meeting for other matters.

Mr. ADAMS. Gentlemen, we thank you for your attention to this hearing.

Mr. EVANS. I should like to have it understood that we may leave here the written statement made by Mr. Burkholder, who is absent now, as Mr. Adams has stated.

The CHAIRMAN. There is no objection to that. You may have it sent to the committee, and it will be filed with your testimony as part of the testimony.

Senator KEAN. And let it be printed.

The CHAIRMAN. Yes, and it will be printed with the other.

The statement above referred to was submitted to the committee during its sitting on April 11, 1902, by Mr. Frank Barry, of Milwaukee, when the following occurred:

Mr. BARRY. Mr. Chairman, I have here a communication from the Missouri, Kansas, and Oklahoma association of lumber dealers, which they desire to submit. A committee representing that association, I understand, appeared before your committee some time ago and were then given permission to submit this paper.

The CHAIRMAN. Have you read it, Mr. Barry?

Mr. BARRY. Yes.

The CHAIRMAN. You vouch for it as being a proper and respectful paper, do you?

Mr. BARRY. Yes. I simply submit it for them, at their request. If it contains anything that is objectionable, you can change it.

The CHAIRMAN. We will accept it, Mr. Barry, if you say it is all right, because I know who you are, and I know you would not ask us to embody anything in this testimony that is not right and proper.

Mr. BARRY. It is all right, Mr. Chairman.

The CHAIRMAN. We are so busy and pressed that we can not read all these documents, before they are printed, in order to ascertain whether they are in proper shape.

Mr. BARRY. I may have some other documents to submit, and so I shall be very careful about them.

Following is the paper referred to:

*To the Interstate Commerce Committee, Washington, D. C.:*

The undersigned, representatives of the Missouri, Kansas, and Oklahoma Association of Lumber Dealers, having been assured that their views in writing, in reference to the needed legislation in the interest of interstate commerce, would be considered, beg leave to submit the following:

The interstate commerce law enacted by Congress in 1887 was the outcome of constant public demand for at least ten years. The conditions existing at that time, and which gave rise to this demand, confront the public to-day in more aggravated form. President Arthur, in his message of December 4, 1882, recommends to Congress the regulation of interstate commerce, arraigns the corporations which own or control the railroads of adopting such measures as tend to impair the advantages of healthful competition, and to make hurtful discriminations in the adjustment of freightage. He points out the fact that these inequalities have been corrected in several of the States by appropriate legislation, but so far as such mischiefs affect commerce between the States, they are subjects of national concern, and Congress alone can afford relief.

In his message in December, 1883, he points out the relations that ought to exist between the public carriers and their patrons, and lays upon Congress the responsibility of granting relief and protection to the general public in the following language:

"While we can not fail to recognize the importance of the vast railway systems of the country, and their great and beneficent influences upon the development of our material wealth, we should, on the other hand, remember that no individual and no corporation ought to be invested with absolute power over the interest of any other citizen or class of citizens. The right of these railway corporations to a fair and profitable return upon their investments and to reasonable freedom in their regulations must be recognized; but it seems only just that, so far as its constitutional authority will permit, Congress should protect the people at large in their interstate traffic against acts of injustice which the State governments are powerless to prevent."

I desire to draw your attention to the time when these messages were delivered; this was prior to the birth of populism; also to the fact that they come from a Republican President of the United States, who gives authoritative expression of existing facts and of a universal demand for needed legislation. The charge has been made that this demand for the amendment of the interstate-commerce law is populistic in its origin and character. It is no more populistic than the origin of the law, and no law has ever been placed on our statute books which gave greater satisfaction to the general manufacturing and commercial public.

The necessity of this law is made apparent by the study of the number and the variety of cases tried and decided by the Commission before its authority was questioned and denied by the courts.

In his message of December, 1896, President Cleveland says: "The justice and equity of the principles embodied in the existing (interstate commerce) law passed for the purpose of regulating transportation charges are everywhere conceded, and there appears to be no question that the policy thus entered upon has a permanent place in our legislation." He states further that the wholesome effects of this law are manifest and have amply justified its enactment and expresses the hope "that the recommendations of the Commission upon this subject will be promptly and favorably considered by Congress." Instead of Congress heeding the advice of the nation's Chief Executive, and the nation's spokesman. and carrying out the nation's wishes in this matter, the Supreme Court acted in 1897 and most effectually deprived the Commission of the power necessary to enforce its findings. The immediate result of this decision was the inauguration of a period of extortionate rates, rank discrimination, and a general hold-up of a forbearing, but a determined and outraged public.

President Roosevelt, voicing the sentiment of the general public, again calls the attention of Congress to the need of legislation along this line. He states "that the cardinal provisions of the interstate-commerce act were that railway rates should be just and reasonable, and that all shippers, localities, and commodities should be accorded equal treatment." That "experience has shown the wisdom of its purposes, but has also shown, possibly, that some of its requirements are wrong, certainly that the means devised for the enforcement of its provisions are defective." He concludes by saying that "the act should be amended. The railway is a public servant. Its rates should be just to and open to all shippers alike. The Government should see to it that within its jurisdiction this is so, and should provide a speedy, inexpensive, and effective remedy to that end. Nothing could be more foolish than the enactment of legislation which would unnecessarily interfere with the development and operation of these commercial agencies. The subject is one of great importance and calls for the earnest attention of Congress."

The observation of these three Presidents covers a period of twenty years. They agree that an adequate interstate-commerce law is a necessity, that it is indispensable to the administration of justice, and that the responsibility for the enactment of such a law rests with Congress. For twenty years and more the general public has demanded this law. In 1887 the Commission was created, as was then supposed, with power to stop and correct abuses; in 1897 the Supreme Court held that their powers were purely advisory. Since then the Commission is practically powerless; it is, perhaps, a little better than no Commission, but so far as granting practical relief is concerned the country would be just as well off without any Commission. It is contended by representatives of the railways that the granting of power to the Commission to substitute a just for an unjust rate, or an equitable for a discriminative rate, is equivalent to depriving the roads from the management of their property and investing the Commission with power to make rates. This was not the intention of the law of 1887, nor the practice of the Commission under that law, neither is it the wish of the business men of to-day; what we contend for is a law which will give the Commission power, after a full, fair, and impartial hearing of both parties in interest to put into effect a just and equitable rate, and this rate to be observed by the roads in question until the decision of the Commission is reversed by the Federal courts.

The prosperity of the railways depends on the traffic given them by the public, just as the success of a bank depends on the deposits and business of its patrons. There is no public institution in the land which is administered more autocratically than our national banks by the Comptroller of the Currency. Yet the only bankers that kick against this supervision are those who are determined to do an illegitimate business. The same is true of railroads. Honest railroad men have nothing to fear;

they know that the public does not want to rob them, and that the law as it now stands affords them ample protection; they also know that it is the inalienable right of their patrons to be protected by law against the unjust methods of unscrupulous railroad managers.

The lumbermen of Kansas and Oklahoma, and the wholesalers shipping to these points have had special experiences with the railroads on the question of lumber rates. The lumber rates to Kansas and to Oklahoma have not only been arbitrarily high but have been in direct violation of the interstate-commerce law, which provides that a greater charge shall not be made for a short haul than for a long haul, under similar conditions. It is a general rule in both passenger and freight traffic that the company having the shortest and most direct route dictates the rate. This is one of the reasons offered by the railroads why Missouri, Illinois, Indiana, and other States have a much lower average rate on lumber than Kansas and Oklahoma, although the distance from the center of production in the Southern forests to the center of consumption is much shorter, and in many instances the lumber passes through Oklahoma and Kansas to reach these more distant points. The argument advanced has been that some railroad having a direct route to some point in the lumber district makes the rate for all roads to these centers. We do not object to this rule, but we do object to railroads using one method of procedure or one law to make rates to one State and another law to make rates to another State.

The rates from the central points of production to the central points of consumption in the various States are as follows:

|  | Average distance. | Average rate. |
|---|---|---|
|  | *Miles.* | *Cents.* |
| Oklahoma | 350 | 29¼ |
| Kansas | 600 | 29 |
| Missouri | 600 | 23 |
| Illinois | 1,000 | 24 |
| Indiana | 1,300 | 25¼ |
| Ohio | 1,500 | 28 |

This discrimination in rates greatly retards building in this territory; it deprives us of all the natural advantages of location in close proximity to the southern forests. This territory has to pay an excessively high rate to enable the roads to give an extremely low rate to more remote points, in order to get into the territory of roads hauling lumber from Northern forests.

The Kansas rate, established more than fifteen years ago, was made via Kansas City. The rate established then to the central Kansas points was 27½ cents per 100 pounds. This rate was made to conform to the existing white-pine rate from the North. Since then white pine has gone out of use, and yellow pine is used almost wholly; in addition diagonal roads were built, running south through Kansas and Oklahoma direct to the forests of Texas, Arkansas, and Louisiana, shortening the distance of the lumber haul 200 miles or more. The route for carrying the Southern lumber product has been changed; the lumber comes no longer by way of Kansas City; and yet these old Kansas City rates are steadily maintained. Kansas City lies 40 miles north of the center of the State, and the opening of the diagonal roads to the south has moved the center of lumber production 80 miles west. This new condition saves to the center of Kansas consumption a haul of over 200 miles, or about 33 per cent of the entire distance. This shortened haul entitles us to a proportionate reduction in rates. But instead of reducing rates, in December, 1899, the roads advanced the rate 10 per cent to this territory, on the plea that they were entitled to share in the general prosperity of the country. Through the efforts of the attorney-general of the State and the political situation in reference to State railroad legislation, we succeeded in getting the advance changed from 2½ cents to 1 cent per hundred pounds. But still there was an advance instead of a reduction.

Another reason why lumber rates should be less than local rates per ton per mile— and unfortunately they are higher in the State of Kansas and the Territory of Oklahoma—lies in the fact that the kind of service required to haul lumber is less expensive than that required for most other commodities. The roads can use a cattle car, a box car, a flat car, or any other kind of car that may be to them convenient; the lumber is moved whenever it suits the road, without any loss to them, except their own delay; the cost of loading and unloading is borne by the consignor and the consignee; the payment of freight is in large amounts and is always cash; the risk is the minimum as compared with the hauling of other commodities, such as live stock, grain, and other commodities even more perishable; no suits confront the roads in the adjustment of losses; besides the distribution of the Southern lumber trade extends over the entire year and over the entire territory traversed north and south; the Southern lumbermen are not dependent on winter snows for logging purposes; their stocks are always full, unless depleted through the channels of trade. The territory intervening between Kansas and the Southern forests is rich in natural resources; every foot of it affords a large amount of traffic in both directions. These considerations ought to be strong factors in determining the rates on lumber. But I shall give you a practical idea of the existing conditions. Let us suppose a train load of lumber originates at Conroe, Tex., on the Atchison, Topeka and Santa Fe Railroad, and let us suppose that this lumber is distributed along its line to Chicago, the distances and rates will be as follows:

| | Distance. | Rate per 100 pounds. |
|---|---|---|
| | *Miles.* | *Cents.* |
| Gainesville, Tex | 342 | 18¼ |
| Ardmore, Okla | 382 | 25 |
| Purcell, Okla | 449 | 26¼ |
| Guthrie, Okla | 513 | 28¼ |
| Wichita, Kans | 653 | 28½ |
| Topeka, Kans | 815 | 26 |
| Lawrence, Kans | 842 | 24 |
| Kansas City, Mo | 882 | 23 |
| Chicago, Ill | 1,340 | 24 |

And all points between Carrollton, Mo., and Chicago on this line get a 24-cent rate. You will notice that the rate from Gainesville, Tex., to Ardmore, Okla., jumps up 6¼ cents per 100 pounds in a distance of 40 miles, or 30¼ mills per ton per mile, whereas the through rate to Chicago is 3.6 mills per ton per mile. The rate increases in inverse ratio to the distance the lumber is carried. This is not an isolated case, but is a fair sample of the lumber rates adopted by all the roads operating in the State of Kansas and in Oklahoma.

Texas originates lumber within its own State, and has a stringent State railroad law; this accounts for the advance in freight as soon as the road strikes Oklahoma, and also emphasizes the necessity of an interstate railroad law. The distance from Conroe to Chicago is more than twice the distance from Conroe to Wichita, and yet the rate to Chicago is 24 cents, while the rate to Wichita over the same road under precisely similar conditions is 28½ cents per 100 pounds.

Under the existing interstate-commerce law the Commission is powerless. We employed the best legal talent obtainable, and were advised by them that the Commission can only advise and intercede with the railroads to do the right thing by its patrons, but has no power to enforce its findings. They can not inaugurate a fair and reasonable rate; neither can we obtain redress in any court of the land, except in so far that we can bring suit for recovery in individual cases where the roads have made excessive and unreasonable charges; but to prosecute a suit of this nature takes years under our present system, while in the meantime the excessive charges are carried on by the roads.

With these facts and conditions confronting us and affecting all lines of trade throughout the nation, and presented constantly and persistently by the Presidents of the United States to Congress for the last twenty years for favorable action, it seems unnecessary for business men to plead with Congress to do what seems to them their plain duty. The men who are pleading with you to place on our statutes (Federal) such a law as is suggested in President Roosevelt's message are not wild-eyed Populists. They are men who own and represent capital. They are men who by brain and brawn develop the varied industries of the nation. They are men who produce the business which makes the railroads a public necessity and a paying investment, men who understand the laws of business, men who realize the cost and appreciate good railroad service and are willing to pay for it.

We desire to draw your attention to the fact that the owners and operators of our great public railroads are men subject to like passions as other men. The fact is that men at the heads of the various departments are able men in the prime of life who have an ambition to make a financial record for their respective departments. To gain their ambition they very often resort to means which are neither just nor legal, and we look to you, the only body of men in the nation who have power to give protection, to pass a law which makes justice available and easy and speedy to the humblest citizen of our land. We know that the interests of the railroads do not weigh heavier with you than the interests of the public, and that you will not by inaction make it possible for unscrupulous railroad men to rob an unprotected public.

I know that factitious and misleading arguments are made by the representatives of the railroads, claiming that this legislation would place the rate-making power in the hands of five inexperienced men, and would deprive them of the management of their business. We do not ask for any such law. We would ask you to pass a law which, while it protects the public, also protects the railroads. Any other law would be unconstitutional. The proposed Nelson bill gives ample protection to both parties in interest, and does not deprive the railroads any more of the management of their business than the rulings of the Comptroller of the Currency deprives national banks of the management of their business, or the rulings of the Treasury Department, in administering the revenue, deprives importers or merchants of the management of their business. These departments see that these lines of business are conducted in a lawful and legitimate way, and the only parties that suffer are those who are guilty of fraudulent methods. The railroads are amply protected in this measure against any mistake made by the Commission, intentionally or otherwise, and can get speedy action in any of the Federal courts.

In conclusion we desire to state that we come not to ask a favor, but simple justice. We do not desire to arraign class against class. We ask you as our representatives and lawmakers to place upon our statute book a law which will prevent this. If in your judgment the general public is to be left to the mercy of conscienceless railroad magnates, either repeal the interstate-commerce law or let it stand in its present worthless form. Their practices of extortion and discrimination turn good and able citizens into anarchists. "Patriotism lives and grows ·on what it feeds upon." Create or tolerate a condition which deprives A of an equal chance with B, which will build up one man by pulling down another, or build up one city, community, or State by tearing down another, and let this condition continue for years against the protest of the greatest and most responsible men of the nation, including our Presidents, and you will create a condition of distrust, dissatisfaction, disaster, and political disaffection.

All of which is respectfully submitted.

> E. M. Adams,
> E. S. Miner,
> E. R. Burkholder,
> *Committee.*

(Dictated by E. R. Burkholder, Hillsboro, Kans.)
April 5, 1902.

At the sitting of the committee on Friday, April 11, 1902, the following-named gentlemen appeared: E. P. Bacon, of Milwaukee, chairman of the executive committee of the Interstate Commerce Law Convention, held in St. Louis in November, 1900; Bernard A. Eckhart, of Chicago, representing the Chicago Board of Trade and the Illinois Manufacturers' Association; Hon. Blanchard Randall, of Baltimore, president of the National Board of Trade; Charles England, of Baltimore, grain commissioner; George F. Mead, representing the Boston Chamber of Commerce and the New England Manufacturers' Association; J. B. Daish, representing the National Hay Association; Aaron Jones, grand master of the National Grange, Patrons of Husbandry, and Frank Barry, of Milwaukee.

## STATEMENT OF E. P. BACON.

The CHAIRMAN. Gentlemen, Mr. Bacon is here and wishes to be heard on what are called the Nelson bill and the Elkins bill. He desires to present the whole question. He has given it a great deal of thought, and, I understand, represents the Interstate Commerce Law Convention that was held in St. Louis some time ago.

Mr. BACON. Consisting of delegates from various commercial organizations.

The CHAIRMAN. Before you proceed with your statement, Mr. Bacon, give us your place of residence and your business.

Mr. BACON. My place of residence is Milwaukee; my business is that of grain commission merchant.

The CHAIRMAN. You can proceed.

Mr. BACON. Mr. Chairman, the convention I represent is termed the Interstate Commerce Law Convention, which was held at St. Louis in November, 1900, consisting of delegates from 41 commercial organizations of various kinds. That convention was called for promoting the passage of the Cullom bill, which was then pending in the Senate, but which, as you all know, failed of passage. That convention appointed a committee, which, in consequence of the failure of the passage of the Cullom bill, proceeded to frame a new bill, removing the objections which had been urged to the Cullom bill but retaining the principal features of that bill, or at least what were considered the most important and vital features of it, only two or three in number, omitting the other provisions, some of which had been objected to in different quarters, the object being to have the interstate-commerce act so amended as to give it greater effectiveness, and it was desired that the committee should concentrate its efforts upon these two or three vital provisions.

I will state that the committee, after framing a new bill, which was introduced in the House by Mr. Corliss, and by Mr. Nelson in the Senate, proceeded to communicate with the various commercial organizations of the country in order to secure their opinions of the provisions of the bill. The committee received responses from a very large number of those organizations in approval of the bill, and stating that they had passed resolutions requesting their representatives in Congress to give it their support. I will state briefly of what those organizations consist: Of national organizations there are twelve, comprising the various classes of business—grain dealers, millers, livestock associations, retail grocers, wholesale lumber dealers, National Dining Table Association——

Senator FORAKER. I suggest that, without reading that list, you hand it to the stenographer to be embodied with your statement, which will give us more time to hear what you have to say.

Mr. BACON. I will do so.

Senator FORAKER. Then we shall have it all before us in print.

Mr. BACON. I would like to state, however, that of State organizations there were 18 in number, representing the various branches of trade and industry; and of local organizations there are about 50 in number, making about 80 in all.

The CHAIRMAN. Then you would like to have this paper incorporated as part of your statement?

Mr. BACON. If you please.

The paper is as follows:

NATIONAL ORGANIZATIONS.

Grain Dealers' National Association.
Millers' National Association.
National Board of Trade.
National Dining Table Association.
National Livestock Association.
National Retail Grocers' Association.
National Wholesale Lumber Dealers' Association.
Winter Wheat Millers' League.
Millers' National Federation.
National Wholesale Druggists' Association.
National League of Commission Merchants.
National Hay Association.

## State Organizations.

Illinois Manufacturers' Association.
Indiana State Board of Commerce.
Kansas Millers' Association.
Michigan State Millers' Association.
Minnesota Retail Grocers and General Merchants' Association.
Missouri, Kansas, and Oklahoma Lumber Association.
New England Granite Manufacturers' Association.
New England Shoe and Leather Association.
Ohio Grain Dealers' Association.
Ohio State Association—Patrons of Industry.
Oklahoma Millers' Association.
Texas Cattle Raisers' Association.
Texas Millers' Association.
Utah Live Stock Association.
Wisconsin Cheese Makers' Association.
Wisconsin Retail Hardware Dealers' Association.
Wisconsin Retail Lumber Dealers' Association.
Nebraska Retail Grocers and General Merchants' Association.

## Local Organizations.

### CALIFORNIA.

Claremont Citrus Union.
Colton, San Bernardino County Fruit Exchange.
Los Angeles Chamber of Commerce.
Los Angeles, Southern California Fruit Exchange.
North Pomona, Indian Hill Citrus Union.
Pomona Fruit Growers' Exchange.
Pomona, San Antonio Fruit Exchange.
Porterville Board of Trade.
Porterville, Tulare County Citrus Fruit Exchange.
San Diego Chamber of Commerce.
Santa Barbara Lemon Growers' Exchange.
Santa Barbara, Santa Barbara County Chamber of Commerce.

### COLORADO.

Colorado Springs Chamber of Commerce.

### ILLINOIS.

Chicago Board of Trade.

### INDIANA.

Indianapolis Board of Trade.
Indianapolis Commercial Club.

### IOWA.

Davenport Business Men's Association.

### KANSAS.

Topeka Commercial Club.

### LOUISIANA.

New Orleans Board of Trade.

### MARYLAND.

Baltimore Lumber Exchange.

### MASSACHUSETTS.

Brockton Board of Trade.
Fitchburg Merchants' Association.
Worcester Board of Trade.

### MICHIGAN.

Detroit Merchants' and Manufacturers' Exchange.

MINNESOTA.

Duluth Produce and Fruit Exchange.

MISSISSIPPI.

West Point, Aberdeen Group Commercial Association.

MISSOURI.

Kansas City Board of Trade.
St. Louis Builders' Exchange.

NEBRASKA.

Lincoln, Retail Grocers' Association.
South Omaha Livestock Exchange.

NEW YORK.

Brooklyn, United Retail Grocers' Association.
Buffalo Lumber Exchange.
Buffalo Merchants' Exchange.
Middletown, Business Men's Association.
New York Lumber Trade Association.
New York Manufacturers' Association.
New York Merchants' Association.
New York Produce Exchange.
New York Stationers' Board of Trade.

NORTH CAROLINA.

Wilmington Chamber of Commerce.

OHIO.

Cincinnati Chamber of Commerce. (Will send representative.)
Toledo Produce Exchange. (Will participate in expense and send representative to Washington.)
Newark Board of Trade.

OREGON.

Portland Chamber of Commerce.

PENNSYLVANIA.

Pittsburg Chamber of Commerce.

WASHINGTON.

Spokane Chamber of Commerce.

WISCONSIN.

Milwaukee Chamber of Commerce.
Milwaukee Merchants and Manufacturers' Association.
Milwaukee Association of Master Steam and Hot Water Heating Engineers.
Wyoming-Muscoda Dairy Board.

Mr. BACON. I would like to state the names of individual States which are represented in this expression: California, Colorado, Illinois, Indiana, Iowa, Kansas, Louisiana, Maryland, Massachusetts, Michigan, Minnesota, Mississippi, Missouri, Nebraska, New York, North Carolina, Ohio, Oregon, Pennsylvania, Washington, and Wisconsin.

Senator DOLLIVER. May I trouble you to state what Iowa organization is represented?

F R P——2

Mr. BACON. The Davenport Business Men's Association is the only one from Iowa.

Senator KEAN. What ones from Massachusetts?

Mr. BACON. The Brockton Board of Trade, the Fitchburg Merchants' Association, and the Worcester Board of Trade.

Senator FORAKER. Be kind enough now to look at Ohio.

Mr. BACON. The Cincinnati Chamber of Commerce and the Toledo Produce Exchange.

Those are the local organizations. There are State organizations, some of which I will mention. Ohio Grain Dealers' Association, Ohio State Association Patrons of Industry. Those are the only two State organizations of Ohio, I believe, that have reported.

Senator KEAN. What from New York?

Mr. BACON. Brooklyn, United Retail Grocers' Association; Buffalo Lumber Exchange, Buffalo Merchants' Exchange; Middletown Business Mens' Association; New York Lumber Trade Association; New York Manufacturers' Association; New York Merchants' Association; New York Produce Exchange, and New York Stationers' Board of Trade.

I will also state that the legislatures of several States have passed joint resolutions recommending the passage of this bill or of the former Cullom bill.

The CHAIRMAN. Do you mean the Nelson bill that we have here before us?

Mr. BACON. I speak of the Nelson bill; yes. But several State legislatures a year ago passed joint resolutions recommending the passage of the Cullom bill.

The CHAIRMAN. That is the bill we had under consideration during the last Congress?

Mr. BACON. Yes, sir.

Senator FORAKER. Please tell us the purposes of the bill, how it is designed to accomplish those purposes; and then point out to us the difference between the Nelson bill and the Elkins bill. I assume you are familiar with them. That is what we want to hear rather than the number of people who have indorsed it.

Mr. BACON. Michigan, Wisconsin, Minnesota, South Dakota, Kansas, Louisiana, and Iowa are the States that have recommended the passage of the bill.

The CHAIRMAN. The legislatures of those States have asked for the passage of the Cullom bill; is that what you mean?

Mr. BACON. Part of them asked for the passage of the Cullom bill and part of them the Nelson bill.

Senator DOLLIVER. I think the legislature of Iowa has taken no action in reference to this bill—at least, no action of that legislature has been sent here.

Mr. BACON. I was informed by Mr. Trewin, a member of the Iowa senate, that it passed the senate on a certain date, and two days afterwards he advised me that it had passed the house.

Senator DOLLIVER. I doubt whether your information is correct.

The CHAIRMAN. Now please address yourself to the merits of these bills, as suggested by Governor Foraker.

Mr. BACON. In the first place, the Nelson bill (S. 3575) provides that it shall be the duty of the Commission, when it finds, upon investigation, after hearing all parties interested——

The CHAIRMAN. That is the Interstate Commerce Commission.

Mr. BACON. Yes. That it shall be the duty of the Interstate Commerce Commission, upon investigation, upon formal complaint filed, if it shall find that the rate in question is unreasonable or unjust, to specify what in their judgment is a just and reasonable rate in that particular case, and that rate shall be put into effect.

That provision is also included in the Elkins bill (S. 3521).

The second provision of the Nelson bill is that the orders of the Commission shall be operative at a time specified in the order of the Commission, which shall not be less than twenty days after the order is issued, unless appeal is taken or unless application is made for a review of the order before a circuit court, in which case it shall be suspended for thirty days; and that the circuit court, if it finds upon examination that the order proceeds upon an error of law or is unreasonable under the facts, it may suspend the order of the Commission for a specified time, or during the proceedings under the adjudication of the order. That, I believe, differs somewhat from the Elkins bill. But that is considered a point of equal importance with that of giving the Commission the authority to prescribe the rate to be substituted for the one found to be wrong, for the reason that the cases that have been taken before the courts contesting the orders of the Commission have been in course of adjudication for a long period of time, and the order consequently suspended during that period.

The commission states in one of its recent reports that the average length of time that these cases have been before the courts has been four years. There are several that have been before the courts from five to seven years. There were two that were decided by the Commission which were eight years before the court. There is one which has not yet been decided although it has been nine years before the court. The result of that, as you can readily see, is to make the rulings of the Commission practically inoperative, of no effect, affording no relief whatever to the complainants. After a competent body, skilled in questions of railroad traffic, has found a rate to be unreasonable or unjust, it is continued in force during all this period of adjudication, and the public is subjected to a continuance of that wrong and that injustice, in the absence of relief of this kind making the order operative. It should continue in operation until the courts have declared it wrong. The Commission is utterly unable to afford any relief to the business community as it is now.

The practice on the part of the railway companies in these cases has been to protract the proceedings to the utmost possible extent, it being readily seen that it is for their interest to do so. If the Commission has ordered a reduction of 20 per cent, the longer the railway company can prevent the putting into operation of that order, the more it is to its advantage, of course; and it has made use of that to a very great extent, so that it has come to be regarded as almost useless on the part of the business men to bring any case before the Commission. In some cases it takes two or three years to get them through the Commission, to hear all the parties concerned, and to bring the matter to a conclusion. Any business man or commercial organization undertaking the conduct of a case before the Commission becomes almost tired out before it reaches a conclusion in the Commission itself; and then the case is subject to a further delay of three to six years while the validity of the order of the Commission is being contested in the courts. This practically renders the interstate-commerce act of no value whatever to the business community.

Senator FORAKER. Does the bill which you favor undertake in any way to have that difficulty remedied in the commission?

Mr. BACON. As to the delays before the commission?

Senator FORAKER. Before the commission itself, yes.

Mr. BACON. There is no special provision made in that respect.

Senator FORAKER. The remedy is aimed simply at the courts, so far as any provision of the bill is concerned?

Mr. BACON. The desire is to avoid any further delay. Nevertheless, the business organizations have urged upon the Interstate Commerce Commission the expediting of cases before the commission, and will undoubtedly continue to do so.

Another provision of the Nelson bill is that the testimony taken before the Commission shall be certified to the court when the order of the Commission is appealed from; and if additional testimony is offered before the court by either party, the court is to refer the case back to the Commisson to take that additional testimony, and to certify the facts to the court as thereafter found. The object of that is to necessitate the carriers presenting all their testimony before the Commission. It has been the practice to present only a part of it, and then when the case is appealed to the courts to introduce additional testimony, and the consequence has been that the decision of the court has been at times on an entirely different case from that before the Commission.

Furthermore, that causes delay. Ordinarily it takes a case a year, or a year and a half, to go through the commission, and once in awhile two to three years. But the carriers, by means of this method of introducing additional testimony before the court, simply subjects the shipper or the commercial organization, complainant in the case, to unnecessary delay. That seems to be one of the means that is taken advantage of for the purpose of promoting delay, and preventing any order of the commission going into effect within a reasonable time.

One of the important differences between the two bills is that under the Elkins bill the order of the Commission is made obligatory for only a period of one year, while under the Nelson bill it is made obligatory for two years. Under the present law there is no limitation to the time of this obligation. The committee that prepared the Nelson bill deemed it best for the protection of the railway interests to provide that the order of the Commission should be in effect only two years. An objection had been made by the railway interests to the effect that the Commission having the power to prescribe the rate to be observed in the future, when it found the existing rate to be wrong, would before many years have made all the rates for the country. To obviate that objection on the part of the carriers, the committee in the preparation of the Nelson bill made this provision: That the order of the Commission should be obligatory only for a period of two years.

Senator FORAKER. That is the order fixing the rate, where complaint has been made and heard?

Mr. BACON. Yes.

Senator DOLLIVER. Did I understand you to say that in case the rate suggested by the Commission is obviously wrong and burdensome to the company, the court would have the right to suspend it pending litigation?

Mr. BACON. That is what I said. Let me read to you the exact provision of the bill in that respect. I read from the second paragraph on page 6 of the Nelson bill:

The filing of a petition to review an order shall of itself suspend the effect of such order for thirty days, and the court before which the same is pending may also, if upon an inspection of the record it plainly appears that the order proceeds upon some error of law, or is unjust and unreasonable upon the facts, and not otherwise, suspend the operation of the order during the pendency of the proceedings in review, or until further order of the court.

Senator CARMACK. The application of itself suspends the order, as I gather from the reading of that.

Mr. BACON. Yes; the application to the circuit court for a review of the order itself suspends the operation of that order for thirty days. I was about to say, in further response to the question asked by Senator Foraker, that the Commission is not authorized under this bill to make any change in rates in order to correct any error found to exist in the rates, except where formal complaint has been filed before the Commission, and that complaint has been investigated and all parties in interest have been given an opportunity to be heard.

The CHAIRMAN. Is it clearly provided that this order of the Commission shall be in force for two years, and that thereafter the railroads shall make a new rate in that given case?

Mr. BACON. The railroad will be free to make a new rate in that case. It is provided, however, as a protection to any interested party in regard to the change of rate, that he may file with the Commission his objections to such change.

The CHAIRMAN. I know; but let us suppose that the Commission makes an order reducing the rate; that order stands good under the Nelson bill for two years, does it?

Mr. BACON. Two years.

The CHAIRMAN. And after that the railroad is at liberty to make another rate?

Mr. BACON. Yes; and if they do make another rate there is this provision: That any party interested may file with the Commission his objections within sixty days, and the Commission "may thereupon order the carrier to restore and maintain the rate or practice required by the original order, pending its investigation as to the lawfulness or reasonableness of such change."

The CHAIRMAN. Suppose that the railroad, after the Commission has made an order, takes no appeal, but goes on to carry out the Commission's order upon an individual case; that order is binding for two years, and only two years?

Mr. BACON. That is right.

The CHAIRMAN. Consequently, the railroad can make any rate it pleases in that case?

Mr. BACON. It can. But anyone interested has the privilege of filing with the Commission objections to that change, and in that way reopen the case before the Commission.

Senator CARMACK. You mean any shipper?

Mr. BACON. Any shipper can file his objections with the Commission itself.

The CHAIRMAN. How long do you think that would keep a rate in force?

Mr. BACON. It would remain in force another two years.

The CHAIRMAN. Can this go on indefinitely?

Mr. BACON. There is no provision as to how often this process may be repeated. But the provision is inserted so that any party interested, feeling that he has been wronged by the change of rate, can have an opportunity to have it considered under the circumstances existing at the time.

Senator CLAPP. At the end of the two years would the subject be thrown back where it was originally?

Mr. BACON. Exactly.

Senator CLAPP. The Commission has jurisdiction to take up another complaint.

Mr. BACON. It would be virtually a new complaint brought before the Commission, to be considered with reference to the changed conditions and circumstances.

Senator DOLLIVER. Does the order of the Commission contemplated here apply to the individual only or to the classification?

Mr. BACON. Simply to the individual complaint. The complaint may, however, be in relation to an unjust and unreasonable rate or to an unjust and unreasonable classification.

Senator DOLLIVER. Suppose it is an unjust personal discrimination, is not the order of the Commission liable to create more discriminations than it cures, by putting that individual case out of relation with everybody else?

Mr. BACON. A personal discrimination is simply a criminal matter, and the parties are proceeded against criminally. Personal discriminations do not require a determination of the question of whether there was discrimination or not; that is, the payment of rebates is by the present law made a crime, and the railway company guilty of it and the party receiving the rebate are both amenable for the violation of the law under criminal proceeding.

Senator DOLLIVER. But the complaint is very general that there is a secret departure from the published rates.

Mr. BACON. That is one of the serious complaints.

Senator DOLLIVER. What is there in this bill to make it more difficult for the railroads to depart from the order of the Commission secretly than there is to depart secretly from their own agreed and published schedule rates?

Mr. BACON. There are provisions in this bill aiming particularly at that evil, making it more practicable for the commission to obtain the necessary evidence to convict the parties of violation of law. But the payment of rebates, like any other dishonest proceeding, will never be wholly prevented by law. It can only be punished when practiced, the same as any other criminal act. But that is an entirely different thing from the matter of exercising supervision over rates.

Senator CARMACK. Is not the matter of rebates the worst trouble in the whole business?

Mr. BACON. I am very much surprised to find that there is entertained very generally by the public that idea, that individual discrimination is the great evil of the transportation business. But from my own observation—and I have made a study of the operation of the interstate-commerce act ever since its original enactment and have followed its workings very closely—my own observation is that that is comparatively a trivial evil. The great evil is the discrimination between localities—discrimination in the published rates—certain localities being discriminated against in favor of other localities.

Senator DOLLIVER. Has Milwaukee escaped that evil?

Mr. BACON. It has not. I do not know of any city in the country that is more discriminated against than Milwaukee. I will say, however, that Milwaukee brought a case before the Commission some six years ago on account of discrimination and obtained a decision in its favor from the Commission. The Commission ordered a reduction, and that order has never been obeyed by the railway companies, for the reason that just about the time the decision was promulgated the decision of the Supreme Court declared that the Commission had not the authority to prescribe what change should be made in the rates when it found existing rates wrong. Under that decision the railway companies absolutely refused to pay any attention to the order of the Commission. And I will say in this connection that up to that time, which was ten years after the organization of the Commission, the Commission had made its orders in just such cases, prescribing what changes should be made in the rates, and those orders were almost universally observed by the transportation companies. The right of the Commission to do that had never been questioned up to that time. The condition of traffic matters throughout the country during that period was the most satisfactory it has ever been either before or since.

The chief purpose of this bill is to restore that condition of things, to give the Commission specifically this authority which it exercised during that period, under what it deemed inferentially to be its power, its right, and not only its power and right, but its duty. The decision of the Supreme Court was not predicated upon any question as to the constitutional right of Congress to vest the Commission with this power, but it was confined to the fact that the power was not specifically conferred in terms by the law.

Senator DOLLIVER. What is the usual motive for discriminating against localities, as in the Milwaukee case to which you have referred?

Mr. BACON. I will answer that question.

Senator CARMACK. It is more frequently discriminated against than some other localities, is it not?

Mr. BACON. The motive is not for the purpose of discriminating in favor of one locality as against another, but it arises from competition for business over a certain territory. Certain railroads taking business from a certain territory to a certain market are in competition with other roads taking the same kind of business to another market, and each of the roads is trying, of course, to get the advantage over the other in the division of the business. In consequence of that the rates become discriminative.

Senator KEAN. Demoralized.

Mr. BACON. Not demoralized, but discriminative as against certain localities. For instance, here are these various seaboard cities—Boston, New York, Philadelphia, and Baltimore. Certain rates are made from the western country to these seaboard cities. Each of the trunk lines is desirous to obtain as large a share of that business as possible, and in making rates each seeks to make rates that will give itself the advantage over competitors. The railroads, in order to break up destructive competition between them, agree upon certain differentials from certain territory to certain markets or certain ports; they agree upon that with reference to the distribution of the business, not with reference to the question of right or equity. It is simply to divide the business as nearly satisfactorily as possible under the operation of the rates between themselves. The result of that often is that certain places are discriminated against and certain other places are favored.

That practice will be continued until some competent authority requires
it to be changed, because it is only natural that the railroad companies
should continue it.

A case of that kind came up a few years ago with reference to Cincinnati and Chicago in regard to the business to the southeast as compared with the business from the seaboard cities to the southeast.  In
that case the Commission decided that the rates from Cincinnati and
Chicago into that territory were unjustly large as compared with the
rates from the seaboard cities into that territory, and the Commission
prescribed a certain difference which should be made in those rates in
order to equalize the two sections of the country with reference to the
Southern trade.  That case was carried into court, appealed to the
Supreme Court, and the Supreme Court denied the right of the Commission to specify what rates should be enforced in future.

In reference to the exercise of this power by the Commission I wish
to read an extract from the annual report of the Commission for 1897,
in which it expressed itself on this subject.  It says:

It (the Commission) understood that when, as in this case, the rates had been
established by the carriers and afterwards challenged or complained of as unreasonable,
and the question of unreasonableness had been tried, the Commission could declare
not only what rate was wrong, but what would be right, and could lawfully petition
the court to enforce the right.  That is to say, when a rate had been established by
the carriers, challenged by or on behalf of shippers, and tried by the Commission in
a proceeding ordered and regulated as near as may be in conformity with United
States court proceedings, the Commission had a right, and it became its duty when
justified by the facts, to declare the rate wrong, decide what rate would be right, and
through the judgment of the court compel the carrier to perform its legal duty to
receive and carry property at rates which are reasonable and just.

The Commission exercised this power in a case commenced in the second month
after its organization and continued to exercise it for a period of more than ten years,
during which time no member of the Commission ever officially questioned the existence of such authority or failed to join in its exercise.  As already stated, the authority
of the Commission to modify and reduce an established rate, and to enforce a reasonable rate for the future, was not questioned in the answer of the defendant in the
Atlanta rate case, decided March 30, 1896 (previously cited), nor had it ever been
denied in any of the answers made to more than four hundred cases previously commenced, many of them alleging unreasonable and unjust charges and praying the
Commission to enforce a reduction and lower rates in the future.

I introduce that to show clearly what the practice of the Commission
had been for that ten years, and also to show the fact that the authority
for the Commission to proceed in that way had never been questioned
during that ten years by any of the carriers.

We were speaking, when I was interrupted, about the limit of time
during which these orders of the Commission should be obligatory,
being two years under the Nelson bill but only one under the Elkins
bill.  I wish to say to the committee that the limitation of one year
strikes business men as being altogether too limited.  Even two years
is regarded by business men generally as a very short time.  The
length of time taken, the amount of labor required to prepare a case
before the Commission and to carry it through to a decision, and then
the possible contest of that case in the courts, entail such an amount
of time, labor, and expense upon the shipper, or upon the commercial
organization conducting it, that if the order were only to be in force
for one year there would not be one case in twenty, to say the least,
that would ever be brought before the Commission; that is, it would
be considered by the party injured that it would not pay him to go to

the labor and expense for the sake of having the prescribed rate in effect only one year.

Senator DOLLIVER. I want to get more clearly the application of this bill. When there has been an adjudication of an individual complaint, would it not be better to have some mechanism by which the order could be made applicable to all such cases?

Mr. BACON. That is the case, sir.

Senator DOLLIVER. Is there any process is the law by which an order made in an individual case shall also be made obligatory upon all cases similarly situated?

Mr. BACON. That is the case as regards what I term personal discriminations—payment of rebates, for instance.

Senator DOLLIVER. Or extortion?

Mr. BACON. That is a different matter. The question of discriminative rates must be determined by the Commission in each case.

Senator CLAPP. You do not understand Senator Dolliver. Complaint is made by an individual that the rate which he is paying upon something is excessive.

Mr. BACON. I understood it.

Senator CLAPP. What the Senator means, as I understand, is how far can the Commission upon that complaint take into account the effect of modifying that rate as to other cases? That is what the Senator is referring to.

Mr. BACON. The Commission takes into consideration the relation of that rate to other rates and determines largely upon that relation as to reasonableness or unreasonableness. It has no power to order a general reduction. It can only order a change in the particular rate complained of in each individual case.

Senator FORAKER. Why not make the rate for every shipper, not for the one shipper?

Mr. BACON. The Commission can go no farther than to change the rate in the particular instance where complaint has been made.

The CHAIRMAN. Suppose that the court after final review at the end of two years should decide that the order of the Commission was wrong, and that the rate fixed by the railroad in the first instance was right. Then what recourse would the railroad have upon the shipper to get back the difference in money?

Mr, BACON. It is impossible to make any such provision. It is simply a question of who shall suffer during the pendency of the proceeding.

The CHAIRMAN. Should not the shipper give bond for the repayment of that money?

Mr. BACON. It is impossible to do that for the reason that the party who has paid the freight has passed it along on his goods sold to the consumer, and so he does not himself sustain any damage.

The CHAIRMAN. Let me go further: Suppose this order had affected one hundred shippers. as Senator Clapp suggests, to a given destination or between certain points; and suppose that the railroad should lose $400,000 to $500,000 by reason of transporting freight at the rate prescribed; would you not suggest some provision or remedy by which, if the court should decide that the Commission had been in error, the railroad could recover back the difference?

Senator McLAURIN. There would be this trouble about that: Sup-

pose A makes application to the Commission for a reduction, and the
Commission orders that reduction, and the order goes into force; the
railroad company during the time that order was in force would have
to reduce the freight rates on that commodity not only to the applicant, but to everybody else.

The CHAIRMAN. That is my question. I said that.

Senator McLAURIN. Practically, it would deter anybody from making application if he had to give bond to idenmify the railroad company against all loss.

The CHAIRMAN. Not one shipper alone, but every other shipper.

Senator McLAURIN. There would be this trouble about that, that
although B might have had nothing to do with the litigation between
the applicant and the railroad company, he would have to become a
bondsman.

The CHAIRMAN. How is the railroad to be protected against hauling
freight at a loss of $400,000 to $500,000? We do not want to confiscate the railroads.

Senator McLAURIN. There would be considerable difficulty about it,
but you might require everybody to pay into some fund somewhere
the difference between the amount of compensation authorized by the
Commission and the amount that the railroad had fixed, and then if
the railroad company should win, that goes to the company; but if
the company should lose, that would go back to the shippers.

The CHAIRMAN. I will suggest, Senator, that these are questions
that we can perhaps discuss better in executive session. I would like
to get in print before the committee the ideas of Mr. Bacon on that
subject. Now, Mr. Bacon, you say, as I understand, that there is no
recourse provided in the bill, and should be none. Is that your posi-
sition or the position of the organizations you represent?

Senator McLAURIN. I ask your pardon, Mr. Chairman. I think
your suggestion is the better way.

The CHAIRMAN. I want the ideas of the parties who desire to support the bill and who hold, as I understand, that the railroad under
this bill has no recourse and should not have any.

Mr. BACON. I do not think it should not have any.

The CHAIRMAN. That is a direct answer to the question.

Mr. BACON. But, so far as I am able to see, it is impracticable to
make such provision, and certainly there is no such provision in the
bill. It is largely a question of the preponderance of right or of the
suffering and hardship. In the nature of the case, one party or the
other must suffer some hardship, and the question is who will suffer
the more—the railway company or the public.

The CHAIRMAN. That is your position.

Mr. BACON. Yes.

Senator DOLLIVER. I find nothing in here that would make the permanent order applicable to anybody else except the complainant.
Why should the rates be suspended as to the whole upon an individual
complaint.

Mr. BACON. It changes the rate, and of course that rate is open to
all shippers.

Senator DOLLIVER. There might be some mechanism to make it
applicable to the complainant only.

The CHAIRMAN. The Nelson bill does not provide for pooling at all.

Mr. BACON. No.

The CHAIRMAN. Are you against pooling?

Mr. BACON. The convention which I represent was silent on that subject; expressed no sentiment on the subject. Therefore, as the representative of that convention, I have nothing to say on that point.

Senator FORAKER. That is a very important question. You are a well-informed man, and I, as one member of the committee, would like to have the benefit of your views on that subject.

Mr. BACON. Let me answer the question put by the Chairman.

The CHAIRMAN. You are now going back to the other question?

Mr. BACON. I am answering your question. I am now going on to say that the protection of the carrier lies in the fact that the Commission which has determined this question is a competent body, and has acquired a knowledge of traffic matters and skill in the adjustment of them sufficient to enable it to promulgate a decision which in all probability will stand the test of appeal to the courts, and the cases in which it will not stand that test will be a very small number; consequently the loss entailed upon the carrier will be exceedingly small. On the other hand, without this provision the public is subjected to a continuance for years of this rate, which has been pronounced by a competent body to be wrong, and the whole community is paying hundreds and thousands, possibly millions, of dollars, while the case is being carried through the courts.

So that it seems to me, as a matter of practical expediency, that there can be no question but the right way is to make the order immediately operative and let the carrier take the slight risk which will result in these exceptional cases, rather than to permit the public to be wronged year after year while the cases are pending. The wrong in one instance is comparstively insignificant, while in the other instance it is enormous.

Senator FORAKER. Will you give me the benefit of your views about pooling? That is a very important subject.

The CHAIRMAN. Perhaps the gentleman who is to succeed you, Mr. Bacon, will address himself to that subject.

Senator KEAN. But Senator Foraker has asked for Mr. Bacon's opinion.

Senator FORAKER. I do not want it unless he is willing to give it; I am sure it would be an intelligent one.

Mr. BACON. I will say that I have a definite opinion on that subject, but as chairman of the committee that has prepared this bill, in which there is no provision in regard to it, I feel somewhat embarrassed in stating that opinion.

Senator FORAKER. I do not want you to be embarrassed at all. Subsequently——

Mr. BACON. Mr. Chairman, I would like about two minutes to answer a question by Senator Foraker. He asked what provision there was in the bill that would be effective in relation to the prevention of discrimination. As an answer to that I will read, beginning at the top of page 9 of Senate bill 3575:

Any circuit court of the United States for a district through which any portion of the road of a carrier runs shall, upon petition of the Commission, or of any party interested, enjoin such carrier or its receivers, lessees, trustees, officers, or agents from giving, and a shipper from receiving, with respect to interstate transportation of persons or property subject to the provisions of this act, any concession from the lawfully published rate, or from accepting persons or property for such transportation if a rate has not been lawfully published; and by "concession" is meant the giving of any rebate or drawback, the rendering of any additional service, or the practicing of any device or contrivance by which a less compensation than that prescribed by the published tariffs is ultimately received, or by which a greater service in any respect than that stated in such tariffs is rendered.

That covers that point.

Senator DOLLIVER. That is the law now, is it not?

Mr. BACON. No; there is no provision of that kind in the present law. But the question has recently appeared before the courts as to whether they can enjoin railroad companies in this way. A temporary injunction has been granted in several cases in Kansas City and Chicago, and we are told authoritatively that it is the opinion of counsel of the various railroad interests that a permanent injunction can not possibly issue. This specifically provides that a permanent injunction may be issued in such cases.

The CHAIRMAN. I believe that we are all in favor of the most drastic provisions in any of these bills that will prevent discriminations or secret rebates. There is no controversy about that. Any suggestion from anybody to make the law stronger than is proposed in either the Nelson bill or the Elkins bill will meet with the favor of the entire committee, I am sure. So on that point there can be no controversy.

Mr. BACON. I want to answer another inquiry by Senator Clapp, in relation to the enforcement of the order of the Commission requiring a differential not greater than 2 cents a hundred on flour as compared with wheat, why that has not been enforced.

Senator CLAPP. No; I did not ask that question.

Mr. BACON. The question was asked by some Senator. The reason is that under the decision of the Supreme Court the Commission has no right to say what change shall be made. Hence the complainants are debarred from going to the courts and asking an order to enforce the order of the Commission.

## STATEMENT OF BERNARD A. ECKHART.

The CHAIRMAN. Will you be kind enough to state whom you represent?

Mr. ECKHART. I represent the Chicago Board of Trade and the Illinois Manufacturers' Association.

The CHAIRMAN. And your business?

Mr. ECKHART. I am in the flour-milling business at Chicago. I will not attempt to discuss the inadequacy of the present interstate-commerce act or the different features of the bills pending before the committee. Those points have been covered largely by Mr. Bacon, and I assume will be discussed by others who have given that branch of the subject considerable attention.

I desire briefly to call your attention to a few important facts in relation to the milling business of this country, and as to how the inability of the Interstate Commerce Commission to enforce its findings affects the millers of the United States.

It may be interesting to state that there are about nine to ten thousand mills in this country, scattered over 33 different States of the Union, and that their annual output is about $600,000,000. The value of the flour alone produced in these mills is about $400,000,000, to say nothing of the by-products and the cooperage, bagging, fuel, and other things consumed. There are mills enough in this country to grind up all the wheat that we raise annually in the course of four or five months.

The difficulty that we have had in the last four or five years has been the freight-rate discrimination practiced by the transportation companies against flour for export in favor of wheat for export.

The CHAIRMAN. By export do you mean to go across the ocean?

Mr. ECKHART. Yes; from the interior of the country to the seaboard, and from there to Europe.

The CHAIRMAN. By discrimination you mean the amount of freight pai for flour over and above what is paid for the transportation of wheat?

Mr. ECKHART. Charging a proportionately higher rate of freight for flour than for grain.

Senator DOLLIVER. Just how is it between Chicago and New York?

Mr. ECKHART. The published rate is about the same, as a rule. But the difficulty we have encountered is that they have made secret and special rates to the grain shippers for carrying wheat that were not made to the millers of the country for flour. In other words, there are instances where they have charged 15 cents a hundred from Chicago to New York for flour, and have carried wheat for about eight or nine cents a hundred, which makes a difference of about twelve to fifteen cents a barrel on flour, thus giving the foreign miller a great advantage over the American miller.

The foreign countries, more especially the United Kingdom, require either our wheat or our flour. They will take our flour, providing the transportation companies do not discriminate against the miller by carrying wheat at a much less rate of freight, or, in other words, make a secret cut rate on wheat for export.

Senator DOLLIVER. Most of the European countries have high tariffs against flour.

Mr. ECKHART. To those countries we do not export flour. We can not.

Senator CARMACK. To what countries do you export most?

Mr. ECKHART. England is the largest buyer of our flour, and Holland comes next.

The American millers can hold their own against the world on an equal basis if the transportation companies cease discriminating against us. We do not enjoy any special privileges, and we have never asked any. We are not a protected industry; we do not need it. But we do feel that the transportation companies should treat us fairly and equitably. We also feel that it would be a great advantage to the transportation companies to carry all of our surplus product in the shape of flour, rather than wheat, because when this cutting of rates is resorted to, as it has been in the past, they get but nominal rates of freight, hardly commensurate with the value, for carrying wheat.

Senator KEAN. Is it not a through rate?

Mr. ECKHART. It is invariably a cut rate.

Senator KEAN. I mean, does it not include ocean transportation?

Mr. ECKHART. Sometimes they give a through bill of lading, but they pay the ocean freight; that is, whatever cut is made is generally made by our own inland lines.

Senator KEAN. By the ocean lines?

Mr. ECKHART. No; by the railroad lines.

The CHAIRMAN. Is it your contention that wheat and flour ought to be made to pay the same rates?

Mr. ECKHART. We contend that it costs no more to carry flour than wheat. That matter was up before the Interstate Commerce Commission two years ago.

Senator DOLLIVER. I understand the published rate is the same for both.

Mr. ECKHART. The published rate is generally the same.

Senator DOLLIVER. Why do you not get an injunction and make them stand together?

Mr. ECKHART. In answer to that question, I will say that the matter was placed by us before the Interstate Commerce Commission, where we showed conclusively by a preponderance of evidence that it did not cost any more to transport flour than wheat, for the reason that the millers invariably fix up their own cars and load them, and when the railroads furnish us large cars we load them to their utmost capacity; whereas, in case of wheat shipment the railway company is obliged to furnish inside car doors and clean and fix up its own cars.

Senator DOLLIVER. What effect would this equality of rates have on the foreign shipment of wheat?

Mr. ECKHART. We would export our surplus in the form of wheat.

Senator DOLLIVER. No wheat would go abroad?

Mr. ECKHART. Very little.

Senator DOLLIVER. How would that leave the wheat raisers of the United States? Would not that leave them in rather intimate relations with the millers?

Mr. ECKHART. No; that would leave them in this position: They prefer to have buyers of wheat the whole year round. The American farmers of to-day are in such a condition that they like to sell their product to competitors. They enjoy marketing their product to the millers, because the millers are located in different sections of the country and are there competing, one against the other, for wheat to grind in their mills.

Senator DOLLIVER. I have heard the matter complained of in our country that competition has been greatly reduced in recent years.

Mr. ECKHART. Well, that may be true to a certain extent; but it is nevertheless true that competition does exist very largely in the wheat-growing States of the United States.

Senator CARMACK. The wheat grower then would find his market entirely with the miller; he would have no market abroad for his wheat?

Mr. ECKHART. Oh, yes; most assuredly. The miller would have to compete with the exporter in the purchase of his wheat from the farmers.

Senator CARMACK. I understand that.

Mr. ECKHART. There would be the same demand for our surplus, and if they could buy cheaper the manufactured article in the markets of the world than they could buy it in the form of wheat, they would certainly buy it in the form of flour.

Senator FORAKER. Can you let us have the benefit of your views as to these pending bills?

Mr. ECKHART. As I stated at the outset, I do not propose to discuss the merits of the bills, for I believe Mr. Bacon and others have given more attention to the bills than I have, and are therefore more competent to discuss them.

Senator FORAKER. Do you prefer the Nelson bill to any of the others?

Mr. ECKHART. No. So far as I am personally concerned, and so far as the interests I represent are concerned, I am not particular what bill is enacted if there shall be some supervision exercised over the transportation companies. We realize that it is the tendency of the times that consolidation and federation are taking place. We realize, too, that the transportation companies, unless some supervision be exercised by the General Government, can build up one set of men at the expense of another set of men; that they can build up one section of the country at the expense of another section, so that our only hope is in national legislation.

Senator DOLLIVER. We have national legislation now that makes criminal the payment of secret rebates. I will state to you that six suits have been brought by the Interstate Commerce Commission against six lines of railway to enjoin them from any secret departure from their published rates; and, as I understand it, they have entered a court of equity and secured a decree to that effect, which would seem to be a pretty effective remedy for the trouble you complain about.

Senator CARMACK. You have read this bill. What is there in it in the way of more stringent regulations against secret rebates?

Mr. ECKHART. I understand that this bill will correct the defects of the interstate commerce law that have been found to exist against the shipping interests. It was supposed when the original interstate commerce law was enacted that it would cure the evils that then existed, but of course it was in the nature of experimental legislation and in many respects was somewhat crude and imperfect, and the decisions of the courts of the country have shorn it of many of its salient features. I understand that the Nelson bill, if enacted, will remedy some of the defects that have been encountered in the execution of the interstate commerce law.

But what I desired was to call your attention to the difficulties under which a great industry like the milling business is suffering and for which they are asking a remedy.

Senator CARMACK. The whole burden of complaint of the milling industry is against secret rebates, I understand.

Mr. ECKHART. I do not share entirely the views expressed by Mr. Bacon that discriminations in favor of persons are but a trivial matter. I believe that the discriminations practiced by the transportation companies in favor of certain persons against others are destructive of our commercial system, and will ultimately result in the absolute destruction or confiscation of the property of certain people and certain industries. While discrimination has been practiced, and can continue to be practiced, in favor of certain sections against other sections, and while that is a great evil, I believe that the evil of transportation companies giving certain people secret rebates, giving special rates and special privileges, to the exclusion of the public, is detrimental to and destructive of our commercial interests.

Senator CARMACK. The secret rebate of which you complain, however, could not be secret as a rebate in favor of certain individuals against certain other individuals. It is a secret rebate in favor of one class of freight against another class of freight, is it not?

Mr. ECKHART. No. I mean to say that transportation companies have practiced secretly in the past the giving of special rates.

The CHAIRMAN. To individuals?

Mr. ECKHART. To individuals.

Senator CARMACK. As I understand your statement, while through rates for flour and wheat are the same, yet by secret rebates there are differences made?

Mr. ECKHART. Yes.

Senator CARMACK. By that do you mean secret rebates to particular individuals, or is it a general system by which flour is discriminated against?

Mr. ECKHART. That is general. But in discriminating against flour they give certain shippers, located in certain sections of the country, a special rate which is not open even to competitors.

Senator KEAN. For instance, Minneapolis would get a special rate while Chicago would not?

Mr. ECKHART. Chicago could get a special rate and Minneapolis not be able to enjoy it.

Senator CARMACK. What is the cause of this action on the part of the railroads in making this discrimination against flour; what object have they in that?

Mr. ECKHART. Of course I only have a general knowledge; what they tell us. They say, for instance, that one of the transportation companies is out for business; wants to increase its tonnage from a certain section. They go out and get business. Their solicitors want business, and they make special rates. Then another transportation company, finding that the traffic is going over another line, says: "Well, some other fellow is making a special rate; we want business, and we will make a special rate also."

Senator CLAPP. Why does not that apply to flour as well as to wheat?

Mr. ECKHART. That is due, possibly, to this fact, that the railroad companies claim that they can get from 150,000 to 200,000 bushels of wheat to move within a very short space of time, whereas flour will come anyway, because the mills have got to grind, and they will keep in operation, and so they will get that product anyway. That is where they are mistaken, for if they carry the wheat to the seaboard and it goes out of this country as wheat the millers of this country will certainly not be able to grind it into flour, and so it is against their own interest, because they would invariably get the same tonnage at a reasonable freight rate, at the tariff or the published rate. It would go forward because the foreign countries have got to have our surplus and will take it. In that respect I think the transportation companies ought to favor this bill in order to protect themselves against each other.

Senator DOLLIVER. Have you ever received an order from the Interstate Commerce Commission declaring that flour should have the same rate as wheat?

Mr. ECKHART. No. It has said substantially that they believe there should be a small differential, and of course we are willing to abide by that. I think the differential is 2 cents a hundred.

Mr. BACON. Not to exceed 2 cents a hundred.

Mr. ECKHART. Not to exceed 2 cents a hundred. We are perfectly willing to abide by that.

Senator DOLLIVER. On what theory is that based?

Mr. ECKHART. On the theory that the Interstate Commerce Commission, after hearing the evidence, believed that it costs a little more to discharge or unload flour at the other end than wheat. Personally, I believe that the differential established by the Interstate Commerce Commission is a little excessive.

Senator DOLLIVER. Is there not a very substantial difference in the value, by weight, of flour as compared with wheat?

Mr. ECKHART. There is some little difference, but it is not very great.

Senator DOLLIVER. To start with, you have to put the flour in the package, whereas the wheat is shipped in bulk.

Mr. ECKHART. That is true, but the package only costs about 10 cents per barrel.

Senator DOLLIVER. It certainly takes more than a bushel of wheat to produce a bushel of flour.

Mr. ECKHART. Oh, yes; and the labor and the package must be added to the value.

Senator DOLLIVER. I mean there must be more wheat than a bushel to produce a bushel of flour.

Mr. ECKHART. Oh, yes.

Senator DOLLIVER. In other words, the wheat is the raw material?

Mr. ECKHART. Let me see if I can explain that. You can get just as much flour into a car as you can of wheat, so that a 50,000-pound car can be loaded with 50,000 pounds of flour. So they lose nothing in that direction.

Senator FORAKER. How much difference would there be between the value of 50,000 pounds of flour and 50,000 pounds of wheat?

Mr. ECKHART. The difference would probably be——

Senator KEAN. About five times, would it not?

Mr. ECKHART. Oh, no. The difference is possibly 25 cents on the barrel of flour, taking the same weight in wheat. In other words, the value would possibly be from 10 to 12 cents a hundred pounds.

Senator KEAN. That is on 50,000 pounds.

The CHAIRMAN. Is it true that if you could get the same rate on flour and wheat to New York and London the mills of the country would grind all the wheat?

Mr. ECKHART. Yes.

The CHAIRMAN. Then there would not be any wheat to export?

Mr. ECKHART. Very little, certainly.

The CHAIRMAN. Do you think this would be in the interest of the American millers?

Mr. ECKHART. Yes; and in the interest of the American transportation companies and American labor.

The CHAIRMAN. Do you think we could pass laws to regulate those matters?

Mr. ECKHART. No, sir; but I do believe that we can pass laws in this country to exercise supervision over our interstate commerce so as to prevent transportation companies who are common carriers from building up one interest and ruining another interest. What we desire is equality. Of course many of the foreign nations go a great deal further than that. France, for instance, protects its millers by giving them a bounty.

The CHAIRMAN. Is this about what you would like to submit?

Mr. ECKHART. Yes.

Senator CARMACK. I want to ask one question. I understand that the Interstate Commerce Commission have made an order in respect to this matter of differential between wheat and flour, with which I understand you are fairly satisfied.

Mr. ECKHART. Yes.

Senator CARMACK. What is the difficulty about enforcing that order?

Mr. ECKHART. They can not enforce it, they tell me, because they have not the power to enforce their finding.

Senator FORAKER. That is, the Commission can not?

Mr. ECKHART. The Commission can not.

Senator CLAPP. I suggest, Mr. Chairman, that the real issue here is as to what can be accomplished by these bills.

The CHAIRMAN. That is correct.

## STATEMENT OF AARON JONES.

The CHAIRMAN. Please state your residence, your business, and whom you represent.

Mr. JONES. Mr. Chairman, my name is Aaron Jones; my residence is South Bend, Ind.; I am a farmer. I am here as the representative of the National Grange, a farmers' organization composed of an active membership of about 500,000 people, all farmers. This organization is a nonpartisan organization. It has subordinate branches which hold their meetings throughout the States. We have a national organization which is composed of delegates from the various State organizations. I appear before you as chairman of the committee on legislation, and also as master of the National Grange.

This question of interstate commerce is one that the farmers of the United States, irrespective of party affiliations, have a very deep interest in. It is one upon which they have thought more earnestly and deeply than perhaps any other single question. The farmers, as you know, are not a class of men very much given to talking. Yet they feel earnestly upon this question, as it underlies the prosperity of the agricultural classes.

I desire to say that our organization and the farmers generally, so far as I know, have the most friendly feeling for the railroad interests of this country, as well as all the other transportation interests of the country. There is not a particle of prejudice in our minds as against any of the transportation companies of the country. We desire that all these transportation companies should be fairly remunerated for the services that they render to the people. But the growing consolidation of these organizations and the increase of freight rates has impressed us with the fact that the time has come when a power beyond that of the railroads themselves should review the prices that they charge for the transportation of commodities and say what is fair and equitable.

We believe that a commission or a committee having this matter in charge should be composed of men not engaged in the business of transportation, either as shippers or carriers; that they should be men of the broadest information and fairness. We believe that that commission, when appealed to, should examine into all the facts relative to the cost of transportation, and that whatever their findings may be, those findings should be binding upon the shipper and the carrier until they have been reviewed by a competent court, and affirmed or over-ruled, as the case may be. This we believe to be equitable and fair.

We are led to this conclusion by the power of the railroad compa-nies to confiscate our property or by excessive charges of freight and passenger take it by the strong hand of the law. State commis-sions appraise and fix upon a valuation of property that is to be used in the building of a railroad; whatever this commission may find to be the true amount of damages is awarded, and the owner of the real estate has no alternative but to accept the award or to appeal to the court, as the case may be. We believe that is right. We believe that railroads could not be built in this country if the law were other-wise.

Now, if State or national law can create a commission, which com-mission can fix the price of citizens, property taken for the building of a railroad, and compel them either to accept the amount awarded as damages or to appeal to the court, it seems to me that, when they are shipping the products of their farm to the markets of the world in order to get any benefits from their land, the same rule of action ought to apply.

We believe that the farmer is more interested in this question than any other class of people in this country. Statistics tell us that 60 per cent of the freights upon the railroads of the United States are the products of our farms. Therefore, as farmers, we are vitally interested in this one proposition, and that is equitable charges.

• I was present this morning and heard arguments as to differences of rates as between one man and another, and also the question of rebates. It might be said that the farmer would have no particular or direct interest in that. But he has, because if there is a rebate or a lower schedule fixed for one shipper that man gets control, and shuts off competition. We believe that equity and fairness in all trade and business, with an open competitive market, is the only salvation for the American Republic. We believe that if you depart from this great principle and allow the consolidation of great interests to dictate and arbitrarily fix prices, which may be just or unjust, and appeal to the people to stand by them and to transact business upon that plan, it will eventually deprive this Republic of all the liberty it has.

The point that we desire to reach is that every man doing business with a railroad corporation shall receive the same service for the same money, and have the same advantages—one with the other—and that all charges shall be reasonable. That gives everyone an equal oppor-tunity. As the practice has been, and is now, we know that that is not the case.

I was here this morning when one of the committee asked the ques-tion if the pending suits would not cover every point that I make upon this subject. If those pending suits are decided in favor of the Gov-ernment, and the permanent restraining order is issued against the railroads, so far so good. But I want to say that the passage of this bill will simply strengthen the law and make sure the decisions of the courts along the lines of equity, and in my judgment could, therefore, do no harm.

My experience among farmers has been quite considerable. I have come in daily contact with the farmers in all parts of the country, and I have ascertained that the conviction has become fixed in their minds that they ought to have some definite relief in reference to this matter.

What we want is that all the railroad and transportation interests of this country shall be placed upon the same plane with each individual of the Republic; that because they are public carriers engaged in public service their rates should be subject to review by a disinterested tribunal, and that the findings of that tribunal should be operative upon the railroads until they have been reviewed and changed by a competent court.

If you should examine the records of our organization, you would find that in our three or four hundred thousand meetings annually all over this country these matters have been brought up and discussed, and that, with hardly one dissenting voice, they have demanded of the highest legislative body in the world that they be given this kind of protection. You would find upon our records resolutions, passed by our subordinate granges, asking this relief; and I think last year I transmitted petitions for the Cullom bill, signed by at least 100,000 farmers—perhaps 300,000—asking for the passage of that bill, because it covered the very points that I understand are in this bill.

Not only that, but our State granges and our national granges have all directed the legislative committee to do what it could to impress Congress with the importance of this measure.

As a farmer, I want to say that the value of all farm lands depends largely upon the enactment of a law of this kind. Our farms are only valued in proportion to the revenues derived from them. If the power is given to the railroads to discriminate and to make unjust and excessive charges, thus robbing us of the benefits of our lands, it results in actual confiscation. I recollect very well of traveling in Kansas and Missouri when the rate was but 13 cents a hundred for corn from Kansas to New York. I recollect after the great corn crop of 1899 that rate was changed to 23 cents. I do not know whether 13 cents a hundred was a remunerative or a fair price, but I know it was the price fixed by the railroads—for which the railroads carried the corn. If that was a fair price, when the price was raised to 23 cents it was an unjust rate, and it took from the farmers of the country over $130,000,000 in the value of one crop of corn. Not only the amount we sell but the amount that we have kept at home is to be considered. Every bushel of corn that is sold in any market of this country is based upon what it is worth in the markets of the country.

This is a matter of vital importance. The matter of hay was discussed this morning in the House committee. As it was not discussed here, perhaps I should not refer to that. But, at all events, the change of rates from $1.50 to $2.60 for shipping hay from Iowa to the seaboard was absolutely prohibitive and did prevent the shipping of hay. The man who made the speech in the House committee this morning said that since this change in the rates he had not bought a single ton of hay west of the Mississippi River, whereas heretofore he had bought a great deal. That is a matter that affects every ton of hay grown in the great West. The same principle applies to every other product requiring transportation from one part of the country to the other.

I want the Interstate Commerce Commission to have the power, after receiving evidence from the shipper and from the transportation lines, to say what shall be a fair and equitable rate. After taking the evidence in the case, as a fair and equitable tribunal, a disinterested tribunal, I would like for that Commission to have the power to prescribe a fair and equitable rate, and when they have so prescribed it

I want the railroads of this country to obey the order of that Commission until the Commission shall be found by a competent court to have been in error in its finding.

Another point: This morning before this committee the gentleman from Chicago (Mr. Eckhart), who represented the milling interests of the country, was talking about the differences between the export rate on flour and the export rate on wheat, and he said that there were rebates given to such an extent as absolutely made it prohibitory to the shipper of flour, because he could not compete with the shipper of wheat. I want to say, as a farmer representing agriculture, that we are vitally interested in having equity between these two classes of men who buy our products. Why? Because then they become competitors one with the other. You may say that millers may combine and establish prices, and that the farmers are willing to put themselves into their hands to be scalped. I am not a particle afraid of that. Why? Because there is the shipper, who will hold him in check to a certain extent. They are competitors for the trade. I want them to be competitors. It is to our interest that they be competitors, and it is to the interest of the entire people. I believe that our prices the year round will be more uniform for our home people—our men who have established their mills in our localities to grind our wheat giving us a uniform market, and we would thereby get better prices.

There is still another ground, a broader and wider ground; not only are we as farmers interested in it, but every business man in this Republic is also interested in it; and that is that it is to the interest of the farmers of this country to have the mills of the country grind our grain, so that we farmers may have the by-products to feed to our stock, by this means keeping up the fertility of our soil. Otherwise our grain would go to foreign countries and go to maintain the fertility of the farms of Europe. As statistics show, year after year we have been depleting the fertility of our soil by shipping out the grain and its by-products; I mean the bran and shorts and all that stuff derived from our cereals, and which ought to go back to our own soil to be reproduced in fine cattle, in good hogs, and in dairy products, thus inuring to the interest of every man in this country, not merely that of the farmers alone. But if we allow this discrimination to take place, our wheat goes abroad, and that source of fertility is lost to the American farmer; and upon that ground I oppose discriminations.

But the broad ground of equity and fairness is the ground on which we stand. And I want to say as a farmer, I want to say as the master of the National Grange, and I want to say in the interest of the people of the United States that they demand of this Congress that it shall pass a law that will give equity to every business interest and every locality in this broad land of ours in the matter of transportation. I want to say also that in my humble judgment the people of this Republic have got their eyes upon this legislation and are determined that they will watch and see to it that they have that kind of legislation.

I want to say that all the railroads of this country ought to be willing to have a disinterested tribunal to review all their acts, to see that to every man is meted out exact justice, exact fairness; to see that the schedules are right and reasonable.

I can not imagine a single objection to the passage of this bill. I believe that Congress, in justice to the American people, in justice to the farmers of this country, ought to see to it that if they have a hundred bushels of corn or wheat to sell or ship to the seaboard, or a single firkin of butter to ship, or a single head of cattle, that they be placed upon an equitable basis, the poor with the rich. I believe that that is the only safety, the only road that leads this Republic to that freedom of all the people which is the incentive to go out and labor.

I base my argument upon the equity of this case. If these bills do not cover the ground, and you understand now fully the purposes I have in view, then I hope the wisdom of this committee will make such changes as in your judgment will serve to carry out these purposes. I believe that one of these bills, the Nelson bill (S. 3575), will fully carry out that purpose, will enlarge the powers and duties of the Interstate Commerce Commission, and secure fairness and equity in transportation.

The CHAIRMAN. I may say that we all agree that we should take all proper steps that we can, and especially as regards secret rebates. On that point I do not think there can be any difference of opinion, either in the committee or in Congress. Everybody is committed to that. We should like to find a remedy and have the law enforced. As to these particular bills, however. we should like to hear from you.

Mr. JONES. May I ask you this question, Mr. Chairman: Are you in favor of submitting the railroad schedules to a disinterested tribunal and compelling the railroad companies to obey that disinterested decision?

The CHAIRMAN. I think both these bills allow that; one of them, I know, allows the Commission, upon complaint, to change the rate. As to pooling, the Commission is to have exclusive jurisdiction over agreements and over every rate and every classification. I am willing to go that far.

Mr. JONES. That is right.

The CHAIRMAN. Here are two questions: Shall we put in the hands of the Commission the power to change the rate? That is the first question. Secondly, shall we allow the railroads to pool under absolute restriction on the part of the Commission to control all contracts for pooling, or to reject in whole or in part? As to discrimination, that is wicked, unrighteous, unjustifiable, and robbery.

Mr. JONES. As to the first question, yes. And all pooling contracts must be approved by the Interstate Commerce Commission before going into effect.

### STATEMENT OF GEORGE F. MEAD.

The CHAIRMAN. Please state your business and whom you represent.

Mr. MEAD. I am engaged in the produce commission business. I represent at this hearing three large business organizations. First is the National League of Commission Merchants of the United States, having constituent bodies in twenty-three or twenty-four cities, and which, at its national convention held in Philadelphia last January, passed resolutions asking Congress to give the Interstate Commerce Commission the requisite power to enforce its findings. The second organization is the Boston Fruit and Produce Exchange, composed of 350 firms and over 600 members, engaged exclusively in the butter, cheese, eggs, provisions, and fruit business. The third is the Massachusetts State Board of Trade, composed of 41 different State organizations throughout Massachusetts.

Everyone of these business organizations has considered this matter. One of them has indorsed specifically the Nelson-Corliss bill, believing that the provisions of that bill will accomplish what they desire. The other two ask generally that Congress shall give whatever power may be necessary to the Commission to enforce its findings, so that it shall be a benefit to the business interests of the country.

We in Boston had an experience with the Interstate Commerce Commission in 1890. We brought a case before the Commission. An exhaustive hearing was had, lasting three or four days, with the final arguments heard here in Washington. The result of that hearing was that the Commission found entirely in our favor—that the rates were exorbitant and oppressive. But the fact that the Commission had not the power to enforce its own findings rendered that decision utterly useless to us. The railroads absolutely refused to abide by the conclusions of the Commission, so that, so far as any practical benefit to us from that decision was concerned, we received none, as the railroads would not abide by it.

So. Mr. Chairman, believing that the business interests of the country demand just this power to be given to the Commission, not primarily to fix the rates, but, after a full and fair investigation, if they find the rates unjust and oppressive, we come to this committee asking that some power be given so that those rates may be in force and in vogue pending revision of the Commission's order by the circuit court or by the Supreme Court.

I notice that the chairman of the committee has a bill here that I have not studied. I have been over the provisions of the Nelson-Corliss bill, and we think that that would meet the necessities of the business community.

If pooling is a distinct feature of the other bill, and if it is to be under the supervision of the Interstate Commerce Commission, I should say that, in my judgment, that ought to be the system.

The CHAIRMAN. That provision is just as strong as it could be made by very able lawyers to put that power in the hands of the Commission. The bill known as the Elkins bill gives the Commission the right and power in a similar case to determine whether the rate is reasonable or not, and to fix the rate as well.

Senator CLAPP. In the Elkins bill the court, on application, being satisfied that the case is one which should call for such a proceeding, may make an order that the decision of the Commission stand in effect pending appeal. Under the Nelson bill it is provided that the decision of the Commission shall stand unless the court makes an order suspending it. That is the practical difference between the two bills—with the pooling clause added to the Elkins bill.

The CHAIRMAN. As to the supervision by the Interstate Commerce Commission, I have made it still stronger—saying that they shall have absolute control in whole or in part of every classification and agreement, and that the agreement shall not take effect until they say so.

Mr. MEAD. Two of the organizations I represent ask for such powers for the Commission as the wisdom of the committee may deem wise to enable the Commission to carry out the provisions of the law—that they may have power to enforce their own orders. We feel now very much as a criminal feels who is brought into court when all the evidence points to his guilt, and where the judge may say, "If you are willing to take a year's sentence, the law will be justified; but I have no power to enforce my decision." Certainly, business men are loath to bring cases and go to the extent of preparing them before the Commission when they know in advance that the railroads, if the decision is against them, will not carry out the orders of the Commission. That keeps them from it.

The other provision, as to rebates and discriminations, has already been so well covered by those who have preceded me that perhaps I should say nothing about it, except that I believe that the business interests of the country feel to-day as they never have felt before regarding that injustice, because that is driving ordinary business men to the wall very rapidly.

Senator CLAPP. As to both bills, if anybody can suggest anything which will provide a more specific remedy, I am sure this committee will jump at it.

Mr. MEAD. I will not say anything along that line, then.

The CHAIRMAN. Senator Clapp is a good lawyer, and if he can make it stronger he will do so.

Mr. MEAD. Congress has already assumed a limited supervision of the railroads, and we believe that work ought to be carried to a conclusion. Monopoly does not control and can not control public service corporations, as we believe that in the end one company will be bought by another, to the disadvantage of the public. The fact is, as stated by the Commission in its report for 1900, that the matter of rates decides very largely who shall do the business and where it shall be done, and we think that, inasmuch as Congress exercises a limited supervision over public service corporations, it ought to exercise full control over them. If the provisions of either of these bills should become law, we feel that it will then put the business men of the country upon an equality. As it is at the present time, the ordinary business man has no show against those great combinations that are enabled to obtain concessions and rebates which give them the power to drive the ordinary competitor to the wall. It seems to me, Mr. Chairman, therefore, that this committee should determine to recommend the provisions of one bill, or an amalgamation of the two.

The CHAIRMAN. Whatever is best in both we are going to try to put into whatever we recommend.

Mr. MEAD. Then I do not think I will take any more time.

Senator CLAPP. Assuming that this provision for pooling puts it completely in the hands of the Commission, I think the committee would like your view as to that policy.

Mr. MEAD. I understand the Nelson-Corliss bill provides that where there is no through rate, and the railroads can not agree upon one, then the Commission are given power to fix it.

Senator CLAPP. That would only be in a case where there was a complaint and after investigation.

Mr. MEAD. Yes.

The CHAIRMAN. The other bill gives the right to pool. A great many railroads are opposed to that. If you have that rate made public, and in the hands of the Commission, then rebates are almost impossible.

Senator KEAN. There is not a railroad west of the Mississippi River that wants pooling.

The CHAIRMAN. No.

Mr. JONES. Senator Elkins, I see that your bill provides that the findings shall not go into effect until after the order of the court.

What is the reason for not letting it take effect the same as is provided for in the other bill?

The CHAIRMAN. My bill says that if, upon full investigation, after a hearing by the circuit judge, the judge finds the case flagrant he can change the rate. The bill leaves the evidence to the court. In accordance with the reasons stated this morning by Mr. Bacon, the rate could be changed if it was found to be wrong, the changed rate to have two years' operation, during which time the railroad might have a loss of $400,000, for which it would have no recourse under these bills, because if it had recourse against the shipper the shipper could not collect it from the consumer. Whereas if the court finds against the railroad the other party has the right to recover, and can recover from the railroad. One is certain always of securing justice if the rate is wrong— the judge sitting there can, under my bill, change it.

Mr. JONES. So he can under the other.

The CHAIRMAN. There is very little difference between the two bills, I can assure you.

Senator KEAN. In the one case you are sentenced first and hanged afterwards and in the other case you are hanged first.

Mr. MEAD. I do not like to answer these hypothetical questions, Mr. Chairman, without having given thought to the matter. I have got myself in trouble several times in that way. It would seem to me, however, that we would rather favor that feature of the bill that allows the Interstate Commerce Commission to fix the rate.

The CHAIRMAN. And makes it operative at once.

Mr. MEAD. Yes. That would reverse the present order of things, but it seems to me that the business interests would be better satisfied with that version.

Mr. JONES. I think all these cases are emergency cases and ought to be tried at once, and that a prompt decision should follow; but if it be put in the shape Senator Elkins has it, of course the corporation should have, as it is usually understood to have, more power than the other fellow, and it might be a long time before any result would follow the decision of the court.

The CHAIRMAN. In some localities, if you give a chance to the jury, the corporation has no show whatever. I am trying to see both sides of this case. I have been on both sides; I know about railroads and their interests as well as about the interests of the other side. I do not want to say what we are going to do here, but it is our duty to look out for the interests of both sides of the question.

Senator CLAPP. I think we should give the Commission power to enforce its orders.

The CHAIRMAN. If we can break up rebates and stop absorption by giving the pooling privilege, then we shall have made a great step. If the court finds that the rate is too high, he should have the power to fix the rate right there and make it operative at that moment, because the case has been flagrant.

Mr. BACON. And when the Commission is in error somebody who is competent should pass upon that error, and that is the court.

Mr. MEAD. The business men, from their expressions that I have heard in the last two or three years, as stated in their organizations, feel that the Commission under present conditions might as well be abolished, and that the cost of its maintenance, approximating some $200,000 a year, might just as well be saved.

## STATEMENT OF JOHN B. DAISH.

The CHAIRMAN. Please state your residence and whom you represent.

Mr. DAISH. I represent the National Hay Association, an organization of about 700 men. The president of the association, Mr. George S. Bridge, resides in Chicago; he appointed me chairman of the special committee to appear on this occasion. My residence is Washington.

Confining myself almost entirely to the two objects that have been outlined by you, Mr. Chairman, the first question has a dual aspect. We have heard from several of the gentlemen as to what the business men want, and what seems to the shipper and the farmer the best thing to do under the circumstances. We are confronted with a situation.

The law passed in 1887 by reason of decisions of the Supreme Court in 1897 became practically ineffective, to a certain degree at least. We have stood under that decision five years, the decision having been rendered in the case of the Interstate Commerce Commission v. the Cincinnati, New Orleans and Texas Pacific Railway upon an act on the statute books which created a body whose powers were supposed to be enforceable, and yet by reason of that decision the statute was rendered ineffective. That decision says in effect to the commission: "You can sit here, but you can not exercise the powers which you have been exercising under that statute." That is where we stand to-day.

The object of these bills, whether the Nelson-Corliss bill or the Elkins bill, is to remedy the existing situation. We have heard from the business side of the question, and so it is not necessary to go into that in any great detail.

We have recently brought a complaint before the Interstate Commerce Commission alleging that because it changed the freight rate on hay, it made that rate unreasonable and unjust. That case is still pending.

Objection has been made in certain quarters to the constitutional features of any bill which provides that the Interstate Commerce Commission may make a rate for the future. It is conceded, I believe, that the power to prescribe a rate lies in the halls of this Congress.

Senator CLAPP. Is it seriously contended that Congress can not delegate that authority?

Mr. DAISH. No, sir. There seems to be no question raised about the right of Congress to delegate authority, but the question has been asked of me, for opinion, stating in substance that a railroad commission or the Interstate Commerce Commission can say that a rate of 30 cents a hundred from Chicago to New York on hay in car lots is unreasonable and unjust, and then can go farther and say to the carrier that "25 cents a hundred is a reasonable and just rate, and we therefore order and decree that you shall not charge more than 25 cents a hundred for this particular service." It is the latter portion of that which is attacked.

The CHAIRMAN. This bill gives that power precisely.

Mr. DAISH. Precisely.

The CHAIRMAN. That power was taken away from the Commission by the Supreme Court because Congress had not given the power. So we propose in both bills to give that power.

Mr. DAISH. That is true.

I wish to cite, for the purposes of record more than anything else, a couple of cases analagous to this, wherein the Supreme Court has decided that such power can be given to a railroad commission. The power given in these bills is not primarily to fix the rate, but to say that a.certain rate is unjust, unreasonable, and exorbitant.

A question was asked this morning concerning the adequacy of the present law, whether the power if within the law itself could be enforced, and reference was made to injunction proceedings. We have read considerably in the press concerning these injunction proceedings. The injunction, as you all know, was a temporary injunction; and if the press correctly reports Judge Groscup, he is reported to have said practically as follows: that "were the objection on behalf of the defendants to this proceeding, I should be very careful in granting that preliminary injunction." That injunction, if I recollect rightly, is to be in force and effect until the final hearing, which is set for the 23d of June. The Government, I understand, rests its case largely upon the Debs case. It has become my duty recently to reread that Debs case; and with the little legal light that has been given me by instruction of professors at various times, and with my little experience, I must say frankly that I can not see the application of the case in re Debs to the rate for interstate traffic. That case was for an obstruction of a public highway dealing with interstate commerce, and that obstruction was held by the United States Supreme Court to be a nuisance.

While the ordinary business man says that it is a "nuisance" for him to pay an excessive rate, it is not a legal nuisance. The fact that it is impossible for me, as a business man, to make shipment of various commodities on account of high freight rates does not constitute a legal nuisance. While I am not a prophet, it seems to me that sooner or later that injunction must be dissolved. As I see it, only some such legislation as is proposed in one of these bills can remedy the existing difficulty with which we are confronted.

Mr. BACON. That is the Nelson bill.

Mr. DAISH. I am referring to either bill at the moment. Either one will cover the point. I shall very soon come to the consideration of the differences between the two bills. The main difference, I take it, between the two bills, is the question of pooling.

The CHAIRMAN. That is the substantial difference.

Mr. DAISH. My instructions in that respect are practically these: That the National Hay Association as an association—we have had no vote of the membership—does not object to a regulated pool, a pool under the supervision, direction, or authority of a competent body.

The CHAIRMAN. Would you name the Interstate Commerce Commission? We can not name any other just now.

Mr. DAISH. We think that Commission is competent to take care of it. We think the members of that Commission are broad minded enough to look out for the interests of the public as well as for the interests of the carriers who would be affected by these pooling arrangements. It is immaterial whether a pooling arrangement is a pooling of earnings or a pooling of tonnage.

I have now given my instructions as an official representative. Personally, as a student of transportation matters, I am an ardent advocate of pooling, on two grounds. Not pooling generally, but regulated pooling. First, it recognizes that movement which is going on

to-day in all classes and lines of business—a movement toward aggregation of capital.  Boots and shoes are made in large factories.  They
are not made by a single individual man, as they were made twenty-
five years ago.  There is a tendency in the same direction on the part
of the railroads.  It is called "community of interest" for want of a
better term.  Legalized supervision of pooling will not only accelerate
the movement of the pendulum in that respect, in my judgment, but
it will help to secure the greater and better interests of all parties
concerned.

The history of the pool which existed prior to 1887 in the Southern
States without doubt shows that not only were freight rates less, that
the service was equally as good, and that no one was injured, but that
on the whole the shippers and carriers were alike benefited under
that arrangement.

The CHAIRMAN. That was pooling, Mr. Daish, without the supervision of a commission.

Mr. DAISH. I was just coming to that.  It was an unregulated pool,
if I may use the term.  I am very fond of using the term "regulate"
in this connection, because it is the word that is used in the Constitution.  You might call that an ex parte pool.  Yet no one seemed to
object; no one raised his hand and said, "You are squeezing me."  At
least, if such objections there were, I have not heard of them.

Take the case of the pool of individual carriers, competent railway
people versed in transportation matters; bring a case before them where
one party says the rate is apparently right, and the opposite party says
that it is apparently wrong; where one party says if the pool rate goes
into effect it will injure a certain trade, a certain locality, or a certain
individual engaged in a particular trade, one who is situated slightly
differently from some other person; let that body give the case careful
thought, and it seems to me that pooling will not only be favored but
advocated.

I have given my personal views on the subject of pooling; and while,
perhaps, I have stated the case more strongly than the hay association
would care to have me do in my representative capacity, yet I earnestly
believe what I have said concerning pools.

There is one other difference, I take it, between the Nelson-Corliss
bill and the Elkins bill, and that is the force and effect to be given to
the decrees of the Commission after hearing before them and pending
appeal.  Suppose, for example, that it will be two or three years
before you get a given case to the Supreme Court of the United
States; in the Nelson-Corliss bill, unless the decree should be manifestly wrong, so wrong that the circuit judge could see in an instant
that the Commission had made a serious error on the facts or the law—
unless that be the case, that decree shall be in force and effect until
the Supreme Court of the United States reverses or affirms it.

Senator CLAPP. On appeal to the Supreme Court, the court is not
authorized to suspend the operation of the order of the Commission.

Mr. DAISH. The Supreme Court can not suspend it?

Senator CLAPP. No.

Mr. DAISH. But after the decree, there are two ways of changing it—
one is that the Commission itself shall modify the decree; whereas
by the Nelson-Corliss bill the circuit judge alone has power to suspend
the operation of the decree.

Senator CLAPP. If the circuit judge were vested with power to suspend the decree, what would you say as to giving the Supreme Court the same power on appeal from the circuit court?

Mr. DAISH. In all right and justice, manifestly I should say the Supreme Court, being the appellate body, and there being no review of its decision, might well be invested with authority to make the change upon proper showing.

SENATOR CLAPP. If the circuit court suspended the order, then it would remain suspended until ordered back into effect by the circuit court.

Mr. JONES. By the Supreme Court?

Senator CLAPP. No; by the circuit court. If the circuit court sustains the order, then the order would be in effect pending appeal to the Supreme Court; and, there being no power in the Supreme Court to suspend it, the circuit court in the first instance could have suspended it when it heard the case.

Mr. JONES. The Supreme Court certainly ought to have that power as well as the circuit court, in my opinion, if they find that it is not just and right.

Mr. BACON. One objection to that is the long delay in adjudicating the case. The carriers avail themselves of every possible means of protracting litigation.

Senator CLAPP. You do not understand the point. This bill, called the Nelson bill, provides that on an appeal to the circuit court the circuit court may, if it deems it wise, suspend the operation of the order of the Commission, provided there was a proper case of complaint and the Commission found that the law was plainly violated. While this same law gives an appeal to the Supreme Court, yet it does not give the Supreme Court that same power which the circuit court has in a given case to suspend the operation of the order of the Commission.

Mr. BACON. That is just as I understand it.

Senator CLAPP. If one court has that power, why should not the other and higher court have it?

Mr. BACON. The objection is that it affords still further opportunity for the suspension of this order which has been found by a competent and skilled body to be necessary in order to do justice.

Senator CLAPP. Then why not give it in the first instance?

Mr. BACON. As a check upon the Commission.

Senator CLAPP. Surely the Supreme Court is as safe to be intrusted with discretionary power to suspend or enforce an order as is the circuit court.

Mr. BACON. But after the circuit court has confirmed the order of the Commission it would seem as if the carrier were sufficiently protected. It would take probably a year to reach the case if carried to the Supreme Court, and it may be delayed a year or two longer by motions and arguments and the like, and then there would be two or three years of additional delay, during which time this unjust rate, which has been so found by a competent body and confirmed by the circuit court, is in effect, and the public must suffer until the final decision is reached.

Senator CLAPP. If you vest the circuit court with power to suspend the order of the Interstate Commerce Commission, it seems a forced construction not to give as safe a tribunal as the Supreme Court that same discretionary power.

Mr. DAISH. To amplify the point a little, suppose the circuit court suspends the order; that would place the traffic back on the higher rate.

The CHAIRMAN. Or the rate made by the railroad.

Mr. DAISH. Yes; we may use that term, presuming it means an unreasonable rate. That puts the traffic back to the railroad rate. As representing a shipper, I should certainly want to apply at once to the Supreme Court of the United States and say to that court that this is so wrong, that the circuit court of the United States has so sadly missed the mark, and that the Commission were so completely right, that I want you, pending full argument, to say that the Commission was right when it determined that the rate was unreasonable and unjust. On the other hand, if the circuit court does not suspend the order, then the carrier, who on appeal should certainly be allowed to have his day in court, could say to the Supreme Court: "The circuit court is wrong, the Interstate Commerce Commission is wrong, and without looking at these papers that have been filed against us, we want you to suspend this order pending proceedings." It seems to me as fair for the one as for the other.

The CHAIRMAN. The Elkins bill provides that the Supreme Court may do it.

Mr. DAISH. If by application in the nature of a petition, or by any interlocutory proceeding, you allow one party that right before the circuit court, then allow both parties the same right before the Supreme Court, because the circuit court may do either one way or the other.

There is another difference between the two bills, and that is as to the length of time that the order of the Commission shall be in force and effect—the difference between one year and two years. For some reasons I am rather inclined personally to favor the one year on certain classes of commodities. I recall distinctly one of the earlier cases before the Commission, dealing with transportation rates on wheat from Oregon to Washington. The order in that case was practically this: That on and after the 21st day of December until the end of the present shipping season—which I think was the 21st of June—it shall be unlawful for the carrier to charge a greater rate than a specified amount. I think Mr. Jones will bear me out that if these orders or decrees could be made to correspond to certain harvest times it would be of advantage.

On the other hand, it may be said that a year is too short a time in which to try the particular rate. Or, again, it may be said that within two years we may have serious business conditions which would practically necessitate asking that the rate be changed.

But I take it that under either the Nelson-Corliss or the Elkins bill, at any time pending the decree, upon the assumption that the carriers obey the order, at any time within a year or two application might be made by the carrier or by the shipper for a modification of the decree. If, for instance, the price of steel rails should go up, or if we should have a panic and the price of steel rails should go down, freights were hard to move, nobody wants anything, and you wish to raise or to lower the rate, let the power be vested in the Commission that they may increase, or allow the carrier to increase the rate, as the case may be.

Mr. JONES. That is in both bills now.

Mr. DAISH. Yes; but the difference is the difference between one year and two years. However, I do not know that the time is material, because the Commission has been given the power in both bills to change or modify the order, so that they may say that, upon a hearing or a rehearing of the case and upon a consideration of new evidence, some other fact has entered into the case, and so they may conclude to modify the order a little.

It seems to me that not only do we want legislation, but we want legislation along one of the lines, either of the Nelson bill or of the Elkins bill. There is no great amount of difference in them in substance.

I appreciate this: That the commercial interests of the country when you come to the subject of pooling, a great number of them consider it a dangerous thing. The word "pool" seems to the minds of some people to mean a great big ghost, something that will hit you when you are not looking. I do not want to charge those people with lack of properly investigating transportation matters, but concerning them it is a word which either in itself, or as it is the result of a pool, has done in the past serious injury to no one. As I said before, it is in the line of aggregation of capital; it is in the line of the regulation of things, setting them in order. But I will say, frankly, that it is considered by a great many people to be objectionable, because their argument to me is that to give the carriers the power to pool would give them such power as would enable them not only to dominate the Commission but dominate the power that created that Commission; and on those lines they have argued to me that a pool is a dangerous thing.

I have not gone very fully into the subject of our grievances, because that has been thrashed over this morning. I think the committee thoroughly understand the question of rebates and discriminations as it has been outlined. Our case was a little different from most cases. Our case was a discrimination, not against persons or localities, but against a particular commodity. If the committee desire, I can prepare for filing in this record, on behalf of the National Hay Association, something of that kind.

The CHAIRMAN. All right; you can do that, if you like.

Mr. DAISH. I have prepared a brief upon the constitutionality, not of any one of these proposed measures, but upon the power of Congress over the Interstate Commerce Commission, which will be filed if you desire.

The CHAIRMAN. Is it in print?

Mr. DAISH. It is in print.

The CHAIRMAN. Very well. You may file it.

Following is the brief referred to:

### POWER OF CONGRESS OVER INTERSTATE COMMERCE.

Congress has power to constitute tribunals inferior to the Supreme Court. (Cons. U. S., section 8, clause 9.)

To regulate commerce with foreign nations and among the several States and with the Indian tribes. (Cons. U. S., section 8, clause 3, article I.)

The making and fixing of rates is a legislative, and not a judicial, function; and the decisions are uniform in declaring that statutes creating railroad commissions, and giving them the power to make and fix rates, are not unconstitutional as delegating a legislative power which belongs only to the legislature itself. (8 Am. and Eng. Ency. of Law, 911; Chicago & N. W. R. Co. v. Dey, 4 Ry. & Corp. L. J., 465, 35 Fed. Rep., 866, 2 Inters. Com. Rep., 325, 1 L. R. A., 744; Granger Cases, 94 U. S., 113–187, 24 L. ed., 77–97; State ex rel. Railroad & Warehouse Commission v. Chicago, M. & St. P. R. Co., 38 Minn., 281, 37 N. W., 782; State ex rel. Board of Transportation v. Fremont, E. & M. Valley R. Co., 22 Neb., 313, 35 N. W., 118, 23 Neb., 117,

36 N. W., 308; Tilley *v.* Savannah, F. & W. R. Co., 5 Fed. Rep., 641; Georgia R.
Co. *v.* Smith, 70 Ga., 694; New York & N. E. R. Co. *v.* Bristol, 151 U. S., 556, 38
L. ed., 269; Reagan *v.* Farmers' Loan & T. Co., 154 U. S., 362, 38 L. ed., 1014, 4
Inters. Com. Rep., 560, and cases quoted; Ames *v.* Union P. R. Co., 64 Fed. Rep.,
165, 4 Inters. Com. Rep , 835; Interstate Commerce Commission *v.* Cincinnati, N. O.
& T. P. R. Co., 167 U. S., 479, 42 L. ed., 243; Texas & P. R. Co. *v.* Interstate Com-
merce Commission, 162 U. S., 197, 40 L. ed., 940; Smyth *v.* Ames, 169 U. S., 466, 42
L. ed., 819).

When the law has confided to a special tribunal the authority to hear and determine certain matters arising in the course of its duties, the decision of that tribunal,
within the scope of its authority, is conclusive upon all others. (Johnson *v.* Tows-
ley, 13 Wall., 72, 20 L. ed., 485.)

The legislature's determination, either directly or indirectly, of what is reasonable,
is conclusive, subject only to charter rights and to the fact that the rates established
will give some compensation to the carrier. (Atty. Gen. *v.* Old Colony R. Co., 160
Mass., 62, 22 L. R. A., 112; Chicago & N. W. R. Co. *v.* Dey, 35 Fed. Rep., 866, 2
Inters. Com. Rep., 325, 1 L. R. A., 744.)

The power to regulate is to prescribe the rule by which the commerce is to be governed. This power, like all others vested in Congress, is complete in itself, may be exercised to its utmost extent, and acknowledges no limitations other than are prescribed
in the Constitution. If, as has already been understood, the sovereignty of Congress,
though limited to specified objects, is plenary as to those objects, the power over
commerce with foreign nations and among the several States is vested in Congress as
absolutely as it would be in a single government having in its constitution the same
restrictions in the exercise of the power as are found in the Constitution of the United
States. (Gibbons *v.* Ogden, 9 Wheat., 1, 197, 6 L. ed., 23, 70.)

It is obvious that the Government, in regulating commerce with foreign nations
and among the States, may use means that may also be employed by a State in the
exercise of its acknowledged powers—that, for example, of regulating commerce
within a State. (Gibbons *v.* Ogden, 9 Wheat., 204, 6 L. ed., 72.)

The power to regulate commerce   *   *   *   amounts to nothing more than a power
to limit and restrain it at pleasure. (Gibbons *v.* Ogden, 9 Wheat., 227, 6 L. ed., 77.)

It may be doubted whether any of the evils proceeding from the feebleness of the
Federal Government contributed more to that great revolution which induced the
present system than the deep and general conviction that commerce ought to be
regulated by Congress. It is not, therefore, matter of surprise that the grant should
be as extensive as the mischief, and should comprehend all foreign commerce and
all commerce arising among the States. (Brown *v.* Maryland, 12 Wheat., 446; 6 L.
ed., 688.)

The power to regulate commerce includes that of punishing all offenses against
commerce. (United States *v.* Coombs, 12 Pet., 72; 9 L. ed., 1004.)

The design and object of that power, as evinced in the history of the Constitution,
was to establish a perfect equality among the several States as to commercial rights,
and to prevent unjust and invidious distinctions which local jealousies or local and
partial interests might be disposed to introduce and maintain. (Veazie *v.* Moor, 14
How., 574; 14 L. ed., 547.)

Commerce is a term of the largest import.   *   *   *   The power to regulate it
embraces all the instruments by which such commerce may be conducted. (Welton
*v.* Missouri, 91 U. S., 280; 23 L. ed., 349.)

The power conferred upon Congress to regulate commerce with foreign nations
and among the several States is not confined to the instrumentalities of commerce
known or in use when the Constitution was adopted, but keeps pace with the
progress of the country, and adapts itself to the new developments of time and of
circumstances. It was intended for the government of the business to which it
relates at all times and under all circumstances; and it is not only the right, but the
duty, of Congress to take care that intercourse among the States and the transmission of intelligence are not obstructed or unnecessarily encumbered by State
legislation. (Pensacola Teleg. Co. *v.* Western U. Teleg. Co., 96 U. S., 9; 24 L. ed.,
710.)

The power to regulate that commerce,   *   *   *   vested in Congress, is the power
to prescribe the rules by which it shall be governed; that is, the conditions upon
which it shall be conducted.   *   *   *   The power also embraces within its control
all the instrumentalities by which that commerce may be carried on, and the means
by which it may be aided and encouraged. (Gloucester Ferry Co. *v.* Pennsylvania,
114 U. S., 203; 29 L. ed., 161; 1 Inters. Com. Rep., 382.)

When a commodity has begun to move as an article of trade from one State to another, commerce in that commodity between the States has commenced. (The Daniel Ball, 10 Wall., 565, *sub nom.;* The Daniel Ball *v.* United States; 19 L. ed., 1002.)

But this movement does not begin until the articles have been shipped or started for transportation from the one State to the other. (Coe *v.* Errol, 116 U. S., 517; 29 L. ed., 715.)

This species of legislation is one which must be, if established at all, of a general and national character. (Wabash, St. L. and P. R. Co. *v.* Illinois, 118 U. S., 577; 30 L. ed., 251.)

For the regulation of commerce as thus defined there can be only one system of rules applicable alike to the whole country; and the authority which can act for the whole country can alone adopt such a system. (Mobile County *v.* Kimball, 102 U. S., 691; 26 L. ed., 238.)

The power to regulate commerce embraces a vast field, containing not only many but exceedingly various subjects quite unlike in their nature. (Cooley *v.* Philadelphia Port Wardens, 12 How., 299, 13 L. ed., 996.)

The power to regulate commerce among the several States is granted to Congress in terms as absolute as is the power to regulate commerce with foreign nations. (Brown *v.* Houston, 114 U. S., 622, 29 L. ed., 257.)

The uses of railroad corporations are public, and therefore they are subject to legislative control in all respects necessary to protect the public against danger, injustice, and oppression. (New York & N. E. R. Co. *v.* Bristol, 151 U. S., 556, 38 L. ed., 269.)

Congress has plenary power, subject to the limitations imposed by the Constitution, to prescribe the rule by which commerce among the several States is to be governed, and may, in its discretion, employ any appropriate means not forbidden by the Constitution to carry into effect and accomplish the objects of a power given to it by the Constitution. (Interstate Commerce Commission *v.* Brimson, 154 U. S., 447, 38 L. ed., 1047, 4 Inters. Com. Rep., 545.)

The making and fixing of rates by either a legislature directly or by a commission do not work a deprivation of property without due process of law. (Munn *v.* Illinois, 94 U. S., 113, 24 L. ed., 77; Davidson *v.* New Orleans, 96 U. S., 97, 24 L. ed., 616; Stone *v.* Farmers' Loan & T. Co., 116 U. S., 307, 29 L. ed., 636; Dow *v.* Beidelman, 125 U. S., 680, 31 L. ed., 841, 2 Inters. Com. Rep., 56; Minneapolis & St. L. R. Co. *v.* Beckwith, 129 U. S., 26, 32 L. ed., 585, and cases cited; Budd *v.* New York, 143 U. S., 517, 36 L. ed., 247, 4 Inters. Com. Rep., 45; New York & N. E. R. Co. *v.* Bristol, 151 U. S., 556, 38 L. ed., 269; Reagan *v.* Farmers' Loan & T. Co., 154 U. S., 362, 38 L. ed., 1014, 4 Inters. Com. Rep., 560.)

The State does not lose the right to fix the price because an individual voluntarily undertakes to do the (public) work. · (Budd *v.* New York, 143 U. S., 517, 36 L. ed. 247, 4 Inters. Com. Rep., 45.)

The Nebraska statute fixing maximum rates is not obnoxious to the fourteenth amendment. (Ames *v.* Union P. R. Co., 64 Fed. Rep., 165, 4 Inters. Com. Rep., 835.)

The compelling of railway companies to comply with the order of railroad commissioners regulating rates is due process of law. (8 Am. & Eng. Enc. of Law, 911; Chicago, M. & St. P. R. Co. *v.* Becker, 32 Fed. Rep., 849; Louisville & N. R. Co. *v.* Railroad Commission, 19 Fed. Rep., 679, 16 Am. & Eng. R. Cas., 1; Railroad Comrs. *v.* Oregon R. & Nav. Co., 17 Or., 65, 2 L. R. A., 195, 35 Am. & Eng. R. Cas., 542; State ex rel. Railroad & Warehouse Commission *v.* Chicago, M. & St. P. R. Co., 38 Minn., 281, 37 N. W., 782; Stone *v.* Natchez, J. & C. R. Co., 62 Miss., 646; Stone *v.* Farmers' Loan & T. Co., 116 U. S., 307, 29 L. ed., 636; State ex rel. Board of Transportation *v* Fremont, E. & M. Valley R. Co., 22 Neb., 313, 32 Am. & Eng. R. Cas., 426; People *v.* New York, L. E. & W. R. Co., 104 N. Y., 58; State *v.* New Haven & N. Ry. Co., 37 Conn., 153.)

The principal objects of the interstate-commerce act were to secure just and reasonable charges for transportation. * * * (Interstate Commerce Commission *v.* Baltimore & O. R. Co., 145 U. S., 263, 36 L. ed., 699, 4 Inters. Com. Rep., 92.)

It is difficult to perceive how the power to fix and regulate the charges for such transportation can be considered in any other light than that of a power to regulate commerce. (Illinois C. R. Co. *v.* Stone, 20 Fed. Rep., 468.)

It is not doubted that Congress has the power to go beyond the general regulations of commerce which it is accustomed to establish, and to descend to the most minute directions, if it shall be deemed advisable. (Cooley, Const. Lim., 732, quoted with approval by Mr. Justice Field in the case of Gloucester Ferry Co. *v.* Pennsylvania, 114 U. S., 196, 29 L. ed., 158, 1 Inters. Com. Rep., 382.)

That this power to regulate by fixing charges for interstate transportation is vested solely in Congress by Article I, section 8, paragraph 3, of the Constitution of the

United States, is, in my opinion, equally well settled by numerous decisions of the Supreme Court of the United States. (Mobile & O. R. Co. v. Sessions, 28 Fed. Rep., 592.)

Several of the State statutes, under State constitutions containing nearly identical provisions on the subject as the Federal Constitution, allowing State railroad commissions to make and fix railway rates for such States, which said rates were to be operative until set aside by the courts, have been upheld as valid and constitutional by the United States Supreme Court. (See Pensacola & A. R. Co. v. State (Fla.), 3 L. R. A., 661, with extensive notes to that case and notes to Winchester & L. Turnp Road Co. v. Croxton (Ky.), 33 L. R. A., 177.)

This Federal Commission has assigned to it the duties and performs for the United States in respect to that interstate commerce committed by the Constitution to the exclusive care and jurisdiction of Congress the same functions which State commissioners exercise in respect to local or purely internal commerce, over which the States appointing them have exclusive control. Their validity in their respective spheres of operation stands upon the same footing. The validity of State commissions invested with powers as ample and large as those conferred upon the Federal Commission has not been successfully questioned when limited to that local or internal commerce over which the States have exclusive jurisdiction, and no valid reason is seen for doubting or questioning the authority of Congress, under its sovereign and exclusive power, to regulate commerce among the several States, to create like commissions for the purpose of supervising, investigating, and reporting upon matters or complaints connected with or growing out of interstate commerce. What one sovereign may do in respect to matters within its exclusive control the other may certainly do in respect to matters over which it has exclusive authority. (Kentucky and I. Bridge Co. v. Louisville and N. R. Co., 37 Fed. Rep., 567; 2 Inters. Com. Rep., 380; 2 L. R. A., 289.)

The power granted to Congress to regulate commerce is necessarily exclusive whenever the subjects of it are national or admit only of one uniform system or plan of regulation throughout the country.  * * *  In the matter of interstate commerce the United States are but one country, and are and must be subject to one system of regulation, and not to a multitude of systems. (Robbins v. Shelby County Taxing Dist., 120 U. S., 489; 30 L. ed. 694; 1 Inters. Com. Rep., 45; Stoutenburgh v. Hennick, 129 U. S., 141; 32 L. ed. 637.)

Congress may, under certain conditions, reduce the rates of fare on the Union Pacific Railroad, if unreasonable, and fix and establish the same by law. (12 Stat. L., 497, chap. 120, sec. 18.)  This statute is discussed by Mr. Justice Brewer in Ames v. Union P. R. Co., 64 Fed. Rep., 165; 4 Inters. Com. Rep., 835, and held not to conclude the State of Nebraska from fixing rates until Congress takes action.

This act (of Colorado) was intended to apply to intrastate traffic the same wholesome rules and regulations which Congress two years thereafter applied to commerce between the States. (Union P. R. Co. v. Goodridge, 149 U. S., 680, 37 L. ed. 896.)

The Interstate Commerce Commission is an administrative board, and the courts are only to be resorted to when the Commission prefers to enforce the provisions of the statute by a direct proceeding in the court, or when the orders of the Commission have been disregarded. (Interstate Commerce Commission v. Cincinnati, N. O. & T. P. R. Co. 162 U. S., 184, 40 L. ed. 935, 5 Inters. Com. Rep., 391).

The entire commerce of the United States, foreign and interstate, is subject to the provisions of the act of Congress to regulate commerce. (Texas & P. R. Co. v. Interstate Commerce Commission, 162 U. S., 197, 40 L. ed. 940, 5 Inters. Com. Rep., 405.)

Upon the power of legislatures to fix tolls, rates, or prices, see note to case of Winchester & L. Turnp. Road Co. v. Croxton (Ky.), 33 L. R. A., 177.

A statute imposing a penalty for charging more than just and reasonable compensation for the services of a carrier, without fixing any standard to determine what is just and reasonable, thus leaving the criminality of the carrier's act to depend on the jury's view of the reasonableness of a rate charged, is in violation of the constitutional provision against taking property without due process of law. (Louisville and N. R. Co. v. Com., 99 Ky., 132; 33 L. R. A., 209.)

Penalties can not be thus inflicted at the discretion of a jury.  * * *  The legislature can not delegate this power to a jury. If it can declare it a criminal act for a railroad corporation to take more than a "fair and just return" on its investments, it must, in order to maintain the validity of the law, define with reasonable certainty what would constitute such "fair and just return." (Louisville and N. R. Co. v. Railroad Commission, 19 Fed. Rep., 679.)

The Supreme Court of the United States, in Railroad Commission Cases, 116 U. S., 336, sub nom. Stone v. Farmers' Loan & T. Co., 29 L. ed. 646, refers to the last-named case and substantially approves it.

Although a statute has been held to be unconstitutional which left it to the jury to determine whether or not a charge was excessive and unreasonable, in order to ascertain whether a penalty is recoverable, yet, where the action is merely for recovery of the illegal excess over reasonable rates, this is a question which is a proper one for a jury. (8 Am. and Eng. Ency. of Law, 935.)

The Iowa railroad commission act was attacked for uncertainty on the ground that it did not prescribe what should constitute a reasonable rate; but as the statute declared that the rate fixed by the commission should be prima facie evidence that it was reasonable, although the accused could show in defense that it was not reasonable, the supreme court of the State held that the statute was sufficiently definite, since the rate was fixed, although it was subject to attack in the courts. To the claim that the commissioners' rate would not secure the accused from conviction if it was excessive, the court declared that the State was precluded from denying that the commissioners' rate was a reasonable one. (Burlington, C. R. & N. R. Co. v. Dey, 82 Iowa, 312, 3 Inters. Com. Rep., 584, 12 L. R. A., 436.)

The same decision in substance was made on this question by Judge Brewer, then of the United States circuit court, in the case of Chicago & N. W. R. Co. v. Dey, 35 Fed. Rep., 866, 2 Inters. Com. Rep., 325, 1 L. R. A., 744.

The Illinois act providing that a charge by a railroad company of more than reasonable rates shall constitute extortion is held to be sufficiently definite when construed with another section which provides that the railroad commission shall make a schedule of reasonable maximum rates. (Chicago, B. & Q. R. Co. v. People, 77 Ill., 443.)

And the validity of this provision of the Illinois statute has been further established by the Illinois supreme court. (See Chicago B. & Q. R. Co. v. Jones, 149 Ill., 361, 4 Inters. Com. Rep., 683, 24 L. R. A., 141; Stone v. Farmers' Loan & T. Co., 116 U. S., 307, 29 L. ed., 636, deciding the same way the Mississippi statute.)

The Georgia statute is not violated unless the rates charged exceed those fixed by the Commission. (Sorrell v. Central R. Co., 75 Ga., 509.)

But, in order to constitute a crime, the act must be one which the party is able to know in advance whether it is criminal or not. The criminality of an act can not depend upon whether a jury may think it reasonable or unreasonable. (Tozer v. United States, 52 Fed. Rep., 917; 4 Inters. Com. Rep., 245.)

An inquiry whether rates of carriers are reasonable or not is a judicial act; but to prescribe rates for the future is a legislative act. That Congress has transferred to any administrative body the power to prescribe a tariff of rates for carriage by a common carrier is not to be presumed or implied from any doubtful and uncertain language. If Congress had intended to grant such a power to the Interstate Commerce Commission it can not be doubted that it would have used language open to no misconstruction, but clear and direct. (Interstate Commerce Commission v. Cincinnati, N. O. & T. P. R. Co., 167 U. S., 479; 42 L. ed., 243.)

In the case of Munn v. Illinois, 94 U. S., 113, 24 L. ed. 77, the Supreme Court of the United States, after a thorough review of the American and English authorities, has laid down the following fundamental principles governing public carriers and other quasi-public institutions:

1. Under the powers inherent in every sovereignty, a government may regulate the conduct of its citizens toward each other, and, when necessary for the public good, the manner in which each shall use his own property.

2. It has, in the exercise of these powers, been customary in England from time immemorial, and in this country from the first colonization, to regulate ferries, common carriers, hackmen, bakers, millers, wharfingers, auctioneers, innkeepers, and many other matters of like quality, and in so doing to fix a maximum charge to be made for services rendered, accommodations furnished, and articles sold.

3. The Fourteenth Amendment to the United States Constitution does not in anywise amend the law in this particular.

4. When the owner of property devotes it to a use in which the public has an interest, he in effect grants to the public an interest in such use, and must to the extent of that interest submit to be controlled by the public.

5. The limitation by legislative enactment of the rate of charges for services rendered in an employment of a public nature, or for the use of property in which the public has an interest, establishes no new principle in the law, but only gives a new effect to an old one.

Thus the highest court has permanently established the broad principle that the public have the right to regulate charges in all enterprises affected with a public use. To this doctrine all the courts have steadfastly adhered. In this leading case it was also held that the courts had no right to interfere with the rates fixed by the lawmaking power. This doctrine, however, has been since somewhat qualified in the case of Reagan v. Farmer's Loan and T. Co., 154 U. S., 412; 38 L. ed., 1028; 4 Inters.

Com. Rep., 1028, and other cases there cited, where it is held that when rates are confiscatory the courts may so declare, and relegate the matter back to the lawmaking power for new rates, by which a reasonable profit is left to the carrier. But the principle that the legislative power, either directly or indirectly, through a commission, can fix rates of freight and passenger traffic within this constitutional limitation, has been uniformly upheld in all the decisions of the United States Supreme Court upon this subject.

## ADDITIONAL STATEMENT OF E. P. BACON.

Mr. Bacon. I want to say a few words further in regard to a question that has been raised as to furnishing bond pending the determination of a case before the Interstate Commerce Commission. It must be borne in mind, in considering this question, that the party who pays the freight, as a general thing, is merely a middleman. He has no direct interest in it. He pays the freight and passes that additional cost along to the prices of the goods which he handles, and the total cost is finally borne by the consumer. Or, in the case of agricultural products, the freight rate that is charged is deducted primarily from the value of the property at the point of shipment, and in that case falls upon the producer.

The Chairman. It comes off of the one or the other.

Mr. Bacon. In either case the man who pays the freight has no interest in it. That statement will probably cover 99 per cent of the traffic of the country. So that while the case is pending and the rate continues to be charged, there is no possibe way of protecting the party who sustains the injury. He can not be reached. He can not be known, in the first place, and if he could be, such cases would be so numerous that it would be next to an impossibility to indemnify the loser.

That fact places the matter of freight charges in an entirely different position from all other questions that arise in litigation, and necessitates, consequently, entirely different treatment. One party or the other has got to suffer; the carrier will suffer if the decision of the Commission was wrong, and it is afterwards reversed, and the order is operative from the time of its issuance; and in the opposite case it will be the consumer or producer, as the case may be, who suffers. On the one hand it is the producer, and on the other it is the consumer who must suffer. So that it is a question of relieving the greatest sufferer—relieving the public, who are in fact the sufferers in case of excessive rates—relieving it from the necessity of bearing that burden throughout the long continuance of these cases in the courts.

I want to say one word further as to the necessity of this legislation at the present time, which necessity is increasing from year to year, arising from the fact of the enormous consolidation of railway interests during the past two years, and which is now going forward. The fact is that the greater proportion of the aggregate mileage of the railroads of this country, some 200,000 miles, is under the control of five or six syndicates, so called, controlled mainly by as many individuals; that is, five or six individuals have obtained the operating control of three-fifths of the railway mileage of the country; and that process is still going forward. It is stated that there is a scheme now under way for the consolidation of the four or five most important Western railroads, aggregating about 20,000 miles, which scheme is expected to be carried out. Another scheme is in progress in the South that will take 10,000 or 12,000 miles more.  So that we shall have 150,000 miles under the control of the very same individuals where they own a majority of the stock and control it in that way, or where the control is obtained by holding companies, as in the case of the Northern Securities Company, about which we have heard so much.  This presents a phase that should commend itself to the serious consideration of legislators.  Here is this vast railway traffic of the country coming into the control of five or six men.

And in connection with this process of consolidation I want to call attention also to the increase of capitalization.  Where railroads have been purchased by other corporations, or consolidated, in almost every case the capitalization has been very largely increased.  Take, for instance, the Chicago and Alton, which was purchased by a syndicate about two years ago.  It was capitalized at $30,000,000, and it was purchased by the syndicate for $40,000,000, subject, however, to $8,000,000 of the underlying bonds.  But it was capitalized by the new corporation at $94,000,000.  The original capitalization was $30,000,-000.  The road evidently had a high value, for they paid $40,000,000 for it, and the new organization was capitalized at $94,000,000.

The Northern Securities Company very largely increased the capitalization of the two railroads which were included in that consolidation—some 60 per cent, I believe.  I have the figures, but I will not take the time to look them up.

But in all those cases of reorganization and consolidation the capitalization has been immensely increased.  There has been for the past year, and there seems to be now, almost a mania on the part of large capitalists to obtain possession of railroad property, get it under their control, by means of which they can force such rates as will afford them very large profits.  All this extra capitalization is effected, of course, with the expectation that the returns from the operation of that property will be sufficient to pay proper dividends upon the increased capitalization.  That must be evident.

Now, it seems to me that these facts render it evident that this subject is one that requires proper and prompt legislation on the part of Congress to protect the people from the improper exercise of this great power to increase charges upon the transportation of the property in which every individual in the country is interested.

Senator KEAN.  Is it not a fact that after all these consolidations have been effected the rates have been reduced?

Mr. BACON.  That is the general impression, but I have found from an examination of the figures that such is not the case.  The rates on merchandise two years ago were increased by general agreement among the various railroad companies.

Senator KEAN.  On account of the increased cost of handling.

Mr. BACON.  Nevertheless, the increase of business was far greater than the increase of capitalization.  The statistics which have been procured by the Interstate Commerce Commission in regard to the results of these operations show that the average earnings per mile were greater during the year 1900 than during the ten previous years, and that the net earnings of the roads were also greater than the average of the preceding ten years.

Senator KEAN.  They were better operated also than ever before.

Mr. BACON.  They were undoubtedly operated at a less cost.  But that should tend to reduce rates, instead of increasing them.  The public should have the benefit of such decreased cost of operation as it is possible to effect.

Senator KEAN. Everything else has advanced in price. Not only have the rates advanced, but the commodities that the railroads carry have advanced in price in every way, have they not?

Mr. BACON. The prices of materials have advanced, to be sure. But the increased volume of the traffic more than compensates for the increase in the value of the freight transported.

Senator KEAN. To what extent have wages advanced in that time?

Mr. BACON. I can not tell you the percentage, but I have given you the result.

Senator KEAN. They have advanced.

Mr. BACON. They have advanced. One result of the operations of the railroads has been very largely increased profits, dividends, and surplus during that period of two years.

And, by the way, I will say right here that I have ascertained from figures furnished by the Interstate Commerce Commission that the amount carried to surplus accounts by the railroads of the country during the past two years, after paying interest and dividends, and after making large expenditures for permanent improvements, aggregates $165,000,000.

Senator KEAN. Is not the same true of nearly all other kinds of business in the United States—that they have had large surpluses in the last two years?

Mr. BACON. There has undoubtedly been a large surplus earned. But railways perform a public service, and that service should be performed at a fairly remunerative rate, affording a fair return upon the capital invested.

I cite this matter in order to show the possibility that is before us—in fact, the probability which confronts us—of a further increase of railroad rates in consequence of this extensive consolidation, and the necessity of providing some corrective, some supervisory control, to prevent abuses of that power at the expense of the people.

The committee adjourned.

***

## EXTRACTS FROM THE PRESS.

### NEW YORK.

*New York Mail and Express.*—The whole matter of regulating interstate commerce is in a state of chaos, though the power of Congress is unqualified, and so far as it is exercised excludes any State interference. Why should it not put an end to the confusion caused by the incorporation laws of different States. and tangling interstate commerce up in a jungle of constitutions and statutes that it will take the most astute lawyers and jurists years to make their way through? Why should not the powers and obligations of corporations engaged in interstate commerce be defined by one clear statute of national authority?

*New York Evening Post.*—The Merchants' Association of New York indorse the Nelson-Corliss bill, because it restores to the Interstate Commerce Commission the powers originally intended to be conferred, of which it has been stripped by the courts. The decisions of the

Commission now, the memorial states, amount to nothing more than mere propaganda, having no binding effect upon any person or corporation, either as shipper or carrier.

It is the big shippers who are in terror lest something should be done by Congress to rob them of their special privileges, and they are speading broadcast the stories of popular discontent with the course of the Administration in enforcing the laws. The railroad companies—those, at least, with progressive men at their heads—are making no fuss at all, but merely expressing their hope that in proceeding with its prosecutions and injunctions the Government will treat all offenders alike, so as not to cast an undeserved stigma upon any one road or group of roads, even for the purpose of getting a test decision.

*New York Times.*—With an effectual supervision by the Government, directed to the enforcement of publicity and reasonable equality of rates, the tendency would, we are confident, be toward progressively lower rates.

*New York Railway News.*—Some effective remedy for the intolerable conditions which prevail under the interstate-commerce law to-day must certainly be provided.

*Wall Street (New York) Journal.*—Our belief is that a permanent solution of the railroad question can only be reached on lines which place the ultimate control of rates in the hands of the public's representative and place in the hands of the railroads the machinery necessary for the maintenance of those rates and the avoidance of discrimination.

The railroads at this moment stand in serried ranks, facing the law, and the settlement of the present dispute involves a settlement on first principles. Abuse of the railroad interests, on the one hand, and of the Interstate Commerce Commission, on the other, at this time is puerile. The former may have been guilty of imprudent action and the latter of dereliction of duty, but these are small matters when questions of first principles have to be settled, as they have at present. Looking at the situation as it exists to-day, we believe that the railroads must, sooner or later, surrender the rate-making power to the Government. By doing so now we believe that they can secure the right to protect themselves in the conduct of their business. Later it may be difficult, if not impossible, to do so.

Many people who are studying this matter are blind to one very important fact, which is that the people are taking alarm over recent events, and that they will demand some kind of protection from Congress. The wiser heads in the railroad world see that there is a chance now, by conceding Government control over rates, to secure Government protection for organization. They see that sooner or later the public will demand rate control, and they see that if that demand be refused it will eventually be enforced without corresponding protection being given.

The Interstate Commission is the natural and proper machinery for bringing about the necessary change in the law. It is absurd to say that an appointive commission can not be trusted to be honest, and it is equally absurd to say that it must necessarily act in a foolish manner, even if it be not actuated by corrupt motives. We fancy that it would be difficult to persuade the average shipper that the danger to him from corruption of public officials is necessarily greater than the danger arising from the self-interest of powerful financiers and corporations.

*Buffalo (N. Y.) Express.*—In deciding to ask Congress to enlarge the powers of the Interstate Commerce Commission, the governors of the Northwestern States have taken at least one step which promises some practical results. The Commission needs all the support it can get. As the establishment of close traffic arrangement in one form or another can not be prevented, the enlargement of the powers of the Interstate Commerce Commission appears to offer the only check that can be found on exorbitant freight rates.

What the outcome of the Commission's efforts will be remains to be seen. If this body is to be continued, it should have enlarged powers, including supervision of rates in a large degree if not completely. The Commission and its friends have no easy task before them, yet, undoubtedly, it is the wish of the country that something be done to clear up this vexing question.

*Brooklyn (N. Y.) Eagle.*—Equality of rates is the great demand of the shipper. He would be reasonably assured of this were the scope of the Interstate Commerce Commission broadened as it should be. If the Commission is to do nothing better than provide for the collection and compilation of statistics it might as well be abolished and its duties, as at present defined, transferred to an ordinary bureau. If it is to remain in existence it should be endowed with the authority to make its decisions worth the paper they are written on.

## MINNESOTA.

*St. Paul (Minn.) Pioneer-Press.*—The vital point is to find a remedy for the evils of combination, whatever form it may assume. The President's view that the remedy is to be found in a larger Government control, through the Interstate Commerce Commission, is that of the Commission itself, and of the best opinion of the country.

Objection is made that there is no use trying to get a measure of that kind through Congress; that all the combined influence of the railroad corporations in this country would be employed to defeat it, as they have heretofore managed to defeat all amendments to the interstate commerce act designed to enlarge and effectuate the powers of the Commission. But if they have easily succeeded in defeating such attempted legislation heretofore, it is because it was backed by no active or urgent popular demand.

So long as the railroads were cutting each other's throats in relentless wars of competition the people were comparatively indifferent to any Government control. But now, after the survivors of the slaughter and the reorganized successors of a multitude of bankrupt railroads have found a way to avoid ruinous rate wars in consolidation or combination, the American people will surely insist upon such adequate protection from any abuse of their powers of taxing commerce and industry as can only be found in an effective Government control. Under existing conditions it is entirely safe to assume that the popular demand for such legislation will become so urgent and imperative that no Congress would dare to disobey it, and that the united influence of the railroad corporations, with all their thousands of millions of capital behind them, will be impotent to resist the mandate of the public will.

*Minneapolis (Minn.) Tribune.*—The measure introduced by Congressman Corliss, of Michigan, appears to be the best susbtitute for the present interstate-commerce law which has appeared.

*Faribault (Minn.) Republican.*—The present helpless state of the Interstate Commerce Commission is indicative of what will be the condition of the public if the railroads are not restricted from effecting unlimited combinations for controlling business in their interests. The disclosures of discriminations and rebates to the larger shippers in direct violation of the law made in the late investigation by the Commission in Chicago show that the law has been but a cobweb before the mercenary forces whose interest it is to disregard it. Representative Corliss, of Michigan, has introduced a bill making amendments to the bill for the purpose of strengthening the hands of the Commissioners, but in view of the ill success of past legislation the outlook is not encouraging.

*Duluth (Minn.) Tribune.*—The bill recently introduced in the Senate to increase the powers of the Interstate Commerce Commission is a step in the right direction. It is in line with the general demand that the Commission should either be abolished or made effective for good by giving it the power to enforce its decrees subject, always, to appeal to higher tribunals.

## INDIANA.

*Muncie (Ind.) Times.*—The Interstate Commerce Commission should have more authority. At present the Commission can do little else than point out where evils exist and suggest remedies.

*Indianapolis Sentinel.*—The Interstate Commerce Commission has made a strong showing of the need for greater power, but there is little probability of Congress giving it. The railroads and trusts do not want the law made effective, and this is a Republican Congress.

The country should not lose sight of the desired amendments to the interstate-commerce law. As the Commission urges, it has no power to accomplish the ends for which it was created.

*Indianapolis Sentinel.*—The Commission has asked for increased powers repeatedly, but the railroad and trust lobby has always been able to defeat the measures. Of course it is possible that the roads might get control of the Commission, if it were given adequate powers, but that is no reason for making it a mere figurehead. It should be given power to regulate commerce or it should be abolished. The bill introduced by Mr. Corliss, of Michigan, ought to be passed.

*Indianapolis News.*—If more power is not granted to the Interstate Commerce Commission by the present Congress, the people in the coming elections will want to know why.

It is useless to talk of the wisdom of the let-alone policy when the railroads themselves are doing everything in their power to destroy those conditions under which alone the let-alone policy can be defended. The theory on which free and popular governments keep their hands off private quasi-public enterprises is that the force of competition is sufficient to protect the people. When, therefore, these enterprises interfere with the free action of that great force, they must expect another one put in motion. No great thing is asked. All that the people want is that existing legal agencies be made effective. It is through them, and them alone, that competition can be preserved.

To doubt that a remedy can be found for the evils from which the country is now suffering, or with which it is threatened, is to doubt the capacity of the people for self-government.

No law should pass Congress that does not permit the decisions of the Interstate Commerce Commission to be binding at the moment of their promulgation, and that does not throw the burden of their reversal on the railroads.

We do not believe our Senators and Representatives realize the depth of public feeling on this subject. For, if they did, they would take up the question and consider it seriously, with an honest purpose to arrive at the solution that would be best for all.

*Indianapolis Sentinel.*—It is hardly necessary to state that the people who want the evil stopped are not in favor of the Elkins bill and are in favor of the Nelson-Corliss bill, which is a good measure. If the power of trusts is to be curbed this law is absolutely necessary, and all who are interested in securing fair and equal rates should write their Senators and Representatives in support of it.

*Indianapolis Sentinel (Dem.).*—The Democratic party is to be congratulated on its square stand for giving the Interstate Commerce Commission power to enforce its rulings. All the trusts have profited by this abuse, and many of them owe their very existence to it. It was railway favors more than anything else that built up the Standard Oil monopoly, the beef trust, and other of the most odious of the combines.

## ILLINOIS.

*Chicago (Ill.) Journal.*—The Interstate Commerce Commission is popularly supposed to be a national board that in a great measure controls the railroads of the country and protects the people from unjust oppression on the part of the roads. This undoubtedly was the original object of the law, which was passed by Congress in 1887, but year after year since then the lawyers of the railroads have torn wider and wider holes in it through which they have not only driven the traditional "coach and six," but great railway trains as well, with the result that nobody now precisely knows what the Interstate Commerce Commission is, or its powers and duties. Congress seems to be powerless, or else unwilling, to patch up the law thus rent in fragments. Every session of the Commission simply adds to the demonstration of its impotence. Congress should mend it or end it.

*Chicago Chronicle.*—It is enough to know that the Commission is practically powerless, and that the law under which it acts is not much better than a dead letter. The real question is whether the law ought to be changed so that it will have some effect to protect the public against the abuses of corporate power against which it purports to be aimed. If not the law may about as well be wiped clean off the statute books and the Commission abolished as a useless and expensive excrescence upon our governmental establishment. There can not be much doubt that public sentiment is overwhelmingly in favor of such action as will make the law of some effect.

The wild and eccentric competition between railroads, by which rates for freight and passengers are indiscriminately cut to meet the rates of some rival bankrupt or reckless line, is the worst evil of railroad commerce. It demoralizes all business of the country which is regulated by the prices for transportation. Under intelligent supervision by proper authority pooling contracts would be equitable to every interest, and would give to railroad commerce a stability of rates with other such other fair regulations as would constitute a substantial reform in the business methods of the country.

*Chicago Post.*—One thing is certain, unregulated monopoly the people will not endure. The corollary of mergers, consolidation, and pooling is systematic and rigid control by a court, commission, or any other agency representing the interests of the people. Transportation will not be allowed to regulate itself. The advocates of the let-alone policy are playing into the hands of those who favor Government ownership. The law should permit consolidation and pooling, but it should also guarantee equal and fair rates. This is the position of the President and the Commission.

*Chicago Post.*—The people of the United States will not tolerate favoritism, discrimination, and abuse of monopolistic power by the railroad corporations. In the words of Chairman Knapp, of the Interstate Commerce Commission, "No service which the Government undertakes can be more useful, and no duty which rests upon it more imperative than to secure for the public always and everywhere equal treatment by every railway carrier." The "let-well-enough-alone" cry is absurd, for the situation is not satisfactory to the majority of shippers. Wherever there is monopoly there must be supervision and regulation in the public interest. The only possible alternative to regulation is Government ownership. "Enlightened self-interest" is a broken reed to lean on where competition fails or finds itself barred by the nature of the industry.

Mr. Roosevelt's policy is fair and reasonable. He offers to aid the railroads in obtaining better and more modern legislation, but present abuses he insists on suppressing. It is idle to threaten him with withdrawal of support. The railroads will not stand together in the contest outlined, and they could not win if they did stand together. The people would be on Mr. Roosevelt's side, and they are more powerful than the railroads. The truth is mighty, especially the truth about the evils of discrimination and favoritism in rate making. The railroads will not carry out the threats they are alleged to have made.

The railroad corporations are not by any means satisfied with the status quo and they have a programme of their own to promote. While they have crippled the Commission, the necessity of resorting to secret rate cutting, rebates and other violations of the law is painful to some of them. Other things equal, they would rather obey the law and adhere to published rates. Unfair competition drives them into practices they can not wish to continue indefinitely. What they want is reasonable freedom of contract and pooling, of association for the regulation and equitable distribution of traffic.

*Chicago Inter-Ocean.*—The agitation against railway consolidation and the demand for equity in railway rates do not arise from a desire to injure anyone. They arise from the perception that transportation has become such a commercial and industrial necessity to the people that equality in charges is almost as vital as equality before the laws.

To many citizens the only safe alternative in the railway problem seems to be Government control of the rate-making power. For many reasons the vast majority of Americans do not desire Government ownership. Yet equality in railway rates they must have, and this equality the railway managers have practically confessed their inability to attain. All their traffic agreements, pools, etc., in the last analysis are no bar to discrimination.

Hence Mr. Cassatt is wise if he supports the plan of effective Government supervision over the rate-making power.  Those who oppose such supervision but strengthen the hands of the confiscators.

*Chicago News.*—How serious is the need of a revision of the law is shown in the annual report of the Interstate Commerce Commission, which does not mince words in denouncing the present evasions of the measure as "surprising and offensive to all right-minded persons." The Commission declare that the criminal provisions of the law need reenforcement.  Unless Congress is disposed wholly to discredit the Commission's report, it can hardly ignore these recommendations, unless it proposes to repudiate the principle of Government supervision of railways.

*Chicago Drovers' Journal.*—As the matter now stands, the Commission can do nothing except to investigate and make a report.  The railroads are said to violate agreements and rules with impunity, because they know that it is highly improbable that a fine will have to be paid.

*Chicago Standard.*—The difficulty with the work of the Interstate Commerce Commission is that it has no power to enforce its mandates. It is to be hoped that Congress will soon come to the relief of the Commission and, disregarding the formidable opposition by the railroad lobby that is certain to be organized, will amend the law in such a way as to give the Commission power to fix at least maximum rates, and to enforce its decisions by direct judicial process under proper limitations.

*Chicago (Ill.) Railway Age.*—Railway legislation is a fact, and, in the absence of Government ownership, will continue to be a fact.  The principal thing just now is to relieve the present intolerable situation, and the Elkins bill as presented seems to fairly promise to do this.

*Springfield (Ill.) News.*—The Interstate Commerce Commission has shown many abuses which need correction, but which it is powerless to correct.  Congress will be supported by public sentiment in any extension of power given the Commission.

*Pekin (Ill.) Times.*—The interstate-commerce law should be amended or repealed.  As a joke it has been carried too far.

*Springfield (Ill.) Journal.*—The Cullom bill has now been replaced by a shorter and simpler one, which will accomplish all that is really necessary and which stands a much better chance of being enacted into law.  These simple amendments will be effective if adopted, because they will close up the loopholes through which the railroads evade compliance with the orders of the Commission.  If they are compelled to observe the orders of that body until the courts reverse them, they will not violate the law with impunity as they have done for years past, and there will be an immediate change in their methods.

*Examiner, Mount Sterling, Ill.*—It is enough to know that the Commission is in fact practically powerless and the law under which it acts is not much better than a dead letter.  There can not be much doubt that public sentiment is overwhelmingly in favor of such action as will make the law of some effect.

*Bloomington (Ill.) Pantagraph.*—A representative of the Chicago Board of Trade and the Illinois Manufacturers' Association has made some important statements before the House Interstate Committee with reference to rate discrimination by the railroads.  He told the committee that the roads made a cheaper rate on wheat from Chicago to New York for wheat than they did on flour. There is a measure under consideration that will correct the evil if it is adopted. It provides that when the Commission after investigation finds that a rate is unreasonable and a reasonable rate is fixed this rate will remain effective until the question is passed on by the courts. Unless some authority like this is given the Commission, the railroads will laugh at its decrees and continue the unjust practice of giving rebates to favored shippers. It is up against this Congress to pass some legislation that will insure fair dealing among shippers, great and small, and if it is not done the country will be disposed to bring to account those responsible for the failure. The matter has been talked up as a campaign issue and staved off at Washington until the people are beginning to see through the scheme and are demanding action as well as words.

*Rock Island Argus.*—Until a bill to strengthen the Interstate Commerce Commission is passed the war against trusts is useless.

*Springfield (Ill.) News.*—There is certainly added force to thè movement for more power for the Interstate Commerce Commission in the report of the Commission just made public. At all events it is plain that, if the Commission is not to be given enlarged powers, some method should be devised by which such orders as can be made may be enforced within a reasonable time. The fact is that the Government can exert a proper control over the railroads of the country only through some such a commission as the Interstate Commerce Commission, and since this organization is in existence, and is composed of men whose abilities, integrity, and good common sense are unquestioned, Congress can reasonably do nothing else but extend the powers of the Commission to the extent that they ought to be. That Congress fails to do its duty in this connection is a matter which the people of the country are coming to regard with suspicion.

### PENNSYLVANIA.

*Philadelphia North American.*—The obvious remedy is that proposed by the commissioners—first of all to require the publication of tariff rates, then their uniform application to all shippers, and finally to permit the inspection of company books by Government agents. Doubtless traffic managers who prefer the lax system under which they now ply trade will find nothing to commend in the commissioners' plan.

*Philadelphia (Pa.) Press.*—The most important reform which the Interstate Commerce Commission urges in its report is the demand that the act of 1887 "should be amended so as to open the books of the carriers to the inspection of the Commission or its agents." Congress ought to pass this law, and pass it at once. There is everything to be said in its favor. There is nothing to be said against it. A railroad corporation is a public carrier. A public carrier is a public servant. Its books ought always to be open for inspection. If it is keeping its rates published, there is nothing to conceal. If it is not keeping these rates, it is committing a crime. In either case public policy requires publicity. Congress would pass this act in a week if members were not influenced in a score of sinister ways by the influence of great railroads which mesh them about with gifts and political aids.

*Scranton (Pa.) Republican.*—The Interstate Commerce law should be amended. There can be no question about that. The act as it now stands is more or less purposeless. A determined effort is being made to amend the law so as to restore full power to the Commission. The Corliss bill should be passed, but it is by no means certain that it will be. The railroads maintain a powerful lobby at Washington, and can make very hard sledding for any measure they may set about to oppose in earnest. The Corliss bill authorizes the Commission to correct rates that may be regarded as unjust and discriminating but does not abolish the right of appeal, and is regarded as a very mild measure by the shippers, who really think they are entitled to far more substantial protection than the bill as it now stands can afford them.

*Scranton (Pa.) Tribune.*—For years there has been a well-founded complaint at the inadequacy of the power vested in the Interstate Commerce Commission to enforce equality among shippers. A bill to supply the deficiency in this direction is now pending in the House, having been introduced by Representative Corliss, of Michigan. The law is to be put into enforcible shape. This should be done or the law repealed. In its present shape it is merely a travesty.

## IOWA.

*Sioux City (Iowa) Tribune.*—Chairman Knapp is trying to get Congress to at least amend the interstate commerce law so the Commission can prevent secret rate cutting and the practice of giving rebates to big shippers. The transportation situation will never be satisfactory till this reform is effected, and as uniformity of rates would be beneficial to the railroads as well as to the public, the former ought to encourage Mr. Knapp.

*Marshalltown (Iowa) Herald.*—The people of this country are practically unanimous that the powers of the Interstate Commerce Commission should be so enlarged that it shall have the power to prevent combinations which may be made to the detriment of the people and to business generally, and that it is the duty of Congress to take prompt and decisive action in this matter, that the relief demanded may not be delayed because of the nonaction of Congress.

*Des Moines Leader.*—That some law along the lines of the Nelson-Corliss bill should be passed under which a board, combining executive and judicial functions, shall have authority, in the name of the nation, to prescribe reasonable rates, is now generally admitted. The principle may be said now to be almost universally admitted. With the elimination of competition in the railroad business, a condition whose coming is clearly foreshadowed, it will become a public necessity to establish public regulation of transportation rates. Otherwise power would be in the hands of a few persons to apply to a degree most oppressive the principle of making the rate all traffic will bear.

*Des Moines Register.*—The Interstate Commerce Commission's recommendation that the law under which it has been attempting to work be amended in such a manner as to give the Commission power to accomplish something will be a great benefit to Iowa if it is heeded by Congress and given recognition in the statutes. A proportionate car load freight rate is just what is needed to build up all the home markets of Iowa—that fact is true as to the home markets of all the other States—and all the people of the nation should steadily labor until that long-needed measure of justice for all has been gained and enforced.

*Des Moines Leader.*—There can hardly be serious disagreement with the opinion that if Senator Dolliver shall decide to introduce in the upper house of Congress the Corliss bill relating to the powers of the Interstate Commerce Commission, he will be acting in line with the sentiment of the State which he represents. The great business interests of the country that are directly dependent for their prosperity on transportation are more nearly aroused than ever before to the necessity of making the Commission a real power instead of a shadow without the substance. It is to be hoped Senator Dolliver will accept the opportunity to do a great service. His public career will lose nothing by it. He will, indeed, find himself one of the central figures in a great fight in which the most powerful special and private interests of the country will be arrayed against him, but he will have the people of Iowa and the business men of the country with him, and in the end he will win. The measure is one that, when properly presented, will command the support of the country.

*Dubuque (Iowa) Times.*—The Nelson-Corliss bill now pending in Congress gives the Interstate Commerce Commission the power to revise tariffs. The objections made to it are more technical than substantial. The bill should become a law at the present session.

*Dubuque (Iowa) Journal.*—Why has Senator Elkins united a pooling proposition with his bill authorizing the Interstate Commerce Commission to make rates on interstate traffic? The question of whether rate cutting could be prevented in the absence of a pool is quite distinct from the question of whether the Commission can be trusted to revise the rates on interstate business. The States successfully regulate rates on business wholly within their own borders without exempting railway companies from the operation of the antitrust laws. The question should be divided. The Commission should be given power to revise rates, and the question of whether pooling must be sanctioned in order to prevent discrimination in favor of big shippers or shipping centers should be left for future determination.

*Dubuque (Iowa) Times.*—Our delegation in Congress may accept the legislature's indorsement of this measure (the Corliss bill) as a faithful reflection of Iowa sentiment respecting the need for legislation that will serve the original purpose of the interstate-commerce law.

*Clinton (Iowa) Herald.*—Under existing circumstances the Commission, which stands in the attitude of the representative of the United States as between carrier and shipper, is absolutely without power to give any utterance of opinion, or to lay down any binding rule. The Commissioners themselves have repeatedly stated this fact. The right of the Commission to prescribe a remedy, subject to appeal to the courts, is fair to shipper and carrier, and would be effective. It is undoubtedly necessary for the proper conduct of the commerce of the United States that there should be some intelligent and responsible body empowered to fix, adjust, and decide rates and all questions arising on complaint between railroad carriers and the shippers.

At the time of the passage of the interstate-commerce act the universal belief was that Congress intended to give the Commission such power. But the act having been construed otherwise by the courts, it now devolves upon the Congress to remodel the law so as to give it the force originally intended. The rehabilitation of the commission has already been too long delayed, and it is not too much to say that the people of this country begin to feel that their patience has been abused.

For the safety of the railroads, as well as the good of the country, there must be some tribunal to which appeal can be made, and which has the power to render quick and full justice and enforce its mandates without delay. The prompt passage of the pending bill would do injustice to no one and give the shipper what he has long sought and waited for—a chance for fair and uniform rates, fair treatment, and a stable and uniform classification.

## WEST VIRGINIA.

*Wheeling Register.*—The Interstate Commerce Commission is after a few of the railroads not respecting the law of the land, and is evidently disposed to do the best it can with these notorious violators of the interstate-commerce laws and the Sherman antitrust law. The whole procedure savors of the ridiculous. A simple bill passed by Congress, regulating rates and providing ample penalties, would be sufficient. The present situation savors largely of farce comedy, and is so esteemed by the public.

It is high time that Congress was supplementing the powers of the Interstate Commerce Commission, which is now without the ability to practically reform railroad abuses. In short the interstate-commerce law is a farce and a dead letter, so far as regulating the railroads or railroad rates are concerned, and the amendments proposed by the Corliss bill, prepared under the direction of the Interstate Commerce Law Convention, should receive the attention of Congress.

*Wheeling (W. Va.) Intelligencer.*—Recent developments have been such as to make it incumbent upon Congress to act. The time is opportune, and further delay would arouse such a feeling of resentment in commercial circles as to render possible serious agitation for radical measures against the carriers. Public opinion is in sympathy with the present movement. This is apparent from expressions by prominent statesmen and business men, by testimony submitted to the Industrial Commission on the subject of transportation, and in the known desire of certain representative railroad men to meet the friends of the proposed legislation in a spirit of compromise. Attention should also be directed to the action of the legislatures of Michigan, Kansas, Wisconsin, and other States, in passing joint resolutions urging upon Congress the necessity for prompt remedial legislation. The firm attitude taken by President Roosevelt in his recent message in discussing this subject is of the deepest significance, and is indicative of the vast change that has taken place in high quarters within recent years. Some relief is demanded, and some must come from the present Congress.

## WASHINGTON.

*Spokane (Wash.) Chronicle.*—If the voters of Washington really want to secure better rates from the railroads, let them do their share to secure laws that will give the people of this nation genuine control of interstate commerce by means of duly appointed commissions. To begin the good work, let them see that no candidate for Congress is nominated next summer who is not pledged to support such legislation as is needed to enable the Interstate Commerce Commission to enforce just freight rates from every State or Territory to every other State.

*Spokane ( Wash.) Spokesman.*—The present law is sadly in need of mending, if the Commission is to perform the work expected of it in the matter of regulating rates. The Commission has had the power to investigate railway abuses and to issue orders, but it has been powerless to enforce them. In several instances it has found rates to be unreasonable, and has ordered that new tariffs be established, but the roads have laughed at the Commission and have ignored its mandates as completely as if it never existed.

## TEXAS.

*Houston (Tex.) Post.*—The Interstate Commerce Commission is an institution that is surely calculated to impress not only the political philosopher but the ordinary business man with the folly of a bureau or department without power. What is the Commission for? What does it do? What good is accomplished by what it does?

For years the Interstate Commerce Commission has reported that the law is constantly violated by railroad corporations. The cardinal provisions of the interstate-commerce act are that railway rates should be just and reasonable, and that all shippers, localities, and commodities should be accorded equal treatment.

There is no doubt as to the duty of Congress. It should give the Commission the power to compel the railroads to disclose all the facts in their possession that would bear on suspected violations of the act. Not only should the legal remedy and punishment for such violations of the law be adequate, but the hands of the Commission should not be tied in making the investigations that the law imposes upon it.

*Houston (Tex.) Post.*—As to the benefit that would result to the people from an interstate-commerce act that could be enforced, it would be enormous. Congress should take up the question of amending the interstate-commerce act and give it immediate and earnest attention.

## MISSOURI.

*St. Louis (Mo.) Republic.*—So practical are the arguments in favor of an amendment to the interstate-commerce act with a view to effectively empower the Interstate Commerce Commission to punish all railroads violating the law against discrimination between shippers that the favorable action of Congress should be certain. The proposed amendment is urged by all the leading commercial organizations in the United States. The point at issue is a plain business proposition, remote from politics, and the public sentiment of the Union, supported by the commercial bodies and the Interstate Commerce Commission, itself should prevail for the general good. The amending of the interstate-commerce act will constitute early action, unless the railroad influence in Congress is too strong to be resisted.

Every Congressman should be made to realize that public sentiment demands the amending of the interstate-commerce act as now contemplated. The time to relax such effort will not have arrived until the interstate-commerce act has been definitely amended.

*Kansas City (Mo.) Star.*—There is evidently need of legislation to make the Commission an efficient body. It must have power to give speedy relief to shippers. and to enforce its rulings without the interminable delays which now make its work futile. If its hands are not strengthened, it might as well disband.

*Joplin Globe.*—It is an absurdity to protest hostility to the beef trust, which confessedly has been able to control markets by rebates on freights from railroad companies, and at the same time refuse to pass the bill for which the Interstate Commerce Commission has for years been begging, to give it adequate powers to compel railroads to make equal rates. If the Commission had that power and exercised it, the ability of the beef trust to control markets would be largely curtailed.

## MASSACHUSETTS.

*Boston Record.* — The Interstate Commerce Commission would assume the position of some dignity if, following the recommendations of the Industrial Commission, Congress should decide to make a definite grant of power to the Commission, never on its own initiative, but only on formal complaint, to pass upon the reasonableness of freight and passenger rates or charges; also definite power to declare given rates unreasonable.

*Christian World (Boston, Mass.).*—The American public has few more burning domestic questions before it now than giving to the Interstate Commerce Commission, or some other body of Federal officials, authority to deal with and punish the railroad corporation officials and captains of industry who violate the laws governing uniformity of rates to shippers.

*Boston (Mass.) Journal.*—The bill has for its single purpose the amendment of the existing act in such a manner as to make it actually effective for the purposes for which it was framed. It is intended, in other words, to confer upon the Interstate Commerce Commission the powers which it was clearly the mind of Congress should be exercised by it, but which have been taken from it by the rulings of the courts.

*Boston Transcript.*—Revision of the Interstate Commerce act is urgently needed. The purpose of the act—to put a stop to discriminations—has not been attained; the evils against which it was directed still flourish. The situation clearly needs amending legislation which shall make the system of public control of the railroads through the Interstate Commerce Commission really effective.

## CALIFORNIA.

*San Jose (Cal.) Mercury.*—During the present session of Congress there should be enacted a Federal law which will have the effect of so strengthening the Interstate Commerce Commission as to make it efficient or should abolish it altogether. For the past several years the cry of its members has been expressed in every annual report for legislation that would enable it to enforce its decisions against carriers who have been treating them with a scornful disregard. There is no question that the necessity of such legislation is urgent. The Commission is at present an expensive and a useless body. Congress has no longer the right to disregard the cry of the Commission and the interests of the public. Better no commission than an impotent one. Let it either be made efficient or wiped out of existence.

*San Francisco* (*Cal.*) *Call.*—Unfair and illegal discrimination is one of the greatest evils that now afflict the industries and the commerce of the people. Some method must be devised for protecting the industries of the country from such evils, and no better plan is at present in sight than that of strengthening the power of the Commission and holding it responsible for the enforcement of the law.

*Los Angeles* (*Cal.*) *Journal.*—Not until the powers of the Interstate Commerce Commission to enforce its rulings are made plenary can the public expect a substantial measure of protection against extortion, discrimination, and oppression practiced by common carriers.

*San Francisco* (*Cal.*) *Call.*—It would be well for merchants, manufacturers, and other large shippers of the country to unite in a concerted movement to bring pressure to bear upon Congress in favor of the measure to enlarge the powers of the Interstate Commerce Commission. It is clearly the duty of Congress to act, but of course Congress is not going to act unless the shippers of the country demand it. So long as the railroads can keep the people divided just so long can they keep Congress quiet and the Commission and the courts powerless.

### VIRGINIA.

*Norfolk* (*Va.*) *Pilot.*—There is, undoubtedly, a large sentiment in the country in favor of giving the Interstate Commerce Commission more power. The bill generally favored w is introduced by Representative Corliss, of Michigan. We believe that the Commission should be given the power to make rates outright, but, failing that, the power to correct rates that will enable it to supply a remedy in case of discriminations. If the published tariff is too high, however, and excessive, the Commission, under this bill, can afford no relief as long as all are treated alike.

*Norfolk* (*Va.*) *Pilot.*—The interstate-commerce law as it exists to-day is the mere headless body of a statute decapitated by the United States Supreme Court.

### NORTH CAROLINA.

*Raleigh* (*N. C.*) *News.*—The present Congress ought not to adjourn until it gives the Interstate Commerce Commission power to regulate rates. The rapid consolidation and mergers of great railway systems has made it vital to give this power to the Commission for the protection of the public.

*Raleigh Observer.*—Full of railroad owners and railroad attorneys, Congress will do nothing toward proper regulation until the people emphatically demand positive action, and back up their demand by a threat to send members of Congress into retirement. That is not now in sight and therefore no remedial legislation may be expected at this session.

### COLORADO.

*Denver* (*Colo.*) *Republican.*—The Interstate Commerce Commission has been deprived of the requisite power to make its decrees effective. It has been necessary for it to appeal to the courts to compel the railroad companies to obey its orders. Thus it has been almost powerless to achieve the things which were hoped for when it was organized.

*Denver (Colo.) News.*—On the Commission itself there have been many eminent lawyers, and since their experience with the Federal courts they are all agreed that the Commission has been shorn of all practical power to name and enforce equitable rates.

*Denver Post.*—The Interstate Commerce Commission was orignally formulated and created for the purpose of standing between the public and the railroads, to prevent extortion, to insist upon certain equities, to have the country as a whole treated equally by the corporations, to give the small shipper the same advantages as the large, and stop railway combinations from imposing upon the powerless public. The Commission has not accomplished this purpose because it has not had the power to do so.

Now it it suggested that it be given the power to fix rates upon a basis so fair that the railroads can always make money and still serve the public wisely and well.

Of course, the railroads object. They want to fix their own rates, although they ask from Congress and the State and communities generally all manner of benefits. The rate-making power should not be in the hands of the railroads. It really belongs to Congress. Originally it was in the hands of that body, and when railways were organized and given vast grants and powers by the National Government, the National Government usually fixed charges, features, and tariffs.

To-day the railroads are exercising a public function, but they have gone far beyond their rights and privileges. The time seems to have arrived for the Government to exercise the power, which no one questions it has, to supervise and control when necessary the acts of railroad officials.

If Congress delegates this power to half a dozen capable, competent, just, and fair men, giving them the right to act in the interest of the public and to treat the railroads fairly, these great commercial arteries should not object. If they do object it should make no difference.

*Denver (Colo.) Times.*—President Roosevelt, the greatest of the servants of the people of America, and his Attorney-General will not fail the nation—that is absolutely certain. But they are alone and can do comparatively little. The time has come for the most radical and sweeping extensions of the power of control and supervision of the Interstate Commerce Commission. Congress can hardly go too far to meet popular approval. But will it rise to the occasion with broadest statesmanship?

## OHIO.

*Columbus (Ohio) Journal.*—Recent developments have been such as to make it incumbent upon Congress to act. The time is opportune, and further delay would arouse such a feeling of resentment in commercial circles as to render possible serious agitation for radical measures against the carriers. Public opinion is in sympathy with the present movement. This is apparent from expressions by prominent statesmen and business men, by the testimony submitted to the Interstate Commission, and in the known desire of certain representatives in a spirit of compromise.

*Cincinnati (Ohio) Commercial Tribune.*—The result of the ruling of the Supreme Court is to put complainants to heavy expense for witnesses and for counsel, merely to find the losing party refusing to delay in going down to the tavern to swear at the court, but enabling him to begin, at once and defiantly, to ask the Commission what it is going to do about it. The Commission exists to-day merely as a gatherer of statistics of no particular value, unless the complainant before it selects to take the record into some court and, after going over the whole case again, asks the justice which was denied him before the Commissioners. Even if justice had been awarded him it would be of no avail, for the reason that the Commission is without power to compel the losing party to respect its decrees.

## LOUISIANA.

*New Orleans (La.) Times-Democrat.*—The Interstate Commerce Commission, which did an immense amount of good for the first few years after its creation in the way of obtaining justice for the shipper of goods by railroad and generally in the way of regulating rates, has now for several years had its efforts frustrated by the Federal courts, which in many cases have rendered decisions in favor of the railroad corporations in litigation with the Commission.

The Commission is, in fact, now almost entirely shorn of its powers, and unless it obtain rehabilitation from Congress through either of the two bills now before that body, it might as well close up its affairs and go out of business, for all the use of which it has recently been, and is.

Unless some legislation is enacted this session to strengthen the hands of the Commission in its continuous fight with the corporations, it is not unlikely that the Commission will go by the board. There is no use for its decisions if its decisions be not backed up by the law.

*New Orleans Item.*—Congress must strengthen the hands of the Interstate Commerce Commission. The railroads see that legislation will soon compel them to do away with their devices of favoritism, and are resorting to the only possible method of defense, that of universal consolidation. But a complete consolidation will never come until the Government assumes charge, and hence it is imperative that Congress shall act and act promptly.

*New Orleans (La.) Item.*—Congress should not delay to clothe the Interstate Commerce Commission with the powers they ask, powers that were intended to be by the original act, but which were wiped away by the Supreme Court.

## NEBRASKA.

*Omaha (Nebr.) Twentieth Century Farmer.*—Public sentiment is rapidly crystallizing in favor of the supervision of corporations engaged in interstate commerce. The demand of the hour is for the fullest publicity in corporate management, and especially in the management of colossal corporations, whether organized as trusts or under cooperative control.

The demand for publicity is no longer confined to the press and public officers holding executive position in the State and nation. It has at last dawned upon the corporation managers and trust attorneys that the well-defined business sentiment against everything resembling a blind pool and in favor of the fullest publicity must be respected and complied with.

*Omaha Bee.*—It would seem that Congress should need no more enlightenment in regard to public sentiment in this matter; that in view of the disclosures of the last three months regarding the widespread and persistent violations of the interstate-commerce law Congress can require nothing more to convince it of the necessity for so amending the act as to make it more effective.

*Omaha Twentieth Century Farmer.*—The advocates of strengthening the law should not weaken or abate their efforts so long as there appears to be a chance of getting what they believe to be essential. They should find encouragement in the fact that they are supported by a stronger public sentiment than ever before since the policy of railway regulation was instituted.

*Omaha Bee.*—The demand for strengthening the Interstate Commerce Commission has an overwhelming public support, and the necessity for it has been most conclusively demonstrated. * * * Congress ought to have the courage to meet this question squarely and determine it as the public interests clearly require.

## MICHIGAN.

*Grand Rapids Post.*—The failure of Congress to act on the proposed amendments to the interstate-commerce law would be a serious blunder, involving dire consequences; and it is not likely that the people of the United States can be induced to demonstrate to the world that democratic governement is incapable of profiting in the dear school of experience. In view of the future magnitude of the transportation interests the importance of placing its control upon sound principles should not be underestimated.

*Grand Rapids Herald.*—Of course the great transportation companies will be on hand with powerful lobbies to oppose; but the friends of the amendment are better organized and more thoroughly in earnest than ever before, and the indications are that the enemies of the change will not be allowed to shelve the measure as they did during the last session.

*Jackson Patriot.*—It is claimed the Commission should be given greater powers. That body should be given authority to determine as to the reasonableness of the rate, and it should have the power to fix rates and put them in operation at once.

*Grand Rapids Press.*—It is going to be Government regulation or Government ownership, and by too strenuously opposing the one the railroads invite the other.

## WISCONSIN.

*Superior ( Wis.) Telegram.*—Without discussing the merits of the Elkins bill, or the probability of its passage, it is proper to notice that it is a step in the direction asked by the Commission.

Now that the railroad officials have admitted the charges of rate cutting, and pleaded necessity in extenuation, then it seems as if the time had come when the Commission should be given more power or less. If it is desirable to have a Commission possessed with powers of investigation and determination as to conditions, then it follows as a natural conclusion that the power to rectify the unfair conditions should be lodged somewhere. It is more natural that it should be with the Commission which is charged with the general consideration of transportation matters. In the past the Interstate Commerce Commission has been more or less of a farce because of its lack of power. This condition was recognized by the President in his message to Congress, and, now that there is such indubitable proof as to this matter, it should be enough to convince even Congress that immediate action should be taken one way or the other.

*Racine* ( *Wis.*) *Journal.*—The Nelson bill, amending the interstate-commerce law, prepared in the interest of the people, seems to fit the case. It is plain enough that if the people are not to be further confirmed in their impression that the Commission is but a plaything—an excuse for a number of estimable citizens to draw commodious salaries—it will be necessary that Congress take some action and endow its measures with the life qualities that will take the dead wood out of it. The Nelson bill proposes to make a distinctive advance, and, if Congress pleases, it can give the Interstate Commission a new lease of life and dress it up with the garment of legal respectability that will bring to it that measure of respect from the transportation companies they have hitherto denied it.

*Oshkosh* ( *Wis.*) *Times.*—With all its defects the interstate-commerce act has accomplished much good. In the first place it has been construed by the Supreme Court of the United States, and the powers of the Interstate Commerce Commission under the act are beginning to be known. The railroads and big corporations under the law.

Congress has no more important and urgent duty before it, in the interest of the great majority of the shippers of the country, than that of amending the interstate-commerce act so as to rendered it more effective. The demand for this is so overwhelming that it would seem hardly possible that Congress can fail to heed it. There is no other question affecting our domestic affairs as to which the commercial interests of the country are so nearly unanimous. Whatever diversity of opinion there may be as to particular propositions, there is a very general agreement that the law should be strengthened and that the Interstate Commerce Commission should have its powers enlarged. Yet there appears to be doubt whether anything will be done, at least at the present session.

*Milwaukee* ( *Wis.*) *Free Press.*—If it is the purpose of the railway companies to create a sentiment of opposition to the enactment of the proposed amendment of the interstate-commerce law, their action seems singularly shortsighted, for the effect is likely to be exactly the opposite, and to lead to a keener realization of the absolute necessity of some Government department or commission standing between the railways and the people to see that exact justice is done.

Some of the more progressive railway officials, like those of the Pennsylvania Company, recognize the growing demand for equality in railway rates, the justice of such a demand, and the certainty that a much longer continued policy of opposition may result in the overthrow of the party in power, and will probably lead to the adoption of much more severe measures than are now proposed.

*Milwaukee* ( *Wis.*) *News.*—The conviction that the only solution of the transportation problem lies in Government ownership and operation is rapidly growing, having received a strong impetus from the recent merging of vast railway interests. With the immense power possessed by the railway corporations, they are enabled to control legislation. They have their representatives in the legislatures.

*Milwaukee ( Wis.) Sentinel.*—The Interstate Commerce Commission merely secures under this act (the Corliss bill) the power which, for instance, is possessed by the Treasury Department, whose orders and decisions are upheld and enforced until decided by the courts to be unlawful or erroneous. In the case of the railroads they would have opportunity to present evidence on their side and to facilitate action of the courts instead of putting obstacles in their way, as heretofore.

*Milwaukee ( Wis.) Evening Wisconsin.*—Here is another demonstration of the necessity of clothing the Interstate Commerce Commission with power to enforce its decisions. It is intolerable that boards of railway directors should be permitted to arbitrarily build up one locality and tear down another, to line their own pockets at the expense of the public which gave them their charters and patronage.

There is at the present time, and there will be hereafter, greater necessity than in the past for the existence of a body like the Interstate Commerce Commission, clothed with full powers to protect the people from injustice at the hands of the common carriers. This necessity is the outcome of the consolidation of railway interests. Consolidation and merging and community of interest arrangements, which tend to unite all the railway interests of the country under a common management, tend also to abolish competition. The decisions of the Interstate Commerce Commission should be made immediately operative and continue in force until suspended or overruled by the courts.

Congress should cloth the Commission with the powers proposed to be conferred upon it by the Nelson bill.

*Milwaukee ( Wis.) Sentinel.*—One of the results of the recent investigations of the Interstate Commerce Commission has been to develop a respect for the interstate commerce law that has lain dormant for several years in the minds of traffic men; and local representatives of Eastern railroads have recently been cautioned by the traffic officials that the law with its severe penalties for violation is still on the statute books and that infractions are very likely to be followed by punishment.

*Milwaukee Free Press.*—The plan of having an impartial administrative board like the Interstate Commerce Commission, composed of experts in matters of transportation and vested with sufficient power to enforce its findings, seems so reasonable as to lead to the hope that the railway companies will not succeed in defeating the bill to be introduced covering the case.

*Atlanta (Ga.) Journal.*—There is a bill now before Congress to do something that will give the Commission the power to do something. Everybody who can vote for Federal legislation in Georgia's name is for this bill, and we hope it will be passed. Unless Congress shall amend the interstate-commerce act and give the Commission power to enforce it, it had better be repealed.

*Birmingham (Ala.) News.*—The Interstate Commerce Commission can not enforce its orders with sufficient celerity or completeness to do any good, and, for that reason, it is largely an ornamental body. Congress should by all means so enlarge its scope as to give it such authority that the edicts which it has been designated to issue can be carried to effect.

Really Congress has no very intricate proposition before it in the double plea of the Commission. Give the Commission, to start with, such scope of authority (and no more) as is proper, then clothe it with power to enforce the orders made within its lawful territory and, finally, open the books of the corporations to the public at such periods and within such limitations, just alike to both sides, and the problem has been solved.

*Willimantic (Conn.) Chronicle.*—The amendment but gives the Commission those powers which the framers of the original interstate-commerce law meant to confer and thought they were conferring, and which the railroad companies accepted as within the jurisdiction of the Commission, until about three years ago, when the Supreme Court made a decision which had the effect of rendering the Commission impotent.

*Wichita (Kans.) Eagle.*—The only way to satisfy the people is an amendment to the law insuring prompt relief from discriminations. This can only be done by strict control through the Interstate Commerce Commission, and our Senators and Congressmen can do no less for their constituents than to support the Nelson-Corliss bill.

*Jackson (Miss.) Clarion-Ledger.*—No question to be considered at this session of Congress is of so much importance to the commercial welfare of the country and to the people generally as that embodied in the bill proposing to strengthen the interstate commerce act so as to make the rulings of the Commission binding and effective until reversed by the courts.

*Newark (N. J.) News.*—Failure in practical power to enforce its own decisions has been the crying defect in the operations of the Interstate Commerce Commission. What good is there in jurisdiction if mandatory power exists only in name? There is a strenuous demand for some effective revision of methods of procedure over the whole country, and the strong pleas of commercial bodies have been affirmed by resolutions of a number of State legislatures. Under the present conditions it is generally known that the decisions of the Interstate Commerce Commission are little more than a dead letter when railroads care to ignore them, which is more often than not.

*Grand Forks (N. Dak.) Herald.*—The present session of Congress should be marked by some action that will increase the powers of the Commission to something like what they ought to be. Should Congress expire without something done we may look for the greatest railroad war in history. Some of the railroad men profess to desire the extension of the powers of the Commission, but the fact is on record that the Commission, even with the powers that it does possess, was only created after twenty years of the most active opposition that the railroads could give it.

*Sioux Falls (S. Dak.) Argus-Leader.*—Ever since the passage of the Cullom law, in 1887, efforts have been made to so amend the law as to make it effective. These all have failed. The railroad companies have been able to control a sufficient number of Congressmen to block any effort to make the law effective. It would now appear, however, that either the big lines have concluded to obey the law themselves and help make the weaker ones do it, or that certain of the Congressional strength has turned against them.

*Sioux Falls (S. Dak.) Argus-Leader.*—The railroads have admitted that they pay rebates to favored shippers; that some men get much lower rates than others, and are thus assisted in driving the others out of business. This being so, any right-minded person will join in the demand that the laws be so reconstructed that this sort of thing will be made impossible, or, when it is committed, the offenders will be brought summarily to justice.

*Memphis (Tenn.) Appeal.*—It is clear that the work of the Commission as now constituted is rather futile. It has not been able to prevent discriminations. It has not been able to have its recommendations respected or its decrees enforced. Now, the objection that the gentlemen composing the Commission are not qualified to fix rates is hardly valid, in view of the fact that a circuit judge might exercise that power.

The only question involved is the most practical way of correcting rate discriminations, which are violations of the law. If this is too delicate a matter for the five eminent lawyers to decide, it is too delicate a matter for a circuit judge, or indeed for any legal tribunal, to decide. We shall either have to conclude that there is no practical remedy for rate cutting and unjust rates, and that the Interstate Commerce Commission ought to be abolished, or the power lodged in that tribunal to enforce its judgments as any other court can do.

*Salt Lake (Utah) Herald.*—If Congress, in spite of the railroad lobby, which may be depended upon to make a hard fight against it, should pass the Corliss bill, a long step would be taken in the direction of proper Government supervision of the railroads of the country. The present powers of the Commission consist mainly of the right to use moral suasion—that is, if it finds that a railroad company is giving heavy rebates to large shippers, as was freely admitted at the Chicago hearing, all it can do is to beg the magnates to be good. Of course, the Commissioners are laughed at. Railroad companies, as a rule, don't treat all men alike, unless they are made to do so. The purpose of the Corliss law is to put all on an equal footing, and it should be passed.

WASHINGTON, D. C., *May 27, 1902.*

Hon. S B. ELKINS,
     *Chairman Committee on Interstate Commerce,*
                    *United States Senate,*
                         *Washington, D. C.*

SIR: The following organizations have indorsed Senate bill 3575, to amend the act to regulate commerce, and have adopted resolutions requesting the Senators and Representatives from their respective States and districts to give the same their active support, in addition to the organizations mentioned in the testimony given by me before your honorable committee on the 9th day of April last, making an aggregate of 94 organizations located in 29 different States.

### NATIONAL AND STATE ORGANIZATIONS.

Indiana Grain Dealers' Association; Massachusetts State Board of Trade; National Grange, Patrons of Husbandry; National Association of Railway Commissioners; Southern Hardware Jobbers' Association; Utah Wool Growers' Association; Western South Dakota Stock Growers' Association.

Colorado.—Lincoln County Cattle Growers' Association.
Connecticut.—Waterbury Business Men's Association.
New Haven Chamber of Commerce.
Georgia.—Atlanta Chamber of Commerce.
Illinois.—Chicago Merchants' Association.
Indiana.—Indianapolis Furniture Manufacturers' Association.
Kansas.—Kansas City Board of Trade.
Missouri.—St. Louis Millers' Club.
New Jersey.—Jersey City Board of Trade.
Ohio.—Columbus Board of Trade.
Cleveland Retail Coal Dealers' Association.
Pennsylvania.—Philadelphia Commercial Exchange.
Wisconsin.—Muscoda Dairy Board.

Very respectfully,     EDWARD P. BACON,
*Chairman Executive Committee,*
*Interstate Commerce Law Convention.*

THURSDAY, *April 17, 1902.*

At the sitting of the committee on Thursday, April 17, 1902, the following-named gentlemen appeared: William R. Corwine, representing the Merchants' Association of New York; John V. Barnes, president of the New York Produce Exchange; Samuel T. Hubbard, president of the New York Cotton Exchange; Robert W. Higbie, representing the National Lumber Dealers' Association and the New York Lumber Dealers' Association; John D. Kernan, representing the New York Produce Exchange; David Bingham, chairman of the committee on freight rates and differentials, of the New York Produce Exchange; Charles N. Chadwick, representing the Manufacturers' Association of New York; Mr. Clapp, representing the New York Produce Exchange; T. W. Tomlinson, representing the National Live Stock Exchange and the Chicago Live Stock Exchange; R. S. Lyon, representing the Chicago Board of Trade; Frank Barry, of Milwaukee; N. B. Kelly, secretary of the Trades League of Philadelphia; George F. Mead, representing the Boston Chamber of Commerce and the New England Manufacturers' Association; and J. B. Daish, representing the National Hay Association.

## STATEMENT OF WILLIAM R. CORWINE.

The CHAIRMAN. Please state your residence, business, and whom you represent.

Mr. CORWINE. I represent the Merchants' Association of New York, under instructions from its officers to attend these hearings here. I am also a member of the executive committee appointed by the Interstate Commerce Law Convention, held at St. Louis in November, 1900, which committee prepared the bill now before Congress known as the Nelson–Corliss bill. The Merchants' Association of New York, which has instructed me to appear here, is a commercial body composed of merchants, manufacturers, bankers, brokers, and business men generally, of nearly all lines of business, aggregating about a thousand members in New York City, and with a large nonresident membership throughout the United States footing up to something like thirty-five thousand merchants, each having what is known as a credit rating. Let me say here that the affairs of the association are controlled by the usual executive officers—a president, first and second vice-presidents, secretary, treasurer, and board of directors. The nonresident members have no voice in the management of the association, but are kept in touch with its work. The subject of this bill came before the board of directors at its meeting in December, and the board adopted a series of resolutions indorsing the Nelson–Corliss bill, a certified copy of which I ask leave to file.

### RESOLUTIONS, ETC., INTERSTATE COMMERCE ACT.

Whereas a bill known as the Cullom bill was pending in the last Congress, but failed of passage, the purpose of which was to restore to the Interstate Commerce Commission certain of its powers which, by the decisions of various courts, had been taken from it; and

Whereas a large number of commercial bodies throughout the United States, over 40 in number, among which was the Merchants' Association, advocated the passage of this bill, the position of the Merchants' Association having been set forth in an argument prepared by William R. Corwine, of the office staff, in which, while the passage of the bill was advocated, certain suggestions were made which, in the opinion of the officers of the association, ought to be incorporated therein in the shape of amendments; and

Whereas the commercial bodies which were in favor of the measure held a convention at St. Louis in November, 1900, at which an executive committee was appointed to take charge of the matters connected with the bill; and

Whereas Mr. William R. Corwine was recently elected by the members of the committee to fill a vacancy thereon, and, with the consent of the officers of the association, accepted that election and is now a member of that executive committee, the full title of the committee being the "Executive Committee of the Interstate Commerce Law Convention, held at St. Louis, Mo., November 20, 1900," of which Mr. E. P. Bacon, of Milwaukee, Wis., is chairman, on which are a number of prominent gentlemen throughout the country representing large commercial and shipping interests; and

Whereas the bill proposed to be introduced in the current session of Congress differs in certain respects from the Cullom bill of last session, and some of the ideas advanced by the Merchants' Association, through its representative, referred to above, have been incorporated in the new bill; and

Whereas the bill as now drawn has been approved by the members of the executive committee above mentioned, and has received, as we understand it, the approval of the Interstate Commerce Commissioners, and we are informed is accepted by many railway officials as being reasonably fair in its provisions; and

Whereas President Roosevelt, in his annual message to the current Congress, has referred to this subject, and in connection therewith has said:

"The act should be amended. The railway is a public servant. Its rates should be just to and open to all shippers alike. The Government should see to it that within its jurisdiction this is so, and should provide a speedy, inexpensive, and effective remedy to that end. At the same time it must not be forgotten that our railways are the arteries through which the commercial lifeblood of this nation flows. Nothing could be more foolish than the enactment of legislation which would unnecessarily interfere with the development and operation of these commercial agencies. The subject is one of great importance and calls for the earnest attention of the Congress;" and

Whereas the principal provisions of the bill are:

First. That the Commission be invested with power when it is found, after a full hearing of all parties in interest, that an existing rate or differential in rates is unreasonable or unjust, to prescribe the necessary change to be made therein to bring them into conformity with the provisions of the interstate commerce act. The Commission is to have the same power in relation to the classification of freight articles.

Second. That the rulings of the Commission, issued in pursuance of such hearing, shall be operative twenty days from the service thereof upon the defendant carriers, subject to appeal on the part of the carriers to a circuit court of the United States, these courts being empowered to suspend the operation of the order of the commission, pending the hearing of the appeal, and it is made the duty of the court to vacate such order if found to be illegal or unreasonable upon the facts of the case. Either party may appeal to the Supreme Court.

Third. That imprisonment penalties be done away with, and proper fines substituted therefor, in case of violation of the act. It is believed that this will facilitate .the obtaining of evidence necessary for the conviction of guilty parties, which the severe penalties of the present act strongly operate against. The act provides penalties for shippers as well as for carriers: Now, therefore, be it

*Resolved*, That in view of the position already taken by the Merchants' Association, based upon the foregoing statement, the directors of the Merchants' Association hereby approve the general terms of the bill referred to, and ask for its careful consideration and passage by Congress, and indorse the appointment of Mr. William R. Corwine upon the "executive committee of the Interstate Commerce Law Convention, held at St. Louis, Mo., November 20, 1900," and request him and the officers of the association to cooperate as fully as possible in obtaining the passage of this bill or of such amended bill as may finally be agreed upon, if amendments be found necessary, as will insure the end desired.

I hereby certify that the foregoing is a correct copy of the preambles and resolution unanimously adopted by the board of directors of the Merchants' Association of New York at a meeting on the 5th day of December, 1901.

Dated New York, April 14, 1902.

[SEAL.]

S. C. MEAD,
*Assistant Secretary, the Merchants' Association of New York.*

These resolutions, in substance, set forth that in the opinion of the directors something ought to be done by which the decisions or rulings made by the Interstate Commerce Commission may be made effective; that in the judgment of the directors the provisions of the bill which had been submitted to them—they having considerable knowledge of the general subject—would produce the results desired by shippers without undue hardships to the carriers.

The question seemed to us to resolve itself into the very simple one of whether or not the Interstate Commerce Commission should be given powers which it seems to the shippers they ought to have, or whether or not the Commission should be abolished. As the Interstate Commerce Commission stands now, it seems to be nothing more than a statistical bureau, composed of very estimable gentlemen, in whose integrity and ability the public have confidence, but whose powers seem to be limited to the issuing of statistical information and propaganda at various times, which people read, but to which they pay no attention. It seems to us that, owing to the changed conditions existing throughout the country, to the community of interest chiefly, which is bringing the great railway systems into closer harmony, it would be wise, in fact, is necessary, that something be done which, on the one hand, will not be too harsh against the railroad interests, which we recognize as being a very important interest in the country, but which, on the other hand, will conserve the interests of the shippers.

How far it is wise to go is of course a question which Congress must determine. I am not here for the purpose of voicing any specific complaints of shippers just at this particular moment. We have had a number of such complaints, and, in fact, our position in this matter grew almost entirely out of the very numerous complaints which were filed with us and which we were asked to consider at the time the railroads, in the latter part of 1899 and in the early part of 1900, arbitrarily and without any hearings or conferences with shippers, attempted to obtain a larger revenue, not by an increase of rates—to which I think as a rule shippers would not have objected, owing to the prosperous condition of the country—but to a very violent change in the method of classification.

It is not necessary to go into the details of that subject. These details were fully laid before you at the last session, when the Cullom bill was being considered. Mr. J. M. Langley, representing our association, testified before this committee, and went into a very thorough analysis of the changes made by the different railways of the country in regard to classifications and the percentages of increase in items, showing the effect of those percentages upon the rates and the average increase of rates which resulted from that change of classification. We felt then and we feel now that the method pursued was not a fair or an equitable method; that it did result and has continued to result in a very serious detriment to many lines of industry, more particularly on account of the arbitrary change which the railroads made in what may be called the widening of the difference between the carload lot and less than carload lot.

I am not an expert on the subject of rates, Mr. Chairman, but there are a few general principles which we all understand fully. In the particular changes I have in mind, where carload lots were classed, say, fifth class, and less than carload lots were classified in the fourth class, the railroads in the new classification of 1900 kept the carload in the class in which it had stood for many years, and advanced the less than carload lots to a higher classification, for instance, the third class, thereby making the difference of two classes between the carload and less than carload lots. This served to advance the rate charged for less than carload lots. We claim, without going into the details as to the effect of this change upon the rate, that it has necessarily worked injuriously to the small shipper through lessening the area of his distribution. The tendency of the times is toward concentration in commercial industries and transportation. There is a very serious endeavor on the part of thinking men of the country to ascertain how far this concentration is being brought about by natural conditions, and how far it is artificial. Monopolies are not desired by the people, but how far legislative bodies ought to go in an endeavor so to regulate the results of conditions as to minimize the evils complained of is a serious problem.

These changed conditions, whether due to natural causes—to the growth of business resulting in the creation of great industries throughout the world—tend to drive the small man out of business or to force him to combine with the larger organizations. We ought not unduly or arbitrarily make it harder for him to live. The narrowing of the area of distribution, whether it be of New York, of Chicago, of St. Louis, of Minneapolis, of Atlanta, or of New Orleans, or any other distributing center, is certain to contract the business of the small man. By widening the difference between carload and the less than carload lots, you make it harder for him to compete with the men who get the carload rate. That is so plain that it seems to me to need no explanation.

As I said, I think, at the outset, there is no disposition on the part of our people to harass the railways. The consideration, originally by the Merchants' Association, of the question under discussion was due to the fact that there were in effect certain discriminations as between localities, which operated unfavorably as against other localities; and as those discriminations operated against us locally, self-preservation forced the organization of this institution, for the purpose of seeing if it were not possible to place New York upon a parity with other localities by doing away with the discriminating rates in freight and passenger business which were being practiced.

I am frank to say, and am very glad to be able to say, that in all the relations which we have had with the railways the latter have been fair with us. They have lived up always, not only to the letter, but to the spirit of the agreements which they have made with us. And I am glad and proud to say that on our part we have done the same. Mr. Blanchard, whom you knew, and who is now dead, put himself on record in writing as to the fairness of the dealings on the part of the Merchants' Association of New York with the great railway interests of the country.

We feel, as I have said, that there ought to be some power somewhere, either in the present Interstate Commerce Commission or in some other body to be created, if need be, by or through which these two great interests of shipper and carrier, which are very largely the bone and sinew of the country, may be conserved fairly and equitably to all. So far as we have been able to study the subject, it seems to us that the provisions of the so-called Nelson-Corliss bill meet the situation as the conditions are to-day.

Several criticisms have been made by those opposed to that bill. One that I have in mind, that has been urged quite strenuously, is that its operations will be unfair to the railroads, because under it the decisions of the Interstate Commerce Commission would go into effect practically immediately, and remain in effect for two years, even though the railroads had the right of appeal to the circuit court, but that, notwithstanding the appeal, the decision of the Commission would remain in force and effect while the appeal was pending. In other words, it is claimed by the legal fraternity, who are investigating the bill from the railroad point of view, that this is a reversal of general legal proceedings, where an appeal from the decision of a lower court stays the effect of the decision which has been rendered until such time as the appeal may have been determined. It seems to me that those who are making that criticism are looking from the wrong point of view. I do not want to be unfair or unjust or appear to be put in the position of asking for that which is harsh or arbitrary. But I do not view the Interstate Commerce Commission quite in that light.

It seems to me—if I may use a phrase which does not, perhaps, exactly fit the situation, but which, in general, describes it—that we may look upon that Commission more as a legislative than as a judicial body. It is not a body appointed, as are the judges of the Supreme Court of the United States and its subordinate branches, with general powers to interpret the laws that are upon the statute books, but is a body of men, five in number, appointed to determine certain minor—or great, if you like—questions of fact raised by the specific act under which that body has been created, and their jurisdiction goes no farther.

been coming to me as a member of this committee, and I presume they have to you, Mr. Chairman.

The CHAIRMAN. Yes.

Senator TILLMAN. There have also come very urgent appeals from apparently a great many sources, but appeals so similar in character that it has occurred to me that they must have originated from one source, in regard to this 20 per cent reduction of sugar bounty, and I have been skeptical as to the necessity of that reduction and as to the responsibility of the parties who have signed those petitions. I should like to have as good evidence as possible to prove that there is a real demand from the citizens of this country for this proposed legislation. I believe there is, and I sympathize with it, and therefore I should like to be able to show that the merchants, manufacturers, and other parties interested would be glad to have Congress give them relief from present unbearable conditions, or abolish the commission and let us quit fooling with it.

Mr. CORWINE. All right; I will arrange that for you. Will you let me put into the record the names of the officers?

Senator TILLMAN. It is not the names of the officers at all that we want.

Mr. CORWINE. The membership has changed very much.

Senator TILLMAN. Why should there be any desire for secrecy on the part of this association in regard to its membership? Are they afraid that the railroads will discriminate against them in business?

Mr. CORWINE. No; they are not afraid of anything on God's footstool.

Senator TILLMAN. Then we ought to have their names.

Mr. CORWINE. They have simply considered it as good business judgment not to publish such a list. That resolution was adopted in 1897, when certain members tried to do certain things not necessary to be disclosed here for the purpose of advertising themselves through their connection with the institution, and it was then determined that it would be best and wisest to keep its membership from being published, and also for the reason that it would keep the members from being subjected to bothersome solicitation.

Senator TILLMAN. Do your members meet in convention, or how do they formulate and prosecute their work? How did they send you here, for instance?

Mr. CORWINE. I was about to explain that when you interrupted me. I was about to offer to furnish the names of the officers when you said you did not care for them.

Senator TILLMAN. I would like to have the whole thing.

Mr. CORWINE. I will say that the Merchants' Association holds its election annually in January of each year, at which the directors are elected. There are fifteen of them, and to them are given the power and authority, under the constitution and by-laws, to manage the affairs of the association. They have the power to do anything they like within the scope of their authority. If any person not a member of the board has at any time a grievance, and thinks the board has managed unfairly or does not fairly represent the sense of the association, that person has the power, under our rules, to have a special meeting of the members called and to protest, and the members have the power to oust the directors at the next election if they conclude that the affairs of the association have not been properly managed.

Senator TILLMAN. You mean the association has that power?

Mr. CORWINE. The members can do it.

Senator TILLMAN. That is a strange power to be lodged in the hands of one member.

Mr. CORWINE. I will here give the names of the officers and directors who are still holding office and will continue in office until the next annual meeting in January, 1903, so far as I am able to refresh my memory from an old letter head which I happen to have with me:

Mr. D. Leroy Dresser, the president, is the head of the dry goods commission house of Dresser & Co., which he started himself when comparatively a young man.

Mr. John C. Juhring, first vice-president, is a member of the wholesale grocery house of Francis H. Leggett & Co., in which he has grown up from boyhood.

Mr. John C. Eames, is second vice-president now. He is the second vice-president and general manager of the H. B. Claflin Company, which concern I take it you all know as being a very large dry goods house in New York.

Mr. Charles H. Webb, treasurer, is a member of the firm of J. H. Dunham & Co., a large dry goods jobbing house in New York, in which he has grown up from boyhood.

Mr. William F. King, who was the founder of the Merchants' Association and its first president, is a member of the dry goods house of Calhoun, Robins & Co., in which he has grown up from boyhood.

Mr. George F. Crane, of Baring, Magoun & Co., bankers; he worked his way up into the firm from a boy.

Mr. Adolph Openhym is a member of the firm of William Openhym & Sons, a dry goods commission house dealing principally in silks and located in New York. That firm was founded by his father, I think.

Mr. George L. Duval is the resident member in the United States of the firm of Beeche, Duval & Co. And, by the way, he worked his way up from boyhood.

Mr. Gustav H. Schwab, the general manager of the North German Lloyd Steamship Company, in New York, with which he has been connected ever since he was a boy.

Mr. Frank Squier, a member of the firm of Perkins, Goodwin & Co., wholesale paper manufacturing and jobbing house. I do not know his history, whether he has been there all his life or not.

In addition, there were elected at the last meeting Mr. William Edmond Curtis, who was formerly Assistant Secretary of the Treasury under Secretary Carlisle during Mr. Cleveland's last Administration; Mr. Herbert L. Satterlee, lawyer, at 120 Broadway, and Mr. Henry R. Towne, the president of the Yale and Towne Manufacturing Company, of New York, with headquarters in New York City. Those three gentlemen were elected last January to take the places made vacant by the retirement of Mr. Alvah Trowbridge, who had been president of the Ninth National Bank; Mr. Corcellus H. Hackett, who is a manufacturer, and of Mr. John H. Starin, of the Starin Transportation Company, of New York. As I say, those three gentlemen's terms expired, and as they did not want to be reelected, the three gentlemen I have named were elected to take their places.

The directors subsequently elected officers, as follows: Mr. D. Leroy

Dresser, president; Mr. John C. Juhring, first vice-president; Mr. John C. Eames, second vice-president; Mr. Charles H. Webb, treasurer, and Mr. W. A. Marble, secretary. Mr. Marble went into the board to fill a vacancy. He is the vice-president of the R. & G. Corset Manufacturing Company. None of the officers or directors draw any salary or compensation of any kind.

I will also say that Mr. James B. Dill had served without charge as counsel for the association from the time of its organization; but, feeling that he could not attend to the work any longer, he resigned in January, when the Hon. John G. Carlisle, formerly Secretary of the Treasury, was unanimously elected by the board as counsel of the association.

That, Mr. Senator, represents the working force of the Merchants' Association.

Senator TILLMAN. I take it that the rank and file are very eminently respectable merchants and manufacturers. Why not send their names also?

Mr. CORWINE. I have no objection to sending you the list, if you really want it. We keep it on a card index, and it will only take a few days to prepare it.

Senator TILLMAN. I hope you do not understand that I have even suspected for a moment that yours is not a bona fide association of very great proportions, and of wealth and respectability. I simply want to have the proof, because when we get this bill before the Senate for consideration, if we ever do, we are going to be met with the charge that this bill emanated from the Interstate Commerce Commission or from those who have been working in its interest. Something like that has been the cry that has been heard ever since this subject was first agitated.

Mr. CORWINE. I think I can get the list for the committee, although in saying that I may be assuming more than I shall have the power to perform.

The CHAIRMAN. All right.

Mr. CORWINE. I have nothing more to say to the committee, I believe.

Senator FOSTER. Before you give way to the next gentleman, I should like to put a question. I understand that you consider that the Commission has been practically shorn, by the decisions of the Supreme Court, of all authority and power; that now it is but little more than a bureau of statistical information, rather than a body armed with the power of control over the subject matter, for which it was originally created. In your opinion, should that Commission be continued unless there be legislation giving it greater power and greater authority for carrying out what we generally believe to have been the objects and purposes of that Commission.

Mr. CORWINE. I do not quite catch your idea, Senator. If I may, I will answer it in this way: I, for one, as a humble layman, believe that when the interstate-commerce law was enacted in 1887—that is the year, if my memory serves me rightly—it was intended that there should be somebody with such powers as are now sought to be embodied in the bill before the committee. That is the impression that I, as a layman, have always had. Not being a lawyer I may not be able to determine the nice distinctions of language, as a court can do. But by the decisions rendered by the Supreme Court, in some cases from New York and elsewhere, it was determined, as I understand it, not that they were shorn of any power, but that they never had had the power. This decision was rendered as a result of the judicial interpretation of the statute which came before the court in these various cases that were carried to the Supreme Court. Therefore, the Commission seems to me to be nothing more nor less than a statistical bureau, and it does not seem to me to be necessary to keep a body of that kind in existence, eminently respectable though its membership be, unless it should be given more power than it now has.

Senator FOSTER. I used the word "shorn." Probably you are right in saying that the Supreme Court decided that it never had the power. But once the Supreme Court has denied the existence of this power, is it useless to continue this Commission?

Mr. CORWINE. As a Commission, I should say no. It seems to me that it would be beneficial for the Government always to maintain some kind of a bureau, perhaps not so expensive and elaborate a bureau as this, in which there can be collated the railroad statistics of the country, which are very useful and serve a most excellent purpose, both for action by Congress and for discussion by the public as to the conditions existing among railroads. They are gotten up in better shape there than anywhere else in the country. They are far better than Poor's Manual, which it would require a railroad expert to understand. They are better than the data furnished by the financial papers of New York and Chicago. But, as a Commission, that body of five members it seems to me ought to go out of existence if they can not serve more useful purposes; and it seems to me, also, that they do not serve those purposes now.

Senator FOSTER. You believe in giving them additional power?

Mr. CORWINE. I do.

Senator FOSTER. That is, your association believes that?

Mr. CORWINE. They do.

Senator FOSTER. That the good of the country will be better subserved by conferring this additional power upon the Interstate Commerce Commission?

Mr. CORWINE. I think it will. I think it will work out great benefit all round.

Senator FOSTER. Have you read the Elkins bill?

Mr. CORWINE. I saw the Elkins bill as it was published in the press at the time it came out. I have understood that there have been some changes made in it or that some are about to be made. I have not seen it in its present printed form, and I should very much like to have a copy of it while I am here. I had intended to get one.

The CHAIRMAN. I hand you a copy of the bill (S. 3521).

Mr. CORWINE. I only saw the substance of it as published in the papers.

The CHAIRMAN. We are very much obliged to you, Mr. Corwine.

Mr. CORWINE. I am very much obliged to you for your courtesy, also.

## STATEMENT OF ROBERT W. HIGBIE.

The CHAIRMAN. Please give your business address and whom you represent.

Mr. HIGBIE. I represent the committee on legislation of the National Wholesale Lumber Dealers' Association. My business address is 45 Broadway, New York. I am also a manufacturer of lumber in the State of West Virginia.

This association which I have the honor to represent before this committee is composed of several hundred of the representative lumber dealers of the United States, with a membership extending from Maine to Minnesota on the north, to the south and southwest, Alabama and Arkansas, and thence across to the Atlantic seaboard.

This association has indorsed the principles of the Nelson bill and also certain features of the Elkins bill for two or three successive years in their annual conventions. The board of trustees of our association appointed a small committee to represent the association before Congress in the advocacy, in a general way, of these two bills, more particularly the Nelson bill.

We feel, Senators, that the necessity exists for some additional legislation by way of amendment to the interstate-commerce act, and the necessity for that is so apparent that it is not necessary for me to take up your valuable time in making any extended argument along that line, but rather to suggest our thought as to how the act should be amended and in what respect the powers of the Commission should be increased.

There are four things, particularly, in which our association is very much interested.

In the first place, we think the railroads should be placed in the position where they should treat all shippers alike; that they should charge like pay for like service under similar conditions.

In the second place, we feel that when an important case has been brought before the Interstate Commerce Commission and they have carefully investigated it and decided as to what is a proper rate or proper adjustment between railroads and shippers, of course conserving the interests of both, that they should have the power to say what is right, and, having said it, that they should have the power to enforce it. This covers the second and third of the additional powers for which we are asking.

In the next and last place, we think that these orders, when once entered, should be made effective within a reasonable time.

The act as originally passed, and as interpreted by the Commission itself, practically covered most of these points which we are now asking. I am not undertaking to say whether the original law actually conferred these powers or not. I simply say that the interpretation of that act by the Commission itself was that they had, and as a matter of fact they used, most of these powers for several years.

The courts have, however, in various decisions in cases coming before them under this act, held that the Commission did not possess certain of the powers which they had been exercising and which they thought the act conferred upon them, and as a result of these decisions the Commission has been compelled to desist from the exercise of those powers.

For instance, one, which is the only one I shall speak of, is that part of the act which is known as the long and short haul clause. As I understand it, this clause was put in the act for the benefit of small individual shippers, whose shipments were made at noncompetitive points. The courts have held, however, that the conditions under which shipments were made by the railroads were such that the railroads in certain cases were justified in charging a less rate for a long haul than for a short haul. The result is that the individual shipper from what we term way stations is left high and dry and is compelled to pay whatever the railroad sees fit to charge him from that particular point, because he has no other way of getting his property to the markets.

I know of no case which better illustrates the necessity of some change in that particular than a case which the association I am representing here at one time brought before the Interstate Commerce Commission. I will very briefly state the case and the developments arising therefrom. The National Wholesale Lumber Dealers' Association lodged a complaint against the Pennsylvania Railroad, the Baltimore and Ohio, and the Norfolk and Western railroads. The basis of that complaint was that shippers on the Norfolk and Western were discriminated against in comparison with shippers from the Chesapeake and Ohio and from the Baltimore and Ohio, and that the rates were very much higher to them than were given to their competitors on other lines, and that those rates were unreasonable, unjust, and discriminative. The testimony in that case brought out these facts: That the three railroads named were under the practical control of the Pennsylvania Railroad and to all intents and purposes were one system. It also brought out this fact: That the three roads had connections with and entrances into the city of Cincinnati; that the rate on lumber from Cincinnati to New York was $21\frac{1}{2}$ cents per hundred pounds; that all of these roads were parallel and shipments were made from all of them to the New York market; and this additional fact, that two of these roads gave to points east of Cincinnati the benefit of the Cincinnati rate. But the Norfolk and Western in their wisdom saw fit to refuse to give the $21\frac{1}{2}$-cent rate to its shippers east of Cincinnati, but charged such shippers an average rate of $27\frac{1}{2}$ cents, and the result was that such shippers on the Norfolk and Western were compelled to pay from 30 to 35 per cent more than the shippers on the two parallel roads.

The Commission, in writing the decision in that case, closed by saying that inasmuch as these three roads were under the control of the Pennsylvania system, they saw no reason why all the shippers on the three lines should not be treated alike. The order that finally came in reference to this matter from the Commission, instead of reducing the rate, as the opinion would seem to have indicated we had reason to expect, only reduced the rate 10 per cent, still leaving us 15 or 20 per cent above the rates for shippers from the other two roads. I infer and assume, although I have no authority for the assumption, that the reason why the larger reduction was not ordered was because the railroads might not have been willing to obey it. But they did obey the order of the Commission. If, however, the Commission had the power which we are asking now to be conferred upon them and had followed logically the line of the opinion in that case, the shippers on those three roads would have been placed upon an equal footing. As it is, the shippers on the Norfolk and Western, of whom I happen to be one, are still at the disadvantage of at least $1 per thousand.

The CHAIRMAN. On the rate to New York?

Mr. HIGBIE. Yes. I have had prepared a table which I will file with the committee, showing the distances, the rate in cents per hundred, per ton per mile, on lumber from some 25 or 30 different points to New York City.

These points cover twelve to fifteen States and fairly represent the shippers of lumber from inland points to New York City. In selecting these various points I wanted to be fair, and so I showed no preference at all and made no selection except the natural one. I had no foreknowledge of what the result would show when tabulated in this form. The result is as follows: The point enjoying the most favorable rate to New York City is Menominee, Mich., which has a rate of 0.423 cent per ton per mile, this distance being 1,182 miles and the rate being 25 cents per hundred. The point which is compelled to pay the highest rate is Elizabethton, Tenn. The distance from that point to New York is barely more than half the distance of Menominee from New York, being but 628 miles. The rate per hundred is 28 cents, or three cents per hundred more for practically half the distance, while this rate per ton per mile is 0.892 cent, or more than double. The intermediate points on the table vary.

The CHAIRMAN. Does your table show what lines those points are on?

Mr. HIGBIE. It does not.

The CHAIRMAN. That would add a valuable feature if you would show the lines.

Mr. HIGBIE. I will be glad to make that addition.

The CHAIRMAN. If it will not interrupt you, and with the consent of the committee, I suggest that you put in an additional column to your table showing. for instance, that lumber from Menominee to New York passes over the following lines, and from Elizabethton to New York over the following lines.

Mr. HIGBIE. I shall be very glad to do that, Senator.

The CHAIRMAN. I think that would look well and would be valuable information.

Following is the amended statement here referred to:

*Statement showing the distance, rate in cents per 100 pounds, and rate per ton per mile on lumber from points shown below to New York, N. Y.*

| Dis-tance. | From— | Rate per 100 pounds. | Rate per ton per mile. |
|---|---|---|---|
| | | *Cents.* | *Cents.* |
| 1,182 | Menominee, Mich | 25 | 0. 423 |
| 1,388 | Duluth, Minn | 33 | .476 |
| 1,348 | Ashland, Wis | 33 | .489 |
| 1,209 | Memphis, Tenn | 31 | .512 |
| 818 | Indianapolis, Ind | 22 | .538 |
| 915 | Chicago, Ill | 25 | .546 |
| 1,097 | Appleton, Wis | 31 | .565 |
| 757 | Cincinnati, Ohio | 21¼ | .568 |
| 980 | Petoskey, Mich | 28 | .571 |
| 865 | Louisville, Ky | 25 | .578 |
| 715 | Bay City, Mich | 21 | .588 |
| 709 | Dayton, Ohio | 21 | .592 |
| 702 | Saginaw, Mich | 21 | .589 |
| 1,273 | Helena, Ark | 40 | .628 |
| 685 | Ironton, Ohio | 21¼ | .628 |
| 683 | Ashland, Ky | 21¼ | .629 |
| 411 | Buffalo, N. Y | 13 | .632 |
| 671 | Kenova, W. Va | 21¼ | .641 |

*Statement showing the distance, rate in cents per 100 pounds, and rate per ton per mile on lumber from points shown below to New York, N. N.*—Continued.

| Distance. | From— | Rate per 100 pounds. | Rate per ton per per mile. |
|---|---|---|---|
| | | *Cents.* | *Cents.* |
| 667 | Huntington, W. Va | 21½ | 0.645 |
| 479 | Grafton, W. Va | 16 | .668 |
| 830 | Murphey, N. C | 28 | .675 |
| 899 | Chattanooga, Tenn | 31 | .689 |
| 615 | Charleston, W. Va | 21½ | .699 |
| 717 | Norton, W. Va | 25½ | .711 |
| 604 | Camden-on-Gauley, W. Va | 21½ | .712 |
| 584 | Wilmington, N. C | 21 | .719 |
| 788 | Knoxville, Tenn | 28½ | .723 |
| 316 | Oswego, N. Y | 11½ | .728 |
| 1,050 | Nashville, Tenn | 38½ | .733 |
| 680 | Panther, W. Va | 25½ | .750 |
| 705 | Asheville, N. C | 27 | .766 |
| 392 | Elizabeth City, N. C | 15½ | .791 |
| 492 | Elkins, W. Va | 21½ | .874 |
| 628 | Elizabethton, Tenn | 28 | .892 |

### MENOMINEE, MICH.

C., M. & St. P. Ry., or C. & N. W. Ry. to Chicago, and via any line east of Chicago

### DULUTH, MINN.

C. & N. W. Ry., or Wisconsin Central Ry., to Chicago; via any line east of Chicago, Ill.

D., S. S. & A. Ry. Canadian Pacific Ry. N. Y. C. & H. R. R. R.

### ASHLAND, WIS.

C. & N. W. Ry., or Wisconsin Central Ry., to Chicago, and any line east of Chicago, Ill.

### MEMPHIS, TENN.

Southern Ry.
Penna. R. R.

L. & N. R. R.
C. & O. Ry.
Penna. R. R.

L. & N. R. R.
B. & O. R. R.
P. & R. Ry.
C. R. R. of N. J.

K. C., M. & B. R. R.
Southern Ry.
Penna. R. R.

K. C., M. & B. R. R.
Southern Ry.
Seaboard Air Line R. R.
R., F. & P. R. R.
Penna. R. R.

### INDIANAPOLIS, IND.

C., C., C. & St. L. Ry.
L. S. & M. S. Ry.
N. Y., C. & St. L. R. R.
} to Buffalo.

L. E. & W. R. R.
L. S. &. M. S. Ry. Co.
N. Y., C. & St. L. R. R.
} to Buffalo.

Penna. Co.
Penna. R. R.

East of Buffalo:
West Shore R. R.
D., L. & W. R. R.
N. Y. C. & H. R. R. R.
L. Valley R. R.
R., W. & O. R. R.
N. Y., O. & W. Ry.

## CHICAGO, ILL.

| | | |
|---|---|---|
| B. & O. R. R. | C., C., C. & St. R. Ry. | L. S. & M. S. Ry. |
| P. & R. Ry. | L. S. & M. S. Ry. | N. Y. C. & H. R. R. R. |
| C. R. R. of N. J. | N. Y. C. & H. R. R. R. | |

| | | |
|---|---|---|
| P., C., C. & St. L. Ry. | P., Ft. W. & C Ry. | Mich. Cent. R. R. |
| Penna. R. R. | Penna. R. R. | N. Y. C. & H. R. R. R. |

N. Y., C. & St. L. R. R.
    to Buffalo.

Grand Trunk Ry. and all lines east of
    Buffalo.

West Shore R. R. ⎫
D., L. & W. R. R. ⎬ east of Buffalo.
Lehigh Valley Ry. ⎭

Wabash R. R. and all lines east of Buffalo.

## APPLETON, WIS.

C., M. & St. P. Ry. or C. & N. W. Ry. to Chicago, Ill., and any lines east of Chicago

## CINCINNATI, OHIO.

| | | |
|---|---|---|
| B. & O. So. W. Ry. | C. & O. Ry. | C., C., C. & St. L. Ry. ⎫ To |
| B. & O. R. R. | Penna R. R. | L. S. & M. S. Ry. ⎬ Buffalo |
| P. & R. Ry. | | N. Y., S. & St. L. R. R. ⎭ |
| C. R. R. of N. J. | | |

| | | |
|---|---|---|
| | | West Shore R. R. ⎫ |
| | | N. Y. C. & H. R. R. R. ⎪ |
| N. &. W. R. R. | N. & W. R. R. | D., L. & W. R. R. ⎬ East of |
| Cumb. Valley R. R. | N. Y., P. & N. R. R. | Lehigh Valley R. R. ⎬ Buffalo |
| Penna. R. R. | Penna. R. R. | R., W. & O. R. R. ⎪ |
| | | N. Y., O. & W. Ry. ⎭ |
| | Erie R. R. | |

## PETOSKEY, MICH.

Grand Rapids & Indiana Ry.
Penna Co.         Penna. R. R.

## LOUISVILLE, KY.

| | | |
|---|---|---|
| B. & O. So. W. R. R. | C. & O. Ry. | C. & O. Ry. |
| B. & O. R. R. | Penna. R. R. | N. Y., P. & N. R. R. |
| P. & R. Ry. | | Penna. R. R. |
| C. R. R. of N. J. | | |

C., C., C. & St. L. Ry. ⎫
L. S. & M. S. Ry.   ⎬ To Buffalo.
N. Y., C. & St. L. R. R. ⎭

L. & N. R. R.
B. & O. So. W. R. R
B. & O. R. R.
P. & R. Ry.
C. R. R. of N. J.

West Shore R. R. ⎫
N. Y. C. & H. R. R. R. ⎪
D., L. & W. R. R. ⎪
Erie R. R.        ⎬ East of Buffalo.
L. Valley R. R. ⎪
R., W. & O. R. R. ⎪
N. Y., O. & W. R. R. ⎭

Southern Ry.
Pennsylvania R. R.

P., C., C. & St. L. Ry
Penna. R. R.

## BAY CITY, MICH.

Michigan Central R. R. to Buffalo.

West Shore R. R.
N. Y. C. & H. R. R. R.
D., L. & W. R. R.
Erie R. R. } East of Buffalo.
L. Valley R. R.
R., W. & O. R. R.
N. Y., O. & W. Ry.

Pere Marquette R. R.
Grand Trunk Ry. to Buffalo.

West Shore R. R.
N. Y. C. & H. R. R. R.
D., L. & W. R. R.
Erie R. R. } East of Buffalo.
L. Valley R. R.
R., W. & O. R. R.
N. Y., O. & W. Ry.

Pere Marquette R. R.

Grand Trunk Ry.
L. S. & M. S. Ry. } To Buffalo.
Mich. Cent. R. R.

West Shore R. R.
N. Y. C. & H. R. R. R.
D., L. & W. R. R.
Erie R. R. } East of Buffalo.
L. Valley R. R.
R., W. & O. R. R.
N. Y., O. & W. R. R.

## DAYTON, OHIO.

C. C. C. & St. L. Ry.
L. E. & W. R. R.
L. S. & M. S. Ry.
or } to Buffalo.
N. Y. C. & St. L. R. R.

West Shore R. R.
D. L. & W. R. R.
N. Y. C. & H. R. R. R.
Erie R. R. } East of Buffalo.
L. Valley R. R.
R. W. & O. R. R.
N. Y. O. & W. R. R.

Erie R. R.

Penna. Co.

Penna. R. R.

## SAGINAW, MICH.

Michigan Central R. R. to Buffalo.

Pere Marquette R. R.
Grand Trunk Ry.
L. S. & M. S. Ry. } to Buffalo.
Mich. Cent. R. R.

Pere Marquette R. R.
Grand Trunk Ry. to Buffalo.

West Shore R. R.
N. Y. C. & H. R. R. R.
Erie R. R.
D. L. & W. R. R. } East of Buffalo.
Lehigh Valley R. R.
R. W. & O. R. R.
N. Y. O. & W. Ry.

## HELENA, ARK.

Ill. Cent. R. R.
Southern Ry.
Penna. R. R.

Ill. Cent. R. R.
K. C., M. & B. R. R.
S. A. Line R. R.
R. F. & P. R. R.
Penna. R. R.

Ill. Cent. R. R.
K. C., M. & B. R. R.
Southern Ry.
Penna. R. R.

Ill. Cent. R. R.
B. & O. So. W. R. R.
B. & O. R. R.
P. & R. Ry.
C. R. R. of N. J.

Ill. Cent. R. R.
L. & N. R. R.
C. & O. Ry.
Penna. R. R.

Ill. Cent. R. R.
K. C., M. & B. R. R.
Georgia R. R.
A. C. Line R. R.
R. F. & P. R. R.
Penna. R. R.

HELENA, ARK.—continued.

Ill. Cent. R. R.
N. C. & St. L. Ry.
L. & N. R. R.
Ches. & Ohio Ry.
Penna. R. R.

St. L. I. M. & Co., Mo. Pac.
to East St. Louis, and
any lines east of East St.
Louis.

ASHLAND, KY.; KENOVA, W. VA.; HUNTINGTON, W. VA.; PANTHER, VA., AND IRONTON, OHIO.

Via Ches. & Ohio Ry.
  B. & O. R. R.
  P. & R. Ry.
  C. R. R. of N. J.

Ches. & Ohio Ry.
Penna. R. R.

BUFFALO, N. Y.

West Shore R. R.
N. Y. C. & H. R. R. R.
Erie R. R.
D., L. & W. R. R.
Lehigh Valley R. R.
R. W. & O. R. R.
N. Y., O. & W. Rwy.

CHATTANOOGA, TENN.

Southern Rwy.
Penna. R. R.

Southern Rwy.
N. & W. Rwy.
Penna. R. R.

Southern Rwy.
O. D. S. S. Co.

KNOXVILLE, TENN.

Southern Rwy.
Penna. R. R.

Southern Rwy.
N. & W. Rwy.
Penna. R. R.

Southern Rwy.
O. D. S. S. Co.

OSWEGO, N. Y.

D., L. & W, R. R.
N. Y. C. & H. R. R. R.
N. Y., O. & W. Rwy.

NASHVILLE, TENN.

L. & N. R. R.
Penna. R. R.

N. C. & St. L. Ry.
Southern Ry.
Penna. R. R.

N. C. & St. L. Ry.
S. A. Line R. R.
R., F. & P. R. R.
Penna. R. R.

N. C. & St. L. Ry.
Georgia R. R.
Atlantic Coast Line.
R., F. & P. R. R.
Penna. R. R.

ASHEVILLE, N. C.

Southern Ry.
Penna. R. R.

Southern Ry.
N. Y., P. & N. R. R.
Penna. R. R.

Southern Ry.
O. D. S. S. Co.

WILMINGTON, N. C.

A. C. Line.
Penna. R. R.

A. C. Line.
N. Y., P. & N. R. R.
Penna. R. R.

S. A. Line.
Penna. R. R.

A. C. Line.
O. D. S. S. Co.

S. A. Line.
O. D. S. S. Co.

S. A. Line.
N. Y., P. & N. R. R.
Penna. R. R.

### ELIZABETHTON, TENN.

| | | |
|---|---|---|
| East Tenn. & W. N. C. R. R. | E. T. & W. N. C. R. R. | E. T. & W. N. C. R. R. |
| N. & W. Ry. | N. & W. Ry. | N. & W. Ry. |
| Cum. Valley R. R. | W. Md. R. R. | B. & O. R. R. |
| Penna. R. R. | P. & R. Ry. | P. & R. Ry. |
| | C. R. R. of N. J., or L. V. | C. R. R. of N. J. |
| | R. R. | |

### GRAFTON, W. VA.

B. & O. R. R.
P. & R. Ry.
C. R. R. of N. J.

### MURPHY, N. C.

| | | |
|---|---|---|
| Southern Ry. | Southern Ry. | Southern Ry. |
| Penna. R. R. | N. Y. P. & N. R. R. | O. D. S. S. Co. |
| | Penna. R. R. | |

### NORTON, W. VA.

| | | |
|---|---|---|
| N. & W. Ry. | N. & W. Ry. | N. & W. Ry. |
| Cumb. V. R. R. | W. Md. R. R. | W. Md. R. R. |
| Penna. R. R. | P. & R. Ry. | P. & R. Ry. |
| | L. Valley R. R. | C. R. R. of N. J. |
| N. & W. Ry. | | |
| B. & O. R. R. | N & W. Ry. | N. & W. Ry. |
| P. & R. Ry. | O. D. S. S. Co. | Southern Ry. |
| C. R. R. of N. J. | | Penna R. R. |

### CAMDEN ON GAULEY, W. VA.

B. & O. R. R.
P. & R. Ry.
C. R. R. of N. J.

### ELIZABETH CITY, N. C.

| | |
|---|---|
| Nor. & So. Ry. | Norfolk & So. Ry. |
| N. Y. P. & N. Ry. | O. D. S. S. Co. |
| Penna. R. R. | |

### ELKINS, W. VA.

| | |
|---|---|
| W. Va. Cent. & Pgh. Ry. | W. Va. Cent. & Pgh. R. R. |
| B. & O. R. R. | Penna. R. R. |
| P. & R. Ry. | |
| C. R. R. of N. J. | |

Senator TILLMAN. Mr. Chairman, my understanding has been that the long and short haul clause had reference to shipments by a given road, not over any general railroad system of the country.

The CHAIRMAN. That was my understanding of it.

Senator TILLMAN. I should think that the information which you are seeking to get, and which we all want, would be fuller if points with-out competitive water rates were named. For instance, Menominee is on the river leading into Lake Michigan.

Mr. HIGBIE. It is right at the mouth of that river.

Senator TILLMAN. So there is really entire water transportation if you choose to bring it through the lakes, down the Erie Canal, and into the Hudson to New York City. Do you not suppose that that accounts for the extremely low rate?

Mr. HIGBIE. It is more than probable.

Senator TILLMAN. Still there must be other points connected with New York by all-rail routes that have no advantage of that kind.

Mr. HIGBIE. Yes; there is Memphis, Tenn.

Senator TILLMAN. That also has an entire water route down the

Mississippi and by the Gulf and Atlantic to New York, but this route is not used at all. Take some point that has no water connection with New York.

Mr. HIGBIE. Indianapolis, Ind.

Senator TILLMAN. Indianapolis and Elizabethton, I should suppose, are practically the same distance from New York.

Mr. HIGBIE. Indianapolis is a trifle farther; it is 818 miles from New York, and Elizabethton is 628 miles from New York. But Elizabethton, which has the shorter distance, has to pay a greater rate.

Senator TILLMAN. Such information is valuable.

Mr. HIGBIE. I thank you for calling my attention to it, Senator.

The CHAIRMAN. I know that Menominee has a water route, but I would like Mr. Higbie to show what roads his land freights would travel over. An additional column can be made to show that.

Mr. HIGBIE. Oh, yes; it will take only very little trouble. In reply to what the Senator has said about the long and short haul clause, I will say that I know it to be the fact that this movement of freight over the Norfolk and Western road from Cincinnati has to pass these same points in going to New York, and which points are compelled to pay a much higher rate than what is known as the Cincinnati rate.

Senator TILLMAN. That would come under the interpretation, as we understand, of the long and short haul clause. My understanding of that clause of the original act is that no given railroad should charge a greater rate to a place 300 miles from a competitive point than to a place 500 miles from such a point.

The CHAIRMAN. The statute states further that the freight must move in the same direction over the same road. Mr. Higbie, if you will add that column to your table, as suggested by me, it will be very valuable to us.

Mr. HIGBIE. I shall be glad to do so, and will mail it to you as soon as I can get it prepared.

Another thing that has changed the conditions since the time when the present act was passed, is competition among the railroads themselves. At that time there was great competition, and that, in many cases, regulated the rates charged and the rates made. But in the change of the method of doing business different systems have been consolidated into one system, and they have entered into what we call a community of interest plan, gentlemen, "agreements and other such arrangements."

Senator TILLMAN. What is understood by the general term pooling.

Mr. HIGBIE. Yes.

The CHAIRMAN. It has gone further, it is absolute ownership.

Senator TILLMAN. Of course; but it is said that they have also combined where ownership does not exist.

The CHAIRMAN. They can not combine now.

Senator TILLMAN. You mean they can not lawfully combine; but still some of us feel pretty thoroughly satisfied that they have combined and are now combining.

The CHAIRMAN. By actual purchase, but not in violation of the Sherman antitrust law. If so, they ought to be prosecuted. Now, Mr. Higbie, I will ask you this question: Have you observed in the last two years, since these consolidations have gone into effect, that the rates are perceptibly higher than they were before?

Mr. HIGBIE. It has not been my experience in the lumber business— I know of no case where the lumber business has been affected in that way. I understand that some other kinds of business have been very largely affected by these consolidations, more particularly in the matter of classifications.

The CHAIRMAN. Then I understand you to say that within the last two years, or since these consolidations, the rates on lumber have not perceptibly advanced?

Mr. HIGBIE. They have not.

It seems to me, Mr. Chairman, that the railroads in setting forth their side of the case in the public prints and otherwise, have rather sought to create the impression that the Interstate Commerce Commission was intended more particularly to represent the shippers, and not the railroads. My understanding is that the Interstate Commerce Commission was created for the express purpose of representing both sides of the question, so that when complaint is made, or when objection is made to an order of the Commission, each side shall have an equal chance to prove its side of the case before the Commission, just as they would in a court of law. The impression has been abroad that in case these additional powers are conferred upon the Commission the Commission will be dangerous, and many other adjectives are used which I will not specify. I can not understand that. They lose sight of the fact that somebody has to make these railroad rates. While we do not intend to ask that the Interstate Commerce Commission should be given the power to take initial action to make a rate—that being left entirely to the railroads, as it always has been—we do feel that in view of the discriminations and secret rate cutting and unreasonable rates that some of the railroads have been charging, the power to regulate and to determine what is reasonable rate should be given to the Commission, and then it should have the power of seeing that that reasonable rate is put into effect.

I think, gentlemen, I will not take any more of your time.

Senator TILLMAN. Before the gentleman closes, I should like to ask him, if he is willing, or is authorized, to give us a list of the membership of his association?

Mr. HIGBIE. I will also mail that with the other statement.

Senator TILLMAN. As I have said, we want to have as much light as possible upon the character, respectability, and wealth of the business interests involved in those who come here appealing for legislation.

Mr. HIGBIE. I will be very glad, indeed, to mail that.

Senator FOSTER. Is it your opinion that the decision of the Commission as to rates should go into operation and effect immediately, or should it be open to appeal to the courts before it becomes effective?

Mr. HIGBIE. In reply to that question, Senator, it seems to me that the rate should go into effect within a reasonable time, say twenty or thirty days. I think the Nelson bill provides that. The trouble has been heretofore that when the decision of the Interstate Commerce Commission has been rendered, the matter has been allowed to take its course through the United States courts, thus consuming much time, until final determination has been had in the Supreme Court.

Senator FOSTER. An instance of the law's delays.

Mr. HIGBIE. Yes.

Senator TILLMAN. It tends to prevent appeal to the courts.

Mr. HIGBIE. And not only that, but it also tends to prevent lodgment of complaint with the Commission in the first instance. The expense of preparing the complaint and the conditions of delay are such that in a great many cases no action is taken at all.

## STATEMENT OF DAVID BINGHAM.

The CHAIRMAN. Please state whom you represent.

Mr. BINGHAM. I am chairman of the board of discrimination of the New York Produce Exchange. We have a membership of between 2,900 and 3,000. We are an incorporated body, and I think we are the largest exchange in the United States or perhaps in the world. The president of the exchange is here to give countenance to what I say; I am to do the talking. I suppose our business in extent comes next to the Chicago Exchange, which I think does a little more business than we do.

We are very anxious to have some legislation which will give to somebody the power to decide questions. It took us nearly ten years to get the first Interstate Commerce Commission appointed. For ten years after that we thought we had something that would give us relief from the discriminations of the railroads, only to find out, when it came to the test, that it was a delusion and a snare, and, so far as the business interests of the country are concerned that we represent, we do not think it is of any particular use. We want particularly to have a body that will give us a decision, and a decision before we die.

Our business is prompt. If we are shipping grain from Chicago to New York, of what earthly use is it to us to get a decision at the end of twelve months that the railroad companies were charging too much? We want a decision at once, even if it be against us. If we are to be hung, we want to know it right away. That is the reason why we are very much more favorably impressed with the Corliss bill than we are with the Elkins bill, as regards that particular point.

The CHAIRMAN. You want the order of the Commission made operative at once?

Mr. BINGHAM. Yes. It looks to us, Mr. Chairman and gentlemen, as if the Interstate Commerce Commission ought to occupy very much the position of the jury while the legal fraternity could retain the position of judge. We are perfectly willing to have the questions of law go to the judges, but when it comes to questions of fact, then we want them to go to the jury, to men who are familiar with the facts.

The New York Produce Exchange has an agreement with the trunk lines for arbitration which works very satisfactorily. We get along with our disputes with that association fairly well. The president of the exchange appoints one arbitrator and the trunk line appoints one; and they two appoint a third, and those three settle any question given to them not involving a large amount.

We are not here complaining particularly of the railroads, so far as New York is concerned. We are here to urge that we may have somebody whose decisions shall carry weight. It seems ridiculous to us that such a great body of men as the Interstate Commerce Commission should be created and given no power at all. The idea among the railroad people of the West when this Commission was created was that it had power to settle questions. Now we find that we want you gentlemen to give them power. We are not very particular about that power, except that we want to have it promptly applied. New York stands a little differently in that respect, I presume, from almost everybody here.

The produce exchange is not opposed to railroads making proper combinations. We would rather do our business with a combination of railroads than with this road, that road, and the other. When we get a number of gentlemen together we can agree upon some tribunal to which we may refer our differences, and in that way we can keep transportation matters in good shape.

The CHAIRMAN. In other words, you think there may be pooling by way of agreements between railroads, subject to the supervision of the Commission?

Mr. BINGHAM. I wish you would change that word "pooling," Mr. President. We think there ought to be an agreement. We do not believe in pooling.

The CHAIRMAN. Well, call it an agreement.

Senator TILLMAN. Why should we beat the devil around the bush in that way? If there is an effective agreement, that is pooling.

Mr. BINGHAM. You have stated it. But a pooling arrangement may be made which will allow one road to be idle. Your grain may be shipped under a pooling arrangement over the Canadian Pacific when you do not want it to go over that road at all. What we want is to have the right of selecting the railroad to carry our grain. Let the best road have the most freight. We have no objection to these roads getting together and making agreements, such as they have in regard to passenger rates. For example, we go from New York to Chicago over the Delaware, Lackawanna and Western and we pay $18. We travel over the New York Central and we pay $20. Let the roads make the same sort of an arrangement in regard to freight, always provided that this arrangement is safeguarded by a competent body. We believe that the Interstate Commerce Commission is a competent body.

Senator TILLMAN. You are not, then, in favor of pooling, as it is usually understood?

Mr. BINGHAM. No, sir.

Senator TILLMAN. You do not believe it is for the best interests of the country?

Mr. BINGHAM. I do not.

Senator TILLMAN. But you do believe that it would be permissible for the roads to agree to give a rate of freight on each line from a given point?

Mr. BINGHAM. Yes, sir.

Senator TILLMAN. What is the use of any agreement at all? Why not let the Commission determine the rate over any given line, provided it shall be reasonably remunerative? It is not proposed anywhere, I believe, to confiscate property by compelling a railroad to haul at a loss. If one line, by reason of its heavy grades or other conditions, can not haul as cheaply as the New York Central can haul along the almost absolute level of the Hudson River from Albany down, where it can haul a hundred cars with one engine, why not give the Interstate Commerce Commission the power to fix rates on each line according to the conditions of that line, instead of letting the lines themselves fix them?

Mr. BINGHAM. Well, Mr. Senator, we believe we are doing that. The lines in the first instance settle the rate, but that rate does not go into effect until the Commission passes upon it. If it is not satisfactory, they throw it back, so you have got to make these rates subject to the approval of the Commission.

Senator FOSTER. Your idea, then, is that this agreement shall be subject to the approval of the Commission?

Mr. BINGHAM. That is my idea. In point of fact, if you care for it, I am willing to read what we would be willing to accept.

Senator TILLMAN. Let it go in your testimony.

The CHAIRMAN. Let it go in as part of your testimony.

Mr. BINGHAM. Very well.

Carriers subject to the provisions of this act, with respect to traffic subject to the act, may form associations to secure the establishment and maintenance of just, reasonable, nonpreferential, uniform, and stable rates, and for the promulgation and enforcement of reasonable and just rules and regulations as to the interchange of interstate traffic and the conduct of interstate business upon the following conditions:

(a) Articles of agreement shall be subscribed by the parties thereto stating, among other things, that they are entered into subject to the provisions of this section; the terms upon which new parties may come in; how the decisions of the association are to be made and enforced, and the length of time for which the association shall continue, which shall not be more than ten years. Such articles, when subscribed and in effect agreeably to the provisions of this section, shall be legally binding upon the parties thereto and be legally enforcible between them.

(b) The articles of association shall be filed with the Commission at least twenty days before they take effect. If the Commission, upon inspection of the same, is of the opinion that their operation would result in unreasonable rates, unjust discriminations, insufficient service to the public, or would in any manner contravene the provisions of this act, it shall enter an order disapproving the same. In connection with such order the Commission shall file a statement of its reasons for its disapproval. Said order shall be final and conclusive.

(c) If the Commission, upon inquiry into the actual operation of the association after the same has gone into effect, is of the opinion that it results in unreasonable rates, unjust discriminations, inadequate service, or is in any respect in contravention of this act it may enter an order requiring the same to be terminated on a date named, which shall not be less than ten days from the making of the order. Such order shall be final, and the effect of it shall be to render such articles of agreement null and void from and after date named, except as to claims between the parties arising prior to that date.

(d) The Commission shall have the right to examine, by its duly authorized agents, the files and proceedings of such association, including all contracts, records, documents, and other papers; and it may require said association to file with it, from time to time, copies of decisions promulgated by it or of other papers received or issued.

All orders issued by associations thus formed that in anywise affect rates shall be filed with the Commission, as provided in the original act in relation to the filing of tariffs.

Every agreement for the establishment and maintenance of rates or for the formation of such associations as are authorized by this section is prohibited, except as hereby authorized, and every carrier or representative of a carrier acting as a member of such an association or committee, whether the same exists by virtue of a definite agreement or not, is made subject to a penalty of $5,000 for each day he so acts or continues a member thereof, which penalty shall be enforced in the manner provided for the enforcement of those penalties imposed by the tenth section of said act.

Senator TILLMAN. Are you willing to give the names of your membership?

Mr. BINGHAM. That is a big book, containing some 23,000 names; but we will give it to the committee.

Senator TILLMAN. I have been twitted time and again in conversations with the fact that nobody reads these statements; that people are satisfied with present conditions; that nobody wants legislation; that nobody appears here but interested parties, and that they get their inspiration from the Interstate Commission itself, which is clamoring for more power; that it has sent out circulars and solicitations to this man and to that association begging them to come here in the interest of that Commission.

Mr. BINGHAM. Here is a man interested in cotton. That comes in his line.

## STATEMENT OF SAMUEL T. HUBBARD.

The CHAIRMAN. Whom do you represent?

Mr. HUBBARD. I am president of the Cotton Exchange of New York. I am authorized by that body to appear and advocate the passage of the Corliss bill. We simply ask that more power be given to the Interstate Commerce Commission; that the orders which they issue may be carried into effect.

There is no need of detaining the committee with any extended remarks. That is the position we feel should be taken in regard to the Interstate Commerce Commission. I shall not detain the committee any longer, unless they desire to interrogate me.

Senator TILLMAN. Is your association in favor of pooling?

Mr. HUBBARD. I do not think we are. The question has not been discussed before it.

The CHAIRMAN. Were you authorized to make any statement in regard to that?

Mr. HUBBARD. No, sir.

Senator TILLMAN. Will you give us your individual opinion in regard to pooling?

Mr. HUBBARD. I do not think pooling would be for the best interests of the country. One road might be eliminated from operation by the payment to it of a certain sum of money, and freight would be lost to it which would otherwise come to it. This would tend to destroy the industries along that road. For instance, you might ship a thousand car loads over the New York Central which would more properly go over the Lehigh Valley; but instead of sending it by the Lehigh Valley road, that road is given $10,000 in cash.

The CHAIRMAN. You think the Interstate Commerce Commission would not agree to anything like that?

Mr. HUBBARD. That is the question of pooling.

The CHAIRMAN. But if you had pooling under the absolute supervision of the Commission, with full power to set aside any pooling contract in whole or in part, what would you say?

Mr. HUBBARD. That is a question which I have not considered, Mr. Chairman.

Senator TILLMAN. You would not be willing to commit yourself personally, and you are not authorized to commit your association to an indorsement of pooling?

Mr. HUBBARD. No, sir; I am not.

## STATEMENT OF R. S. LYON.

The CHAIRMAN. Please give us your residence and your official position.

Mr. LYON. I reside in the city of Chicago. I am a layman now; I have heretofore been president of the Chicago Board of Trade; I was in 1899. I am a member of the transportation committee of that board now.

The CHAIRMAN. And authorized to appear here?

Mr. LYON. My credentials are here.

The CHAIRMAN. That is sufficient. You appear here on behalf of your board of trade?

Mr. LYON. Yes, sir.

The CHAIRMAN. Please make your statement.

Mr. LYON. It would seem possibly a little superflous to one at this day to appear before a committee of Congress and show that the inter-state-commerce law had been violated, or to bring any evidence to that end. You have had abundant evidence and are surfeited no doubt with facts showing this to be the case; consequently I will not attempt to take up any of your valuable time to that end. Representing, as I have the honor at this time, the great grain and shipping trade of the board of trade of the city of Chicago, I come before you to urge some change in the interstate-commerce law that will give to us equal, stable, and uniform rates to and from all points.

The Chicago Board of Trade, handling as it does the greatest bulk of grain of any market in the world, reaching out in all directions, west, northwest, and southwest, to bring this grain to the market, and in turn supplying the markets of the world, both domestic and foreign, must of necessity be the barometer of prices. So that any deviation from tariff rates, known always, whether made in the country west, tributary to Chicago, whereby grain is diverted from its natural chan-nel, or even by our own members, competitors with one another, is immediately felt, and the market price of commodities dealt in on the Chicago market is influenced to a greater or less degree.

Transportation is necessary to the people. It is as absolutely a neces-sity to the prosperity of our nation as the air we breathe. Every one should be treated alike, whether a large shipper supplying the wants of foreign countries or a small shipper taking care of the needs of this country. All sorts of devices known to shippers and railroads should be open, and the great transportation lines of this country should treat each and every one alike. To use the language of one of our learned judges, "Freight rates should be as stable as postage rates, to every-where and from everywhere alike." This is all we ask, and for such a law properly carried out we are willing to stand, to survive or fall.

I am a member of a grain firm and have been for the past twenty-four years. Formerly we belonged to that coterie of grain shippers designated as "small shippers." Previous to and about 1890 we sought to supply the wants of grain men in New England, New York, Pennsylvania, and Ohio, and throughout the Southern States, doing nothing but a domestic trade, and did exclusively a shipping business. We were, in fact, distributers of grain and its products from the West to that class of smaller merchants and mills throughout the above ter-ritory, who in their turn filled the wants of the farmers for these com-modities; generally merchants who purchased in small quantities, single car lots, whose capital often prevented their carrying large lines, or who did not have extensive storehouses to care for the same. Nor did they seek to use the cars of the various railroads to store their grain in. As fast as their single car lots were disposed of they were in the market for further supplies.

We did strictly a domestic shipping business, and were not of that class of grain dealers who sought an export trade, shipping in large quantities by water and rail to the seaboard and solely to supply the wants of the export trade. I speak of our own firm merely as an example, but our own experience is that of many. Gradually this trade became smaller by reason of the encroachment of larger shippers, more favored by rates; and we were at last driven almost entirely out of the shipping business and obliged to take up other branches of the grain business. There are combinations of Western elevator companies with railway managers on different lines of roads, and all more or less competitors. Each railway wants the business. They are secret and powerful combinations, with mutual desires for securing traffic. The rates and devices known only to railroad men are mere playthings.

The act to regulate commerce was passed solely to secure an equable distribution of the benefits of transportation and to correct abuses which had imperceptibly and gradually crept into the administration of the vast powers conferred upon railroad corporations, not for the corporations alone, but for the people in the prosecution of their business enterprises. This Interstate Commerce Commission was not framed to impair business interests, but to conserve and protect. In the words of the Interstate Commerce Commission, "It had for its object to regulate a vast business to the requirements of justice, and was not passed for a day or a year; it had permanent benefits in view, and to accomplish these with the least possible disturbance to the immense interests involved." But, as the years since the enactment of the law have gone on and law itself tried, it seems to-day as if the Commission (without reflecting in any manner upon the character and ability of its members) has signally failed in the exercise of controlling power; its mandates have either been supinely forced or altogether evaded. The great complaint against the law and the Commission to-day is that it is a creation powerless to enforce its decrees.

I am of the opinion that the bill now before the committee, and known as Senate bill No. 3575, will meet the requirements and give to the interstate-commerce law greater effectiveness. I believe the interstate-commerce law should be so amended as a whole that under the light of experience and decisions of the courts of the United States the rights and interests of the people in general should be properly safeguarded under it, and defined by it, and the responsibility of carriers carefully fixed and defined in it, and the power and scope of the Interstate Commerce Commission, including the right to fix rates and enforce their decisions, properly established by it.

I am not wise enough nor am I lawyer enough to go into the details of this bill. . Its common sense appeals to me, and I leave it to others, and no doubt you have heard them, to argue out the amendments proposed in the bill now before you. My own experience in freight matters makes me believe that such portions of the bill now before you as relate to the imprisonment clause in the original law should be dropped and that fines against corporations violating the law be imposed. Railroad officials and agents hold social positions among themselves and in the community; different shippers are personal friends of one another; to complain one of the other, and send them to imprisonment for violating a law which we know emanates from corporations themselves, goes against our best feeling. But if a fine could be imposed on corporations, who are in reality above agents and general managers, and in fact the real offenders, our courts would now be full of violators of the law.

The temper, if not the spirit of railway managers, toward the successful administration of the interstate-commerce law has become more hurtful to the railways than to the public. But these corporations are in no sense exempt from public opinion because of the nearly universal, if not organized, opposition to laws enacted for the purpose of regulating their relations with the people. It is not too much to assume that the people hold these laws in higher and higher esteem to the ratio of contempt for them and the constant violation of their terms by the railways. This conflict between the railways and the interstate-commerce enactment has well-nigh exhausted the patience of the people and those who are appointed to execute its provisions. That the law itself has demonstrated that it needs some changes to make it more applicable to present needs, none will deny. The public demands at the hands of Congress some radical improvements. What we need in reference to the Interstate Commerce Commission is that its powers shall be more definitely specified; that it shall have greater powers to enforce its orders. We need an interstate-commerce law, and that the powers of its commission be defined. I believe that there is but one way to maintain reasonable, fair, and just rates, and that is by giving the railways the right to establish a rate, and then go to the Commission and have that rate indorsed, publish the rate, and live up to it. In a word, be honest. Heretofore Congress has seemed slow and apparently indifferent, but we believe needed changes in the law will be obtained and justice be done to all.

Senator TILLMAN. Will you please tell us what your association thinks of pooling?

Mr. LYON. I can not tell you. I do not believe our association has put itself on record one way or the other as an association. Our directors have from time to time opposed it, and they are the controlling power.

Senator TILLMAN. What is your individual opinion?

Mr. LYON. My own opinion is decidedly against it—always has been and always will be—because it smothers competition.

Senator TILLMAN. Will you leave with us a list of the membership of your association?

Mr. LYON. We have a book that should be on file in Congress, certainly, in the form of our board of trade reports from 1870. Those are now on file in the library. We send them every year.

Senator TILLMAN. You know what I want, from what I said to the other gentlemen.

Mr. LYON. We will send them, and will be glad to do so.

Senator TILLMAN. I want some testimony as to the character and respectability of the men who are asking relief.

Mr. LYON. Many members of the New York Produce Exchange are members of our board of trade, and many of the members of our board of trade are members of the New York Board of Trade. We also have members in Europe, and one, I believe, in Australia.

Senator FOSTER. Do you believe that the railroads should establish a rate, submit that to the Commission, and then that the Commission should either ratify or reject it?

Mr. LYON. I think the Commission should have power to say whether a rate is reasonable or not, and then should also have the power to compel the railroads to live up to it.

Senator TILLMAN. You mean that after they have establsihed it they should not change it without the permission of the Interstate Commerce Commission?

Mr. LYON. Yes, sir.

Senator TILLMAN. And have no secret rebates?

Mr. LYON. No, sir; not at all.

Senator FOSTER. Suppose the Commission should establish unjust rates?

Mr. LYON. The Nelson bill provides for that. We indorse the Nelson bill, that the rates be in force for two years.

Senator TILLMAN. You mean that the Commission should be given the power to fix what it decides to be just rates, with right of appeal?

Mr. LYON. With right of appeal to the courts. Let that power be enforced.

Senator TILLMAN. While litigation is going on?

Mr. LYON. Yes, sir.

## STATEMENT OF CHARLES N. CHADWICK.

WASHINGTON, D. C., *April 16, 1902.*

*The Honorable Committee on Interstate Commerce, United States Senate.*

GENTLEMEN: At a meeting of the Manufacturers' Association of New York, on the 17th day of February, 1902, the following resolution was unanimously adopted:

*Resolved,* That this Association favors the enactment of H. R. bill No. 8337, and urges upon our representatives in Congress to use their best endeavors to secure passage of said bill. The undersigned was appointed a delegate to appear at Washington as a representative of the association to advocate the enactment of the above measure and for the following reasons:

First, under the interstate-commerce act, as it now exists, orders of the Commission can only be made effective by judgment of the courts. The pending amendment provides for a remedy to give effect to the orders of the Commission while securing to the defendants the right of appeal. This appears to us to be eminently just and fair.

Second. These amendments do not confer upon the Commission any general rate-making power. This power is still left with the common carriers. It seeks to give the Commission power to correct rates which have been shown by judicial investigation to be unreasonable, unlawful, and discriminative, and the orders of the Commission to be obligatory only for a period of two years. Inasmuch as common carriers are recipients of favored legislation, it is but right they should be subjected to governmental control. Under the circumstances it is not a dangerous precedent, and if wrong be done remedy lies with the courts. It reverses present conditions and makes the railroads the defendants rather than the public. Because of the varying conditions, the implied contract between the public and the common carrier must be, to a great extent, a matter of continuous interpretation. Common sense and fair dealing would seem to point to some authority with full power to enforce the needed remedy.

Third. To leave the jurisdiction of conflicting interests to the courts provides only a remedy and compensation for the particular question under consideration. The condition still remains unchanged unless power lodges with some body to rule effectively upon the question and make the needed change, which shall be continuous.

Fourth. The added powers and penalties provided for in these amendments seem to meet the situation and make the interstate-commerce act a mandatory rather than an advisory measure. As an advisory measure it is an absurdity, because it can compel no action. As a mandatory measure it places control over the common carrier, where it belongs, with the Government as a representative of the people, and insures, so far as human limitations admit, substantial justice to all.

For these and other reasons, would respectfully urge that these amendments be enacted into law. I have the honor to be,

Respectfully, yours,

CHARLES N. CHADWICK,
*Delegate of the Manufacturers' Association of New York.*

The committee adjourned to 10 a. m. to morrow.

FRIDAY, *April 18, 1902.*

At the sitting of the committee on Friday, April 18, 1902, the following-named gentlemen appeared: William H. Chadwick, representing the Chicago Board of Trade; T. W. Tomlinson, representing the Chicago Live Stock Exchange; J. B. Daish, representing the National Hay Association; F. B. Thurber, representing the United States Export Association; and John D. Kernan, counsel for the New York Produce Exchange.

## STATEMENT OF WILLIAM H. CHADWICK.

The CHAIRMAN. Please state whom you represent.

Mr. CHADWICK. I will read my credentials first; and in fact I will read the whole of what I shall say, with the permission of the committee. I think that is the better way. I will now read my credentials, so that you can see the charter I have.

BOARD OF TRADE OF THE CITY OF CHICAGO,
*Chicago, April 9, 1902.*

Mr. WILLIAM H. CHADWICK,
*Chairman Transportation Committee.*

DEAR SIR: I have the honor to inform you that I have appointed you to represent the Board of Trade of the city of Chicago at hearings in Washington before the committees of the Senate and House upon the subject of granting additional powers to the Interstate Commerce Commission.

While the association has indorsed the Nelson-Corliss bill, and you are to use your endeavors toward the passage of that bill, you are granted discretion to agree to such compromise as may seem necessary in your judgment to secure the relief sought.

Respectfully,

WM. S. WARREN, *President.*

If the committee wish any information in regard to the Chicago Board of Trade, I shall be pleased to furnish it.

To draw our attention to conditions which formerly prevailed and which led to the enactment of the act to regulate commerce, I now quote, from the proceedings of the National Board of Trade in Washington, December 15, 1897, the statement of Hon. George F. Stone, secretary of the Board of Trade of the city of Chicago, as follows:

The proposition to establish pooling is not by any means new, and we are therefore not left in doubt as to its effects upon the business interests of the country. The first prominent pool was the Chicago-Omaha, and was formed in 1870, and was found in its operation immensely profitable to railroads, so that in the year 1887 practically all competitive traffic was pooled.

During those years business suffered, localities and shippers were discriminated against, secret rebates to a greater extent than before or since were granted. Discrimination in favor of industries in which some of the parties to the pool were financially interested placed other industries under great and sometimes fatal disadvantages.

One of the most mischievous and demoralizing pools that were established about this time was the Southwestern Railway Association, a vampire which for a decade sucked the life-blood of the commerce of the Missouri Valley. The Southwestern Railway Association solved the problem of how to get rid of competition and to rob the people within the letter of the law. Kansas City built a line to the South and thought she had a line that could be used to fight this pool. It had not been in operation a year before this association, with subsidies, had it bound hand and foot. Another outlet to the East, via Omaha and Council Bluffs, was also shut up, leaving the Missouri River country absolutely at the mercy of the pooling lines.

At every acquisition of competing lines, rates were moved up a notch, until they reached an appalling figure. When this association was organized, in 1876, the rate on first-class matter between Missouri River Valley and Chicago was 60 cents. It was at once advanced several cents, and in 1880 had reached 75 cents on east bound and 85 cents on west bound. In a few months it was moved up to 90 cents. When the association was organized, it included the Burlington, Chicago and Alton, Missouri Pacific, Rock Island, and Wabash. The system was soon found incomplete, in that there were several loopholes by which the people were enabled to avoid the association's higher tariff.

One of these was the Missouri Pacific in Kansas. The business of ten points on the Gould system—Parsons, Chanute, Garnett, Ottawa, Humboldt, Fort Scott, Paola, Burlington, Emporia, and Junction City, since known as the ten junction points— was sent to St. Louis over Gould's southern line, avoiding the pool points. In order to divert this traffic through the pool, by which means alone the higher rates could be maintained, the association entered into an agreement to pay the Missouri Pacific a liberal percentage of the gross earnings of the pool, on condition that this business be sent via pool points. The amount paid the Missouri Pacific in 1885, on account of the ten junction points, was $660,000, the agreed percentage of the receipts of the association, which amounted to $11,000,000.

During several years of the existence of this pool the shippers of the Missouri Valley had occasionally taken advantage of the rates offered by the Milwaukee and St. Paul Railroad to ship via Omaha and Council Bluffs. The pool, in order to prevent this, found it necessary to bind the Missouri Pacific and Council Bluffs Railroad from making special rates to Omaha and Council Bluffs. Here again a money plaster was applied, the pool agreeing to pay the two lines a percentage of the gross earnings, amounting to $75,000 a year; the lines on their part to charge the full local rates between the pool points and Omaha and Council Bluffs.

The object of this was to make the rate via the northern roads the same as that via the association or pool roads, in order to keep all the business in the pool, as shippers would not use the Milwaukee or Northwestern at the same rates, owing to the greater length of those lines. The Burlington and Missouri River coming into competition with the central branch of the Union Pacific (a pool line), the association, in order to maintain rates and have the business pooled, subsidized the competing line to the amount of $250,000 a year; the same principle was applied to the St. Louis, Fort Scott and Wichita after its extension into southern Kansas. The Fort Scott and Wichita, in consideration of the maintenance of rates and pooling business of its lines, received of the association a percentage of the gross earnings of the pool amounting to $225,000 a year. All the competitors who could be taken into the pools were thus brought in. The commissioner in the meantime turned his attention in other directions. Immediately upon the completion of the Kansas City, Springfield and Memphis, in 1883, the Fort Scott began to compete for the St. Louis business in conjunction with the St. Louis and San Francisco; by its connection with the latter at Springfield it was enabled to cut the association rate to St. Louis and still get a fair remuneration. In order to stop this, the association entered into an agreement with the Fort Scott and Frisco roads by which the latter were paid $8,000 a month on condition that they keep out of the St. Louis business.

Such instances and similar combinations might be multiplied almost indefinitely, but sufficient is shown to indicate the nature of railway pools; they are inimical to the public interests; they are in restraint of trade; they prevent competition; they are monopolistic in purpose and effect; they are odious in law; they are subversive of the very interests which railways were created to conserve, viz, the general welfare, in so far as that welfare relates to the functions and obligations of a common carrier.

I have read this simply to take your minds back to the reason why there ever was created an interstate commerce commission, and why the law was ever framed to bring about that result, to get a body of men who could do the things that were apparently intended by the authors of the law to be done; but I have always thought that if able men had written that law with the contrary intent it could not have been found more fatally weak.

Year after year we plain people have been coming to committees of the Senate and the House seeking and asking relief from conditions which are a disgrace to the Republic and which never should have been tolerated in this country.

The people have long known and testified what the conditions have been, and their statements have had such full corroboration recently that their case is completely established beyond refutation.

I think that we may fairly assume, without argument or dispute, that discrimination, rate cutting, and rebate granting have been common and widespread practices for a number of years. These are the chief causes of complaint, and I have never heard them defended as just, fair, or right.

The complaint is that discrimination has been practiced for the benefit of some to the injury of others, and to the complete destruction of the business and substance of not a few.

The general public appears to be well represented in asking that the powers of the Interstate Commerce Commission be enlarged so that certain conditions which are represented as evils may be properly and justly regulated.

The end thereby sought appears to be that the common interstate carrier must perform every service, to all patrons, without any discrimination whatever—the same price to each for an identical service.

New conditions are now fast making, and with the control of vast systems vested in the hands of a few men, the problem is likely to become more complex through a return to the practices of the old pooling days.

The great danger threatened in this country is railroad monopoly, which will produce an extortionate rate.

Five syndicates, in each one of which some one man is the dominating spirit, control more than 100,000 miles of railroad. If you add to each one of these systems one of five lines which are still independent, and which will not aggregate over 25,000 miles, making 125,000 miles in all, you have railroad monopoly. There are 75,000 miles left, but those railroads are absolutely dependent on the others. The effect of this is already to be seen. Rates are advancing. The grain rate is an illustration. In 1890 the Commission held that 23 cents was a reasonable rate from the Mississippi River to New York; in the winter of 1892 the published rate was 29 cents; in the winter of 1899 the published rate was 13½ cents, and later 12 cents from the Mississippi River to New York. That was due to competition between carriers. That rate is to-day 18¼ cents.

In other words, while it was a few days ago 12 cents per hundred, on Monday of the current week it was increased to 18½ cents, which is an increase of more than 50 per cent.

The higher rate has been made possible by the combinations of lines between Chicago and the seaboard. The Pennsylvania has acquired the Baltimore and Ohio, the Norfolk and Western, the Chesapeake and Ohio, and lines north of the Pennsylvania have come mainly under the control of the New York Central and Mr. Morgan.

A year ago the published rate on grain from Chicago to New York was reduced from 16 cents to 13½ cents. At the same time the railroads agreed to charge a secret rate of 11 cents. April 14, 1902, the published rate was advanced from 13 cents to 16 cents.

The CHAIRMAN. That is the rebate.

Mr. CHADWICK. Secret rebates, of course. I do not know that I ought to say that it is always in the way of rebate.

The CHAIRMAN. That is the effect of it?

Mr. CHADWICK. That is your deduction.

This rate they must expect to maintain, for certain of the most important lines are under injunction to maintain the published rate. Apparently it is the intention to maintain a rate 5 cents higher this season than last season between Chicago and the seaboard.

When five or six men can sit down in New York and determine what the grain rate shall be from Kansas City to the Atlantic seaboard, from the Mississippi River to the Atlantic seaboard, and from the grain fields to St. Louis, Chicago, and Duluth, there is really no longer any competition in the transportation of grain, and that condition is practically here.

Senator KEAN. Is not that exactly what you are asking to have done?

Mr. CHADWICK. I will come to that later, Mr. Kean. I think it is better to state definitely what we do ask than to make deductions, so far as individual statements go, if that is agreeable to you.

Mr. KEAN. Certainly.

Mr. CHADWICK. To return to this matter about the railroads:

| | Miles. |
|---|---|
| The Vanderbilt system | 20,000 |
| Pennsylvania system | 18,000 |
| Gould system | 16,000 |
| Morgan-Hill (including Southern Railway, controlled by Mr. Morgan) | 37,000 |
| Harriman system | 17,000 |
| Total | 108,000 |

In the Harriman system I leave out all reference, for good reasons, to the Illinois Central.

The five combinations which are now independent and which have to-day 108,000 miles under the control of five men are:

IMPORTANT INDEPENDENT SYSTEMS.

| | Mileage. |
|---|---|
| Atchison, Topeka and Santa Fe | 7,481 |
| Chicago, Rock Island and Pacific | 3,818 |
| St. Louis and San Francisco | 2,887 |
| Colorado and Southern | 1,142 |
| Chicago, Milwaukee and St. Paul | 6,461 |
| Pere Marquette | 1,747 |
| Atlantic Coast Line | 2,177 |
| Seaboard Air Line | 2,600 |
| Plant System | 2,207 |
| New York, New Haven and Hartford | 2,038 |
| Boston and Maine | 3,338 |
| Total mileage | 35,896 |
| Illinois Central | 5,000 |

VANDERBILT SYSTEM.

| | Mileage. |
|---|---|
| New York Central System (including the main line, the Beech Creek, the Fall Brook, the Mohawk and Malone, the New York and Harlem, the Rome, Watertown and Ogdensburg, the West Shore, and many others) | 3,107 |
| Lake Shore and Michigan Southern | 2,084 |
| Michigan Central (including the Canadian Southern) | 1,635 |
| New York, Chicago and St. Louis (Nickel Plate) (including the Pittsburg and Lake Erie) | 523 |
| Chicago and Northwestern (including the Chicago, St. Paul, Minneapolis and Omaha, and the Fremont, Elkhorn and Missouri Valley) | 8,769 |
| Cleveland, Cincinnati, Chicago and St. Louis (Big Four) | 2,287 |
| Boston and Albany | 394 |
| Lake Erie and Western | 725 |
| Total mileage | 19,524 |

### PENNSYLVANIA SYSTEM.

|  | Mileage. |
|---|---|
| Pennsylvania R. R. (east of Pittsburg and Erie) (including the New Jersey lines, the Allegheny Valley R. R., the Philadelphia and Erie, the Northern Central, and many others) | 5,530 |
| Pennsylvania R. R. (west of Pittsburg and Erie) (including the Pennsylvania Company, the Peoria and Western, the St. Louis, Vandalia and Terre Haute, the Pittsburg, Chicago, Cincinnati, and St. Louis, the Cleveland, Akron and Columbus, the Grand Rapids and Indiana, and others) | 4,405 |
| Long Island | 391 |
| Baltimore and Ohio (including the Cleveland, Lorain and Wheeling, the Baltimore and Ohio Southwestern, and others) | 4,025 |
| Total | 14,351 |

### GOULD SYSTEM.

| | Mileage |
|---|---|
| Controlled by the Gould-Sage interests: | |
|   Missouri Pacific and Iron Mountain | 5,372 |
|   International and Great Northern | 891 |
|   Wabash (including the Wheeling and Lake Erie and the Omaha and St. Louis) | 2,968 |
|   St. Louis and Southwestern | 1,293 |
|   Texas and Pacific | 1,619 |
| Rockefeller and Gould interests: | |
|   Missouri, Kansas and Texas | 2,480 |
|   Denver and Rio Grande (including the Rio Grande Western) | 2,301 |
| Total mileage | 16,924 |

### MORGAN-HILL SYSTEM.

| | Mileage |
|---|---|
| Controlled jointly: | |
|   Northern Pacific (which owns 23,000,000 acres of land) | 5,487 |
|   Great Northern | 5,417 |
|   Chicago, Burlington and Quincy | 8,171 |
|   Erie | 2,605 |
|   Lehigh Valley | 2,178 |
| Controlled by Mr. Morgan: | |
|   Philadelphia and Reading (including the Central of New Jersey) | 1,677 |
|   Hocking Valley (including the Toledo and Ohio Central and the Kanawha and Michigan) | 882 |
|   Chicago, Indianapolis and Louisville | 546 |
|   Southern Railway (including the Central of Georgia, the Alabama Great Southern, the Cincinnati, New Orleans and Texas Pacific, and the Mobile and Ohio) | 10,627 |
| Total mileage | 37,590 |

### HARRIMAN SYSTEM.

| | Mileage |
|---|---|
| Union Pacific (including the Southern Pacific, the Oregon Railroad and Navigation Company, and the Oregon Short Line) | 15,163 |
| Chicago and Alton | 918 |
| Kansas City Southern | 873 |
| Total mileage | 16,954 |

It is true, it is forceful, for a man to sit down and look at this matter dispassionately. A man not interested in railroads and being put in possession of these facts would throw up his hands in holy horror. I really do not believe that those who have not studied the question thoroughly can realize it at all.

While the powers of the judiciary should not be conferred on the Commission, it may safely be granted the right to arbitrate.

We consider another provision absolutely essential to reasonably safeguard the interest of the public if this bill shall pass; namely, that as the Interstate Commerce Commission is composed of men who can have no personal interest in the matters brought before them under the provisions of this bill, the order of the Commission should stand, unless and until it be suspended or revoked by the circuit or other court or judge, as may be provided.

The powers of the Commission are now simply advisory.

For the first ten years the Commission exercised the power of revising rates, which proved quite satisfactory to the country.

The decisions of the Supreme Court about 1897 terminated that power. The consequences have been most serious during the succeeding five years. Of about 135 orders made by the Commission, I think that 68 of them dealt with unjust and unreasonable rates; and for the correction of such wrongs I have not been able to learn of a single instance where the remedy sought has been obtained.

If the Nelson bill is to become substantially the law, we earnestly hope and recommend that it be amended, so that any definite order made by the Commission, as provided in the bill as printed, shall be reviewable by but one particularly designated court of the United States, which shall have jurisdiction in all parts of the United States and Territories, or shall be reviewable by one particularly designated judge of some court of the United States, who shall have the same jurisdiction, for the reviewing and passing upon such orders, so that all causes which may be heard under the act may have the benefit of expert service of the highest order.

Is there any argument in that particular suggestion? Here is a board, the Interstate Commerce Commission; they and their agents are experts. A case is taken to them, they are expert in their judgment of the matter; that is, they apply to the case the results of all the researches and study they have given to former cases and decisions and to such new ones as are necessary, and they come to a decision based upon that expert investigation. The case is then thrown by appeal into the courts. It comes before good lawyers, true; before good judges, true; is argued by able attorneys, true. But it is to be considered by men who never before have had such a case before them and may never have another. They have to decide the case without previous experience in such cases. Whereas if the case were to be considered by experts all the way through, would not that be ideal? And when the ideal is obtainable why not have it?

The CHAIRMAN. Is it your idea that such cases should be taken before the courts of the District of Columbia, or some other court specially designated?

Mr. CHADWICK. They should go to some court somewhere. It might be a loafing court. It is for you to formulate these things. I think it is possibly one of the wisest suggestions that could possibly be made for your consideration, that if you are going to have these matters go ultimately to a court it should be a court that shall have, per se and de facto, expert knowledge. It must be so. It can not be otherwise than expert.

The railroads ask for protection against each other. Are they not willing that the public be granted similar protection against the railroads themselves? Why not?

My personal experience with railroad managers has led me to believe that individually they are the peers of any class in the Republic.

Evidence was recently made public showing the following state of affairs:

That Richardson of Chicago, operating grain elevators and doing a grain business on the Santa Fe system, and Hall & Robinson of Kansas City, operating in grain on the Missouri Pacific, partially in common territory, each received from their respective railroads a private, and to all intents and purposes a secret, rebate of 5 cents per hundred; and that the Santa Fe authorized and employed the Richardson concern to purchase the grain at certain stations, paying to them a stipulated commission of one-fourth of a cent per bushel for handling the grain for the account and risk of the Santa Fe, which thus departed apparently from its proper functions as a common carrier, and thereby instead of performing its duty as the servant of the public, became the competitor of those legitimately so trading, engrossing their business.

Why should they collectively take any different course than each would follow of his own volition individually?

I am not willing to concede that the tariff rates of freight on grain of late have been, or now are, too high, nor do I complain that the different railroads, even in this period of great commercial activity and admitted prosperity, are collecting more pay for their services than honestly may be defended as fair and reasonable; for surely profits may be had more easily and paid with better grace in prosperous than in pinching times.

A crying and annoying evil which works hardship in many cases, and seems to be indefensible, is the irregular, heterogeneous classification of freight; and in this day of organization and method it seems strange that it has not heretofore been regulated.

Whenever any bill is passed it should provide protection for the carrier and the public by making it a misdemeanor, punishable by an exemplary fine, for any person, acting either as principal or otherwise, to obtain transportation at less than tariff, by misrepresentation of classification, weight, character, or any other fraudulent means.

As stability of rates, when fair, is a great desideratum, the orders of the Interstate Commerce Commission should be continued in force and obeyed for two years from the time they become originally operative and observed.

Of course, you know the vexing delays that have occurred all along the line. You know that has been one of the reasons why no one tries to do anything now. How can a man with a small fortune bet it all as against a tremendous corporation loaded with millions and hundreds of millions?

The people are here again with a bill—those same people who have been here time and again—seeking relief from evils which are now undenied and undeniable. It may seem strange that they continue to come again and again, but as you well know, they have no other hope save in you—you who stand morally pledged to do the fair thing, the reasonable, the proper, the possible thing, the thing that is right for the whole community of interests—trade, producer, consumer, shipper, carrier.

Devices for evading the interstate-commerce law have been abundant in the past, and as fast as one is uncovered and corrected, wholly or in part, a new device has been found, and who can say when and where the end will be?

Probably you—each of you—know much more than I do about this question of the regulation of common carriers, and I do not doubt that you know that the abuses which exist ought to be abated, and that we ought to obtain from you at the earliest day possible a full measure of relief from discrimination.

I am not prepared to indorse any proposition to confer upon any commission whatever the power to primarily institute and make a "just and reasonable rate."

It seems, however, that it is entirely proper and right that the Commission may examine into all the conditions surrounding, pertaining to, affecting, or affected by any rates or practices which may be established by carriers, and if after a full hearing the Commission finds grounds on which they consider an order justifiable, then, as arbitrators, the order of the Commission should stand until and unless revoked by the court of review, for the making of the rate or the practice by the railroads is necessarily in the first instance ex parte and should not stand unless confirmed by the arbitrator, the Commission.

Relief from the evils of discrimination of every kind and degree, relief from the evils of unreasonably high rates, and to secure the benefits of uniform rates are what we intend to seek through the Nelson bill.

This is our charter to-day, and we think that the bill will accomplish the end sought, but if it will not accomplish that, show us how to amend it, so that justice may be done the public and the railroads alike, and you will confer an inestimable boon on millions who are affected by the matters under discussion.

I have the honor to represent before you the most important commercial organization of the world—an organization comprised of business men, merchants in and about Chicago and in all parts of the country, and also in those countries which are in close commercial touch with the United States.

The vessel and the railroad interests are strongly represented in our membership, as well as all the important banks and kindred interests.

We are in close touch with all the agricultural interests of the continent, and may fairly claim to know and reflect the crying needs of the people, and this we intend to do, and believe we are now doing.

Year in and year out for more than—think of the time the country has suffered!—more than thirty years, for the Chicago-Omaha pool was formed in 1870, and was grinding on like the car of Juggernaut in full vigor thirty years ago. The public has carried this Old Man of the Sea on its shoulders through a generation. This is no dream, for the vast volume of evidence given before the committees of Congress, before the Commission, before the courts, is perhaps so small in proportion to the amount that would be forthcoming should every man tell what he knew about railroad discriminations, as to constitute but an insignificant per cent of the whole; and yet what a mass of testimony has been printed upon these subjects!

Our prayer is before you. You are the only people who can assist us in this stage of the proceedings. You are the people on whom rests the responsibility for withholding from the people their rights and from granting the railroads the privileges which they deserve to enjoy. Few, if any, will complain that the people have not done their duty fully.

Two bills have been introduced in this session to amend the "Act to regulate commerce," and they are quite dissimilar in scope and in character.

I have been in hopes that some action would be taken whereby the members of the Interstate Commerce Commission would not be left subject to the political fortunes of party, but that their tenure of office would be certain and assured and their income comport with their position.

Give us the best courts possible, give Congress a fair bill, and practically what the railroads honestly know they need and what the public has a right to demand—reasonable safeguards; and, I am convinced, a large part of the present opposition will disappear, and I see now no good reason why the different interests should not come together, and, fairly safeguarding every interest, unite upon a fair, reasonable bill, and this we respectfully and earnestly petition you to do, and lift the traffic of the country out of the slough of despond in which you now see it.

In support of this statement I ask permission to file with this committee a document or report of the Interstate Commerce Commission printed in 1901 and denominated "In the matter of rates, facilities and practices applied in the transportation, handling, and storage of grain and grain products carried from western points to Atlantic seaboard and other Eastern destinations."

Senator KEAN. That is that Chicago case, is it?

The CHAIRMAN. Do you wish this document to go into the record, or is it accessible?

Senator TILLMAN. Is it a Government document?

Mr. CHADWICK. Yes.

The CHAIRMAN. Then we do not want to print it.

Mr. CHADWICK. I am going to put it in here if you will permit.

The CHAIRMAN. If it is a Government document and accessible, we do not need to reprint it.

Mr. CHADWICK. You can refer to it, of course.

The CHAIRMAN. Is it to be filled with your testimony?

Mr. CHADWICK. Yes.

Senator TILLMAN. I suggest to Mr. Chadwick that he will better accomplish his purpose if he will designate in specific terms just what portion of the document he refers to, so that anyone, in the extreme pressure of work here, can get it at once.

Senator KEAN. It is page 279.

Senator TILLMAN. Mr. Chadwick has not said anything about page 279. I suggest to him to designate what portion of that document bears out the statement he made a few moments ago.

Mr. CHADWICK. You get this matter on page 279.

The CHAIRMAN. You say the matter you refer to appears on page 279 in the document mentioned, and let that go in your testimony.

Mr. CHADWICK. If you so instruct me.

The CHAIRMAN. I make that suggestion, thinking it will reach what Senator Tillman wants.

Mr. CHADWICK. I shall finish in a moment.

This seems to me one of the most flagrant of all the numerous instances of wrongdoing on the part of the railroad fraternity which recently has come to my attention.

It seems to me that if we do not promptly enact a law which will not only check but abate such practices by the common carriers, we may expect them to encroach more and more on the province of the legitimate merchant in all directions, which can not fail to lead to and produce most deplorable results.

What will happen if the railroads go on and engross the business of the lumbermen, the iron dealer, the miller, the merchant, and so on, as they, in the instance cited, have treated the grain men in the territory named? What can the answer be but anarchy?

Now, Senator Tillman, I am at your disposal.

Senator TILLMAN. What I wanted was to have you designate specifically, so that it would be of easy reference to any Senator who may send for the document if this matter should come up in the Senate for consideration. If you understood the immense pressure that is on even the laziest of us here to try to keep in touch with what is going on, you would understand the value of such specific statements and references to data that can be secured in a moment. It will not do to proceed upon the assumption that men will read it, for they will not. But I want you to specify in as condensed shape as possible just what portion of that document bears out the statement you have just made as to the Santa Fe going into the grain business and hiring agents to monopolize the grain trade on the line of its road.

The CHAIRMAN. How recently was that? What year?

Mr. CHADWICK. It was recent enough. It is hard to find, because these hearings are printed without any proper heading or reference.

Senator TILLMAN. I suggest that we allow the stenographer to put it in when Mr. Chadwick finds it.

Mr. CHADWICK. I will try to help you. It was notably the testimony of one Robinson, of the firm of Ball & Robinson, and of Paul Morton, vice-president of the Atchison, Topeka and Santa Fe.

The CHAIRMAN. What year was that?

Mr. CHADWICK. Perhaps it was last year.

The CHAIRMAN. It must have been last fall.

Mr. CHADWICK. I see the date here "Washington, January 9" for one of them.

The CHAIRMAN. Last year was when it happened, I think. May I suggest that you fix this with the stenographer to give this data as Senator Tillman suggests. Is that all you have to submit?

Mr. CHADWICK. Yes, unless I am asked questions.

The CHAIRMAN. Does any member of the committee desire to ask any questions?

Senator TILLMAN. I did not hear all of Mr. Chadwick's statement or evidence or argument. I would like to ask him whether he thinks that the business interests of the country could stand a pooling arrangement among railroads? He may have answered that question in his statement, but I want to know specifically. One of these bills provides for pooling, subject to ratification by the Interstate Commence Commission. I want his opinion or that of those whom he represents as to that matter.

Mr. CHADWICK. I will say in reply to the question of the Senator that it is generally understood that railroad men are better able to understand all the elements involved in the law granting to the Commission the power to make rates; that railroad men are probably better experts to judge of what are proper rates, and therefore railroad men feel as they say they do, and consequently seek a bill providing for pooling by the railroads. If we once admit that they are the best judges in this matter, it seems to me, if you heard the premise that the railroad people are so——

Senator TILLMAN. So expert and honest?

Mr. CHADWICK. No; but so free from suggestion of self-seeking that they are really and truly experts, experts who will do justice in any case that comes before them, then your question is answered.

On the other hand, while the people are complaining against railroad practices, the railroads themselves have their own troubles, and one special feature before this Congress is the production of a bill to protect the railroads against each other. This confession—for it seems to be such—should appeal to the honest man in whatever walk of life, and should influence him to urge speedy action for the solution of the problem.

As pooling was practiced in the past it seemed to make rates unduly high and onerous. One great desideratum with us is uniform rates. We seek to escape discrimination. That is the greatest evil, as we consider. The great desideratum is to have uniform and steady rates, rates that are not changed by mere whim, but when made shall be made on some proper basis, and not as in the old pooling times, when the railroads skinned each other.

Instead of having pooling based on net earnings, we think pooling should be based on other considerations, namely, that they should take into consideration the equipment and the opportunities of earning money. They should take into consideration whether the equipment has been allowed to deteriorate, because I take it if the spirit of emulation is removed—which, of course, is a good spirit, needing only to be properly safeguarded—we shall have a drop, and equipment and service will deteriorate. I never heard anyone suggest that it would not, if let alone.

Pooling, pure and simple, would be something, of course, that would be a disgrace to the country, and not up to the times. So, when you ask me that question, I would answer by asking you another, seeking to get light before I give an answer: Would not pooling tend to stifle competition and lead to deterioration in service and equipment? If the spirit of emulation be removed, will not the whole railroad service deteriorate in all these features and become inadequate to the needs of the country? Could not the individual lines evade their responsibilities?

Senator TILLMAN. Are you through with your question?

Mr. CHADWICK. No; I want to answer your question, Senator, honestly, if you want me to. You do not want to cut me off, do you?

Senator TILLMAN. Not at all.

Mr. CHADWICK. The Board of Trade of the city of Chicago represents a great number of people—has a tremendous clientele. Representing that great number of people, they are in favor of having relief. We pray for relief. We want relief. But we want all conditions safeguarded on both sides of this controversy—I take it that it is called a controversy. We want everything safeguarded fairly. If there is any person living who can formulate the terms under which pooling can be permitted I wish that person would give you the benefit of his suggestions. There is nothing wicked, per se, in pooling. The wickedness in any of these things is the result to the person who is outside of the control and also outside of the benefits of the pool. The railroads have heretofore had vast benefits from pools, but the people have suffered.

If there is such deterioration of service and equipment, can all be cared for under a pooling bill? What difference does it make? Everybody is served alike. It is the very thing we ask for. If we have good service under proper conditions the railroads will not become a laughing stock, but will be as they are now, a thing in which we take great pride.

It seems to me that the people have suffered so long that we can not do otherwise than to take the best we can get. But we ought to insist upon having the best obtainable. Therefore, Governor Tillman, I will say that in the matter of pooling I am on the fence. I do not care a fig if we do have pooling, provided it is surrounded with proper safeguards. My people do not care, and the people at large do not care. You did not hear the first of my statement.

Senator TILLMAN. No.

Mr. CHADWICK. I wish you had, because I showed the horrors of the pooling arrangements in the West and Southwest, and I think I gave a very fair statement in regard to it; don't you, Mr. Chairman?

The CHAIRMAN. Yes.

Senator TILLMAN. Now, can I ask a question?

Mr. CHADWICK. Certainly.

Senator TILLMAN. In asking your questions a moment ago you said your answers were given in some measure by interrogatories?

Mr. CHADWICK. I was merely endeavoring to attract your attention to the point.

Senator TILLMAN. Then, instead of making a direct statement, with your opinion, you merely asked some questions, from which you drew deductions. Those deductions, to my mind, seemed to show that you were in favor of pooling, provided it should be safe-guarded by impossible conditions. In other words, you do not regard it as possible, do you, that human nature will lose its selfishness or that unlimited power will ever restrain itself so as to protect the masses against monopoly? Did I understand you correctly?

Mr. CHADWICK. I certainly would not have the safe-guards against pooling tied with a rope of sand.

Senator TILLMAN. What I was after was to get your opinion, as a business man representing business men, as to the feasibility, the practicability, the desirability, of some compromise arrangement, if that be possible, that would give relief from the present unbearable conditions, and at the same time not jeopardize the great interests of transportation. I do not think any reasonable person wants to ruin the railroads or unduly to hamper them or destroy their profit-earning capacity. The real question, after all, is to give the business interests of the country proper transportation facilities, to guard against discriminations, and you want a uniform, steady, and just rate—the justice being the most essential of those three features of the rate. You do not want any secret rebate given to competitors who are getting advantages from the railroads. Those are the elements.

Mr. CHADWICK. Certainly.

Senator TILLMAN. Do you believe that human nature can stand the strain of being allowed a rope and not using it? In other words, if you give the railroads the power to pool, if you do not hold the club over their heads by some statutory provision, will they not abuse it?

Mr. CHADWICK. The real thought that is in my mind, Governor, and which has crystallized itself from all the conferences in which I have participated, is that another bill should be drawn and perhaps adopted as a substitute by the committee for both these bills.     I am chairman of the transportation committee of the Chicago Board of Trade, and all these matters come under my administration.     I go before our local body there, the board of railroad and warehouse commissioners, and I am pretty well versed in all these things pertaining to transportation, as well versed as many laymen; and I know that if a proper bill is drawn, and honestly drawn, that will do all it pretends to do—which the original bill did not, because it was deftly drawn, in my opinion—then that bill ought to be submitted to this committee.

Now, I say if an honest bill is drawn, by honest men, and submitted to a jury of their peers, and subjected to scrutiny on the floor of the Senate and of the House, and then if you will have another meeting of the committee while it is under your consideration, so that people can come here and criticize it and tell you where the loopholes are, it is my belief that you can get a bill which will better serve your purposes than these bills.     But if you Senators try to deal with this question on the floor of the Senate with only such information as is brought before the committee without dispute, then the case is hopeless, and must be.     I wish to say to you now that what I have said, if you will permit me, by way of a partial answer to the questions that have been asked me, is exemplified by the testimony of Mr. Counselman, of Chicago, a brainy millionaire broker, a broad man, who knows all about this subject, as printed in Senate Document 39, Fifty-fifth Congress, first session.     Mr. Foraker presented the report to the Senate, and it was ordered to be printed April 15, 1897.     He testifies here——

The CHAIRMAN. Give us a reference to the page, if you please.

Mr. CHADWICK. He testifies on page 25 as follows:

Senator CHANDLER. Do I understand Mr. Counselman, as a shipper of grain, to say that the reduction of rates from Chicago to New York made last fall, which Mr. Blanchard has described, was an injury to the people of the United States?

Mr. COUNSELMAN. I believe that the reduction made in the way it was, day by day, rapid as it was, was an injury to the people of the whole Western country.     I do not know whether it was an injury to the consumer.     He got some benefit from it.

Senator CHANDLER. But to the producer you think it was an injury?

Mr. COUNSELMAN. Yes, sir.

Senator CHANDLER. Please explain that a little more fully.

Mr. COUNSELMAN. As the rates went down the prices at the seaboard declined. We therefore had to make our buying price accordingly as the rate went down.

Senator CHANDLER. Did that reduction grow out of the manipulation of the market?

Mr. COUNSELMAN. No; but of the rates.

Senator CHANDLER. It did not necessarily or logically grow out of the reduction of rates?

Mr. COUNSELMAN. Necessarily, and, I think, logically.

Senator CHANDLER. Logically the reduction of freight rates from Chicago to New York is an injury to the farmer who produces the corn?

Mr. COUNSELMAN. In this way: We will say 25 cents is the market price, and that there is a reduction of 5 cents a hundred, if you choose.     You reduce that rate 5 cents per hundred and he can reduce his price 2.80 per bushel, because you can get corn in Chicago and ship it to New York for 5 cents per 100 pounds less than he used to, or 2.80 per bushel less.     "I am not going to pay 40 cents when I can get it for 2.80 less," he says.     The rate from the West to Chicago is not changed in this trouble.     It is the same.     How is the Chicago shipper to protect himself unless he buys that grain just in proportion as the eastern rate is reduced?

Senator CHANDLER. It seems to me to be a paradox—I may be able to work it out— that the reduction of rates from Chicago to New York hurts the producer, the farmer.

Mr. COUNSELMAN. Just remember in your reflections on the subject, and it may not appear so paradoxical, that the freight rate from the West to Chicago is undisturbed, and that the disturbance in this instance was from Chicago East. It cost just as much to get the grain to Chicago, but the rate was reduced from Chicago eastward. Therefore, way back West we look finally where we are going to land, as the Chicago price is reduced in proportion to the reduction in freight eastward.

Senator CHANDLER. If the rate from Chicago to New York were suddenly put up from 25 cents to 30 cents the farmer would gain?

Mr. COUNSELMAN. He would.

Senator CHANDLER. He would get a higher price for his product?

Mr. COUNSELMAN. Yes, sir. The freight makes the price at the seaboard.

The purport of that testimony is that an advance in the rate of freight is a benefit to the farmer. That does not require any argument at my hand, does it?

Senator TILLMAN. Is it not so absurd on its face that nobody would swallow it?

Mr. CHADWICK. I am only showing what comes before committees, and that when such testimony comes to be considered on the floor of the Senate or the House, upon the strength of which you make such and such assertions, I think you will then see that you have not secured the evidence you ought to have. If you are going to try to amend any of these bills now pending, I think you should have the proper kind of testimony before your report is made to the Senate. In order to secure this testimony you should allow the people to appear before you and criticize the proposed amendments and the bill as a whole.

Senator CLAPP. I think you have struck a practical keynote. There are two bills here, one of which provides for pooling. Have you examined that?

Mr. CHADWICK. Yes.

Senator CLAPP. If there could be a proper provision made for pooling which you would indorse, what suggestion have you to make as to the improvement of that provision?

Mr. CHADWICK. I could not answer you offhand in this way.

Senator CLAPP. But you say that we ought to get the opinions of people as to the defects of the bills. That is what we want, as I understand.

Mr. CHADWICK. But being called upon suddenly I can not give an offhand opinion that would be of value.

Senator CLAPP. We do not ask it offhand. Take that bill and study it, and give us your views.

Senator TILLMAN. That bill has not been reported to the Senate yet, and therefore it is not a matter that would meet his requirements.

Senator CLAPP. It is a tentative proposition upon which we should have the opinions of just such men as Mr. Chadwick. First, is it advisable to admit pooling under all circumstances? If so, then does this bill properly safeguard it? I would like his suggestions.

Senator TILLMAN. I want an answer from anybody who can give it.

The CHAIRMAN. Mr. Chadwick is a very intelligent gentleman. He has read the pooling clause of what is known as the Elkins bill, and I will state to Mr. Chadwick, as I have stated before, that I propose to make that as strong as it can be made by the help of intelligent men, leaving it within the power and jurisdiction of the Interstate Commerce Commission to approve or to disapprove in whole or in part of any pooling contract, agreement, or arrangement between railroads, this action to be taken by the Commission before such pooling arrangement shall become effective, so that no pooling agreement can go into effect without the consent of the Commission. Section 2 of that bill is strong as it stands, but I will state that I have on my table a proposed amendment which will make it still stronger. That proposed amendment I shall submit to the committee, and when we come to its consideration we shall be glad to have the testimony of so intelligent a witness as Mr. Chadwick, who has evidently given the subject much thought. The question has been put by Senator Clapp and Senator Tillman in the best possible way: First, is it desirable? secondly, if so, what would you suggest? The law says the railroads must fix freight rates and publish them. The Supreme Court of the United States says that the railroads shall not make agreements as to rates, because that would be a violation of the Sherman Act. The railroads must be given some latitude, but how are they to make any agreement fixing rates? As it is, three or four railroad men are afraid now to get together in a room.

Mr. CHADWICK. The last utterances of the legislature would control, would they not?

The CHAIRMAN. Of Congress, you mean?

Mr. CHADWICK. Yes; any legislative body. The last utterances of any legislative body control. Is not that a principle of law?

The CHAIRMAN. Until something else is enacted.

Mr. CHADWICK. That controls, I say.

Senator CLAPP. There is no question about that.

Mr. CHADWICK. The last utterance of Congress on this subject, I think, was the Sherman antitrust law, and your bill might deal with that in plain English. But that law was drawn with great care, and it might seem presumptuous for a layman to make any suggestion in regard to your action in reference to that law.

Senator CLAPP. Do not understand us as expecting you to commit yourself offhand to anything in this bill.

Mr. CHADWICK. If it be the pleasure of the committee, I will appear before it at a later day, after I shall have had more time to think about this.

Senator CLAPP. But you said that the proper way to deal with this is for a bill to be prepared, and then let men who are familiar with the subject come before us and point out its defects.

Mr. CHADWICK. Yes.

Senator CLAPP. For one, I will say that I should like to have men of experience, like yourself, point out the defects of these bills and suggest improvements; and I think the committee agrees with me in that.

The CHAIRMAN. Certainly I do.

Senator TILLMAN. If I may be permitted, some of those gentlemen who were here yesterday appeared to me, while stating their grievances, to be liberal in their desire to safeguard the railroads. I make the suggestion that it might facilitate our work as a committee if these various boards of trade and chambers of commerce, through their representatives, would take these two bills as a basis, and from them prepare a bill; then after they have exhausted their ingenuity, ability, and experience in fixing up what they want, let us have a hearing from the railroads to show us wherein their opponents are wrong. I am willing to work a reasonable amount of time two or three days in a week at hearings of an hour or two each day. If we should request that, and ask them to act promptly in taking up these two bills as a basis for the preparation of another bill, I think something practical might result. The railroad people would in that way have a chance to show us wherein these merchants and business men are trying to tamper with, injure, or destroy the railroad interests by this proposed legislation. Then we would get into a practical situation, from which could possibly be evolved some valuable legislation.

Senator CLAPP. I want to make an additional suggestion, Mr. Chairman, and which I can not help but think would be a better one. If these gentlemen should formulate a bill it would necessarily be, as between themselves, a compromise, and the views of the different men, which might be of great value to the committee, would be lost so far as they were swallowed up in the compromise bill. Now, my idea would be for these men to take these bills, which are purely tentative; Mr. Chadwick may have one view, and some one else may have another. I say, let these men get together and present their views on these distinct propositions, and then let us have the benefit of the views that they entertain, which would otherwise be lost in a compromise bill from them.

The CHAIRMAN. That is a very good suggestion.

Mr. CHADWICK. I will say that we have been over these bills time and again; we have discussed them line upon line and precept upon precept. But it would be unfair to ask me to get up here and state a definite conclusion without time for consideration, and if I did so perhaps it would not be heard. A bill of this character should have the most careful consideration and scrunity—every word of it. I will state to the committee that I expect to leave the city this afternoon for New York State, and on Monday I expect to be in Baltimore, on this business. Quite recently I have interviewed some of the greatest men in the country; the last man I left was Mr. MacVeagh, yesterday, I think. We are working along on the lines not for compromise. The people will never compromise a hair in this matter. We will fight to the last gasp but what we will have the law properly safeguarded this time. The only place where we can not be heard is when you get into action. That is the time when the men who are in the ranks are set aside, and the journals get together and fight it out among themselves; but they do not know what they are about, and that is the great trouble.

Senator FOSTER. Let me make a suggestion: Here are two bills before the committee now, both more in a tentative shape than otherwise. The principal object of these hearings is to get views and opinions as to the merits and demerits of these bills. Then the committee, after hearing parties favorable to or opposed to these measures, will probably shape the bill to be reported to the Senate.

Mr. CHADWICK. Here is where it ought to be done.

Senator FOSTER. We have heard your evidence and the evidence of others for and against the propositions. When the bill shall be presented to the Senate those favoring or opposing the bill will be armed with full information of all the facts that you gentlemen can give to us. That is what we are trying to reach now.

The CHAIRMAN. I suggest that when you return next week or the week following, Mr. Chadwick, you appear again and give us the result of your conferences.

Senator FOSTER. The suggestion of Senator Clapp strikes me as preeminently practical, that you gentlemen take these two bills, examine them thoroughly, analyze every provision in both of them, and then come before the committee to-morrow, or next day, or next week.

Mr. CHADWICK. How do we know when we can get before the committee?

The CHAIRMAN. I will let you know.

Mr. CHADWICK. We will do what you want us to. But here is the point. You are now hearing one side of the case. Heretofore there has been delay by the railroad people putting things off forever and a day. If you will fix a day when both sides can be heard then we shall all be on a fair footing. But there is no use for us to try to patch up bills, and then have the railroad people come in here and deftly suggest some law that will have the effect of skinning us alive.

The CHAIRMAN. Do you not think it would be fair to suggest, for our guidance, just what you think would be a proper remedy?

Mr. CHADWICK. Why in the meantime can you not hear the railroad people, and get the thing to a focus?

Senator TILLMAN. I will tell you why: The railroads do not want anything; they are not taking steps to facilitate legislation; they are obstructing that, so far as I can understand the situation, and they will never move until you have lined up in battle array and moved forward to give battle.

Mr. CHADWICK. The point I am trying to make, Governor Tillman, is that the railroads shall not be heard except purely in rebuttal; then if they do not come in here and take a stand, they will be out of the fight. Set a day beyond which they shall not come in, and give them plenty of time and opportunity.

The CHAIRMAN. We are going to hear the railroad people, and I hope you will find it consistent to act upon the suggestion of these Senators, and perhaps come in here next week with your suggestions embodied in a paper, so as to be able to say to us that if you were drawing the bill you would make it that way, or suggest this amendment or that provision. We will hear you with pleasure. I will call a special meeting for that purpose. You shall not go without a hearing and you shall be facilitated.

Senator FOSTER. Please impress upon Mr. Chadwick, Mr. Chairman, the advisability and importance of his people discussing among themselves and suggesting legislation or no legislation upon this question of pooling.

Senator TILLMAN. Pooling, on the one hand, with its benefits to the railroads, and, on the other, giving the Interstate Commerce Commission the power to fix rates to go into effect immediately and stay in effect until reversed. Those are the two issues.

Senator FOSTER. Those are the two preliminary issues before the committee.

APRIL 18, 1902.

Senator ELKINS, *Chairman.*

SIR: As I am obliged to go to Chicago to-day, may I ask you to kindly permit the following suggestions to go to the Committee on Interstate Commerce:

The rate, or relation of rates, being fixed primarily by the carrier, is, therefore, ex parte.

Objection being raised by any party in interest, both sides are heard by the Commission, which, acting as arbitrator in the hearing, determines what is proper and necessary to correct any wrong which may be found to exist, and issues an order as provided.

An appeal may be taken from the decision of the Commission.

Thus far the question has been treated by experts—carrier, shipper, Commission.

That all the proceedings may continue to enjoy the benefits of expert treatment, why may not the Attorney-General of the United States be vested with power to name any three judges of the United States district courts to constitute a special court with jurisdiction in all the States and Territories to review all causes which may arise under the provisions of the act to regulate commerce, and to administer all receiverships, etc., in common carrier causes?

From the findings of such court appeal to be only to the Supreme Court.

The creation of the court of appeals since the act to regulate commerce became a law has increased considerably the time and expense of reaching the final decision.

England, through the Parliament, has created a court composed of one judge, one railroad man, and one business man.

The findings of that court are, I understand, conclusive except on questions of law. They make the rates, which, however, are commonly said to be very high on freights.

They provide that there shall be no discrimination between parties and places.

If this country forms some such court as I have suggested to administer railroad receiverships the effect would seem to be beneficial to vested interests.

The bankrupt road could not be used as a club, as formerly, to distress solvent and prosperous roads who would have to pay interest, dividends, etc.

I hope I have been able to partly outline this subject and regret having to annoy you with so much manuscript.

I am, sir, with high respect, your obedient servant,

WM. H. CHADWICK,
*Chairman Transportation Committee, Board of Trade of Chicago.*

## STATEMENT OF T. W. TOMLINSON.

The CHAIRMAN. Please state whom you represent here.

Mr. TOMLINSON. I am the railway representative of the Chicago Live Stock Exchange. I have the honor to represent not only that exchange, but the Cattle Raising Association of Texas, and cojointly with Judge Springer I have also the honor to represent the National Live Stock Association. That association comprehends practically all the live stock associations in this country, and I believe you can safely say that I represent the live stock industry of this country—a very poor representative it is true, but at least I have that honor.

The CHAIRMAN. We shall be glad to hear you. There are just two points here that give us concern, and we must settle them. Can you give us light on the point of giving power to the Interstate Commerce Commission to change rates and the power to pool under proper restriction?

Mr. TOMLINSON. The live stock industry objects to any pooling bill. The railroads indorse that, and want pooling for no other purpose than to increase their rates. We believe that in the aggregate the earnings of the railroads to-day give them a very fair return upon their investment. We will not indorse any machinery that will enable them to extract any more money without some absolute assurance that if they get more of this competitive traffic affected by the pool that additional traffic will be handled at lesser rates.

As to the making of the orders of the Interstate Commerce Commission effective immediately, the bill which we indorse, the Nelson bill, gives, as I read it, fifty days practically for the court to pass upon the order of the Commission. We think that is ample and long enough. The bill of your honorable chairman recognizes at least that the rates of the Commission ought to be in effect a year. As a matter of fact, if you can not get some immediate results from the order of the Commission the conditions will doubtless change in the course of a year so that it will be of no benefit to anybody at the end of that time.

Further than that, you must always bear in mind that there are many people interested in rates other than those who actually pay the freight. In other words, the producer and consumer may be indirectly affected, and yet not be the ones who actually pay the freight. Hence those people would have no redress in a court from unreasonable charges.

We are certain of our position on those two points. I trust I have made it plain to you, and I shall now be very glad to answer any questions.

Senator TILLMAN. You are very strenuous in your statement. The matter has gone beyond a plea, as I understand, for action by Congress in restraint of the condition of confusion worse confounded in which the roads are left practically free to do as they please.

Mr. TOMLINSON. Yes; that is the condition. The situation has been very serious. There have been very portentious changes in the railroad situation, but every change has been such as to strengthen their grasp upon the country. There used to be competition, but that is now a word almost without meaning as regards the railroad transportation facilities of the country. It is a very, very serious matter. The public should be safeguarded better than is even provided in the Nelson bill. While we indorse the Nelson bill, I feel personally that legislation ought to go farther.

Senator CLAPP. What would you suggest in addition to the Nelson bill?

Mr. TOMLINSON. I do not know that I could suggest anything except to make the decision of the Commission absolutely final.

Senator CLAPP. Without appeal to the courts?

Mr. TOMLINSON. Yes. I do not know why we can not rely upon the Commission as well as upon the courts. If the members of that Commission are not to be relied upon, they ought not to be there.

Senator CLAPP. Have you ever thought of the proposition that an action which involves property rights must have its day in court somewhere?

Mr. TOMLINSON. Yes. I have thought the matter over very carefully, and I am quite satisfied in my own mind that the interests of the entire country would be just as well safeguarded by having the Commission's decision final.

Senator CLAPP. I think you do not understand my question, which was as to the validity of a law which affects property rights without giving the parties their day in court.

Mr. TOMLINSON. I assume that they fully have their day in court when they appear before the Commission.

Senator TILLMAN. In other words, Mr. Tomlinson, you consider that as the court itself is an appointive one, created by the President with the consent of the Senate, the Interstate Commerce Commission, getting its authority from the same source, backed by act of Congress, ought to be fully as able to render a final decision as a court devoted to ordinary legal matters?

Mr. TOMLINSON. You have stated my view practically.

Senator CLAPP. That is not the question. The question I asked is whether, under our Constitution, we can delegate authority to a tribunal to make an order which affects property rights without giving the owners an opportunity to appeal to the courts. Have you ever given that point consideration?

Mr. TOMLINSON. I do not believe I can make any further answer than I did a moment ago. I am not a lawyer and I have not paid very much attention to it from a legal standpoint. I am only expressing my views as to the equity and fairness of the matter as they occur to me.

The CHAIRMAN. In expressing your views about pooling, do you express the views of all the parties you represent?

Mr. TOMLINSON. Yes.

The CHAIRMAN. They have had that matter under consideration?

Mr. TOMLINSON. They have.

The CHAIRMAN. And authorized you to make this statement?

Mr. TOMLINSON, Yes.

Senator CLAPP. That is, the statement that there should be no appeal from the order of the Commission?

Mr. TOMLINSON. That there should be no appeal?

Senator CLAPP. That is what the chairman meant.

Senator TILLMAN. No. He was speaking of pooling. He said he was not entirely satisfied with the Nelson bill; that he thought it did not go far enough; and that personally he was in favor of going to the point of leaving no appeal.

Senator CLAPP. I understood the chairman's question to go to that point, but he did not so understand it.

The CHAIRMAN. It covered both points.

Mr. TOMLINSON. The association which I have the honor to represent indorses and supports the Nelson bill.

Senator TILLMAN. And that gives the right of appeal.

Mr. TOMLINSON. Mr. Chairman, before I leave the stand I wish to say that Mr. Barry asked me in his absence to file with you a petition from merchants, members of the Baltimore Chamber of Commerce, in support of this Nelson bill, and with your permission I will file it for the purpose of having it appear in the record.

The CHAIRMAN. Very well.

The petition referred to is as follows:

BALTIMORE, MD., *April 1, 1902.*

The INTERSTATE COMMERCE COMMITTEE OF THE HOUSE OF REPRESENTATIVES,
*Washington, D. C.*

GENTLEMEN: The undersigned merchants, members of the chamber of commerce, Baltimore, respectfully petition your honorable body to favor the adoption of the interstate commerce legislation now before you, embodied in a bill known as H. R. 8337, amending the interstate commerce law and giving it authority and force.

It is plain to all men that a few more years of discrimination and favoritism on the part of the railroads in the interest of the few shippers as against the many, will make business, except for the very wealthy, an impossibility. Already we have seen our fellow-merchant shrivel up and drop out by the wayside, ourselves have suffered and must in turn be driven from the marts of trade, if this unfair favoritism is continued. All we ask is a fair field and no favor, and this we hope is found in H. R. 8337, which we pray you will speedily enact into law.

W. G. Bishop & Co., George Frame, James J. Comer & Co., W. M. Knight, Frank Kraft, H. A. Lederer, H. C. Wright, The Baltimore Pearl Hominy Co., H. D. Eidman & Bro., J. A. Loane & Co., Andrew W. Woodall, C. Bosley Littig & Co., John R. Hudgens & Co., I. K. B. Emory & Co., Dudley & Carpenter, Edelen Bros., Wm. G. Scarlett & Co., C. S. Schermerhorn, Robert Marye, John S. Smith & Co., Geo. P. Williar & Son, Pitt Bros. Co., John S. Hayes & Co., Frank Mudge, W. Rühl & Sons, W. A. Simpson & Co., D. C. Timanus & Bro., Frank M. Cline & Co., J. H. Sherbert, F. Megenhardt, Rich'd S. Wells, Saml. J. Diggs & Son, J. A. Manger & Co., John C. Legg & Co., Wm. Simpson, R. L. Burwell, J. Oliver Neal, J. H. Maynadier, Robinson & Jackson, James Lake, J. M. Wharton, Loney & Co., James J. Swaine, Wm. H. Spedden & Bro., Thos. M. Dinsmore & Co., Daniel Rider, Seaton Bros. & Co., H. S. Belt, O'Neill & Co., Charles C. Gorsch, Jas. T. Clendenin, Chas. England & Co., S. M. Lyell & Co., Jos. T. Flautt, sr., Fahey & Ryley, Chas. H. Gibbs, Stagle & Myers, C. B. Watkins, Hilldorfer & Schuchhardt, E. Stern & Bro., E. B. Owens & Co.

Senator CLAPP.    Is this Judge Springer you speak of, ex-Congress-man Springer?

Mr. TOMLINSON.  Yes.

Senator CLAPP.  He was also a judge in Oklahoma Territory; is that the man?

Mr. TOMLINSON.  Yes.  I said that cojointly with him I have the honor to represent the National Livestock Association, whose headquarters are in Denver.

Senator TILLMAN.  I should like to ask you, if you are willing to express an opinion offhand, as to what effect the Nelson bill, for instance, would have in giving protection to the shippers, provided that the railroad consolidation has been effected, such as we were told this week had taken place, and we do not know but that it is true, by which every road from here to Texas, south of the Potomac and Ohio rivers, comes under one management.  Would not that be a railroad pool that would practically leave the roads in absolute possession of the field, and we should have no protection whatever unless Congress specifically regulates the rates?

Mr. TOMLINSON.  With the passage of the Nelson bill, the public would be at least assured of a tribunal who would have the power, after hearing, to say what was a reasonable rate.  No tribunal has that power now.

Senator TILLMAN.  Then you think that it is absolutely essential to the business interests of the country that Congress should do something by way of protection against this absorption or consolidation of the roads which tends toward making all roads practically one road throughout the United States?

Mr. TOMLINSON.  I think that is absolutely necessary.

### STATEMENT OF JOHN D. KERNAN.

The CHAIRMAN.  Please state your name, business or occupation, and whom you represent.

Mr. KERNAN.  My name is John D. Kernan; my office is at 39 Liberty street, New York City.  I appear here as counsel for the New York Produce Exchange.

The CHAIRMAN.  Proceed with your statement.  We shall be very glad to hear you.

Mr. KERNAN.  You know this subject is one to which a man may devote a good deal of his time, day and night, and then feel that he has not very greatly succeeded; but I shall endeavor to be brief.

I am here to say that since the passage of the interstate-commerce act I have given much thought and study to the operations of that law. I was the first chairman of the New York State railroad commission, serving in that capacity from 1873 to 1877, when I resigned.  Since then I have been engaged in a great many cases brought before the Interstate Commerce Commission, representing the produce exchange and others, and that duty has led me to give thought, study, and investigation to the question.

We think that the Nelson-Corliss bill, with some amendments and perhaps additions, is one that meets the recognized necessities of the situation, that something should be done.  If the interstate-commerce law is to be continued as the policy of the Government for the purpose of regulating the relations between the carriers and the people, something must be done to increase the efficiency of the orders made by the Commission after investigation, and to facilitate and hasten the remedy when rates are found to be unjust and unreasonable.

I may say at the outset that I think you will find 99 per cent of the complaints made before the Commission since its organization have not been upon the subject of the rates being too high. I do not think to-day that that is of any material importance. While there was an increase in rates of 35 per cent on the 1st of January, 1900, yet that was no more, I thought, than the increase ought to be in fairness, in view of the long period of disaster through which the railroads had passed and the reduction of rates that had occurred during that period. It is not the matter of high rates. The difficulty we have got to think about and the difficulty that this bill needs to remedy is the relation of rates to the competition between business men. I do not care whether the rate from New York City to Chicago on my freight is 50 cents per hundred, 60 cents, or 75 cents. But I do very much care that upon my freight reaching my customer in Chicago the relation of my competitors' rights to mine shall be relatively fair, that one man shall have no more advantage in Chicago than I have.

This can only be secured by a body having the power to take in hand the actual situation and investigate in reference to it. The remedies proposed by this individual man or that individual man have ceased to be of use, as applied to this situation, where the great question between all the manufacturers and business men of the country is not as to just how much they pay, but that their relations to their competitors in reaching common markets shall all be fair and just.

I must first say that that bill, with some additions, would, in my opinion, be all right. In the first place, the most important amendment to be suggested, to my mind, is that on page 6.

The filing of a petition to review an order shall of itself suspend the effect of such order for thirty days.

I think that ought to be sixty days.

And the court before which the same is pending may also, if upon an inspection of the record it plainly appears that the order proceeds upon some error of law, or is unjust and unreasonable upon the facts, and not otherwise, suspend the operation of the order during the pendency of the proceedings in review, or until the further order of the court.

These words ought also to be stricken out—they have no business in the law—from the word "also" down to the word "suspend;" so that if both these amendments be adopted, it will read:

The filing of a petition to review an order shall of itself suspend the effect of such order for sixty days, and the court before which the same is pending may suspend the operation of the order during the pendency of the proceedings in review, or until the further order of the court, etc.

You can not undertake to break down the jurisdiction of the courts of the United States in that way. A railroad comes before the court and says, "Here is an order of the Interstate Commerce Commission that is unjust; we want to appeal; we want a stay pending appeal." The court says, "Under the ordinary equity jurisdiction of a United States court you should present a case where it is justifiable for us to suspend the operation of an order pending appeal; but we find that Congress in this new act has stated that it must plainly appear to us— that is, it must more plainly appear to the court than in an ordinary

case—that it has jurisdiction—before we could grant the petition."
I think that would be unconstitutional. You can not enact worse
legislation than that. I think, also, when you enter upon legislation
in regard to this railroad question you can not accomplish anything
good by any law or device unless it is absolutely right. Otherwise it
does more harm than good.

Then, on page 8:

If a carrier neglects or refuses to obey an order which is obligatory upon it as
above—

I think that would be made clearer by saying, "obey a lawful order."
Nobody is obliged in this country to obey any order unless it is a lawful order. So I suggest that after the word you strike out "an" and
insert "a lawful" in line 10.

If those two changes be made I think there is no danger whatever
in this bill of the railroads, through this power vested in this Commission, being injuriously affected in any way by any order. They are
not obliged to obey any order but a lawful order. The remedies of
the United States courts, through injunction proceedings, etc., with
this power to suspend the application of the order and to remain suspended pending appeal, should all be left just exactly as now, without
any attempt in this bill to change the powers of the court. I think
those are two important changes that ought to be made.

I can not go through the bill in detail, but I will refer to one other
matter. It provides that corporations shall be punishable by fine.
That is right. Under the present law you can not punish a corporation, which is the only one that ought to be liable to punishment. It
removes imprisonment, which is all wrong. You can not accomplish
anything by a provision to imprison the officers of a corporation.
That provision only embarrasses the application of the law. It drops
imprisonment and provides penalties only.

One of the bills that has been introduced provides that pooling may
be authorized. I want to state briefly the objections to that, and I
shall not state them in my own language, but in the language of the
ablest railroad man this country has ever produced. I think he was
recognized by railroads as having the ablest mind on this traffic question of any man who ever held a position in railroad management in
this country. I refer to Mr. Alfred Fink. His training began in this
business by employment on some of the railroad systems of the country when he was 45 or 50 years old, at first being traffic manager of
the Louisville and Nashville. When the Interstate Commission was
organized he was recognized by the Commission as the ablest man in
the country upon questions the Commission had to meet. I examined
him at great length on the pooling question.

I may say here that I appeared before the Interstate Commerce Committee at one time when it held sessions in New York City, when I
talked two or three days as a witness, and as a result of my testimony
there I was requested to communicate with the committee and assist in
drawing a bill. The suggestions I made, and which were adopted,
were based upon the English act of 1854 in all provisions, except as to
the appointment of the Commission, and the bill is substantially to-day
as I drew it. I advised against the prohibition of pooling. I thought
it wise to leave pooling as it was under the common law, which prohibited carriers from enforcing pooling agreements among themselves.

Leaving it in that way I thought they would work out the problem so that in the end it would lead to something in that line which would be a public advantage. But the House, you know, put that provision in there, through Mr. Reagan.

A pool is only possible in two ways, as Mr. Fink said when I examined him upon the question, and Mr. Fink's strong point was this: He knew everything upon this question from the railroad standpoint, but he was the only railroad man I ever knew who could get up and state the people's side of the question as well as the railroad side. He knew the whole subject on both sides, and he could reach as just conclusions as any man I ever heard talk upon the question. For instance, as regards legislation by Congress, many of his railroads kicked against it; but he always insisted that it was a matter of safety and protection to have an interstate-commerce law which should protect the railroads as well as protect the people. He was always right. He was a German, of philosophic mind, and could take in all the bearings of the whole question.

There are two kinds of pooling and only two kinds that have ever been practiced: One is a money pool. For instance, there are two lines between New York and Chicago competing for business as between themselves. They agree that one company shall take 75 per cent of the traffic and the other 25 per cent. I asked Mr. Fink, "How about a money pool?" A money pool would be one where, if the line entitled to the 25 per cent found at the end of its traffic period that it had only received 10 per cent, the other line would pay the remaining 15 per cent in money. Some agreements are to repay the difference in money. Mr. Fink said the difficulty about a money pool was this: That it had been found impracticable, because a road can not live without traffic. He said that many of the big lines in competition with the 25 per cent road would be perfectly willing to take the whole 100 per cent of its traffic for one or two years and pay it three times the money that it would have earned if it had carried its portion of the traffic. But that was impossible. Why? Because it wiped out that road in the end. A road can not live without traffic. It has its equipment to keep up, its employees to pay, and it must have traffic to keep going. A money pool, therefore, simply means the extinction and wiping out of the small members of the pool in the course of two or three or four years.

What is the other kind of pooling? That is traffic pooling. That is where they agree that each of the lines in the pool gets its percentage of the traffic. Mr. Fink always maintained that that was the only practical way of pooling. But the inherent difficulty about that, the difficulty for which no remedy has been proposed—and I think the gentlemen who are in favor of pooling will have great difficulty in proposing an adequate remedy—is that it can not be maintained without violating the inherent right of every shipper to route his own traffic. You are at Chicago, and you want to ship grain to New York; you want your grain to go by the Pensylvania road, not by the New York Central, because the Pennsylvania is the shortest, quickest, and best equipped.

But that being so, if 25 per cent of your traffic, under a pooling arrangement, has got to go around three or four hundred miles farther by the Canadian Pacific or the Grand Trunk, then your right to route your traffic has got to be violated by the sending of your

I want to submit to the committee a suggestion, that there be added to the bill a provision which I think would substantially accomplish all that is aimed at in the direction of giving the railroads the right to pool. You want to draw the distinction between pooling and what I suggest.

Senator TILLMAN. May I. ask what are your relations to the Produce Exchange?

Mr. KERNAN. I am its counsel.

Senator TILLMAN. Do they instruct you to appear here?

Mr. KERNAN. I am employed by them as counsel.

Senator TILLMAN. Were you sent here specifically to appear before this committee?

Mr. KERNAN. I came over with a committee, but the other members of that committee had to go back. They did all the talking first. I appeared before the House committee this morning, and have just come from there.

The CHAIRMAN. You stated a moment ago that you have a remedy of some importance that you want to suggest.

Mr. KERNAN. Yes, sir. I think it is not wise to eliminate pooling, because it violates rights, as I have said. I think it is wise to provide that carriers subject to the provisions of this act shall have the right to form associations to secure the establishment and maintenance of just, reasonable, nonpreferential, uniform, and stable rates, to be promulgated and enforced under reasonable rules and regulations as to interstate traffic, those rates to be filed with the Commission, subject to their approval or disapproval.

The Interstate Commerce Commission is not to be authorized to take the initiative, however. The railroads are the ones to take the initiative, and they should be allowed to make agreements as they please. All that the Government should do in the matter through any of its agencies is to inspect the provisions of such agreements and see whether there be anything in them which violates public rights. This is not pooling. This is to authorize the association of railroads so that they may agree upon rates, fix tariffs, uniform tariffs throughout the United States as to rates, and to impose penalties to be recovered of each other in case they fail to maintain the tariff rates. There you see the beauty of it is that they fix their own penalties for their own violations of their contracts. Therefore there is no injustice done in leaving them to recover from each other whatever they can.

They should also agree upon a uniform classification throughout the United States, which is a very important subject. I think that is all right.

I think that is giving the railroads a great deal—all they need and all they ought to have. They ought to be authorized to form traffic associations by which they can keep, by agreement among themselves, jurisdiction over these subjects as to the establishment and maintenance of rates, as to penalties for rate cutting, and as to uniform classifications. They can not do that now, because there is no authority for it.

The CHAIRMAN. The decision of the Supreme Court of the trans-Missouri case says that they can not agree now.

Mr. KERNAN. Yes. That removes the difficulty really as to the prohibition against pooling. But it tends to prohibit the formation of such associations for the purpose of doing what is entirely right and just.

The CHAIRMAN. Will you leave that language in your testimony?

Mr. KERNAN. I think the Corliss bill should be amended in the particulars I suggest, and in one other particular. It provides that "every violation of this act shall be prosecuted," etc. I think that should read: "Every willful violation of this act." An innocent violation ought not to be punished.

The CHAIRMAN. That word "willful" ought to go in there.

Mr. KERNAN. And I think the word "lawful" should be inserted before the word "order" in line 10 on page 8, as I have already suggested. Then I think those words "also, if upon an inspection of the record it plainly appears that the order proceeds upon some error of law, or is unjust and unreasonable upon the facts, and not otherwise," as they appear in lines 11 to 14 on page 6, should be stricken out. Whatever power is to be given to the United States courts, under their ordinary constitutional jurisdiction to suspend the operation of the Commission's orders issued in their discretion, I think no new rule of that kind would be justifiable, and I do not think it would be constitutional.

The CHAIRMAN. Will you give us that memorandum which you have on the subject of pooling?

Mr. KERNAN. With pleasure.

Carriers subject to the provisions of this act, with respect to traffic subject to the act, may form associations to secure the establishment and maintenance of just, reasonable, nonpreferential, uniform, and stable rates, and for the promulgation and enforcement of reasonable and just rules and regulations as to the interchange of interstate traffic and the conduct of interstate business upon the following conditions:

(a) Articles of agreement shall be subscribed by the parties thereto, stating, among other things, that they are entered into subject to the provisions of this section; the terms upon which new parties may come in; how the decisions of the association are to be made and enforced; and the length of time for which the association shall continue, which shall not be more than ten years. Such articles when subscribed and in effect agreeably to the provisions of this section shall be legally binding upon the parties thereto, and be legally enforceable between them.

(b) The articles of association shall be filed with the Commission at least twenty days before they take effect. If the Commission upon inspection of the same is of the opinion that their operation would result in unreasonable rates, unjust discriminations, insufficient service to the public, or would in any manner contravene the provisions of this act, it shall enter an order disapproving the same. In connection with such order the Commission shall file a statement of its reasons for its disapproval. Said order shall be final and conclusive.

(c) If the Commission, upon inquiry into the actual operation of the association after the same has gone into effect, is of the opinion that it results in unreasonable rates, unjust discriminations, inadequate service, or is in any respect in contravention of this act, it may enter an order requiring the same to be terminated on the date named, which shall not be less than ten days from the making of the order. Such order shall be final and the effect of it shall be to render such articles of agreement null and void from and after the date named, except as to claims between the parties arising prior to that date.

(d) The Commission shall have the right to examine by its duly authorized agents the files and proceedings of such association, including all contracts, records, documents, and other papers, and it may require said association to file with it from time to time copies of decisions promulgated by it and of its minutes of proceedings or of other papers received or issued.

All orders issued by associations thus formed that in any wise affect rates shall be filed with the Commission as provided in the original act in relation to the filing of tariffs.

Every agreement for the formation of such associations as are authorized by this section is prohibited except as hereby authorized, and every carrier or representative of a carrier, acting as a member of such an association, or acting for a member of such association, whether the same exists by virtue of a definite agreement or not, shall be deemed guilty of a misdemeanor and shall, upon conviction thereof, be subject to a penalty of $5,000 for each day said carrier or representative continues a member thereof or so acts, which penalty shall be enforced in the manner provided for the enforcement of those penalties imposed by the tenth section of said act.

The CHAIRMAN. Section 16 of the law of 1887, the original interstate-commerce act, formerly overlooked, has been interpreted by Judge Groscup, where they were unable to punish shippers and carriers for violating the law as to rebates or discriminations.

Mr. KERNAN. Under that act the shippers could not be punished at all, whereas they ought to be punished just as well as the railroads.

The CHAIRMAN. The present law is:

That whenever any common carrier, as defined in and subject to the provisions of this act, shall violate, or refuse or neglect to obey or perform, any lawful order or requirement of the Commission created by this act, not founded upon a controversy requiring a trial by jury, as provided by the seventh amendment to the Constitution of the United States, it shall be lawful for the Commission, or for any company or person interested in such order or requirement, to apply in a summary way, by petition, to the circuit court of the United States.

I want to draw your attention to that. It seems now that the provisions of section 16 had been overlooked, limiting the power to compel all railroads, whether in associations or not, to observe the fixed rates and maintain them, by injunction on petition to the circuit court of the United States in equity. Has your attention been drawn to that decision?

Mr. KERNAN. I know that decision.

The CHAIRMAN. Have you anything to say on that point?

Mr. KERNAN. As to whether that gives us a sufficient remedy? It is partial only. You will find that this is the present condition and difficulty: That owing to the methods of United States courts, the delays, the waiting, practically you can not get anything decided in time to be of use.

Take, for instance, the import-rate case that I carried through for the New York Board of Trade and Transportation before the Interstate Commerce Commission, involving a very important question, the question whether the rate upon imports should be the same as the domestic rate between the seaboard and interior points or whether it should be lower. It also involved the same question as to exports, whether there could be a lower export rate than the domestic rate to the seaboard, in order to meet the conditions of foreign markets. All the trunk lines made defense before the Commission. It took a year and a half to get that case through the Interstate Commerce Commission. We took a great deal of testimony and heard everybody.

The Commission finally made an order in our favor, and eighteen railroads, including the great trunk lines, obeyed the order; one or two disobeyed it. Then I took the case to the United States court in 1892; it was expedited and carried through the circuit court of appeals, and then to the Supreme Court. After the first argument before the Supreme Court they ordered a reargument. It was reargued, and then decision was delayed for sixteen months. It actually took four years and a half to get a decision of that question.

This shows that this question of whether the original act is in force is a very serious one. The Commission itself, all the railroads, and all the shippers supposed for ten years, until that decision was rendered, that Congress had given the Commission all the power asked for.

In that import-rate case, how was it decided against us? I had Wallace, circuit judge; I had the three judges unanimously in the circuit court of appeals; I had Harlan, Brown, and the Chief Justice in the Supreme Court. In other words, I had seven out of the twelve judges who passed upon the question holding that the power was given. But five happened to be in the court of last resort, where they could finish me, and so it was decided that the interstate-commerce act could not be construed as containing any of these powers. So you see it has been a pretty close question among lawyers and judges whether this act did not originally give the power which ought to have been given.

Another thing I want the committee to remember, bearing upon the danger of giving to a commission the power sought here. There has never been a decision of any United States court, where the question was made, that the order of the Commission was not decided to be intrinsically fair and just, so far as the amount, the rate, or the discrimination was concerned. It has all finally turned simply on the question whether the Commission had the power.

I thank you, gentlemen, for your attention.

The committee adjourned.

———

At the sitting of the committee on Friday, May 23, 1902, the following-named gentlemen appeared: H. H. Porter, of New York; Albert W. Sullivan, of Chicago, assistant second vice-president of the Illinois Central Railroad Company; H. R. Fuller, representing the Brotherhood of Locomotive Engineers and other organizations of railroad employees; Hon. C. J. Faulkner, representing the Southern Railway Company; Hon. Martin A. Knapp and Hon. James D. Yeomans, members of the Interstate Commerce Commission; Edward A. Moseley, secretary of the Interstate Commerce Commission; Col. John Cassells, representing the Pennsylvania Railroad Company; W. B. Thompson, of Thompson & Slater, Washington, D. C.; A. B. Browne (of Britton & Gray, Washington, D. C.), representing the Atchison, Topeka and Santa Fe Railroad Company; and F. G. Gannon, third vice-president of the Southern Railway Company.

## STATEMENT OF H. H. PORTER.

The CHAIRMAN. Please state your name, present place of residence, and your business.

Mr. PORTER. H. H. Porter; now resident in New York; connected with railroads.

The CHAIRMAN. I sent you copies of the three bills under consideration by this committee, and we should be glad to have a full and free expression of your views as to what ought to be done by this Congress.

Mr. PORTER. From having been connected more or less with railroad operations under the interstate-commerce law, my conclusion is that the first thing to do is to repeal that law from beginning to end. By that I do not mean that it has been entirely a mistake, for the people have learned something, and the railroad officials have learned something since that law was originally enacted; and I think there is a general desire on all sides to have the present law repealed and a new and simplified law enacted in its place. There is in the present law too much detail, so that I think the best thing to do is just what a new management in a corporation often has to do when starting out under old by-laws, and that is to repeal them and begin again at the foundation. I believe the public have learned that there is a great deal in the present law that is worse than useless, and is destructive to the interests of both the public and the railroads. The public want steady rates; they want fair rates between people and places all over the United States; and then they want those fair rates enforced. They do not want on the statute book a set of arbitrary laws, or laws full of arbitrary details, to which it is impossible to conform.

The suggestion I have to make is very simple. It is that the law be simplified down to a declaration in the plainest language that the rates shall be stable, that they shall be fair, and that they shall be just between people and places.

That is a very easy statement to make, but it is much harder to enforce, because there is a quality in railroad rates, just as there is in almost everything else. There is quality in sugar, in silk, in wheat, corn, etc., and so there is quality in railroad rates; and if you enforce the same rates for good railroad transportation and financial responsibility that you enforce on poor roads with poor equipment and facilities, you are going to have chaos.

My idea is that railroad companies should have the privilege of making any agreements that they choose between themselves; that they should be held responsible for violating those agreements; and then, they having made those agreements, I would give the courts the absolute power to enforce them. And I would give the Interstate Commerce Commission just the same power of temporary injunction that the courts now have, subject, of course, to approval or disapproval upon review by the courts. This would make it simple, and the railroads could attend to the pooling question to suit themselves within the principle of the law. Leave out all possible details in the law, and let the railroads in their own way, from their own experience, correct the evils which have grown up, but make them absolutely responsible. Let them make any tariffs or any arrangements with each other consistent with the law that they choose, because that is absolutely necessary in order to have steady rates where some railroads have inferior lines as against better ones.

The first pool I ever knew to be made was the most successful and long-enduring one that was ever made in my opinion. The Rock Island and the Northwestern railroads, both entering Omaha, got into a quarrel, and they were carrying freights at all kinds of rates. The same man was elected president of both roads, and, of course, he wanted that quarrel stopped. Just at that time the Burlington Railroad opened its line into Omaha, and thereupon a third element came into the problem. At that time I was in the directorate of both the Northwestern and Rock Island railroads, and we finally agreed that there was no solution of this difficulty except through pooling, and we made a verbal pool.

We knew there was nothing in the law authorizing a pool. (When I speak now of railroads being allowed to pool, I want the pool to be legal and to hold. I do not want verbal pools. I want the law to provide for their enforcement.) Mr. Harris was president of the Burlington, and we sent for him. He came and said, "Well, we are just opened; we do not know exactly how the business is, and we have got to have our chance to test how much business we can get." After discussing the matter for half an hour, Mr. Harris said, "Mr. Tracey, what proportion of the business are you going to give us if we go into this?" Mr. Tracey said, very emphatically, "You will fight until you get it. We will each take one-third." And thereupon the pool was made.

Senator MILLARD. I remember that was a strong pool.

Mr. PORTER. Railroads will fight to get their share of the business. Self-protection, the first law of nature, demands this. Let this simple principle be at the foundation: That the railroads can have all freedom to agree with each other if they can, within the principle of the law. If they can not, of course that is the end of it, and they must fight until they can. If they make any particular rate or rates in their tariffs that the Interstate Commerce Commission thinks wrong, let the Commission stop the particular item or items; those rates not objected to to continue in effect. If they went into court, the court would grant a temporary injunction. Give the Interstate Commerce Commission power to grant the same temporary injunction. Until we have a law of that kind we shall have to continue under the present demoralizing conditions, which involve disrespect of law, and, on the part of the railroad companies, disrespect of each other.

I think we have demonstrated thoroughly in the United States to-day that the putting together of properties is to the benefit of all interests. I think some of you gentlemen will bear me out in the assertion that more than twenty-five years ago Jay Gould was called the most unpopular monopolist in the United States. W. H. Vanderbilt and others then controlled the Western Union Telegraph, and Gould was building telegraph lines here and there and cutting into the telegraph business everywhere he could. The Western Union necessarily followed him in the competition by cutting the rates in two, and then cutting them again. Every legislature was trying some legislative cure for that unstable transportation difficulty.

The telegraph lines were all broken up and values chaotic, and then Jay Gould conceived the idea of putting telegraph properties together. He did it, and he did it so quickly that the legislatures could not act in time to stop him. Every newspaper and the whole public sentiment was opposed to it on the ground that they were not going to be able to secure freedom of information, and cost would be increased; that Jay Gould would be able to secure information for personal speculation to individual and public injury. Notwithstanding that opposition on the part of the newspapers and public, however, there has not been for years a serious complaint against the telegraph. His remedy was perfect and the public's fears found groundless.

If you analyze it there are three kinds of transportation—transportation of people, transportation of property, and transportation of thought. The transportation of thought by the Western Union was on the same right of way and on lines parallel with the rails of the railroad lines used for the transportation of people and of property. The delivery is the same; the classification is the same. If you travel on a limited express you have to pay an extra price. If you send a banker's message you have to pay an extra price. If you send a package by express or by fast freight you have to pay an extra price. Ordinary passage and freight are the same as ordinary day messages. Cheap passage and coarse freight are the same as night messages.

But whatever you do you will be criticised. I have been connected with railroads since 1853, and I never yet made a tariff that some one could not show me some rate in it that it would be better to change in all interests.

Give the railroads full freedom. If they quarrel among themselves let them fight it out within the principles of the law. If they fight over stable rates they will get over it. They can gain nothing. They must consider quality as an element as well as quantity in transportation. Make the law constitutional and make it short. When a man takes an employee into his service he gives him power and discretion. He does not supervise everything that the employee does; but if the employee does something the employer does not like, he disapproves of it and takes such measures as he thinks proper to see that it does not occur again.

Senator MILLARD. Your idea is that the present law should be repealed and begin again?

Mr. PORTER. Yes; entirely repeal the old laws and begin again. Make the new law constitutional. Give the railroads the power to make agreements, and give the Commission the authority to disapprove and stop the operation of any particular items in such agreements until the courts say what is right and what is wrong. This you can do under the Constitution. I do not know whether I have made myself understood, but I have tried to do so.

The CHAIRMAN. What you have stated is very much to the point. Is there anything else you want to state?

Mr. PORTER. I came here after the original law had been enacted, and had conversations with Judge Cooley, a very able man, the first chairman of the Interstate Commerce Commission, who came here full of hope and died disappointed because people would not do what he expected, without regard to their moneyed interest.

I think some one should be appointed on that Commission who has had experience in railroad transportation. The responsibility of disapproval of a railroad agreement being upon the Commission, the members of that Commission should have among them one who has had sufficient railroad experience to help the Commission judge whether the agreement is wise or not.

Senator FOSTER. Do you believe that the Elkins bill provides for pooling?

Mr. PORTER. I do not like the word pooling. But I believe that it is within the power of Congress to enact a law providing that rates shall be stable, and that is one of the most important elements. I have seen merchants ruined by over-buying goods in order to get them shipped at low rates, and later in consequence having to sell them at a sacrifice. The rates ought to be stable, and should be just between places and people. Of course there should be no favored shippers. It costs the railroad just as much to carry freights when the rates are cut as it does when they are carried at stable tariff rates. I would give to the railroads just the same freedom I would give to anyone— to make any kind of a legal agreement among themselves, and have that agreement enforceable.

Take the Wisconsin lumber trade when I operated there. The lumbermen used to pile the lumber at their mills. I used to go to them and say, "Let me haul it down to your yards in Kansas and Nebraska when I want to, and I will give you a 10 or 15 per cent lower tariff." Why did I do that? Because I could do that at a time when grain was going eastward very heavily, and if I took the lumber westward it would save hauling empty cars one way. It was a commercial transaction. I would have made more money, the lumbermen could save money, and the consumer in Kansas and Nebraska would have had to pay no more for his lumber. I grant you that can not be done now. People could not understand it. But I saved thousands of miles of empty-car mileage in that way, and without that right it must cost railroads more to do transportation.

## STATEMENT OF HON. MARTIN A. KNAPP.

The CHAIRMAN. Do you want to make a statement this morning, Mr. Knapp?

Mr. KNAPP. I am entirely at the service of the committee.

The CHAIRMAN. The committee wanted to hear some of these other gentlemen on the automatic-coupler bill, but we will hear you now.

Mr. KNAPP. Mr. Chairman and gentlemen, it was my misfortune not to arrive here in time to hear Mr. Porter's entire statement, but I think perhaps I got the drift of it from his closing remarks. So much may be said upon the subject embraced in the pending bills that I hardly know where to begin or how, in a brief statement, to say anything which is likely to aid your consideration.

For ten years and more I have endeavored to make this question a subject of conscientious study, with the result of having some rather definite convictions. My observation and experience lead me to be very conservative. I certainly would not advocate any radical change in the existing laws, except in one respect, to which I shall presently allude, with your permission. Nor do I think it necessary to go further, for the present at least, than to give the regulating statute that degree of efficiency which it was supposed to have at the time of its passage.

The bill introduced by Senator Nelson, as you doubtless know, embraces, so far as it goes, some of the specific recommendations of the Commission. With reference to the subject-matter of that measure I need only say that it meets the approval, I think I am warranted in saying, of the entire Commission. I mean by that, as to its general aims and purposes. It has some minor provisions which I think of doubtful validity and which I should not be prepared to indorse.

The bill introduced by the chairman—a revised edition, if I may so characterize it, of which has been introduced in the House and is known there as the Wanger bill—apparently aims at the same purposes and is designed to accomplish substantially the same results as the Nelson bill by way of amending the law. It differs in form materially, however, because it is in form an independent measure, whereas the Nelson bill in form is an amendment of specific sections of the present act.

But the subjects which are in a way covered or treated by the Nelson bill and the corresponding provisions of the Elkins and the Wanger bills are not essentially dissimilar. While, as I said, there are some things in the Nelson bill which I am not prepared to indorse, there are some things also in the Elkins bill which I think might be modified to advantage, not in essential respects, but with reference to making its meaning more certain and relieving it from possible ambiguity, because we all concede that it is desirable in legislation to avoid the necessity of resorting to the courts for judicial interpretation, so far as possible, and to enact such amendments as shall be plain, simple, and readily comprehended.

The two measures differ, however, in one very material respect.

The Elkins bill confers upon carriers, subject to the provisions of the act, rights of association and to contract with each other, which rights existing laws deny.

The Nelson bill is entirely silent on that subject.

Speaking for myself, and not undertaking to voice the united opinion of the Commission, I am very much in favor of changing the law in that respect. My study of this question, Mr. Chairman, led me quite early to perceive the fundamental inconsistency between the aims and purposes of the "act to regulate commerce" and the prohibition of pooling contained in its fifth section. To my mind the idea that all rates shall be just and reasonable, that there shall be no discrimination between persons or localities—in other words, that the announced tariff shall furnish a standard of compensation binding upon the carriers and the public, and to be invariably observed in all cases—is a rule practically inconsistent with competitive relations. There can be no actual competition in railway rates, as the term "competition" is ordinarily understood, and at the same time an actual observance of published tariffs.

I think it is the misfortune of this law that a provision inconsistent with its general purpose was incorporated in it, and a still greater misfortune, because of its far wider application, was the so-called Sherman antitrust law, which the Supreme Court has said applies in all its provisions to railway operations. It might be, if we had the choice between large numbers of actually separate and independent railroads and the legalized association of those roads, that we should hesitate to confer a right of association which is now denied and which is contrary, in a general way, at least, to the trend of judicial utterance for more than two hundred years. But we have not any such choice, and I think the right of contracting, which the Elkins bill confers, could be defended, if upon no other ground, for the reason that it is desirable to preserve as much railway competition as you can.

So the practical choice, in my judgment, is between a degree of independence (the preservation of a considerable autonomy) and some check upon the tendency to railway combination—the choice between that and practically universal consolidation of our American railways—which shall eliminate their competition with each other.

You can not have continued competition that is legitimate, that is honest, of which everybody has the advantage; you can not have that without permitting the roads, by amendment of this law, to put some sanctioned restraint upon competition with each other; and I regard a measure which embodies that principle as not only in harmony with the aims and purposes of a published regulation, but practically essential to the realization of those purposes.

The very obvious fact to my mind is that railway competition, whatever may have been its effects years ago in breaking down railway rates, has not in recent years, broadly speaking, had much influence in reducing published tariffs. That competition has found expression, and does find expression to-day, mainly in secret arrangements and preferential bargains by which the larger shippers profit.

It is very difficult for me to see where the ordinary man of affairs—the farmer, the crossroads country dealer, or the wage-earner of any class or description—gets any benefit from the policy of railway competition which we have endeavored to enforce. Practically speaking, that policy has powerfully aided the great combinations of this country, because it has resulted in giving influential shippers of large tonnage an advantage which the smaller dealers have not been able to secure.

I think it not too much to say, Mr. Chairman, that the evils of present railway management and operation are mainly described by the single word "discrimination." That discrimination takes a twofold form. It may manifest itself in the secret rate by which a large shipper or combination of shippers gets a secret advantage, or it may manifest itself in such an adjustment of rates as between different localities and different articles of traffic as to prejudice the one and unduly favor the other. Those evils and both those forms of discrimination are mainly caused by what we call railroad competition. I am not optimistic enough to expect that those evils will be removed so long as the cause is perpetuated, but I think the time has come when we should recognize the origin of these evils and endeavor to get at the root of the difficulty and correct it from the bottom.

Therefore it seems to me that the amendments of this law which are most needful are those amendments which are most likely to secure the absolute preservation of tariff rates. I say that not only because of its abstract justice, and not only for the reasons I have already suggested, but for another reason, which to my mind is even more convincing, whatever may be said to the contrary—and I certainly express no opinion as to the merits of any particular case—and that is, that there are a great many complaints at the present time that rates are too high. Those complaints, I may say, are mainly, if not altogether, confined to the advances in rates affecting several hundred articles which were affected two years ago by a simple change in classification. Aside from those advances so brought about, nearly every complaint which has reached the Commission has, in its final analysis, resolved itself into a complaint of discrimination.

The most offensive and demoralizing of all evils connected with railroad operation is the giving of a rebate, and I think the first duty of Congress is to provide a legislative remedy against that evil. As I have already said, I think no remedy is adequate which does not include in its provisions the right of association and contract between railroads, which present laws forbid.

I say that for another reason. If it be true that tariff rates are in any case excessive, if it be true that in any community a commodity is burdened with an unjust transportation tax, I believe there is no influence so powerful to bring about a reduction of that burden as to compel everybody to share it equally. Just so long as the carrier, by yielding to the pressure of some great shipper or combination of shippers, by giving to some interest a private and preferential rate, can hold up its tariffs as to everybody else, it is perfectly natural that that should occur.

The carrier is aided to that result by its own interest and by the implied demand of the powerful shipper who gets the preferential rates. So if the question of the reasonableness of railway charges is a question between the public on one side and the carrier on the other, you have, under conditions of actual railway competition—conditions which are enforced by our present legislative policy—you have a division of the public, its most powerful members in a particular locality being ranged on the side of the carrier; and just so long as the interest on one side is divided and the powerful shipper is allied with the carrier, just so long it is natural, if not inevitable, that the tariff rates will be disregarded and the great majority of men be required to pay a high rate and their more important and influential rival allowed a lower rate.   I believe there is no influence which will be so powerful, no authority which you can confer upon the Commission which will be so effective, to bring down rates which are too high as to compel the absolute observance of tariff rates under all circumstances and to all shippers.

For when it comes to pass that an Armour or a Havemeyer or a Counselman can not get a carload of freight carried for one mill less than the weakest and least consequential competitor, then you will have the entire influence of large shippers and small concentrated in an effort to bring about a reduction of rates, and that effort will ordinarily succeed, because, as a general proposition, I do not believe that any railroad or combination of railroads can long maintain a rate which is demonstrably excessive or unreasonable against the united demands and the united insistence of the community or the dealers in the commodity to which those rates apply.   Therefore I believe that the most wholesome and powerful agency which can be introduced to bring about the purposes for which this law was enacted is that which shall secure to every shipper, large and small, precisely the same charge; and that, as I have already said, I do not believe, as a practical matter, can be accomplished without allowing the railroads the right of association with each other.

The CHAIRMAN.  We shall be pleased, Judge Knapp, if you will continue these remarks at our next meeting.

Mr. KNAPP.  That, Mr. Chairman, covers all I want to say.

---

COMMITTEE ON INTERSTATE COMMERCE,
*United States Senate, June 6, 1902.*

At the regular weekly meeting of the committee (present, Senators Elkins (chairman), Kean, Dolliver, Millard, Foster, Carmack, and McLaurin), Mr. Joseph Nimmo, jr., made a statement on the bills before the committee to amend the interstate-commerce act as follows:

## STATEMENT OF JOSEPH NIMMO, JR.

### THE CIVIL REMEDY PROVIDED BY SECTION 16 OF THE ACT TO REGULATE COMMERCE.

Mr. NIMMO.  Mr. Chairman, since bills were introduced in both branches of Congress at its present session for the amendment of the act to regulate commerce, the whole situation has been changed by judicial procedure instituted by the Interstate Commerce Commission at Chicago.   After fifteen years of efforts by the Commission to enforce the criminal provisions of sections 10 and 12 of the act to regulate commerce, recourse was had during the month of March last to the civil remedy provided in section 16 of that act.   It is yet too soon to predict what may come of the attempt to enforce this provision of the statute.   The only information of value upon the subject is contained in the remarks of Judge Grosscup just before issuing his order for a temporary injunction on March 24 last. The language of the learned judge upon that occasion is as follows:

The question presented by this application is a new one and a very great one, and I will not pass upon it finally until there have been elaborate arguments on each side. If the United States courts sitting in equity have the power called for, it will make them master of the whole rate situation, for an inquiry instituted by them to inquire whether the injunction has been violated or not will, much more readily than criminal proceedings, probe to the bottom of the railroad's doings. For my own part, I believe that railroad rates ought to be as stable as postage rates, so that every shipper would know, as certainly as the sender of a letter, how much it would cost him, and the fact that no one else could send it for less. An injunction something like this has been granted in other cases, notably in the Debs case, but an important distinction between that case and this is that in the Debs case the things complained of were in their nature temporary, while in this case the injunction will be against conduct running continuously into the future. The interstate-commerce act has hitherto been ineffectively executed, but the taking of such power by the courts, as this injunction implies, might turn out to be the vitalizing of the act.

This is a mere forecast by Judge Grosscup, but it contains a word of hopefulness. It tells the important fact that the appeal of the Commission to section 16 is a new one—so new indeed that the court will require elaborate argument of the question on both sides before deciding it. It declares further that if the courts have the power called for "it will make them master of the whole rate situation." It next states the opinion of the learned judge that the new or civil process "will much more readily than criminal proceedings probe to the bottom of the railroad's doings," that "the injunction will be against conduct running continuously into the future" and thus exercise a deterent influence, the finest expression of governmental power, and that while criminal procedure has proved ineffectual, the taking of power under section 16 "might prove to be the vitalizing of the act."

This, Mr. Chairman, is the opinion of a learned and astute judge concerning a possible remedy for the specific difficulties which have been made the occasion for the introduction of the various bills now before Congress for the amendment of the act to regulate commerce. So the fact appears at this late day that the interstate-commerce act has two arms—the right arm of civil remedy and the left arm of criminal remedy. Hitherto the interstate commerce has confined its attempts at regulation to the left arm of criminal remedy, but it has at last had recourse to the right arm of civil remedy provided in section 16 of the act. After waiting fifteen years to inaugurate such action, why not, I ask, postpone legislation upon the subject until it can be ascertained what will become of this injunction proceeding, which, as Judge Gresham observes, is not only promising of good results with respect to rate cutting, but also to the whole broad subject of railroad regulation. The motion was set down for hearing on June 9, but I think it has been postponed to a later date in order that similar procedure before a United States judge at Kansas City may be taken under consideration at the same time.

There is another matter which I would refer to, and that is that section 3 of the Corliss bill proposes to take the vital principle out of this vitalizing section 16 of the act. I need not attempt to explain the phraseology which makes this change, for it is evident upon the reading of the act and of the bill, but will simply say that the bill proposes to repeal all of section 16 on pages 15 and 16 of the act to regulate commerce, as printed, and to substitute in lieu thereof obedience to definitive orders of the Commission with respect to prescribing rates for the future, a matter which has no place in the law as it stands.   In the opinion of an able lawyer "it would seem to have the effect of establishing the Commission as the sole tribunal to deal with the subject and ousting the courts of their important jurisdiction."   For this reason above all others, I would say postpone action on this Corliss bill or any other bill involving an attempt to paralyze section 16 of the act to regulate commerce, at least until after the courts have had a chance to decide upon its efficacy for the abatement of the evils on account of which it has been invoked.

### STATEMENT OF THE QUESTION AT ISSUE.

I invite your attention next to the various attempts of the Interstate Commerce Commission to acquire both judicial and legislative power.

1. The Commission at first assumed that it was invested with dispensing power in the matter of granting relief from the provisions of section 4, the long and short haul provision, but it was soon overwhelmed with applications for relief and reversed its policy, declaring that the companies must first decide for themselves whether they are or are not authorized by the law to charge more for the shorter than for the longer haul, and that in case of complaint the Commission would hear and determine each case upon its merits.   The latter method of procedure has been found to be entirely adequate to the prevention of unjust discriminations of this particular character.   It is the legal method of procedure in regard to controversies in contradistinction to the American and autocratic method of exercising dispensing powers not subject to judicial review.

2. The Commission having assumed to exercise the judicial function in the case of the Kentucky and Indiana Bridge Company v. Louisville and Nashville Railroad Company, Judge Jackson, in the United States circuit court for the district of Kentucky, decided in the month of January, 1889, that the Commission is not a court, and that Congress has no power to invest an administrative body with the judicial function. (37 Fed. Rep., 613.)

In its annual report submitted November 29, 1890, the Commission denied the doctrine of constitutional law announced by the court and stoutly maintained that with respect to administrative questions its "conclusions should be a finality even though their enforcement might require judicial aid." (4. I. C. C. R., p. 13.)

A bill expressive of its peculiar ideas was then drawn by the Commission, and at its instance was introduced in the Senate on December 15, 1891.   (Senate bill 892, Fifty-second Congress, first session.)   At hearings before the Senate Committee on Interstate Commerce from February 3 to February 24, 1892, the proposition was strenuously opposed by eminent counsel, mainly upon the elementary principle of constitutional law and of rational government that it is absurd to attempt to invest a single governmental agency with the functions of detective, witness, party complainant, prosecutor, and judge in the same proceeding.   That savored too much of the Pooh Bah style of government.

The attempt of the Commission to secure the desired power was disregarded by the Senate Committee on Interstate Commerce before which the hearings took place.

3. In the maximum-rate case the Commission assumed, by an order dated May 29, 1894, that by necessary implication the act to regulate commerce conferred upon it the power to prescribe the relation of the rates which should prevail as between points north of the Ohio River and points in the South Atlantic and Gulf States with reference to rates from points in the North Atlantic States to the same southern points. The result of this order of the Commission, if it had been allowed to take effect, would have been to endow the Commission with absolute control not only over the transportation interests but also of the commercial interests of the country, thereby eliminating the courts from any power to restrain the action of the Commission in the issûance of such orders. But the Supreme Court of the United States in its decision rendered May 27, 1897 (167 U. S.), overruled the order of the Commission. At every subsequent Congress, however, the Commission has been a somewhat importunate claimant before Congress for the powers which the Supreme Court of the United States declared were not conferred upon it by the act to'regulate commerce.

Furthermore, the Supreme Court ruled, in the maximum-rate case, that if such power over rates as that claimed by the Commission were conferred upon it by Congress it would be in the nature of a delegation of legislative power, and as such be exempt from all judicial control or modification, and therefore constitute practically a grant of absolute or autocratic power.

This conclusion of the Supreme Court of the United States was also strenuously denied by the Commission, and ever since the Commission and its coadjutors have been strenuously engaged in the attempt to secure the power to prescribe absolute and relative rates for the future. The present contention before the two committees of Congress grows out of this struggle for power.

## THE JUDICIAL VIEW OF THE PROPOSITION TO GRANT TO THE COMMISSION THE RIGHT TO PRESCRIBE RATES FOR THE FUTURE.

In the course of the controversies upon the general question of granting to the Commission the power to prescribe rates for the future, the advocates of the measure have had much to say to the effect that such power if granted would be subject to judicial review. This is strenuously denied. The question being vital to the whole subject of governmental regulation of the railroads, it seems proper to consider it upon its merits.

The Supreme Court of the United States, in the maximum-rate case, already cited, announced the following rule of constitutional law:

It is one thing to inquire whether the rates which have been charged and collected are reasonable—that is a judicial act; but an entirely different thing to prescribe rates which shall be charged for the future—that is a legislative act.

And again:

The power to prescribe a tariff of rates for carriage by a common carrier is a legislative and not an administrative or judicial function. (167 U. S., 479.)

In a word, the Supreme Court has declared that it will have nothing to do with a rate for the future made under legislative authority. The business of the judiciary relates to legally contested cases. Its normal expression is the lawsuit—not the administration of the affairs of the busy world. It looks to the past and not to the present or the future. This constitutional view was accepted and has been clearly expressed by members of the Interstate Commerce Commission.

In commenting upon these and related judicial utterances, Hon. Martin A. Knapp, chairman of the Interstate Commerce Commission, made the following statement on March 10, 1898, before the Senate Committee on Interstate Commerce (page 9):

One doctrine is now settled—that whereas the investigation of the question whether an existing rate is a reasonable and lawful one or not is a judicial question, the determination of what the rate shall be in the future is a legislative or administrative question with which the courts can have nothing to do.

• Again, on page 26 of the same hearing, Mr. Knapp said:

This is the theory of it: This Commission, for the purpose we are now discussing, represents the Congress of the United States, and when it has made an order, in a certain sense it is like an act of Congress.

On page 118 of Hearings before the Committee on Interstate Commerce of the United States Senate, February 20, 1900, Hon. Charles A. Prouty, Interstate Commerce Commissioner, also an attorney at law, said:

The prescribing of a rate is, under the decisions of the Supreme Court, a legislative, not a judicial function, and for that reason the courts could not, even if Congress so elected, be invested with that authority.

At a recent hearing in another place Mr. Knapp said, on page 296:

While the determination whether a given rate is—that is, has been—reasonable or not, is a judicial question, the determination of the rate to be substituted in the future is not a judicial question, can not be made a judicial question, and that authority, if exercised at all under the circumstances, must be exercised either by the legislative body itself or by an administrative tribunal to which some portion of the legislative power is delegated. Now, that being so, of course you must bear this in mind, that it is incorrect and misleading to speak of an appeal from the order of the Commission.

In the recent case of Louisville and Nashville Railroad Company v. Kentucky, decided January 6, 1902, the Supreme Court said:

It is scarcely necessary to say that courts do not sit in judgment upon the wisdom of legislative or constitutional enactments.

In the case of San Diego Land Company v. National City, the Supreme Court of the United States held as follows (174 U. S., 739–754):

Judicial interference should never occur unless the case presents clearly and beyond all doubt such a flagrant attack upon the rights of property under the guise of regulation as to necessarily have the effect to deny just compensation for private property taken for public use.

Similar judicial opinions are abundant and need not be cited here.

An exceedingly able and distinguished lawyer, who has given practically his entire time to the study of transportation questions since the act to regulate Congress was passed, has recently expressed the following opinion upon this vitally important point:

As the power to make future rates is a legislative power, Congress can not, in my opinion, constitutionally confer upon the judicial department any power to review or reverse the action of the Commission in making future rates. The only power that would be left to the judiciary or that could be conferred upon the judiciary by Congress would be the power to decide whether those rates (made by the Commission) were confiscatory in character.

And again:

No court can determine whether an act of Congress is upon the facts unjust or unreasonable or whether an act has been passed under some error of law.

While it is unquestioned constitutional law that no carrier can be compelled to carry freights at rates which are in effect confiscatory, yet a broad line of distinction lies between remunerative and confiscatory rates, which in practice excludes the courts from the power to condemn any rate made in pursuance of legislative enactment upon the ground that it is unjust or unreasonable. Without doubt the discretionary power proposed embraces the entire range of commercial profits which in practice justifies both the construction and the operation of railroads. In a word, it is an absolute and practically autocratic power.

The idea that the Federal judiciary will ever allow itself to be used for the purpose of eliminating its own authority in the realm of justice seems too preposterous for serious consideration. It can be safely predicted that in reply to any such proposition the judiciary would again be forced to the indignant exclamation, "Could anything be more absurd?"

I think, Mr. Chairman, that certain members of the Interstate Commerce Commission are fully aware of the import of the bill now before you as I have stated it, namely, that it eliminates the judiciary and confers upon the Commission practically autocratic powers, and have been forced to the conclusion that it is impracticable. In an address delivered before the Illinois Manufacturers' Association on April 2, 1902, Mr. Commissioner Prouty said:

Personally I have for a long time insisted that these questions could only be properly dealt with by the creation of a new and special tribunal for that purpose.

And on page 238 of the hearings, in another place, Mr. Prouty said on April 22:

I think if you could create a special court which dealt with these questions alone, which was chargeable in the public mind with the proper disposition of these questions, and which would speedily become an expert body, you would solve that difficulty.

Governor Fifer, also an Interstate Commerce Commissioner, indicated the same purpose, and pointed to the deterrent influence of judicial procedure, an expression of governmental authority which does not attach to mere administrative authority. The same idea was expressed to me several years ago by another member of the Commission.

In a word, too, the Commission appear already to see the absurdity involved in the autocratic control of the commercial and transportation interests of this country freed from all judicial restraint.

There is no intimation of any such grant of power in the act to regulate commerce. This was emphatically declared by the Supreme Court of the United States in the Maximum Rate Case (167 U. S.) and the fact that ample remedy for all the evils complained of is afforded by section 16 of the interstate-commerce act is indicated by Judge Grosscup in his recent judicial utterance at Chicago.

### MERITS OF THE QUESTION INVOLVED.

And now I come to the merits of the whole contention, namely, the question as to whether the grounds of complaint are of such a character and are sufficient in importance to justify the action proposed in the Corliss bill. The question at issue relates to three causes of complaint, namely: (1) Discriminating rates; (2) exorbitant rates, and (3) violations of published or legal rates.

First I invite your attention to the subject of

## DISCRIMINATING RATES.

On April 16, 1900, Senator Elkins, then a member, and now chairman, of this committee, introduced in the Senate a resolution calling upon the Commission for the following information:

The total number of cases heard and determined by the Commission during the last ten years, the number of such cases which have been appealed to the courts, the number of such cases in which the decisions of the Commission have been sustained, the number of such cases in which the decisions of the Commission have been reversed, and the number of such cases which have not been determined.

This resolution was at once considered and agreed to. It is known as Senate resolution No. 267, Fifty-sixth Congress, first session. On the 28th of April the Interstate Commerce Commission transmitted its reply to the Senate (Senate Doc. No. 319, Fifty-sixth Congress, first session). From this answer the history of the cases decided from April 16, 1890, to April 16, 1900, appeared to have been, summarily, as follows:

Total number of cases decided by the Commission.............................. 180
Number appealed to the courts..................................................... 35

This showed that in the millions of freight transactions in the United States during the ten years from April 16, 1890, to April 16, 1900, only 180 cases, or 18 a year, came to a hearing, and that of these only 35, or 3½ a year, were appealed to the courts, of which in only 4 cases in ten years was the Commission sustained by the courts.

The 35 cases appealed to the courts during the ten years were disposed of as follows:

Commission sustained ............................................................ 4
Commission reversed ............................................................. 17
Cases pending................................................................... 12
Cases withdrawn ................................................................. 2
                                                                          ——
    Total.................................................................... 35

The above result showed that of the 21 cases appealed from the decision of the Commission to the courts and decided, the Commission was overruled in over four-fifths of those cases. This, in connection with the fact as to the small amount of litigation involved, was exceedingly detrimental to the claim of the Commission.

The bill (S. 1439, Fifty-sixth Congress, first session) was reported adversely from the Senate Committee on Interstate Commerce and failed of consideration in the Senate.

In its last annual report the Commission says, "The great mass of complaints are handled and disposed of by the Commission by preliminary investigation and correspondence. The total number of proceedings brought before the Commission during the year were 340, but only 19 formal proceedings were instituted before the Commission, or only one in 18 of the complaints preferred. There were only ten cases decided by the Commission during the year, or one in 34 of the complaints entertained. Of the ten cases decided seven were cases of unjust discrimination. This admirable result indicates the high degree of perfection to which the railroad system of the country has attained. It is also creditable to the cct to regulate commerce and to its administration.

In an argument which I had the honor to make before the Senate Committee on Interstate Commerce on April 3, 1894, I was able to present the following statement:

In the exercise of its function of preventing unjust discriminations and exorbitant charges the work of the Interstate Commerce Commission has been crowned with abundant success. Although several hundred complaints as to alleged violations of the act to regulate commerce were made during the year ending December 1, 1893, only sixteen cases came to a formal consideration and hearing, all the rest having been settled by the mediatorial offices of the Commission. In only one of the cases decided was the reasonableness of rates called in question, and in that single instance the claim was decided to be not well founded. One of the Commissioners has informed me that only about two-thirds of the cases decided sustain the charges preferred. This indicates that the actual number of proven cases of unjust discrimination did not exceed eleven and constitutes a most gratifying proof of the success of this nonjudicial tribunal in the exercise of its appointed function. Mr. Chairman, I venture the assertion that no court in this country inferior to the Supreme Court of the United States has had so few cases appealed from its decision in a single year.

All this proves beyond question that unjust discriminations and preferences of all sorts have been reduced to a minimum, and that they furnish no reason whatever in justification of the appeal of the Commission for more power. This the Commission practically concedes. Accordingly it has abandoned unjust discriminations in rates as a basis for its demand for autocratic powers, and now bases such claims almost, if not exclusively, upon rate cutting.

### EXORBITANT RATES.

In its seventh annual report, submitted December 1, 1893, the Commission said at page 12: "To-day extortionate charges are seldom the subject of complaint." In its twelfth annual report, submitted January 9, 1899, at page 27, the Commission said: "It is true, as often asserted, that comparatively few of our railway rates are unreasonable." From time to time the Commission has had quite a good deal to say about "unreasonably low rates."

In its last annual report the Interstate Commerce Commission stated that "the total number of proceedings brought before the Commission during the year was 340. These include formal as well as informal complaints. But only ten decisions were rendered by the Commission during the year, all of which were on formal complaints. Of these, however, only two involved unreasonable or exorbitant rates, or one in 170 complaints.

On March 18, 1898, Hon. Martin A. Knapp, the present chairman of the Interstate Commerce Commission, stated before the Senate Committee on Interstate Commerce that "the question of excessive rates—that is to say, railroad charges—which in and of themselves are extortionate, is pretty much an obsolete question."

The Supreme Court has in no case decided that a rate charged was in itself exorbitant, and I think I am not mistaken in saying that the question as to the reasonableness of any rate per se has never been presented to that court. I think also that I am not in error in stating that no rate has ever yet been proven to be unreasonable in the lower Federal courts.

The record of constantly reduced freight·charges in this country since the year 1870, as published by the Interstate Commerce Commission and by the Bureau of Statistics of the Treasury Department, affords overwhelming proof not only of the fact that rates are not excessive, but also that they are very low. During the last thirty years rates have steadily declined in every section of the country. This is shown on page 397 of the Statistical Abstracts for 1901 as follows:

*The average receipts per ton per mile on railroads of the United States during the years 1870, 1890, and 1900.*

| Railroad lines. | 1870. | 1890. | 1900. |
|---|---|---|---|
| | *Cents.* | *Cents.* | *Cent.* |
| Lines east of Chicago | 1.61 | 0.63 | 0.55 |
| Western and Northwestern lines | 2.61 | 1 | .89 |
| Southwestern lines | 2.95 | 1.11 | .91 |
| Southern lines | 2.39 | .80 | .63 |
| Transcontinental lines | 4.50 | 1.50 | .93 |
| Average | 1.99 | .91 | .70 |

The average charge per ton per mile for the United States fell from 1.99 cents in 1870 to 0.70 cent, or 7 mills per ton per mile in 1900. This shows that the average rate in 1900 was only a little more than one-third of the average rate in 1870—thirty years ago.

At the same time the facilities for railroad transportation have been enormously increased and wonderfully improved. The service during the year 1900 was very much more efficient than in 1870.

The following table compiled from the data of the Interstate Commerce Commission for the years 1890 and 1900 indicates the fall in rates by groups and for the whole country. It closely verifies the statement made by the Bureau of Statistics:

*Revenue per ton per mile charged by railroads of the United States according to statistics of the Interstate Commerce Commission.*

[Data from page 72 of report for 1890 and from page 95 of the report of the Commission for 1900.]

| | 1890. | 1900. | Reduction. |
|---|---|---|---|
| | *Cents.* | *Cents.* | *Per cent.* |
| Group I | 1.373 | 1.152 | 16 |
| II | .828 | .613 | 26 |
| III | .695 | .546 | 21 |
| IV | .844 | .595 | 29 |
| V | 1.061 | .808 | 24 |
| VI | .961 | .806 | 16 |
| VII | 1.360 | 1.064 | 22 |
| VIII | 1.152 | .964 | 16 |
| IX | 1.303 | .938 | 28 |
| X | 1.651 | 1.067 | 35 |
| United States | .941 | .729 | 22½ |

The facts thus stated prove beyond all doubt that in all our splendid American railroad system embracing about 200,000 miles of road, over which moves about $25,000,000,000 worth of merchandise annually or more than twice the value of the entire railroad system of the country, and involving millions of transactions every year, only 3½ cases a year of unjust discriminations were proven in formal hearings before the Commission during the ten years from April 16, 1890, to April 16, 1900, a fact stated by the Interstate Commerce Commission in Senate Document No. 319 of the Fifty-sixth Congress, first session. Of this small number less than one case a year of unjust discriminations was sustained by the courts. Furthermore, not a single case of unreasonable or exorbitant rates has been sustained by the Federal courts during the fifteen years since the Interstate Commerce Commission was organized.

Mr. Commissioner Knapp has attempted to overcome the effect of the foregoing official record showing the general and very marked reduction in rates by asserting that the apparent reduction in rates is the result of a disproportionate increase in the quantity of low-grade freights, such as iron ore and coal transported during the last ten years. This statement is without any foundation in fact, the tonnage of merchandise transported other than coal and iron ore having increased faster from 1890 to 1900 than did the tonnage of coal and iron ore transported. But this assumption has no foundation whatever in the facts of experience. This is clearly indicated by the following table, which shows the tons carried 1 mile on railroads, the tons of coal marketed, and the tons of iron ore produced in the United States in 1890 and in 1900:

|  | 1890. | 1900. | Increase. |
|---|---|---|---|
|  | *Tons.* | *Tons.* | *Per cent.* |
| Tons carried one mile[a]................................... | 76,207,047,298 | 141,599,157,270 | 0.86 |
| Coal marketed[b] .........................:........... | 114,628,266 | 199,977,758 | .74 |
| Iron ore produced[c]....................................... | 16,036,043 | 27,553,161 | .......... |

[a] Interstate Commerce Commission statistics.
[b] Statistical Abstract of the United States.
[c] Mineral Resources of the United States, 1900, Geological Survey, pp. 43–44.

From this table it appears that the increase of railroad traffic, as expressed by tons of freight carried 1 mile, according to the statistics published by the Interstate Commerce Commission, exhibited an increase of 86 per cent during the ten years 1890 to 1900, whereas the coal marketed and iron ore produced in the United States during the same period showed together an increase of only 74 per cent, so that the attempted argument that the apparent reduction in the average rate per ton per mile during the ten years from 1890 to 1900 is due to the enormous increase in the tonnage of coal and ores transported is seen to be utterly fallacious.

The contention that rates have not been greatly reduced during the last ten years is as glaringly untrue in detail as in the general expression already given for the whole country. For example, the tons of freight transported 1 ton a mile over the lines embraced in Group II of the Interstate Commerce Commission's subdivision, including the States of New York, New Jersey, Pennsylvania, Maryland, and Delaware, increased from 23,236,827,478 in 1890 to 41,275,547,319 in 1900, an increase of 77.63 per cent, while the coal produced in the States of Pennsylvania, Maryland and West Virginia exhibited during the same period of ten years an increase of only 65 per cent, viz, from 88,860,072 tons in 1890 to 146,323,336 tons in 1900.

It also appears from the statistics of the Interstate Commerce Commission that the average rate charged on the lines of Group II fell from 0.828 of a cent in 1890, to 0.613 of a cent in 1900, a reduction of 26 per cent, thus clearly indicating a large and important reduction in the rates charged on the four leading trunk lines of the East—the New York Central, the Erie, the Pennsylvania, and the Baltimore and Ohio, together with their branches and connections in Group II.

### SECRET VIOLATIONS OF RATES.

And now, Mr. Chairman, I come to the ground upon which, at the present time, the Commission bases its demands for practically autocratic power over the commercial and transportation interests of this country.

### SECRET VIOLATIONS OF PUBLISHING RATES.

Having been forced to abandon all other reasons for its persistent claim to autocratic power, the Commission has had recourse to secret rate cutting as the gravamen of its complaint. Here again facts are against the Commission. (1) It has steadfastly denied that it is in any especial manner responsible for the prevention of rate cutting. (2) It has opposed any amendment to the act to regulate commerce designed to afford to the Commission greater facility for the enforcement of the penal provisions of the statute. (3) It has been derelict in the discharge of its duties with respect to the prevention of rate cutting. (4) The remedy proposed by the Commission is not applicable to the cure of the evil complained of, and (5) The remedy proposed by the Commission is misdirected. These points will be considered in the order stated.

##### THE COMMISSION HAS STRENUOUSLY MAINTAINED THAT IT IS NOT RESPONSIBLE FOR THE PREVENTION OF RATE CUTTING.

By the second section of the act to regulate commerce every departure from tariff rates is expressly forbidden and is declared to be illegal. By section 6 it is provided that in order to compel every common carrier to publish and file with the Commission its tariff rates, fares, and charges the "writ of mandamus shall issue in the name of the people of the United States at the relation of the Commissioners," and section 12 provides that "the Commission is hereby authorized and required to execute and enforce the provisions of this act," for which purpose the Commission is given the widest possible powers of investigation, including the power to require by subpœna the attendance and testimony of witnesses and the production of all books, papers, contracts, and agreements and documents relating to any matter under investigation. The law distinctly provides that it may by one or more of its members prosecute any inquiry necessary to the discharge of its duties in any part of the United States. It has also the power to require every district attorney in the United States to prosecute all necessary proceedings for the punishment of violations of the act, and its findings in all judicial proceedings are made prima facie evidence as to each and every fact found.

Furthermore, it is provided by section 16 of the act to regulate commerce that if it is made to appear to any United States court "that the lawful order or requirement of said Commission drawn in question has been violated or disobeyed it shall be lawful for such court to issue a writ of injunction or other proper process, mandatory or otherwise, to restrain such common carrier from further continuing such violation or disobedience of such order or requirement of said commission and enjoining obedience to the same."  ·

Notwithstanding these clearly-prescribed powers and duties, the Commission has, from the beginning, sought to repel the idea that by the act to regulate commerce it is especially charged with the duty of enforcing the provisions of the act against secret rate cutting—the paramount purpose of the act. In proof of the correctness of this assertion the following facts of record are adduced:

In its annual report to Congress for the year 1893, at page 7, the Commission declared that it "is wholly without authority as respects those discriminations between individuals which are made misdemeanors by that enactment," that "it is endowed with none of the functions pertaining to the detection and punishment of delinquents except such functions as may be exercised by private citizens," and (on page 8) it deprecated the idea that it has anything to do with "uncovering the guilty transaction and bringing to justice those who engage in it."

In a letter addressed to Hon. William E. Chandler, a Senator of the United States from New Hampshire, under date of October 17, 1895, Hon. Martin A. Knapp, then an Interstate Commerce Commissioner and now chairman of the Commission, strenuously maintained that the prevention of the crime of rate cutting is a thing "with which the Commission has no power to deal." (Senate Doc. 39, Fifty-fourth Congress, first session, p. 14.)

For this and other declarations of similar import Senator Chandler administered to Mr. Knapp and to the Commission a sharp rebuke.

Mr. Knapp appears to have been then, as he has been ever since, laboring under the delusion that the duty of preventing rate cutting and other penal offenses denounced by the act to regulate commerce is incompatible with and beneath the function of revising all the freight tariff of the country, of prescribing rates for the future, and of determining the relative advantages to be enjoyed by competing towns, cities, and sections, and by competing industries throughout this vast country, a conception which he described in his letter to Senator Chandler as "my high ideal of the work in which the Commission is engaged," an idea which as I have endeavored to show is expressive of a malignant form of bureaucratic government, and as such utterly inconsistent with the governmental institutions of this country.

In its persistent denial of the fact that it is explicitly charged by the act to regulate commerce with the duty of preventing rate cutting the Commission flatly opposes its opinion to that of the Supreme Court of the United States. In the Maximum Rate Case (167 U. S., 479) the court said:

"It (the Commission) is charged with the duty of seeing that there is no violation of the long and short haul clause; that there is no discrimination between individual shippers, and that nothing is done by rebate or any other device to give preference to one against another; that no undue preferences are given to one place or places or individual or classes of individuals, but that in all things that equality of right, which is the great purpose of the interstate-commerce act, shall be secured to all shippers."

But, as before stated, in this as in other respects the Commission has not and does not to-day hesitate to oppose its opinion to that of the Supreme Court of the United States regarding the interpretation of the statutory or constitutional law of the land.

THE COMMISSION HAS REPELLED ANY ATTEMPT TO GIVE IT GREATER POWER IN ENFORCING THE PENAL PROVISIONS OF THE ACT TO REGULATE COMMERCE.

Not content with a denial of its duty to prevent rate cutting the Commission has deprecated the idea of increasing its power to prevent the commission of misdemeanors, particular reference being had to rate cutting. On page 7 of the seventh annual report of the Commission is found the following declaration:

But the main point to be considered is that Congress has no power to clothe the Commission, or any similar tribunal, with authority to execute the penal provisions of this statute other than to aid prosecuting officers in procuring evidence against suspected parties.

And, again, at page 8:

No amendment of this statute, therefore, is necessary or suitable with the view of giving greater power to the Commission in enforcing its penal provisions.

But when driven from the charges of exorbitant rates and unjustly discriminating rates, as possible excuses for demanding of Congress autocratic power, the Commission glaringly stultifies itself by seeking to secure amendment to the act to regulate commerce for the purpose of preventing rate cutting through an expedient which, as herein shown, is not only out of all proportion to but totally inapplicable to the offense, besides being essentially revolutionary.

The repudiation by the Commission of responsibility for the prevention of rate cutting, and its simultaneous effort to prevent any strengthening of its powers for that purpose, which would be subject to judicial review, clearly indicates its fixed purpose and desire to free itself of any sort of cooperation with or dependence upon the judiciary in the discharge of its official function.

#### THE COMMISSION HAS BEEN DERELICT IN THE DISCHARGE OF ITS DUTY WITH RESPECT TO THE PREVENTION OF RATE CUTTING.

The Commission has neglected the duty of using its best efforts to aid in detecting and in bringing to punishment persons who have been guilty of the offense of rate cutting and other misdemeanors, a duty plainly incumbent upon it under the provisions of sections 2, 6, 10, 12, and 16 of the act to regulate commerce. This seems to be the result of the extreme aversion entertained by the Commission toward that class of duties.

In the fifteenth annual report of the Commission, submitted January 17, 1902, at page 8, appears the following:

To convict for unjust discrimination it is necessary to show not merely that the railway company paid a rebate to a particular shipper, but it must also be shown that it did not pay the same rebate to some other shipper with respect to the same kind of traffic moving at the same time under similar conditions. As a practical matter this is almost always impossible.

The rule of law here stated by the Commission was announced by Judge Grosscup, of the northern district of Illinois, in a decision rendered June 20, 1896, in the case of United States *v.* Hawley, 71 Fed. Rep., 672, with which case the Commission had nothing to do. It is as follows:

This case illustrates that whatever difficulties there are in the enforcement of this act are not so much due to the law itself as to the failure of the prosecution to gather up and lay before the grand jury the essential facts of a case. The facts difficult to obtain—the transaction between the carrier and the favored shipper—are fully spread upon this indictment. The facts not difficult to obtain—the identity of the shipper discriminated against—constitute the fatal omission. Ordinary alertness and intelligence would have avoided this pitfall.

Herein the court declared that the facts as to the identity of the shipper discriminated against are "not difficult to obtain" and sharply animadverted upon the failure to obtain them, whereas the Commission in its annual report dated January 17, 1902, has declared that the discovery of such facts "is almost always impossible."

In this the Commission flatly opposes its opinion to that of the judiciary and of every freight-traffic manager in the country. I mention this contrariety of opinion upon a matter easily susceptible of proof as one worthy of Congressional inquiry.

The judicial opinion just cited relates particularly to the offense of unjust discrimination. But in the same case the court stated the fact that it is a violation of the law to charge less than the tariff rate. Even this offense, not involving any charge of unjust discrimination, the Commission seeks to ignore, declaring that the law "does not punish (it) otherwise than by a possible nominal fine." The law, however, explicitly prescribes for this particular offense a fine of "not to exceed $5,000."

The declaration of the Commission that the act to regulate commerce does not confer upon it ample power to prevent rate cutting is strenuously denied by able lawyers and jurists who hold that sections 2, 6, 10, 12, and 16 of the act gives it ample power to correct and prevent such offenses. If, however, the law is in this respect defective, by all means let it be amended so that the procedure may be freed from any practical difficulty.

Differences of opinion prevail as to the nature of the remedy which should be adopted for the prevention of rate cutting. In its fifteenth annual report, submitted January 17, 1902, the Commission suggests as a remedy for rate cutting that the corporation as well as its officers should be subject to the penalty prescribed in the act. The general solicitor of one of the great trunk lines of the country suggests that the corporation alone ought to be subject to the penalty. The question is one to be determined by Congress and is worthy of careful consideration.

It is believed that any proper amendment to the act in regard to rate cutting would be cheerfully accepted by the principal railroad managers of the country, and that they would cordially cooperate in the enforcement of the law. The public attitude assumed by the leading railroad officials of the country toward this subject seem fully to sanction this statement.

In this connection it is worthy of observation that the Commission fails to show in how many cases it has given the courts a chance to consider rate cutting upon evidence which the court declares not difficult to obtain, or to adduce evidence upon which the courts may impose what the Commission calls "a possible nominal fine," but which may amount to $5,000, and which with ordinary diligence can be imposed.

It is believed that if the Commission had been half as earnest in the attempt to prevent rate cutting as it had been in its efforts to secure autocratic power, the misdemeanor complained of would now be very much less the subject of complaint. It is believed also that a thorough Congressional investigation of this particular subject would clearly expose a manifest dereliction of duty on the part of the Commission.

The history of the case exposes the aversion of the Commission to a duty clearly imposed upon it by the interstate-commerce act, and this is exhibited nowhere so glaringly as in the oft-repeated assertion of the Commission that it has been deprived of the power to afford relief to complainants against wrongs incident to infractions of the law, and that it is not responsible for the prosecution of specific violations of the provisions of the act to regulate commerce, both of which statements are strenuously denied.

A recent news item indicates that at last the Commission has awakened to a realization of the fact that the law imposes upon it a duty with respect to the suppression of rate cutting, and that it is disposed to try to set in motion the means for accomplishing that object before the courts as provided in the act to regulate commerce.

### THE REMEDY PROPOSED BY THE COMMISSION IS NOT APPLICABLE TO THE CURE OF THE EVIL COMPLAINED OF.

The plan of conferring upon the Commission the power to prescribe rates is totally inapplicable to the offense of rate cutting. It has no relation to such offenses as of means to an end. The Commission has never sought to show that it has such relation. There is not the slightest reason to believe that rates made by the Commission would be any more exempt from rate cutting than are rates made by the companies. The true remedy pointed out by the judiciary and by the lessons of experience lies in a faithful enforcement of existing laws, which the Commission has spurned and neglected to enforce. Such laws, however, may be amended or supplemented by others which would facilitate the administrative work of the Commission, for the question is one of procedure, and not one as to the power to act.

The history of the course pursued by the Commission in this matter clearly indicates that the idea of asking Congress for autocratic power over the commercial, industrial, and transportation interests of this country in order to suppress rate cutting is an afterthought. Rate cutting is now brought to the front apparently from the fact that the Commission sees no other means of advancing its claim to the exercise of autocratic power either in exorbitant rates or in unjustly discriminating published rates.

Secret violations of published rates have their origin in the competition of rival commercial forces and are expressions of such struggles. This is apparent to merchants and to railroad managers throughout the country, and as such is deprecated by them. The fact is also clearly perceived that the remedy for such evils lies primarily in railroad self-government dictated by enlightened views of self-interest, the inspiring motive of all wholesome statutory enactments. Unfortunately the Commission has frowned upon such self-restraint and sought to substitute therefor its claim to the exercise of arbitrary power.

The question is one of vast political import and should not be left to the discretion of any administrative body—certainly not to any bureau of the Government bent upon the acquisition of autocratic power over the commerce and industry of this country. It is eminently a question for Congressional determination.

Besides, it may be observed in this connection that the duty imposed upon the Commission by the twenty-first section of the act to regulate commerce, to recommend to Congress such additional legislation "as the Commission may deem necessary" does not extend to great questions of public policy or to political questions which would naturally command the attention of Congress, but, in the language of Mr. Justice Shiras in Texas and Pacific Railway v. Interstate Commerce Commission (162 U. S.), should "be confined to the obvious purposes and directions of the statute." It is to be regretted that the Commission has not been guided throughout by this obvious rule of propriety.

### THE REMEDY PROPOSED BY THE COMMISSION IS MISDIRECTED.

Beyond all question the remedy proposed by the Commission is misdirected. There are always two parties to offenses involving contractual relationships. In the case of rate cutting these are the shipper and the carrier. The shipper is invariably the promoter to the offense, for it is always to the interest of the carrier to secure tariff rates and to the interest of the shipper to secure less than tariff rates.

The concrete cases which supply the text and ostensible cause of the present movement of the Interstate Commerce Commission for the purpose of preventing rate cutting is furnished mainly by the persistent efforts of certain large shippers of packing-house products of the West to secure less than tariff rates for the carriage of their products. It is an old story to which public attention has been several times directed during the last two years. So uniform, however, has been the "cut" by the several competing companies that it constitutes practically a common rate, lacking only the legal requirement of publicity. The rates actually charged would avoid the censure of being "cut rates" if they were published. They involve no material discrimination with respect to producers, localities, or shippers, but do involve most outrageously discriminations with respect to carriers. All this is clearly stated by the Commission in its annual report just published. Therein it adduces the fact that at one time a particular road "was carrying into Kansas City 33½ per cent of the cattle slaughtered there and carrying out of that city only 2 per cent of the product."

The Commission also shows, in the report mentioned, that the cut rates are a source of benefit to the producer, the consumer, and the packer. At the same time they involve enormous loss to the carriers. This is stated by the Commission in reply to two self-addressed inquiries: First, "Who has the benefit of the reduction in these rates?" and, second, "Does it result in advantage to the producer and consumer, or is it absorbed by the packing house itself." The answer of the Commission to these questions is as follows:

> It seems probable that in case of a reduction like this, which seems to be tolerably uniform and long continued, the general public must obtain some advantage, but we think that in the main these sums swell the profits of the packers. The number of these great concerns is only some five or six, and there does not appear to be much discrimination between them. Each usually knows about what the lowest rate is and usually manages to obtain that rate.

This clearly expresses the whole matter at issue. The cut rate is practically a common rate and irregular only because not published as required by law. This results in some benefit to the producer and the consumer, much more to the packer, and appalling loss to the carrier—the railroad company. This conclusion has been laconically expressed as follows by one of the Interstate Commerce Commissioners since his recent return from Chicago: "The fact is that five or six big shippers have for years been sandbagging the railroads." Hence the question arises, Why attempt to punish those who are sandbagged instead of having recourse to some plan to punish the sandbaggers? But it is just this injustice and manifest solecism into which the Commission has unconsciously stumbled in its most unreasoning desire to acquire a coveted power by visiting upon the railroad companies the severest and most humiliating punishment, namely, that of depriving them of the right to contract freely with the general public as to the commercial value of the service which they render and with no other apparent excuse than an utter inability to base their claim to autocratic power upon any other plausible pretext.

What has been said of rates on packing-house products applies substantially to complaints as to "cut rates" on wheat and flour. The latter involves a long and sharply debated question as to the relative rates on wheat and flour. This is a complex and involved commercial and economic question. The general but rather vague conclusion of the Commission in regard to it is expressed as follows on page 16 of its last annual report:

To an extent the rate upon flour in the foreign market must be higher than that upon wheat. This is decreed by physical conditions which no statute and no commission can alter. To that extent this industry must expect to operate at a disadvantage.

In the light of all these facts the proposition to have recourse to the haphazard and absurdly misdirected remedy of governmental rate making for the cure of problematical evils attending the transportation of provisions, flour, and wheat, and the commerce in these commodities would be as absurd as it would be monstrous.

A Congressional investigation, as thorough and as impartial as that known as the "Cullom investigation of 1886," would not fail to set all these difficulties in their true light and to disclose a remedy which would be properly directed and efficacious.

I have sought neither to palliate nor to defend rate cutting. Its extent and effects have been greatly magnified for the purpose of predicating upon it the Commission's claim to the exercise of autocratic power; but it is an undoubted evil, and has no defenders other than those shippers who practice it to their own advantage and to the detriment of their competitors and of the carriers. Beyond all doubt it is an evil which can be abated and as successfully prevented as are other misdemeanors which are mala prohibita.

The art of playing off one railroad against another in the matter of securing cut rates in the interest of large and constant shippers was invented about thirty years ago by one endowed with the very genius of commercial affairs, and the game is apparently as successfully played to-day as it was in the beginning. It remains to be seen whether the courts are possessed of the power to circumvent and prevent this nefarious practice, under the provisions of section 16 of the act to regulate commerce, which section was recently invoked for the first time by the Interstate Commerce Commission.

It is stated by The Railway Age in its issue of April 4, at page 578, that the entire movement of packing-house products was not in excess of 800,000 tons for the latest year. The total movement of freights on the railroads of the country during the year 1900, the latest year of commercial statistics, amounted to 1,101,680,238 tons. From this it appears that the packing-house traffic amounted to less than one-tenth of 1 per cent of the total freight traffic of the country.

## THE POLITICAL ASPECTS OF GOVERNMENTAL REGULATIONS.

Mr. CHAIRMAN: In his recent testimony before the Committee on Interstate and Foreign Commerce of the House of Representatives, Commissioner Prouty stated at page 238 that 807 complaints against advances in rates or against rates which are alleged to be too high have been filed with the Commission during the last three years. A similar statement was made by Commisstoner Prouty in an address delivered at Chicago, on April 2, 1902, before the Illinois Manufacturers' Association.   On the latter occasion he said:

While it (the Commission) can not grant relief, there are now pending before it for investigation complaints involving millions of dollars—I think I might say millions annually.

Manifestly these statements were intended to convey the impression that the charging of exorbitant rates is now rampant throughout the country.   But this is absolutely refuted by the annual reports of the Commission, which show that during the last three years only 23 cases in all were decided by the Commission upon formal hearings, which cases embrace only eight complaints of unreasonable rates per se.   Of these the unreasonableness of only four was sustained by the Commission, constituting less than one-half of 1 per cent of the 807 complaints alleged to have been made to the Commission, or less than one case in 200 complaints.   This would indicate either that the Commission has been derelict in the discharge of its duties or that nearly 800 of the 807 complaints were inconsequential or outside the function of the Commission.   The latter is undoubtedly the correct view of the case.   Besides, the fact that not a single case of exorbitant rates has been sustained in the courts during the fifteen years of the life of the Commsssion raises the presumption that not one of the four cases of exorbitant rates in the entire United States as determined by the Commission during the last three years would stand the test of judicial inquiry.

The total number of cases decided by the Commission each year during the last three years, and the number of cases of unreasonable rates tried and sustained, according to the last three annual reports of the Commission, are stated in tabular form as follows:

| Year. | Total number of cases decided. | Number of cases of unreasonable rates. | Number of complaints of unreasonable rates sustained. |
|---|---|---|---|
| 1899 | 5 | 1 | 1 |
| 1900 | 8 | 4 | 1 |
| 1901 | 10 | 3 | 2 |
| Total | 23 | 8 | 4 |

The data from which this statement was compiled are found on pages 20 to 43 of the report of the Commission for 1899, on pages 34 to 48 of the report for 1900, and on pages 22 to 39 of the report for 1901.

Hon. Martin A. Knapp also attempted to create the same impression as to the charging of exorbitant rates, notwithstanding the fact that the statistics of the Commission indicate an average reduction of $22\frac{1}{2}$ per cent for the entire country from 1890 to 1900 and a substantial reduction in the average rate in each one of the ten groups into which the railroads of the country are divided by the Commission.

## THE POLITICAL ASPECTS OF THE CASE.

The fact adduced by Commissioner Prouty that during the last three years 807 complaints of unreasonable rates were filed with the Commission, of which only four, or less than one-half of 1 per cent were proved to be well founded, has a much more important significance than the members of the Interstate Commerce Commission seem to have imagined. It serves to illustrate a fact of controlling force respecting the broad subject of regulating commerce among the States, namely, the fact that from the beginning the complaints which have been filed with the Commission have had their origin chiefly in the discontent incident to struggles for commercial advantage. Such discontent, however, is the chief stimulant to commercial enterprise. It involves problems which must be wrought out by human intelligence, enterprise, and interaction, and not by any sort of governmental interference, for we live in a world in which we are all debating. Every individual and every section, State, city, town, village, and hamlet in this country is at rivalry with competitors near and far, and it is preposterous for any governmental agency to attempt to reconcile these commercial antagonisms. They are intangible to any sensible or just method of governmental regulation.

Besides, the exemption of such antagonisms from governmental interference is a natural and proper expression of the freedom of commercial and industrial intercourse, and has been so regarded in this country since the foundation of our Government. Faith in the conservatism which inheres in this conflict of commercial forces has begotten the maxim " Competition is the life of trade," a maxim which has found its way into our statute laws and has become a tenet of judicial faith and practice. So firmly are the people of this country imbued with this sentiment of nonpolitical interference with commercial struggles that for nearly a hundred years after the founders of our Government had incorporated into the national Constitution the provision that " Congress shall have power to ' regulate commerce among the States," no systematic attempt was made to exercise that power, and clearly owing to the danger attending any attempt to meddle with a commercial interaction which is not and can not properly become the subject of governmental concernment.

But at last by the act to regulate commerce, approved February 4, 1887, an apparent, but carefully limited and clearly defined, exception was made to this policy of noninterference with commercial struggle. The restraints provided by that act, however, applied exclusively to the struggle of railroad transportation, and not to the struggles of trade or of industrial pursuits. Moreover, the restraints imposed by the statute had already become approved as proper methods of railroad self-government after the various lines of the country had become closely connected and cooperative members of one great transportation organism—the American railroad system. As such these restraints already constituted a part of the American common law of the railroad, being based upon the lessons of experience and that consensus of public sentiment which Lord Bacon has characterized as leges legum.

Unfortunately, and as subsequently was proved without any sanction of law, the Interstate Commerce Commission assumed in the Maximum Rate case, decided by it in the year 1894, that the act to regulate commerce authorized it to prescribe both absolute and relative rates for the future. This assumption of authority clearly and inevitably embraced the power to determine the relative commercial status of competing cities, towns, States, and sections affected by that decision. This monstrous assumption of political power was denied by the

Supreme Court of the United States in the year 1897 (167 U. S., 479), and the attempt to secure it by legislation has ever since been denied by Congress. It is a political heresy which should be resisted in its beginning, and under every guise and pretense of limitation.

That the attempts of the Commission to secure the rate-making power intentionally and of necessity involves the Eutopian idea of securing control of the internal commerce of the country is evident from the utterances of the Commission during the last ten years, but perhaps nowhere more strikingly than in the following declaration, found on page 10 of its seventh annual report:

> To give each community the rightful benefits of lŏcation to keep different commodities on an equal footing, so that each shall circulate freely and in natural volume, and to prescribe schedule rates which shall be reasonably just to both shipper and carrier is a task of vast magnitude and importance. In the performance of that task lies the great and permanent work of public regulation.

This expression of its "high ideal" of the work of regulation is a clean-cut proposition by the Commission to commit the Government of the United States to the task of determining all the struggles involved in the commercial and industrial interaction of the wealthiest, the most enterprising, and the most virile nation on the globe, a matter with which the Government should not meddle, and which is opposed to its settled and time-honored policy. It is rank political heresy. It is wildly impractical. It is such a departure from the time-honored policy of this nation that it may properly be , characterized as revolutionary.

The fact that of the 807 complaints of unreasonable rates filed with the Commission during the last three years only four, or less than one in two hundred, were susceptible of demonstration under known principles of adjudication, indicates that nearly 400 of the 407 complaints were struggles which can not properly be made the subject of governmental concernment. This clearly exposes the absurdity of the proposition "to give each community the rightful benefits of location," to adjust the commercial and industrial interaction of this great and growing nation, and to accomplish that purpose by setting up at the seat of the National Government a bureau endowed with the function of prescribing rates for the future, with the chimerical object in view of "keeping different commodities on an equal footing" throughout the length and breadth of this land. This is a wide and most absurd departure from the views of public policy touching the interaction of commercial and industrial forces which were entertained by the founders of our Government, which operated as a barrier to any system of regulation of the highway for ninety-eight years, and which are dominant in this country to-day.

The fact is that the great mass of the complaints made to the Commission relate to fancied grievances, to the results of commercial struggles, which are not and never should be the subject of governmental concernment, and to the frictional resistances and incidental evils affecting the grandest system of transportation ever seen on this planet. In the face of all these evils, real or fancied, the American railroad system may fairly be said to be almost perfect.

As a further illustration of the fact that the complaints which are addressed to the Interstate Commerce Commission are mainly of the class not subject to governmental concernment, the fact may be mentioned that in its last annual report the Commission said: "The total number of proceedings brought before the Commission during the year was 340. These include formal as well as informal complaints." But only 10 decisions were rendered by the Commission during the year on formal proceedings, only 2 of which involved unreasonable rates or 1 in 170 complaints preferred. In a word, the complaints of all sorts brought to the notice of the Commission had their origin mainly in commercial and industrial conditions completely outside the purview of governmental regulation.

I think, Mr. Chairman, that if you will carefully review the testimony of all the representatives of the various trades and industrial bodies who have laid their grievances before you during the last four years, you will find such grievances to be of the intangible character already described, being merely expressions of struggle for commercial advantage and not based upon any clearly defined errors or acts of injustice on the part of the railroad carriers.

It would be exceedingly difficult for Congress to differentiate between complaints which are based upon the conditions of commercial struggle and those complaints which are valid subjects of regulation under the terms of the act to regulate commerce, except in general terms expressive of the firmly established policy of the Government upon the subject. The distinction in concrete cases must be based upon the specific facts which govern in each particular case. The only object had in view in this connection has been to utter a word of warning against a policy which would devolve upon the National Government full responsibility for the course of the commercial and industrial development of this country, with all the dangers of sectional political struggle which would be engendered by such a departure from the principles of commercial freedom upon which our governmental institutions are founded.

There is another political aspect of the proposition to confer practically autocratic power upon the Interstate Commerce Commission to which I would here briefly allude. On pages 15 to 22 of my recent pamphlet entitled A Political and Commercial Danger, I stated at some length the reasons which sustain the belief that any provision of law granting to the Commission the power to prescribe rates for the future would eliminate the Federal judiciary from the function of passing upon the reasonableness of rates. This view is fully sustained by Mr. Commissioner Knapp, on page 296 of the present hearing, as follows:

While the determination whether a given rate is—that it has been—reasonable or not is a judicial question, the determination of the rate to be substituted in the future, is not a judicial question, can not be made a judicial question, and that authority, if exercised at all under the circumstances, must be exercised either by the legislative body itself or by an administrative tribunal, to which some portion of the legislative power has been delegated. Now, that being so, of course you must bear this in mind, that it is incorrect and misleading to speak of an appeal from the order of the Commission.

Mr. Knapp has made a labored argument to the effect that the determination of the Commission—a mere administrative body without permanent tenure of office, and subject at all times to the play of political forces—would be made in a judicial manner, and therefore would have practically the same effect as decisions rendered by the courts. This is too feeble for serious consideration. It would be superfluous to attempt any labored argument upon this point before a committee of the Senate of the United States.

The fact that the Federal judiciary is an independent branch of our Government has made it the bulwark of the liberties of the people. So long as the courts have final determination of all questions of commercial right, the time-honored policy of noninterference in the competitive struggles of trade will be maintained; but when the courts are eliminated from the determination of such questions the storm of political demand for commercial advantage will break loose, and the Commission and the political representatives of the people in Congress will bend to the blast. Besides, it is clearly evident that the sectional political struggles which would ensue from such a policy would endanger the permanence of our governmental institutions.

The exceedingly limited, and in most cases utterly ineffectual, way in which commission rate making exists in certain of the States of the Union affords no conception of the results which would ensue from placing the interstate and foreign commerce of the country under the control of a body characterized by Commissioner Prouty as "partly political and to an extent partisan."

## COMMISSIONER CLEMENT'S ANALOGY.

At a recent hearing Interstate Commerce Commissioner Clements based his argument in favor of granting to the Commission absolute authority over the commercial and transportation interests of this country upon the regulation of cab drivers in our large cities—a mere matter of municipal police. Mr. Chairman, the attempted analogy is strained to the last degree. There is no elementary principle of human government more clearly established than, that, in framing rules of public policy every tub must stand on its own bottom. Unless we observe this rule we shall stand our civilization on its head by forced analogies; for the course of human affairs does not run along any unbroken chain of causation except in the story books written for children. Every rule of public policy must be based upon its own peculiar state of facts and conditions.

It is difficult to conceive of anything more absurd than the idea that the regulation of the charges imposed upon the poor fellows who make a living by crying "Keb!" "Keb!" "Kerridge!" "Keb!" justifies the policy of placing the internal commerce and the transportation interests of this vast country at the absolute dictation of five men, without the possibility of submitting the reasonableness of their decisions to the Federal judiciary. No, sir; this country is not prepared for any such bureaucratic rule in the face of the fact, clearly proved by the experiences of the Commission, that extortionate rates have no existence in this country; that on the average less than one case a year of unjust discriminations is proven in our courts, and that the great mass of complaints which salute the Commission arise from mistaken notions of right, and from those competitive struggles of commercial interaction which never have been and never will become the objects of governmental concernment in this land of liberty.

## PREDICTIONS AS TO EXORBITANT RATES IN THE FUTURE.

Appreciating the fact that the experiences of the past afford no reason to apprehend an increase, but rather a decrease, of rates in the future, attempts are being made to arouse the impression that the strangulation of competition through combination will eventuate in a very large and disastrous increase in rail rates throughout this country. The Interstate Commerce Commission has lent itself to the propagation of this theory. It is without any foundation in the facts of experience or in the probable outcome of present tendencies. Certain reasons for this opinion may be mentioned:

First. The general results of rates now in vogue upon railroad properties is well known and constitutes evidence as to their reasonableness, which could be invoked in any court in case of an attempt to raise rates to an unreasonable or exorbitant standard.

Second. The competition of rival commercial and industrial forces constitutes a potential restraint upon any attempt to advance rates above what is just and reasonable. There is an irresistible tendency toward a parity of values throughout the commercial nations of the globe and the effect of this is constantly to depress transportation charges.

Third. There is another safeguard against excessive rates, and that is the use of substitutes. For example, if the price of beef goes too high we shall have improved cooking with substituted nutritious vegetable food. The same principle applies quite generally in regard to other commodities which constitute a considerable part of the railroad traffic of the country.

But it is unwise generally to expend time or anxiety in attempts to provide against imaginary troubles, so the cure of the evils of excessive freight charges in the future may well be allowed to await developments.

## THE EVOLUTION OF THE AMERICAN RAILROAD SYSTEM.

Mr. CHAIRMAN: Our intimately connected railroad system, which, in so far as relates to the interests of the traveler and the shipper, is operated as though it were a single organization under the control of one executive head, is the product of an evolution. At the beginning and until about the year 1855 each railroad was operated with no reference to any other railroad. Not only was the connection of lines avoided, but joint traffic had no existence. That, however, is of the dead past. The act of Congress of June 15, 1866, commonly known as The Charter of the American Railroad System, was the outcome of a general demand for railroad unity, embracing the juncture of tracks, the common use of cars over connecting lines, and those almost perfect facilities which we now have for continuous traffic over coterminous lines, embracing joint rates and joint traffic arrangements, which secure the practical unification of the railroad transportation interests of the country.

The organic unity of the railroads of the United States involved the necessity for railroad self-government, without which organic unity was of course impossible. This evolution and the consequent organization of lines into one great system of transportation involved as rules of self-government every one of those specific regulations which constitute the essential features of the act to regulate commerce. In fact, that act was builded upon those rules of self-government. Among those regulations are those relating to published classifications of merchandise, published rates, the prevention of fluctuating rates, the prevention of violations of published rates, the prevention of unjust discriminations, the prevention of unjust or undue preferences, the continuous carriage of freights, and the prevention of sudden fluctuations in rates. By the force of coercive experiences all those requirements became the common law of the railroad in this country, and as such they only needed the sanction of statutory enactment to give them the character of governmental regulation. This was accomplished by the act to regulate commerce, February 4, 1887.

That act was no experiment based upon the fancy or the hypothetical conception of any dreamer. It was the carefully wrought out product of practical statesmanship, based upon economic and commercial usages, sought out and set in order by railroad managers under the stress of the stern lessons of experience and amid the conflicts of contending commercial and industrial forces. In proof of this, allow me to read to you a few historic passages from a report made to me in the year 1875, in my then official capacity as chief of the division of internal commerce, by Mr. Albert Fink, one of the ablest railroad men of the country at that time, a leader of men in the formation of the American railroad system. In this admirable report is sketched the ethical and commercial considerations which, in the view of its gifted author, should govern the railroad transportation interests of the American railroad system, and which subsequently, as the result of the patient investigations of Senator Cullom and his coadjutors on this committee, acquired the force of law in the so-called interstate-commerce act. I quote as follows from Mr. Fink's report, written twelve years before that act became law, and made a part of the appendix of my first annual report on the internal commerce of the United States:

A common carrier should strictly adhere to the rule to charge the same rate for transportation for the same articles between the same points, only discriminating on account of quantity as far as it influences the cost of transportation. He should not make any arbitrary distinctions, merely depending upon his will. Discriminations in rates of transportation should be based upon conditions and facts which can not be controlled by the railroad companies, and upon principles recognized as correct in all other business transactions. (See page 9.)

Under the present system of the management of competitive business of transportation lines and from the want of systematic cooperation between so many parties interested in this subject, nothing else can be expected but the constant fluctuation of rates of transportation, railroad wars, and unjust discrimination. Concert of action and cooperation become absolutely necessary in order to establish rates of transportation upon a proper basis and to maintain the same with some degree of permanency. (See page 10.)

The result is fluctuations in rates, unjust discrimination between shippers in the same locality, or between shippers in different localities. Rebates are generally paid and special contracts are secretly made, all in direct violation of the law that should govern common carriers. (See page 12.)

Not only the public suffer from these evils, but from the causes which produce them the proprietors of the railroads greatly suffer. (See page 13.)

I make part of my answer an article which I prepared explanatory of the principal features of the plan of organization and its operation, and point out to what extent the aid of the Federal Government may be required to carry more completely into effect the operation of the organization. (See page 13.)

In a word, this able report by Mr. Fink, written twelve years before the act to regulate commerce was enacted, stated clearly the principles of self-government and the particular expedients upon which that system of government of the American railroad system is based, which principles and expedients later on, as anticipated and hoped for by Mr. Fink, became incorporated into the interstate-commerce act.

I have said this much in regard to the origin and principles upon which the act to regulate commerce is based in order to prove to you that it is firmly based upon the American common law of experience, and that it does not in the slightest degree impinge upon that freedom of commercial intercourse which is the outcome of commercial struggle and interaction, with which the National Government has never interfered. I have also sought to show to you how strangely this beneficent act contrasts with that idealistic attempt of the Interstate Commerce Commission to acquire autocratic control of the commercial and transportation interests of this country, an attempt which in the maximum-rate case caused the Supreme Court of the United States to exclaim, "Could anything be more absurd!" and again to suggest that the Interstate Commerce Commission seemed "to evolve, as it were, out of its own consciousness, the satisfactory solution of the difficult problem of just and reasonable rates for all the various roads in the country."

## THE IMPORTANCE OF A THOROUGH CONGRESSIONAL INVESTIGATION OF THE WHOLE TRANSPORTATION QUESTION.

Mr. Chairman, I would fall very far behind my object at this time if I should fail to submit to you some considerations in favor of a thorough investigation of the whole transportation question in its varied and vitally important aspects.

The many vitally important questions which confront the country, touching any attempt at a radical change in our laws relative to the regulation of the railroads, seem to point unerringly to the necessity for a thorough Congressional investigation of the subject in advance of any attempt to legislate upon it. In this we may profit very much from the example set by the people of Great Britain.

As early as the year 1840 questions arising out of the independent corporate ownership and control of the railroads agitated the public mind in Great Britain. The old British ideas of liberty involved in the consideration of monopoly, competition, and combination, which from time immemorial had been the subject of heated public discussion and of reflective judicial debate, gave rise to just such apprehensions and political theorizing as those which now seriously affect public sentiment in the United States. A British statesman of influence declared at an early date that "the state must govern the railroads, or the railroads would govern the state." George Stephenson, eminent as a civil engineer, declared that "where combination is possible competition is impossible. These expressions were for years accepted in Great Britain as politico-economic dogmas, but have ceased to have any influence whatever upon the public mind in that country.

In the year 1844 a strong parliamentary committee was appointed for the purpose of inquiring into and providing against the assumed danger. The Hon. William E. Gladstone was chairman of that committee. Its labor resulted in an act of Parliament (Acts 7 and 8 Victoria, c. 85) passed in the year 1844, wherein it was provided that the Government might, upon terms stated in the act, at the expiration of fifteen years after completion, purchase any railroad constructed after the passage of the act. In a word, the British Parliament provided, conditionally, for governmental ownership and control of the railroads. But that power has never been exercised, and the public sentiment of Great Britain to-day utterly repudiates any such policy. This has come about as the result of the lessons of experience and of patient and persistent parliamentary inquiry, reference being had particularly to the parliamentary investigations of 1840, 1844, 1846, 1852, 1865, 1867, 1872, 1881, 1888, and 1893–94. The results of these ten parliamentary inquiries were that the asserted dogmas hereinbefore quoted have been exploded, while other baseless notions such as those which now to a greater or less degree possess the public mind in this country have been dispelled; and the ancient principles of liberty and methods of justice still prevail in the regulation of the railroads of Great Britain. In this regard railroad regulation in that country strikingly illustrates the favorite British maxim, "We have government by discussion."

But how different has been the practice in this country. With an area—exclusive of Alaska and our insular possessions—twenty-five times that of Great Britain and Ireland, and a railroad mileage of 192,161 miles, as against 22,000 miles in Great Britain, we have had only one thorough Congressional investigation, namely, that conducted in the year 1886 by the Senate Committee on Interstate Commerce. The act to regulate commerce, drawn by Senator Cullom, chairman of that committee, is loyal to the fundamental American principle of government that all contested questions affecting the commercial interests of the country shall be subjected to the test of judicial inquiry and determination. But the populistic proposition confronts the country in favor of eliminating the courts from this domain of justice, and in lieu thereof of substituting an autocratic rule of administrative authority without any Congressional investigation whatsoever.

There are also other and exceedingly important questions which demand Congressional investigation and public scrutiny in the light of such inquiry. Some of these questions are more important than those determined by the Senate investigation of 1886.

The magnitude and importance of the commercial, financial, and industrial interests involved repel the very idea of any radical legislation in advance of such inquiry as that here suggested.

Beyond all doubt a thorough Congressional investigation of the various commercial, economic, and political questions involved in the general subject of railroad regulation in this country would develop results quite as salutary as those realized in Great Britain. It may also be stated in favor of such action that the two committees of Congress as at present constituted are admirably fitted for such inquiry.

In his recent annual message to Congress President Roosevelt referred to the railroads as "the arteries through which the commercial lifeblood of this nation flows," and in urging the importance of investigation said: "The whole history of the world shows that legislation will generally be both unwise and ineffective unless undertaken after calm inquiry and with sober self-restraint."

### SENATOR DOLLIVER'S INQUIRY.

In the course of my hearing before this committee on June 6, Senator Dolliver, of Iowa, propounded to me the following question:

"WILL NOT THE COMBINATION OF LINES EVENTUALLY GIVE THE RAILROADS SUCH CONTROL OVER RATES AS TO ENABLE THEM GREATLY TO ADVANCE THEIR CHARGES?"

This inquiry touches the pivotal point of the present hearings.

As at the beginning of our national life, so now we have no way of judging the future but by the past and by the force and evident trend of existing conditions. Guided by such indications, I shall to the best of my ability attempt to answer the Senator's important inquiry.

From 1867 to 1902, a period of thirty-five years, the consolidation of competing and connecting railroads proceeded steadily. From time to time during that period the prediction was confidently made that such combinations would result in the absolute control of rates by railroad magnates, and that in consequence rates would be greatly advanced. But the historic record of railroad operations in this country proves those predictions to have been absolutely erroneous. During the period mentioned the control of rates exercised by railroad managers was weakened rather than strengthened. Freight charges fell constantly, and at times to such an extent as to force many hundreds of millions of dollars worth of railroad property into bankruptcy. The decline of rates from 1870 to 1900 is stated in the following table, taken from page 397 of the Statistical Abstract of the United States, published by the National Government:

*Average reductions in the freight charges per ton per mile on the railroads of the various sections of the country from 1870 to 1900.*

| Lines. | 1870. | 1880. | 1890. | 1900. |
|---|---|---|---|---|
| | Cents. | Cents. | Cents. | Cents. |
| Lines east of Chicago ............................... | 1.61 | 0.87 | 0.63 | 0.55 |
| Western and Northwestern lines.................... | 2.61 | 1.44 | 1.00 | .89 |
| Southwestern lines ............................... | 2.95 | 1.65 | 1.11 | .91 |
| Southern lines ................................... | 2.39 | 1.16 | .80 | .63 |
| Transcontinental lines............................ | 4.50 | 2.21 | 1.50 | .93 |
| Average ................................... | 1.99 | 1.17 | .91 | .70 |

This table shows that as the result of the interaction of all the forces and influences which prevailed during the thirty years from 1870 to 1900 the average rate on railroads east of Chicago, in the Western and Northwestern States, and in the Southwestern States during the year 1900 was only about one-third the rate in 1870; that the average rate on railroads of the Southern States east of the Mississippi River during the year 1900 was only about one-fourth the rate in 1870, and that the average rate on the various transcontinental lines during the year 1900 was only about one-fifth the rate during the year 1870. The average rate on all the railroads of the country during the year 1900 was only a little more than one-third the average rate during the year 1870.

According to the data of the Bureau of Statistics as stated in the above table the average rate per ton per mile fell from 1.99 cents in 1870 to 0.70 cent in 1890, a reduction of 1.29 cents per ton per mile. Multiplying this last-mentioned sum into the tons carried 1 mile in 1900, namely, 141,599,157,270 tons, we find that it amounted to $1,826,629,128, which enormous sum the people of this country would have paid for freight charges in excess of what they did pay if the tonnage carried in 1900 had paid the rates charged only thirty years before. This saving of $1,826,629,128 exceeded the value of the exports from the United States during any one year. It is also 184 per cent in excess of the amount actually collected by the railroads from freight during the year 1900.

This wonderful reduction in rates has been going on steadily during the last ten years and has not yet been arrested. The Interstate Commerce Commission states that during the year 1890 the average rate per ton per mile was 0.941 cent, and that in 1900 it was only 0.729 cent, a fall of 0.212 cent, which upon 141,599,157,270 tons carried 1 mile amounted to the sum of $300,190,213 in excess of the amount actually collected by railroads from freight during the year 1900.

The foregoing statements are not materially affected by differences in the character of the freight transported on different lines, nor by changes in the character of the freights transported in the different years.

Prior to and during the entire period to which the above statement relates the consolidation of lines proceeded rapidly in all parts of the country. For example, the Pennsylvania Railroad Company in 1854 had under its control only 248 miles of road. In part by construction, but mainly by the acquisition of the lines of other companies, it controlled 10,202 miles of road in 1891. The Chicago and Rock Island Railroad Company, with an original mileage of only 185 miles, has by construction, but mainly by the acquisition of the lines of other companies, become the "Rock Island System," operating 6,979 miles of road. The Atchison, Topeka and Santa Fe Railroad Company owned and controlled 470.58 miles of road in 1873, but in 1901 it controlled 8,257 miles of road, mainly acquired from other companies.

The historic fact, therefore, stands unimpeached and incontrovertible that the consolidation or combination of railroad interests has not resulted in any advancement of rates, but has been followed by greatly reduced rates. It has also been followed by an enormous increase and wonderful improvement in the facilities for railroad transportation, and by an immense expansion of the commercial advantages afforded by such facilities.

### THE CONSIDERATION AS TO THE RELATIVE IMPORTANCE OF THINGS.

There is an economic view of the question propounded to me by Senator Dolliver to which I would particularly invite the attention of the committee. I refer to the consideration as to the relative magnitude and influence of the various forces of transportation and of trade which govern the whole rate situation. I refer particularly to the comparative value of railroad earnings from freight, gross earnings, the value of railroad properties, and the value of merchandise transported on the railroads of the United States during the year 1900. This is exhibited as follows:[a]

| | |
|---|---|
| Freight revenue | $1,049,256,323 |
| Gross earnings from operation | 1,487,044,814 |
| Total capital or liabilities | 11,891,902,339 |
| Estimated annual value of merchandise transported | 25,000,000,000 |

From this comparative statement it appears that the commercial value of the goods transported on railroads of the United States is about twice the value of the railroads of the United States, about seventeen times the total amount of railroad earnings from freight and

---

[a] The first three items of this statement are taken from the statistical report of the Interstate Commerce Commission, while "value of merchandise transported" is the result of careful estimates.

passengers, and about twenty-four times the receipts of the railroads from the transportation of freights. In a word, the forces of trade, measured by money value, are about twenty-four times those of transportation. This, of course, raises the strong presumption that transportation is the servitor of trade and not trade the servitor of transportation. It also suggests a cause of the reduction of rates.

### THE MANNER IN WHICH THE COMPETING FORCES OF TRANSPORTATION AND OF TRADE ARE OPERATIVE.

In this connection the practical question naturally arises—in what manner and with what effect upon freight charges are the competing forces of transportation and of trade operative? Upon this point I would remark that there is a coercive, a constant, and a world-wide tendency in trade toward a parity of values as the direct result of the competition of product with like product commonly designated as the competition of commercial forces. This tendency toward a parity of values expresses itself in a constant stress upon transportation charges, for the evident reason that the rate on a given article between any two points must always be less than the difference in the price of such article at the point of shipment and at the delivery. The railroad tariff maker is never able to analyze this stress of prices upon rates, so as to exhibit its various elements. He simply designates it by the general expression "What the traffic will bear," by which he means that any price in excess of a certain standard would injuriously diminish or perhaps entirely arrest some particular traffic movement. The commercial fact therefore stands unimpeached that the tendency toward a parity of values, otherwise known as the competition of commercial forces, has in the past, does to-day, and necessarily will in the future exert a potential influence in preventing any advance in freight charges to whatever extent railroad combinations may be effected.

### THE EFFECT OF THE COMPETITION OF RIVAL TRADE CENTERS UPON RAILROAD FREIGHT CHARGES.

The competition of rival trade centers and of other sources of traffic exerts both directly and indirectly a very potential influence upon rates. It brings to bear upon the rates to and from every town and city the influence of the entire property interests of such centers of trade. Besides, the traffic interests of every railroad are greatly dependent upon the commercial prosperity of its termini and other traffic centers on its line. Hence the prosperity of the principal and other direct sources of traffic of each line must be protected by rates which will prevent any diversion of trade to rival trade centers. Thus every railroad company is bound by motives of self-interest to loyalty to its special sources of traffic, while at the same time necessarily reaching out for additional traffic from every available source. All this imparts an intense degree of complexity to the railroad-traffic situation. Its obvious and most important effect is to prevent any advancement in rates. Its actual result has been to reduce rates.

### COMPETITION BETWEEN RIVAL RAILROAD COMPANIES.

The direct competition between rival lines of railroad transportation has exerted a most potential influence in the reduction of freight charges. While closely related to each other in cooperative traffic movements, and bound together by the rules essential to the orderly conduct of the American railroad system, the lines of the various companies have been from the beginning and are to-day at sharp rivalry with each other with respect to competitive traffic. The situation presents exceedingly complex and varied illustrations of unity in diversity, which for many years has confounded the wisdom of the wise and baffled the skill or the most astute. Such competition in the past has tended powerfully to reduce rates. At times there have been destructive railroad wars. During these contests ruinous rates have prevailed, and the task of subsequently raising rates to a remunerative standard has usually been a very difficult one.

### GENERAL DEDUCTIONS FROM THE FOREGOING STATEMENTS.

1. The predictions made from time to time during the last thirty-five years that railroad proprietors would speedily secure the absolute control of rates as the result of combinations and consolidations have been disproved by the results of experience. The control exercised over rates by railroad managers has decreased, and rates have continued to fall.

2. The average charge for railroad transportation in this country is less than in any other country. Approximately the average charge in the United States for 1900 as reported by the Interstate Commerce Commission—0.729 of a cent per ton per mile—was only about one-third the average rate in England and in France, and only about one-half the average rate charged in Germany, notwithstanding the fact that the cost of materials and the wages paid to railroad employees in the United States are higher than in the countries of Europe. This grand result is due mainly to the excellent manner in which the American railroad system is administered, and to the better equipment and the superior economic use of equipment in this country.

3. The constant reduction in the actual cost of transportation due to improved economies in the construction and management and to the enormous increase in the volume of traffic have permitted the constant reduction in freight charges to go on without any general reduction in net revenues and without impairing the value of railroad properties of this country.

### THE RESULTS OF RAILROAD COMBINATION IN THE FUTURE A CONJECTURE.

In the face of the foregoing facts in regard to the fall of rates and the decreasing power of railroad managers over rates, I clearly apprehend that the inquiry propounded to me by Senator Dolliver is based upon the assumption that the combinations recently formed, or which may be formed, in the not distant future may become so great as to overpower those restraining influences of competition which in the past have resulted in the reduction of rates.

This is an hypothesis not susceptible of exact demonstration either as to its correctness or incorrectness. It abandons the lessons of experience and leads into a field of speculation. Still, the idea has gained such lodgment in the public mind as to command the attention of the legislator.

In order to weigh the possibilities and probabilities involved in the inquiry it appears necessary to consider the purposes which are sub-served by competition and combination in the economies of life, with special reference to railroad transportation in this country.

We live in a world in which we are all debating. Competition is the first expression and enduring motive in the struggle. On the other hand, an equally virile trait—the social. instinct—leads men to associate themselves together in cooperative enterprise. Since the world began man's faith in his fellow-man was never before so pro-nounced as it is to-day. This is manifested in innumerable forms of social, industrial, and intellectual association. Combination has for its economic basis and justification three principal objects:

First. It is resorted to as a condition of good. In all ages, many of the world's activities have demanded joint physical and intellectual effort and the use of aggregated capital. The great industrial enter-prises of the present day, and notably those of mining, manufacture, and the construction and management of railroads, are the product of such combinations. Thus far these agencies have wrought beneficially and produced grand results. Any proposition to curtail or forbid the use of aggregated capital would now be regarded as a vagary of the most absurd character.

Second. Cooperative rules and regulations in the nature of combi-nation, are incidental to self-government among those who unite their efforts and capital for the accomplishment of any common object and are necessary for the maintenance of order and justice.

Third. During the last forty years the most impelling motive to combination has been its adoption as a restraint upon competition which when unrestrained runs to disorder and ruin. As such, combination has become the balance wheel of competitive enterprise. Labor com-binations upon the trades-union plan are securely based upon this expedient. Such combinations, regarded a hundred years ago as con-spiracies against the public interests. because in restraint of free com-petition, are to-day subject to no legal or judicial limitations other than those which pertain to the maintenance of order and a proper regard for public and private rights—limitations to which all combinations should be, and, as a rule, are subject.

The absolute necessity and the proven beneficence of the regulation of competition through combination has exposed the absurdity and flagrantly erroneous character of the familiar maxim, "Competition is the life of trade." Fifty years ago Judge Howe, of Wisconsin, afterwards a Senator of the United States from that State, clearly stated that competition is quite as often destructive of trade as pro-motive of trade, and the experiences of the last fifty years have afforded abundant proof of the correctness of that view. Under the intensely virile economic and commercial conditions of the present age competition is continually running to disorder and ruin. It has been proved a thousand times that its possibilities for good are subject to the limitations imposed by the restraints of combination of some sort. There is no economic proposition of the age more firmly established in the public mind. Human intelligence and acquisitiveness consti-tute the life of trade, and competition and combination are merely self-adjusting expressions of the interaction of forces.

The exploded adage "Competition is the life of trade" has in turn begotten the idea that any restraint upon competition is necessarily unjust restraint upon trade, and this idea has even found expression in judicial utterance, but it is a fallacy which long ago ought to have been consigned to the rubbish heap of exploded economic notions. The idea that any restraint upon competition is necessarily an evil goes in the face of all the analogies in the conduct of human affairs, for our civilization is based upon a complex and nicely-adjusted system of restraints and limitations, wrought out by the teachings of experience throughout the ages. We are all tethered in a thousand ways for our mutual comfort and advancement. The world recognizes to-day that the assumed inviolability of competition is an idle dream.

## THE BENEFICENCE OF COMBINATION IN RESTRAINT OF COMPETITION STRIKINGLY ILLUSTRATED IN THE AMERICAN RAILROAD SYSTEM.

The three incentives to combination just mentioned have had their most striking illustration and justification, in this country, in the construction and management of railroads, and in the conduct of their traffic interests. This is indicated in the following brief historical sketch:

Prior to the close of the civil war the railroads of the United States, as a rule, were physically and commercially disassociated. But the physical unity of the various lines and the continuity of traffic over connected lines was soon thereafter seen to be a national necessity. This thought was inspired by political as well as by commercial and economic considerations, for it was clearly perceived that the Union which had been saved by the force of arms was most likely to be reinvigorated and maintained by means of the facilities for direct and speedy commercial intercourse. The desired junction of lines, and continuity of through traffic over connected lines were fully legalized by the act of Congress of June 15, 1866, commonly known as "The charter of the American railroad system." The establishment of our national railroad system was also greatly promoted by the action of State legislatures which offered solicitous invitations to the railroads of other States to extend their lines across State boundaries and to engage freely in interstate traffic.

The juncture of tracks and unity of traffic interests forming one great combined national railroad system begat the second form of railroad combination above noted, namely, organic union involving rules and regulations in the nature of self-government. This was obviously necessary for the maintenance of the orderly conduct of the railroad system; for there can be no organic unity without a governing organization. Such government was established by means of joint traffic associations in various parts of the country.

But by far the most impelling motive to railroad combination has been that dictated by the necessity of imposing restraints upon a competition which when left uncontrolled ran at once and almost invariably to the ruin of the railroad companies and the demoralization of commerce. The fact that the railroads were so closely bound together physically by political and commercial necessities gave to their competitive struggle an intensely destructive character not experienced by disassociated competitors. This compelled the restraint of competition by combination. Such restraint was effected by traffic agreements between rival lines and coterminous lines. These agreements, in the nature of compromise, were highly beneficial to the extent to which they were adopted and honestly maintained. But they were greatly weakened by what, in the light of subsequent events, appears to have been a legislative misadventure. I refer to the act of July 2, 1890, entitled "An act to protect trade and commerce against unlawful restraints and monopolies." If the spirit of that statute, as clearly indicated by the words "unlawful restraints" in its title, had prevailed it would have been a beneficent act, conformed to the principles of justice and economic soundness upon which our governmental institutions are founded, but by what seems to have been an inadvertence the statute forbade "every contract in restraint of trade."

Being deprived of the power of self-government essential to the control of their own interaction with the specific object in view of placing cooperative restraints upon a fierce and destructive competition, certain of the railroads of the country have had recourse to a merger of their interests as a substitute for that restraint of cooperation upon competition which is conformed to sound economic principles and which the lessons of experience have proved to be just and beneficent, but which the Federal judiciary had declared to be forbidden by the act of July 2, 1890. (166 U. S., 290.)

It appears therefore that railroad combination, instead of being a simple proposition, dependent solely upon the volition of railroad managers, is an exceedingly complex proposition. As before shown, it had its origin and has as its main support to-day an important political object, and also vitally important commercial objects upon which the trade and industrial interests of the country securely rest. Besides, as shown, it has a substantial economic basis. Railroad combinations, such as those in regard to which apprehensions have been raised, are in fact but corollaries to that combination of lines and of traffic operations dictated by overpowering political and commercial considerations. It is unnecessary here to follow out the deductions which must readily occur to the minds of the members of this committee as to the delicacy and importance of the issues raised by the proposition to radically change the policy of the Government in regard to a system of transportation which has wrought so beneficially for the country upon the ground of a mere apprehension that its future operations may be detrimental to the public interests.

### RÉSUMÉ.

I have thus attempted to throw the light of fact and of reasoning upon the important question propounded to me by Senator Dolliver, which I here repeat:

"WILL NOT THE COMBINATION OF LINES EVENTUALLY GIVE THE RAILROADS SUCH POWER OVER RATES AS TO ENABLE THEM GREATLY TO ADVANCE THEIR CHARGES?"

By way of recapitulation of all I have said in reply to this inquiry I respectfully submit the following:

1. During the last thirty-five years the combination of competing railroad lines has been going on, and at the same time the companies have been compelled greatly to reduce their rates.

2. The consideration of the relative magnitude of the forces of commerce and of transportation indicates that transportation is the servitor of commerce and not commerce the servitor of transportation.

3. The influences of competition, which have resulted in the reduction of rates and in weakening the power of railroad managers over

rates, have been exerted under the following conditions: (a) The most potential and persuasive form of competition has been that of commercial forces which expresses itself in an irrepressible tendeney toward a parity of values. (b) The competition of rival towns and cities and other traffic centers has exerted a very potential influence over rates. (c) The competition of rival railroads has been a very effective influence in demoralizing and permanently reducing rates.

4. The combination of competitive forces occurs under three distinct conditions: (a) As a condition of good, with respect to industries which can be more successfully prosecuted by associated than by individual capital and effort. (b) In that form of combination which is incidental to associated enterprise for the purposes of self-government. (c) In the restraint of competition by combination for the prevention of the disorder and ruin incident to unrestrained competition.

5. The railroads of the United States are combined under the following conditions: (a) Under the political condition of reinvigorating. and maintaining the union of States, as provided in the act of June 15, 1866. (b) Under the commercial condition of supplying the means of uninterrupted facilities for joint traffic over connected lines. (c) With the economic object in view of restraining and regulating competition between rival lines which if unrestrained by combination invariably degenerate into disorder, to the detriment of both commerce and transportation.

6. The recent merger of railroad interests has been very largely the result of the decision of the Supreme Court of the United States in the trans-Missouri case, that combination in restraint of competition is forbidden by the act of July 2, 1890, commonly known as "the antitrust act."

CONCLUSION.

In view of the foregoing I respectfully submit that neither the lessons of experience nor the apparent trend of existing conditions indicate that in the future there can be or will be any material advancement in railroad freight charges. Certainly the mere apprehension that such advancement in rates may occur affords no possible excuse for that proposed radical change in the national policy which is embodied in the bills now before this committee for its consideration, having reference especially to the measure which is known as the Nelson-Corliss bill.

It seems to be a well-established historic fact that the most important object of the Constitution of the United States was to prevent the several States from employing the taxing power or any other attribute of sovereignty for the purpose of discriminating against other States, and thus of promoting their respective commercial and industrial interests. This cause of dissension and danger of dissolution was removed by conferring upon the Congress of the United States the sole power of regulating commerce among the States. The power thus conferred has ever since been exercised by simply refraining from any statutory provision in the nature of affording commercial or industrial advantage to any town, city, State, or section of the country. It is a latent power. By adhering rigidly to this governmental policy of noninterference the absolute freedom of trade has been preserved within our borders. The struggles of commercial and industrial endeavor have been left absolutely to the conservatism which inheres in the untrammeled interaction of forces.

The interstate-commerce act contains not a word in derogation of this principle, for, as explained elsewhere in my hearing before this committee, that statute is firmly based upon the evolved law of the American railroad system, wrought out in the hard school of experience and of adopted usage, and may therefore be characterized as American common law. In the face of all this the Interstate Commerce Commission, and by its promptings certain representations of trade organizations, have appeared before you in favor of a policy which would confer upon the Commission the power to determine the course of the commercial and industrial development of this country. This appeal comes up to you in the wake of unsuccessful efforts on the part of the Commission to assert the right under the provisions of the act to regulate commerce to exercise the judicial function, to prescribe rates for the future, to eliminate the Federal judiciary from the consideration of vital questions of right and justice in the conduct of the internal commerce of this country, and of efforts to gain the power to exercise the revolutionary function of determining the relative commercial status and prosperity of different sections of this country, an attempt which the Supreme Court of the United States denounced in the maximum rate case with expressions of reprobation. (167 U. S. 479.)

The record of the proceedings of the Interstate Commerce Commission affords abundant proof of the wisdom of the policy of commercial freedom established in this country at the beginning. During the fifteen years of its existence the Commission has not discovered a single case of exorbitant charges which has been sustained by the courts, and it has been able to prove before the courts less than one case a year of unjust discrimination. This is the splendid official record of a railroad system embracing nearly 200,000 miles of road, over which many millions of transactions are recorded yearly, the total value of the goods transported aggregating about $25,000,000,000 annually.

During the last three years 807 complaints were submitted to the Commission, which, however, gave rise to only 23 formal decisions by the Commission, involving only 8 cases of unreasonable rates, of which only 4 cases were sustained by the Commission. The great bulk of the complaints preferred to the Commission and which gave rise to informal hearings have had their origin in the incidental evils and frictional resistances of the most splendid system of transportation the world ever saw, and in complaints based upon discontent arising out of the competitive struggles of rival towns, cities, and industries for commercial advantage, with which struggles the Government of the United States has never meddled, and with which hopefully the Congress of the United States will never interfere while the intelligence and civic virtue of the American people shall endure.

PETITIONS, MEMORIALS, AND RESOLUTIONS OF STATE LEGIS-
LATURES AND COMMERCIAL ORGANIZATIONS TRANSMITTED
THROUGH THE UNITED STATES SENATE TO THE COMMITTEE ON
INTERSTATE COMMERCE DURING THE FIRST SESSION FIFTY-
SEVENTH CONGRESS WITH REFERENCE TO S. 3521 (THE ELKINS
BILL) AND S. 3575 (THE NELSON BILL).

∴

*Resolution adopted by the Grain Dealers' Association in convention at Des Moines, Iowa,*
*recommending the amendment to the interstate-commerce law.*

[Presented by Mr. Cullom December 4, 1801.]

*To the Senate and House of Representatives of the United States, to assemble in the Fifty-*
*seventh Congress:*

The Grain Dealers' National Association in convention assembled at the city of
Des Moines, Iowa, on the 3d day of October, 1901, does hereby memorialize your honorable bodies to enact into law such amendments to the existing interstate-commerce
act as will effectually remedy the defects that have been found to exist therein and
will insure its proper enforcement in the protection of the public interest in relation
to transportation, and yet will in no way impair the just rights or privileges of common carriers.

It is the belief of this convention that the present law has been rendered practically inoperative by recent decisions of the Supreme Court, and that the public is
without redress from unjust and unreasonable exactions and discriminations on the
part of common carriers.

Your petitioners, therefore, earnestly pray that your honorable bodies will give
the subject the consideration which its great importance demands and provide speedy
relief to the public by the enactment of such amendments to the law as will give it
full force and effect.

---

2.

*Joint resolution relating to S. 1439, commonly called the "Cullom bill," adopted by the*
*Wisconsin legislature at its session in 1901.*

[Presented by Mr. Spooner January 7, 1902.]

Whereas various decisions of the Supreme Court of the United States during the
past few years have rendered many of the most important provisions of the interstate-commerce law inoperative, in consequence of which the law in its present
form fails to afford the relief to the shipping interests of the country which was
the purpose of its enactment; and

Whereas a bill is now pending in the United States Senate known as S. 1439, commonly called the "Cullom bill," which is understood to have been framed by a
member of the Commission with the approval of that body, comprising such amendments to the interstate-commerce act as, in its belief, will remedy the defects found
to exist therein and render it effective in accomplishing the purposes of its original
enactment; and

Whereas the said bill has received the indorsements of the principal commercial
organizations of this State and of most of the similar organizations of importance
throughout the country, and of the National Board of Trade, and its passage was
urgently recommended to Congress by a national convention held at St. Louis
November 20 last, consisting of delegates from ten national trade organizations, representing various lines of business, and twenty of the most important State and local
organizations of similar character in this country: Therefore, be it

*Resolved by the assembly (the senate concurring),* That the Congress of the United States
be, and is hereby, requested to speedily enact said Senate bill No. 1439 into law, and
we urgently request that the Senators and members of the House of Representatives from this State cooperate in promoting the passage of said bill, and use their

best endeavors in securing for it precedence over other pending legislation as its great public importance demands.

*Resolved,* That the governor be, and he is hereby, requested to transmit copies of this memorial to the President of the Senate, Speaker of the House of Representatives, and to each of our Representatives.

---

3.

*Petition of Grain Dealers' Association of Des Moines, Iowa, praying for an amendment to the interstate-commerce law.*

[Presented by Mr. Dolliver, January 7, 1902.]

DES MOINES, IOWA, *October 3, 1901.*

*To the Senate and House of Representatives of the United States assembled in the Fifty-seventh Congress:*

The Grain Dealers' National Association in convention assembled, at the city of Des Moines, Iowa, on the 3d day of October, 1901, does hereby respectfully memorialize your honorable bodies to enact into law such amendments to the existing interstate-commerce act as will effectually remedy the defects that have been found to exist therein, and will insure its proper enforcement in the protection of public interest in relation to transportation, and yet will in no way impair the just rights or privileges of common carriers.

It is the belief of this convention that the present law has been rendered practically inoperative by recent decisions of the Supreme Court, and that the public is without redress from unjust and unreasonable exactions and discriminations on the part of common carriers.

Your petitioners therefore earnestly pray that your honorable bodies will give the subject the consideration which its great importance demands, and provide speedy relief to the public by the enactment of such amendments to the law as will give it full force and effect.

The foregoing memorial to Congress was unanimously adopted by the Grain Dealers' National Association in convention, at the place and on the date above mentioned.

B. A. LOCKWOOD, *President.*

Attest:

CHARLES S. CLARK, *Secretary.*

---

4.

*National Live Stock Association, praying for legislation giving the Interstate Commerce Commission adequate power to correct discriminating rates, etc.*

[Presented by Mr. Frye January 7, 1902; also by Mr. Warren; also by Mr. Elkins.]

The following memorial was unanimously adopted by the fifth annual convention of the National Live Stock Association held in Chicago, Ill., December 3, 4, 5, 6, 1901:

*To the Honorable President, the Senate, and the House of Representatives of the United States:*

The National Live Stock Association respectfully represents that it is an organization composed of over 150 of the principal stock raisers, feeders' and breeders' organizations, live-stock exchanges, stock-yards companies, and various commercial organizations of the United States whose names we append hereto; that it represents more than $4,000,000,000 of invested capital, and that it was organized for the purpose of promoting the best interests of the live-stock industry of this country.

This association in behalf of its constituency earnestly urges upon Congress the great importance and increasing need of Federal legislation which will give to the Interstate Commerce Commission adequate power to correct discrimination, remove preferences, abate unreasonable rates, and, where necessary, to prescribe the maximum and minimum rates, making its decision effective, pending any appeal to the courts.

When the present interstate-commerce law was enacted in 1887 it was at least popularly supposed, and we believe clearly intended, that it gave to the Interstate Commerce Commission, after due hearing and investigation, the power to say what was a reasonable or unreasonable rate, and to enforce its decisions.    Court decisions have since declared that the Interstate Commerce Commission does not have the power to fix rates for the future either directly or by indirection.    As substantially every complaint that has been or would be brought before the Commission involves the question of the reasonableness of rates, it can be readily seen that these court decisions practically wipe out the only real power the Commission was supposed to have, and limits its usefulness to the collection and promulgation of statistics.

While governmental control over railroad charges through the medium of the Interstate Commerce Commission has been gradually fading away, the general railroad situation has undergone portentous changes.    Little independent carriers have been forced to the wall and absorbed by their larger competitors, which in turn have combined with or sold out to other larger competing systems, until to-day, by this centralization, the rail transportation facilities of this country are practically controlled by scarce half a dozen different interests.    By these transitions, reorganizations, and combinations added burdens have not only been placed upon the man who pays the freight by reason of increases in the fixed charges or indebtedness of the railroads, but his sole remaining safeguard by free competition has been virtually eliminated, so that the public, which now has greater need of intelligent and effective Federal supervision and regulation of railroad charges, has less protection to-day than previous to the enactment of the present interstate-commerce law.

The general and marked advance in rates during the past three years of unexampled prosperity to the railroads were apparently unnecessary and seemingly unwarranted upon any other theory than the intent of the railroads to exact all they could.    The multiple economies of railroad operation, together with the enormous increase in the volume of the traffic, would seem to logically suggest a reduction instead of an advance.    Their action, however, enables us to unmistakably forecast what they would do, unrestrained by Federal control, when by further consolidations or by other agencies competition becomes entirely stifled.

The members of the National Live Stock Association recognize that the railroads are powerful agencies of progress, and that more than any other factor they have contributed to the development of the country.    The superb service they perform merits our commendation.    We expect to pay the railroads the cost of the service they render, together with a reasonable profit on their investment; we do not want the service for any less, nor ought we to be compelled to pay more.    We are not presuming to say what are or may be reasonable and fair rates, but we do emphatically protest against the railroads being the sole arbiters of their charges and exacting what they think the traffic will stand, or, in plainer language, all they can get.

If railroad rates are fair and reasonable, the railroads should not fear any investigation of them by an impartial tribunal.    The objections they make against the proper Federal supervision of rates by an expert commission confirms the suspicion that railroad rates need regulating.

Either the Government must assume at once an intelligent and comprehensive control over railroad charges or prepare for absolute ownership of the transportation facilities of this country.

For these, among many other patent reasons, the members of the National Live Stock Association respectfully request Congress to give early attention to this much needed legislation, which has already been too long delayed.

Attest:                                                    JOHN W. SPRINGER, *President.*
                                                           CHAS. F. MARTIN, *Secretary.*

---

MEMBERSHIP ROLL OF THE NATIONAL LIVE STOCK ASSOCIATION.

*Arizona.*—Arizona Wool Growers' Association; Live Stock Sanitary Board, Arizona.

*California.*—Kern County Cattle Growers' Association; Southern Pacific Railway Company; Central California Stock Growers' Association.

*Canada.*—Dominion Short Horn Breeders' Association.

*Colorado.*—Custer County Cattle Growers' Protective Association; Denver Union Stock Yards Company; Southern Colorado Stock Growers' Protective Association; State Veterinary Sanitary Board; Fort Collins Sheep Feeders' Association; Logan County Cattle and Horse Protective Association; Lincoln and Elbert County Wool Growers' Association; Lincoln County Cattle Growers' Association; San Luis Valley Cattle and Horse Growers' Association; Roaring Fork and Eagle River Stock Association; Eastern Colorado Stockmen's Protective Association; North Fork Valley Cattle Growers' Association; Weld County Live Stock Association; Park County Cattle Growers' Association; Eagle and Grand River Stock Growers' Association; Denver Chamber of Commerce and Board of Trade; Gunnison County Stock Growers' Association; Colorado Midland Railway Company; Colorado and Southern Railway Company; Crystal River Railroad Company; North Park Stock Growers' Association; White River Stock Growers' Association; Grand River Stock Growers' Association; Saguache Stock Growers' Association; Western Slope Wool Growers' Association; Cattle and Horse Growers' Association of Colorado; Denver and Rio Grande Railroad Company.

*Idaho.*—Blaine, Lincoln, and Cassia Counties Wool Growers' Association; Sheep and Wool Growers' Association of Idaho; Sheep and Wool Growers' Association of Southern Idaho; Fremont County, Idaho, Wool Growers' Association; Oneida County, Idaho, Wool Growers' Association; Washington County Wool Growers' Association.

*Illinois.*—Illinois Central Railroad Company; Chicago and Northwestern Railroad Company; Chicago Live Stock Exchange; American Short Horn Breeders' Association; St. Louis Live Stock Exchange; St. Louis National Stock Yards Company; National Irrigation Association; Union Stock Yards and Transit Company, Chicago; State Board of Live Stock Commissioners.

*Indiana.*—American Shetland Pony Club; American Shropshire Registry Association; Polled Durham Cattle Club of America.

*Iowa.*—Sioux City Live Stock Exchange; Sioux City Stock Yards Company; Iowa Improved Stock Breeders' Association.

*Kansas.*—The Kansas Improved Stock Breeders' Association.

*Kentucky.*—American Saddle Horse Association.

*Michigan.*—National Lincoln Sheep Breeders' Association.

*Minnesota.*—Minnesota Live Stock Breeders' Association; South St. Paul Live Stock Exchange.

*Missouri.*—American Hereford Cattle Breeders' Association; American Angora Goat Breeders' Association; American Galloway Breeders' Association; Kansas City Stock Yards Company; St. Joseph Stock Yards Company; South St. Joseph Live Stock Exchange; Kansas City Live Stock Exchange; The Wabash Railroad Company; The Commercial Club of Kansas City.

*Montana.*—Montana Stock Growers' Association; Eastern Montana Wool Growers' Association; Central Montana Wool Growers' Association; North Montana Wool Growers' Association.

*Nebraska.*—Union Stock Yards Company, of Omaha; South Omaha Live Stock Exchange; Nebraska Stock Growers' Association; Fremont, Elkhorn and Missouri Valley Railway Company; Union Pacific Railway Company.

*Nevada.*—Nevada Wool Growers' Association.

*New Mexico.*—Black Range Protective Association; Sheep Sanitary Board, New Mexico; Cattle Sanitary Board, of New Mexico; Pecos Valley and Northern Railroad Company; Sheep and Wool Growers' Association of New Mexico.

*New York.*—National Association of Exhibitors of Live Stock.

*Ohio.*—American Rambouillet Sheep Breeders' Association; Cincinnati Union Stock Yards Company; Cincinnati Live Stock Commission Merchants' Association; Red Polled Cattle Club of America.

*Oklahoma.*—Oklahoma Live Stock Association.

*Oregon.*—Pacific Northwest Wool Growers' Association; Oregon Stock Breeders' Association; Oregon Railway and Navigation Company; Oregon Wool Growers' Association.

*Pennsylvania.*—West Philadelphia Stock Yards.

*South Dakota.*—Western South Dakota Stock Growers' Association; Missouri River Stockmen's Association.

*Tennessee.*—State Board of Agriculture.

*Texas.*—Fort Worth Stock Yards Company; Cattle Raisers' Association of Texas; Texas Live Stock Association; El Paso-Rock Island Railway Company.

*Utah.*—Utah Wool Growers' Association; Utah Live Stock Association; Dairymen's Association of Utah; Oregon Short Line Railway Company; State Irrigation Association of Utah.

*Wyoming.*—Wyoming Stock Growers' Association; Fremont County Wool Growers' Association; Sweetwater Hereford Cattle Breeders' Association; Uinta County, Wyoming, Wool Growers' Association; Snake River Stock Growers' Association; Board of Sheep Commissioners, Wyoming; State Agricultural College, Wyoming; Northern Wyoming Wool Growers' Association; Eastern Wyoming Wool Growers' Association; Carbon County, Wyoming, Wool Growers' Association; Natrona County Wool Growers' Association.

INDIVIDUAL MEMBERSHIP.

John Cleman, North Yakima, Wash.
A. C. Huidekoper, Meadville, Pa.
E. C. Huidekoper, Yule, N. Dak.
John Clay, jr., Chicago, Ill.
E. D. Brown, Scottsville, N. Y.
S. W. Allerton, Chicago, Ill.
C. M. O'Donel, Bell Ranch, N. Mex.
Frank Rockefeller, Belvidere, Kans.
I. T. Pryor, Kansas City, Mo.
James Leonard, Denver, Colo.
A. B. Urmston, El Paso, Tex.
A. T. Atwater, Kansas City, Mo.
Alex Bowie, Chugwater, Wyo.
Emil Taussig, New York, N. Y.
Frank P. Bennett, Boston, Mass.
Nelson Morris, Chicago, Ill.
F. E. Warren, Cheyenne, Wyo.
George Y. Wallace, Salt Lake City, Utah.
H. H. Huffaker, Silver City, Iowa.
Richard Walsh, Clarendon, Tex.
J. W. Martin, Richland City, Wis.
H. M. Hunter, Port Hope, Manitoba, Canada.
D. B. Zimmerman, Dickenson, N. Dak.
F. C. Lusk, Chico, Cal.
Overton Lea, Nashville, Tenn.
Charles W. Barney, Gillette, Wyo.
Theodore Cuyler Patterson, Philadelphia, Pa.

R. M. Allen, Ames, Nebr.
Mrs. Lillian Gregory, Kansas City, Mo.
J. G. McCoy, Wichita, Kans.
John M. Holt, Miles City, Mont.
John Sparks, Reno, Nev.
Peter Jansen, Jansen, Nebr.
A. B. Robertson, Colorado, Tex.
F. M. Stewart, Rapid City, S. Dak.
J. D. Wood, Spencer, Idaho.
D. N. Stickney, Laramie, Wyo.
H. A. Jastro, Bakersfield, Cal.
George F. Patrick, Pueblo, Colo.
Addison C. Thomas, Chicago, Ill.
C. C. Goodwin, Salt Lake City, Utah.
J. R. Stoller, Kansas City, Mo.
E. H. Callister, Salt Lake City, Utah.
C. S. Barclay, West Liberty, Iowa.
John F. Hobbs, New York, N. Y.
D. W. Willson, Elgin, Ill.
Theo. L. Schurmeier, St. Paul, Minn.
H. H. Hinds, Stanton, Mich.
W. C. McDonald, White Oaks, N. Mex.
W. L. Foster, Shreveport, La.
A. P. Bush, jr., Colorado, Tex.
John C. Johnson, Bridgeport, W. Va.
Ed. H. Reid, Colorado Springs, Colo.
R. C. Judson, Portland, Oreg.

------

5.

*Memorial of the legislature of the State of Wisconsin, praying for the enactment of legislation to make more effective the work of the Interstate Commerce Commission.*

[Presented by Mr. Quarles, January 7, 1902.]

*Joint resolution adopted by the Wisconsin legislature at its session in 1901.*

Whereas various decisions of the Supreme Court of the United States during the past few years have rendered many of the most important provisions of the interstate-commerce law inoperative, in consequence of which the law in its present form fails to afford the relief to the shipping interests of the country which was the purpose of its enactment; and

Whereas a bill is now pending in the United States Senate, known as S. 1439, commonly called the "Cullom bill," which is understood to have been framed by a member of the Commission, with the approval of that body, comprising such amendments to the interstate-commerce act as in its belief will remedy the defects found to exist therein and render it effective in accomplishing the purposes of its original enactment; and

Whereas the said bill has received the indorsements of the principal commercial organizations of this State and of most of the similar organizations of importance throughout the country, and of the National Board of Trade, and its passage was urgently recommended to Congress by a national convention held at St. Louis November 20 last, consisting of delegates from ten national trade organizations, representing various lines of business, and twenty of the most important State and local organizations of similar character in this country: Therefore, be it

*Resolved by the assembly (the senate concurring),* That the Congress of the United States be, and is hereby, requested to speedily enact said Senate bill No. 1439 into law, and we urgently request that the Senators and Members of the House of Representatives from this State cooperate in promoting the passage of said bill and use their best endeavors in securing for it precedence over other pending legislation as its great public importance demands.

*Resolved,* That the governor be, and he is hereby, requested to transmit copies of this memorial to the President of the Senate, Speaker of the House of Representatives, and to each of our Representatives.

---

6.

*Petition of the National League of Commission Merchants of the United States, praying for legislation to enforce the findings of the Interstate Commerce Commission.*

[Presented by Mr. Frye, January 20, 1902.]

JANUARY 18, 1902.

Hon. WM. P. FRYE,
   *President United States Senate.*

DEAR SIR: At the tenth annual meeting of the National League of Commission Merchants of the United States, held in Philadelphia, Pa., January 8–10, 1902, it was—

"*Resolved,* That the National League of Commission Merchants of the United States petition Congress to pass such legislation as will confer upon the Interstate Commerce Commission power to enforce their findings."

   Very respectfully,            A. WARREN PATCH,
                                          *Secretary.*

---

7.

*Petition of the Wisconsin Cheese Makers' Association praying for the enactment of legislation to make more effective the work of the Interstate Commerce Commission.*

[Presented by Mr. Quarles, January 28, 1902.]

*Resolved,* That this convention regards the present freight rate of 33 cents per hundred pounds on cheese from southern Wisconsin points to Chicago as unjust, burdensome, and out of proportion to the rate on articles of like character and of more than double the value.

*Resolved further,* That a committee of three be appointed to devise ways and means to cause a reduction of said freight rate to a just amount.

*Resolved by the Wisconsin Cheese Makers' Association,* That our representatives in Congress, both Senators and Representatives, be urgently requested to use their best efforts to secure the passage of the amended laws on interstate commerce to make the decision of the Commission effective, and that the secretary be directed to write to every one.

*Resolved,* That this association indorses the movement by Manitowoc and Calumet County cheese makers of forming an association for practicing and furthering their interests.

The committee on legislation heartily approve and indorse the resolution offered by the committee on resolutions recommending that the State traveling cheese instructors have a general supervision of the sanitary conditions of cheese factories and the milk product delivered at cheese factories.

*And be it further resolved,* That we favor a suitable appropriation from the State to make a proper exhibit of the dairy industry of the State of Wisconsin at the St. Louis World's Fair in 1903.

8.

*Resolution passed by the Retail Dealers' National Association October 3, 1902, favoring the passage of a law extending the powers of the Interstate Commerce Commission.*

[Presented by Mr. Gamble, January 30, 1902.]

DES MOINES, IOWA, *October 3, 1901.*

*To the Senate and House of Representatives of the United States, assembled in the Fifty-seventh Congress:*

The Grain Dealers' National Association in convention assembled, at the city of Des Moines, Iowa, on the 3d day of October, 1901, does hereby respectfully memorialize your honorable bodies to enact into law such amendments to the existing interstate-commerce act as will effectually remedy the defects that have been found to exist therein and will insure its proper enforcement in the protection of public interest in relation to transportation, and yet will in no way impair the just rights or privileges of common carriers.

It is the belief of this convention that the present law has been rendered practically inoperative by recent decisions of the Supreme Court, and that the public is without redress from unjust and unreasonable exactions and discriminations on the part of common carriers.

Your petitioners therefore earnestly pray that your honorable bodies will give the subject the consideration which its great importance demands, and provide speedy relief to the public by the enactment of such amendments to the law as will give it full force and effect.

The foregoing memorial to Congress was unanimously adopted by the Grain Dealers' National Association in convention, at the place and on the date above mentioned.

B. A. LOCKWOOD, *President.*

Attest:

CHARLES S. CLARK, *Secretary.*

---

9.

*Petition Chamber of Commerce of Colorado Springs, Colo., for amendment to interstate-commerce law.*

[Presented by Mr. Teller, February 11, 1902.]

*Resolved,* That the Chamber of Commerce of Colorado Springs, comprising a membership of 320 representative citizens and business men in all walks of life, resident in and about Colorado Springs, does hereby indorse and recommend the passage of the bill (known as bill H. R. 8337) to amend the "Act to regulate commerce," introduced into the House of Representatives January 9, 1902, by Hon. John B. Corliss of Michigan; but we are of the opinion that said act should be further amended by giving the Interstate Commerce Commission full rate-making powers. We make this recommendation for the reason that the recent combination of great railway systems, either by amalgamation or community of interest relations, will, in a large measure, destroy the competition that has heretofore existed, and for this reason it is highly essential for the protection of the people of this country that the Interstate Commerce Commission have full power to adjust and fix railway rates.

CHAMBER OF COMMERCE OF COLORADO SPRINGS, COLO.,

D. B. FAIRLEY, *President.*

GILBERT McCLURG, *Secretary.*

---

10.

*Resolution of the Jobbers Union of St. Paul, Minn., protesting against the enlargement of the powers of the Interstate Commerce Commission.*

[Presented by Mr. Nelson, February 17, 1902.]

ST. PAUL, MINN., *February 8, 1902.*

Hon. KNUTE NELSON,

*Senate Chamber, Washington, D. C.*

DEAR SIR: At a meeting of the executive committee of the St. Paul Jobbers Union the following resolution was unanimously adopted:

"*Resolved,* That in the opinion of the members of this association the powers of the

Interstate Commerce Commission should not be enlarged, and that it would not be in the interest of shippers to transfer the rate-making power to men unacquainted with local conditions and necessities throughout the country. That the powers of the commissioners are ample to carry out the purpose for which they were created. That the demand for increase of power comes almost entirely from the members of the Commission, certain interested railroads, and not from shippers.

"*Resolved*, That the president and secretary be instructed to forward a copy of this resolution to each of the Senators and Representatives from Minnesota."

J. W. COOPER, *President.*

H. P. HALL, *Secretary.*

---

### 11.

*Petition of Goshen Milling Company, of Goshen, Ind., praying for the passage of the proposed amendment to the interstate-commerce law.*

[Presented by Mr. Fairbanks, February 19, 1902.]

GOSHEN, IND., *February 14, 1902.*

Senator FAIRBANKS, *Washington, D. C.*

DEAR SIR: Please do all that you can to promote the passage of the proposed amendment to the interstate law, giving the Commission power to enforce its findings.

Just at present manufacturers of flour are unjustly discriminated against by the railway companies, being compelled to pay higher rates on export flour than is charged on the raw material—wheat.

Yours, very truly,

THE GOSHEN MILLING COMPANY,

F. E. C. HAWKS, *Secretary.*

---

### 12.

*Resolution of the legislature of the State of South Dakota and of other States, and of commercial bodies, favoring enactment of legislation enlarging and extending the powers of the Interstate Commerce Commission.*

[Presented by Mr. Gamble, February 22, 1902.]

WASHINGTON, D. C., *February 20, 1902.*

DEAR SIR: Permit me to call your attention to the following expressions, as evidence of the strong public desire and need for prompt amendment of the "act to regulate commerce."

President Roosevelt, in his message to the Fifty-seventh Congress, said:

"The act should be amended. The subject is one of great importance and calls for the earnest attention of the Congress."

The last State legislature of Michigan, by concurrent resolution, appealed to Congress to amend the act "so as to enable the Interstate Commerce Commission to put into full force and effect its rulings and decisions."

The last State legislature of Wisconsin, by concurrent resolution, petitioned Congress to "speedily amend the act," and requested the Senators and Representatives of that State "to cooperate in promoting the passage of the measure to that end."

The last State legislature of South Dakota, by concurrent resolution, memorialized Congress, urging prompt amendment of the act, "authorizing and empowering the Commission to fix reasonable and just rates, and also adequate and well-defined procedure for the proper enforcement and carrying into effect its decisions and orders. This enlargement of the statute is imperatively needed to give the law efficiency, so that the objects and benefits originally designed may be fully secured to the people."

The last State legislature of Kansas, by concurrent resolution, petitioned Congress to amend the act "so as to enlarge the powers of the Interstate Commerce Commission and give to it authority to prevent unjust discrimination in the interstate carrying trade."

The last State legislature of Louisiana, by concurrent resolution, petitioned Congress to amend the act and requested the Senators and Representatives of that State "to urge upon Congress the passage of amendments defining with more precision the powers and duties of the Commission."

These and other State legislatures, recognizing the demand of the people for relief from present intolerable conditions, have been content to appeal to the United States Congress for remedial legislation.

The Industrial Commission of the United States, in its final report to Congress, says:

"It is incontestable that many of the great industrial combinations had their origin in railroad discriminations. A great change in the status and powers of the Interstate Commerce Commission has taken place since its institution in 1887. The decisions of judicial tribunals have greatly modified and, in general, reduced the powers and functions which the Commission was at first supposed to possess. We recommend that the authority of the Interstate Commerce Commission necessary for the adequate protection of shippers, and clearly intended by the framers of the law, be restored, and that the powers and functions of the Commission be enlarged."

The Interstate Commerce Commission, in its fifteenth annual report to Congress, reiterates its appeal for speedy amendment of the act, and says:

"The Commission has nothing new to propose. Knowledge of present conditions increases the necessity for legislative action upon the lines already indicated."

The National Association of State Railroad Commissioners, in convention at San Francisco, June 5, 1901, by resolution appealed to the United States Congress to amend the act, and said: "Congress is earnestly urged to the prompt enactment of legislation to clothe the Interstate Commerce Commission with power and authority to fix charges when its judgments need to be so perfected;" and again, in convention at Charleston, S. C., February 15, 1902, reiterated its appeal in forceful language.

The National Grange Patrons of Husbandry, in annual convention, appealed to Congress for amendment of the act, and said:

"We furnish nearly 60 per cent of all freight carried by the railroads of this country. We believe that the Commission has tried to carry out the act, but by virtue of judicial decisions it has ceased to be a body for the regulation of interstate carriers. We approve the recommendation as to enlarging the powers and duties of the Commission, giving it and charging it with the duty of fixing maximum rates."

The National Board of Trade, in annual convention in 1901, and again in 1902, urged Congress to promptly amend the act, and said:

"*Resolved*, That the act to regulate commerce should be amended so as to empower the Interstate Commerce Commission to enforce its findings."

The National Live Stock Association, in annual convention, appealed to the United States Congress to amend the act "so that the Interstate Commerce Commission be granted adequate powers to pass upon questions of unreasonableness and unjust railroad rates, and that some legal effect be given to their decisions when rendered."

The Grain Dealers' National Association, in annual convention assembled, at Des Moines, Iowa, October 3, 1901, memorialized the United States Congress "to enact into law such amendments to the existing interstate-commerce act as will remedy the defects that have been found to exist therein and insure its proper inforcement."

The League of National Associations, in convention assembled, with delegates from 41 organizations, petitioned the United States Congress to amend the act "so as to insure its more effective operation in removing existing inequalities and unreasonable exactions in transportation charges and prevent the practice of discriminations now so prevalent."

The Millers' National Association of the United States, in convention assembled, petitioned the United States Congress to amend the act "to restore to the Commission the powers necessary for the protection of the public and enable it to enforce its findings and orders."

The National League of Commission Merchants, the National Hay Association, the National Business League, the National Wholesale Lumber Dealers' Association, the National Wholesale Druggists' Association, and over 125 prominent organizations of shippers—national, State, and local—have in convention, by strong resolutions, petitioned the United States Congress for legislation amendatory of the "Act to regulate commerce." These petitions and appeals have all been filed with Congress and are of record.

With the recent disclosures as to inequality of rates, discriminations, rebates, and utter disregard of published tariffs by the transportation lines of the country, evidencing the impotency of the act, and the expressions cited above, can it be maintained that the present law is sufficient and may be enforced or that there is not a strong demand from the people for prompt relief from Congress?

Respectfully,

FRANK BARRY, *Secretary.*

13.

*Petition of Indiana State Board of Commerce, of Indianapolis, Ind., praying for certain amendments to the·interstate-commerce law.*

[Presented by Mr. Fairbanks, February 23, 1902.]

Whereas discriminations in freight rates are resulting in great injustice to individuals and great damage to industries in Indiana; and

Whereas the interstate-commerce act as at present constituted is inadequate to relieve this state of affairs; and

Whereas it is the sense of the Indiana State Board of Commerce that amendments to the interstate-commerce act should be speedily adopted which will give the Commission greater power, and which will expedite the final adjustment of cases decided by that Commission:

*Resolved,* That we urge the Senators and Representatives from the State of Indiana to do all in their power to advance on the Calendar and push to early favorable vote the amendments to the interstate-commerce act known as the Nelson bill in the Senate and the Corliss bill in the House, and that copies of this resolution be forwarded to the above-mentioned Senators and Representatives and to the chairmen of the Committees on Interstate Commerce in both Houses, and that a copy of this be forwarded to the executive committee of the Interstate-Commerce Law Convention at St. Louis, Mo.

C. J. MURPHY, *Secretary.*

---

14.

*Resolutions of Granite Manufacturers' Association of New England, favoring increasing the power of Interstate-Commerce Commission.*

[Presented by Mr. Gallinger, March 7, 1902; also by Mr. Elkins.]

BOSTON, *February 25, 1902.*

Hon. JACOB H. GALLINGER, *Washington, D. C.*

DEAR SIR: At the annual meeting of the Granite Manufacturers' Association of New England, held at Barre, Vt., the 12th instant, the following resolution was unanimously adopted:

RESOLUTION.

Whereas the interstate-commerce law declares that railway rates shall be just and reasonable and shall not discriminate between persons, localities, or commodities, and creates a Commission for the purpose of securing to the public the benefit of these provisions; and

Whereas that Commission, in view of the interpretation which the courts have put upon the original act, has not at the present time the necessary power to secure shippers and the public just, reasonable, and nondiscriminatory rates, and can not even exercise the authority which it did in this respect during the early years of its existence:

*Resolved,* That the "Act to regulate commerce" should be so amended as to give the Interstate-Commerce Commission the means to enforce the provisions of that act, and especially in the following particulars:

1. To give the Commission power, after it has upon formal complaint and hearing determined that a rate or a practice is in violation of law, to prescribe the thing which the carrier shall do to bring itself into conformity with the law. There is no way, in our opinion, in which the public can be secured in the enjoyment of a just rate except by compelling the carrier to make that rate.

2. To make the orders of the Interstate Commerce Commission effective of themselves, subject to the right of the carriers to review the lawfulness and reasonableness of these orders in the courts. Under the present system it has required on the

average more than three years to compel a railroad to obey an order of the Commission. After a shipper has tried his case before the Commission and obtained an order for relief he must still spend three years in litigation before that relief is available. No such system can in most cases be of any benefit to the public.

3. To require a uniform classification. The present power of the railways to change classifications at will puts the shipper completely at their mercy. This is illustrated by the action of the railways in putting in effect their new classification January 1, 1900.

4. To compel the railways to keep their accounts in a specified manner and to make those accounts open to Government inspection. This is no more than is now required in case of national banks, and would be the most effective means of preventing the payment of rebates and similar unlawful practices.

We believe these amendments are embodied in Senate bill No. 3575, introduced February 5, 1902, and House bill No. 8337, introduced January 9, 1902, and we urge upon our Senators and Representatives in Congress to give these bills their careful consideration and support.

Yours, respectfully,

WM. H. MITCHELL, *President.*

---

15.

*Petition of the Granite Manufacturers Association of New England, praying for the passage of Senate bill 3575.*

[Presented by Mr. Frye March 7, 1902.]

BOSTON, *February 25, 1902.*

Hon. WM. P. FRYE, *Washington, D. C.*

DEAR SIR: At the annual meeting of the Granite Manufacturers' Association of New England, held at Barre, Vt., the 12th instant, the following resolution was unanimously adopted:

### RESOLUTION.

Whereas the interstate-commerce law declares that railway rates shall be just and reasonable and shall not discriminate between persons, localities, or commodities, and creates a Commission for the purpose of securing to the public the benefit of these provisions; and

Whereas that Commission, in view of the interpretation which the courts have put upon the original act, has not at the present time the necessary power to secure shippers and the public just, reasonable, and nondiscriminatory rates, and can not even exercise the authority which it did in this respect during the early years of its existence.

*Resolved,* That the "Act to regulate commerce" should be so amended as to give the Interstate Commerce Commission the means to enforce the provisions of that act and especially in the following particulars:

1. To give the Commission power, after it has upon formal complaint and hearing determined that a rate or a practice is in violation of law, to prescribe the thing which the carrier shall do to bring itself into conformity with the law. There is no way in our opinion in which the public can be secured in the enjoyment of a just rate except by compelling the carrier to make that rate.

2. To make the orders of the Interstate Commerce Commission effective of themselves, subject to the right of the carriers to review the lawfulness and reasonableness of these orders in the courts. Under the present system it has required on the average more than three years to compel a railroad to obey an order of the Commission. After a shipper has tried his case before the Commission and obtained an order for relief he must still spend three years in litigation before that relief is available. No such system can in most cases be of any benefit to the public.

3. To require a uniform classification. The present power of the railways to change classifications at will puts the shipper completely at their mercy. This is illustrated by the action of the railways in putting in effect their new classification January 1, 1900.

4. To compel the railways to keep their accounts in a specified manner and to

make those accounts open to Government inspection. This is no more than is now required in case of national banks and would be the most effective means of preventing the payment of rebates and similar unlawful practices.

We believe these amendments are embodied in Senate bill No. 3575, introduced February 5, 1902, and House bill No. 8337, introduced January 9, 1902, and we urge upon our Senators and Representatives in Congress to give these bills their careful consideration and support.

Yours, respectfully,

WM. H. MITCHELL,
*President.*

* * *

*Petition on behalf of the Pacific Coast Lumber Manufacturers' Association, urging the passage of H. R. 8337, to enlarge the powers of the Interstate Commerce Commission.*

[Presented by Mr. Foster, of Washington, March 10, 1902.]

SEATTLE, WASH., *February 28, 1902.*

Hon. A. G. FOSTER, Hon. GEO. TURNER, Hon. W. L. JONES, Hon. F. W. CUSHMAN.

GENTLEMEN: At a meeting of this association, representing an annual output of 1,350,000,000 feet of lumber and 2,000,000,000 shingles, held in Tacoma on Wednesday, February 26, the following resolutions were adopted by unanimous vote:

"*Resolved,* That the interests of the country at large, and particularly of this State and of the lumber and shingle manufacturers, will be promoted by the passage of the bill now before Congress, enlarging the powers of the Interstate Commerce Commission.

"That the Pacific Coast Lumber Manufacturers' Association heartily indorses the pending measure, known as H. R. bill No. 8337.

"That the secretary is hereby directed to submit a copy of this resolution to each of the Senators and Congressmen from this State, and request that their influence be exerted in support of the measure."

In accordance with the foregoing instructions I urge upon you to give the measure your unqualified support. The present interstate-commerce law is practically a dead letter, as far as its enforcement is concerned, and shippers of lumber products from this State have and are suffering from the effects of the inability of the Commission to enforce the law, and the flagrant abuses consequent upon its nonenforcement.

Sincerely, yours,

VICTOR H. BECKMAN, *Secretary.*

* * *

17.

*Petition of the Granite Manufacturers' Association of New England, praying for legislation giving the Interstate Commerce Commission power to carry out the provisions of the interstate-commerce act.*

[Presented by Mr. Proctor, March 13, 1902.]

BOSTON, *February 25, 1902.*

Hon. REDFIELD PROCTOR, *Washington, D. C.*

DEAR SIR: At the annual meeting of the Granite Manufacturers' Association of New England, held at Barre, Vt., the 12th instant, the following resolution was unanimously adopted:

#### RESOLUTION.

Whereas the interstate-commerce law declares that railway rates shall be just and reasonable and shall not discriminate between persons, localities, or commodities, and creates a Commission for the purpose of securing to the public the benefit of these provisions; and

Whereas that Commission, in view of the interpretation which the courts have put upon the original act, has not at the present time the necessary power to secure shippers and the public just, reasonable, and nondiscriminatory rates, and can not even exercise the authority which it did in this respect during the early years of its existence;

*Resolved,* That the "act to regulate commerce" should be so amended as to give the Interstate Commerce Commission the means to enforce the provisions of that act, and especially in the following particulars:

1. To give the Commission power, after it has upon formal complaint and hearing determined that a rate or a practice is in violation of law, to prescribe the thing which the carrier shall do to bring itself into conformity with the law. There is no way, in our opinion, in which the public can be secured in the enjoyment of a just rate except by compelling the carrier to make that rate.

2. To make the orders of the Interstate Commerce Commission effective of themselves, subject to the right of the carriers to review the lawfulness and reasonableness of these orders in the courts. Under the present system it has required on the average more than three years to compel a railroad to obey an order of the Commission. After a shipper has tried his case before the Commission and obtained an order for relief, he must still spend three years in litigation before that relief is available. No such system can, in most cases, be of any benefit to the public.

3. To require a uniform classification. The present power of the railways to change classifications at will puts the shipper completely at their mercy. This is illustrated by the action of the railways in putting in effect their new classification January 1, 1900.

4. To compel the railways to keep their accounts in a specified manner and to make those accounts open to Government inspection. This is no more than is now required in case of national banks, and would be the most effective means of preventing the payment of rebates and similar unlawful practices.

We believe these amendments are embodied in Senate bill No. 3575, introduced February 5, 1902, and House bill No. 8337, introduced January 9, 1902, and we urge upon our Senators and Representatives in Congress to give these bills their careful consideration and support.

Yours, respectfully,

WM. H. MITCHELL, *President.*

---

18.

*Petition of the Chamber of Commerce of Milwaukee, Wis., praying for the passage of the so-called Nelson-Corliss bill to amend the interstate-commerce act.*

[Presented by Mr. Quarles, March 17, 1902.]

CHAMBER OF COMMERCE,
*Milwaukee, March 12, 1902.*

Hon. J. V. QUARLES,
*United States Senate, Washington, D. C.*

DEAR SIR: The following resolutions were adopted at a meeting of the board of directors of this chamber of commerce, held March 11, 1902:

" Whereas the Milwaukee Chamber of Commerce has heretofore placed itself on record on several occasions in favor of such amendment of the interstate-commerce act as will give it greater effectiveness; and

" Whereas a bill is now pending in Congress for this purpose, known as the Nelson-Corliss bill, designated in the House as H. R. 8337 and in the Senate as S. 3575: Therefore,

"*Resolved,* That the board of directors of the said chamber of commerce hereby respectfully requests the Senators and Representatives in Congress from this State to give the said bill their active support and to use their influence in every proper way to secure its early enactment.

"*Resolved,* That the secretary be requested to forward a certified copy of the foregoing preamble and resolution to each of the said Senators and Representatives."

Very truly, yours,

W. J. LANGSON, *Secretary.*

19.

*Petitions of Blanton Milling Company, of Indianapolis; of the Harvest Queen Milling Company, of Elkhart; of the Bremen Roller Mills, of Bremen; of Igleheart Brothers, of Evansville; of Harris Milling Company, of Greencastle; of the Goshen Milling Company, of Goshen; of the Mayflower Mills, of Fort Wayne; of C. Tresselt & Sons, of Fort Wayne; of the Lebanon Roller Mills, of Lebanon; of the Gem Flouring Mill Company, of Rushville; of Willard Kidder, of Wabash; of Valley Roller Mills, of Connersville; of William Suckow, of Franklin, all in the State of Indiana, praying for the passage of the so-called Nelson-Corliss bill (S. 3575.)*

[Presented by Mr. Fairbanks, March 18, 1902.]

INDIANAPOLIS, IND., *March 12, 1902.*

Hon. CHARLES W. FAIRBANKS,
  *United States Senate, Washington, D. C.*

DEAR SIR: We desire to respectfully call your attention to bill 3575, known as the Nelson–Corliss bill.

Doubtless you are aware that among the very fundamental industries of the country is the flour-milling business, which represents the largest investment of capital, with few exceptions, of any home industry. Furthermore, activity and prosperity in the flour-milling trade is productive of a corresponding prosperity amongst workingmen, farmers, merchants, manufacturers, bankers, and railroads.

It is an industry which is particularly rooted in all of its ramifications, directly or indirectly, with all classes of people. It is a representative American industry. The wheat grown in this country should be milled in America. Owing to the increased acreage in the wheat-growing country there has been a gradual increase in our wheat production. The most of this wheat should be milled in America, not foreign countries. The export of wheat should be in a less ratio than formerly, by reason of the increased milling facilities and capacity of this country and the increased activity on the part of the millers in building up a foreign trade for American flour. Unfortunately exports of wheat have increased at a greater ratio than the exports of flour. In fact, the increase in the exports of wheat in the past two years has been very noticeable and the ratio of flour exported, compared with wheat, has decreased abnormally. This, we believe, is contrary to the fundamental American idea of trade expansion. No country in the world is better equipped to mill its own wheat than America; hence the exportation of flour should be encouraged and aided by our governmental policies, commercial, legislative, as well as executive.

About three years ago the Central Traffic Association, also independent railway and fast freight lines, made the freight rate to the seaboard lower than on flour, the product of wheat. This was made, as claimed by the transportation companies, for the reason that it cost more to transport flour than it did wheat, but the difference in the cost, per admission of railway officials, was less than 1 cent per 100 pounds. The transportation companies, in defending their position, failed to tell your honorable Congressional committee that flour millers have to pay a charge of 1½ cents per 100 pounds over and above the published tariff rates for the privilege of stopping and milling the wheat in transit.

This charge is a heavy embargo on the milling trade for this privilege merely. As everyone connected with the millers as well as the transportation companies knows, this is far in excess of the actual cost of this milling-in-transit privilege. Several times statistics and facts have been produced proving the assertion of the transportation companies to be wrong. In fact, the transportation companies are showing a better net profit on the transportation of flour than on wheat. The milling industry of this country is suffering because of this added embargo on the transportation of flour. Steamship companies have made more favorable rates on the transportation of wheat because of the different and unlike conditions to any that railway companies have to meet.

The export trade of this country has been gradually and is now rapidly being diverted to foreign millers. Such millers are enabled to buy American wheat, lay it down at Liverpool, for illustration, mill it, and undersell us at a profit to such an extent that the export flour trade of America at this time is unprofitable. The primary cause of the distress in the flour-milling trade is due to this discrimination in freight rates. The millers of the United States do not ask for more favorable rates on flour than wheat, but simply for equal rates plus 1½ cents per hundred charged for milling in transit. Are you in favor of seeing justice done to the American millers? We believe, upon inquiry from men directly or indirectly interested in the export flour trade, that you will find the above statements verified. We therefore respectfully ask you to consider our request for the support of the above-named measure, now pending in your branch of Congress.

We believe this measure will enlarge the executive and police powers of the Intertate Commerce Commission, so that discrimination in freight rates on commodities which should be carried on an equal rate will be obviated.

Kindly signify your intentions with regard to this measure.

Yours, truly,

BLANTON MILLING Co.
Per H. D. YODER,
*Secretary and Treasurer.*

----

ELKHART, IND., *March 13, 1902.*

Hon. C. W. FAIRBANKS, *Washington, D. C.*

DEAR SIR: There has been introduced in the Senate a bill designated as S. 3575 and in the House as H. R. 8337.

It is of the greatest importance that these bills, which are the same and are known as the Nelson-Corliss bill, be enacted into law.

No matter where the mill is located, or how small, all are affected directly or indirectly, and it is a question of life or death to the milling interests, and we therefore urgently request you to support Senate bill 3575.

Very respectfully,

THE HARVEST QUEEN MILLING Co.
Per W. S. HAZELTON, *Manager.*

----

THE BREMEN ROLLER MILLS,
*Bremen, Ind., March 13, 1902.*

C. W. FAIRBANKS, *Washington, D. C.*

DEAR SIR: All millers are quite familiar with the serious effect of the discrimination in freight rates against flour for export. For the purpose of correcting this evil it is proposed to amend the interstate-commerce law, giving the Commission power to enforce its findings. To this end there has been introduced in the House a bill designated as H. R. 8337 and in the Senate as S. 3575. It is of the greatest importance that these bills, which are the same, known as the Nelson-Corliss bill, be enacted into law. No matter where the mill is located, or how small, all are affected directly or indirectly, and it is a question of life and death to the milling interests, and I therefore urgently request that you support bill S. 3575 and hope to receive your favorable action on same.

These bills were prepared with much care and have had the personal attention of millers, so we know them to be what we want.

Yours, truly,

W. F. SCHILT.

----

EVANSVILLE, IND., *March 12, 1902.*

Senator FAIRBANKS, *Washington, D. C.*

HONORABLE SIR: The flour-milling interests of the United States are making a last life and death struggle to regain the export trade they have lost, and we ask your urgent support in the passing of the bill H. R. 8337, known as the Nelson-Corliss bill. This bill is with the view of correcting the evil of discriminating in freight rates against flour exports in favor of wheat.

Every intelligent person knows that no country can excel by exporting raw products, and if this policy were carried out in all other lines of manufacture our nation would become an inferior nation in time.

Can not you assist us in correcting this stupendous outrage upon a milling interest which represents $300,000,000 invested capital and indirectly affects the farmer as well as the milling interests?

Yours, truly,

IGLEHEART BROTHERS.
By A. W. IGLEHEART,
*Secretary and Treasurer.*

GREENCASTLE, IND., *March 12, 1902.*

Mr. C. W. FAIRBANKS, *Washington.*

DEAR SIR: There has been introduced in the Senate a bill known as S. 3575, which, if passed, will greatly help out the winter-wheat millers. We most respectfully urge you to give this bill your support, as it is of vital importance to all of us.

Yours, truly,

HARRIS MILLING CO.,
E. L. HARRIS, *Proprietor.*

---

GOSHEN, IND., *March 12, 1902.*

Senator CHAS. W. FAIRBANKS, *Washington, D. C.*

DEAR SIR: We beg to call your attention to the bill S. 3575, and hope that it will have your valuable consideration and active support.

Some legislation of the sort is imperatively needed to prevent the total annihilation of the milling industries of this country by the action of the railway companies in making a much lower rate on the raw material, wheat, for export than on the manufactured product, flour.

The mills of the United States have outgrown this market and must have a foreign outlet. On even terms they can compete successfully with the foreign miller, but when our own railway companies discriminate in his favor it is impossible for flour manufactured in the United States to be exported at a profit.

Yours, very truly,

THE GOSHEN MILLING CO.,
F. E. C. HAWKS, *President.*

---

FORT WAYNE, IND., *March 12, 1902.*

Hon. C. W. FAIRBANKS, *Washington, D. C.*

DEAR SIR: We write you with a view of calling your attention to the Senate bill 3575, which has been drafted and introduced by practical millers with a view of overcoming the discrimination in freight rates against flour and in favor of wheat, as at present the railroads are carrying wheat to the seaboards at a considerably less price than they will carry the manufactured product, which puts the milling industry in this country at a very great disadvantage, as you can readily see, and hurts both the large and small miller from one end of the country to the other.

Trusting you may lend your best efforts to passing this bill, we beg to remain,

Very truly, yours,

THE MAYFLOWER MILLS.

---

FORT WAYNE, IND., *March 12, 1902.*

Hon. CHAS. W. FAIRBANKS,
*United States Senate, Washington, D. C.*

DEAR SIR: We respectfully beg to call your attention to the Nelson-Corliss bill, now pending, we believe, as S. 3575. The object is, as no doubt you are aware, to do away with unjust discrimination against millers in freight rates. Under existing conditions there is serious danger of crippling the milling industry of the United States, as foreigners now can buy American wheat, laid down in Europe, so low as to exclude our home millers to compete with the foreign miller, and all on account of discriminating freight rates. We earnestly beg of you to use your influence to have said S. 3575 become a law, and remain,

Yours, repectfully,

C. TRESSELT & SONS.

---

THE LEBANON ROLLER MILLS,
*Lebanon, Ind., March 12, 1902.*

Hon. C. W. FAIRBANKS, *Washington, D. C.*

DEAR SIR: We desire to call your careful attention to S. 3575, a bill to increase the powers of the Interstate Commerce Commission, which we believe will be of great advantage to the Western millers doing an export business, and also to us smaller millers, by relieving us from the crushing influence of the great millers, aided by the advantage given them by the railways.

Hoping this bill will have your favorable consideration, we are,

Truly, yours,

MEANS & WITT.

RUSHVILLE, IND., *March 12, 1902.*

Hon. C. W. FAIRBANKS, *Washington, D .C.*

SIR: The passage of S. 3575 is of the greatest importance to the millers of this and adjoining States. The discrimination in rates is disastrous to the millers of this State, especially those of smaller capacity. The large mills of the Northwest get advantages in rates, and the grain shippers through this country get a lower rate on their shipments than the miller gets on grain products, so we have to compete with both the Northwest mills and with the grain shippers of this State, thus practically barring us from the markets. The flour-milling industry seems to be a necessity, yet not one in fifty succeed in operating on a profitable basis, while many are closed down, so we feel that such legislation as will encourage the manufacturing of flour is a necessity, and respectfully ask you to look with favor on S. 3575 as a means to an end so necessary to the largest single industry in this State outside of railroads.

Respectfully,

THE GEM FLOURING MILL COMPANY,
Per C. B. RILEY, *Manager.*

———

TERRE HAUTE, IND., *March 12, 1902.*

Hon. C. W. FAIRBANKS, *Washington, D. C.*

DEAR SIR: The effect of the discrimination in freight rates against flour for export has been so disastrous to the millers in this country, especially in the winter-wheat belt, I feel that you will excuse me for calling your serious attention to the bill S. 3575, known, I believe, as the Nelson-Corliss bill. If this bill can be passed and its provisions enforced, I believe it will help us to again compete with the foreign, millers.

Whatever you can do to insure the passage of this bill will be highly appreciated by

Yours, truly,

WILLARD KIDDER.

———

VALLEY ROLLER MILLS,
*Connersville, Ind., March 12, 1902.*

Hon. C. W. FAIRBANKS,
*United States Senate, Washington, D. C.*

DEAR SIR: No doubt you have before this been made familiar with discrimination in freight rates against flour for export. Such discrimination is working a great injury to the milling business, and we therefore beg leave to ask your kind assistance in passing bill S. 3575.

Yours, very respectfully,

UHL & SNIDER.

———

FRANKLIN, IND., *March 12, 1902.*

Senator FAIRBANKS, *Washington, D. C.*

DEAR SIR: No doubt you are quite familiar with the serious effect of the discrimination in freight rates against flour for export. We believe that bill S. 3575 will remedy this, and earnestly request you to support this bill. We believe if you will take this matter up at once and push it to the extent of your ability it will be enacted into law and afford relief to the millers. It is a question of life and death to the milling interests.

Yours, very truly,

WM. SUCKOW,
Per WEAVER.

20,

*Resolution of Eastern Washington and Northern Idaho Lumber Manufacturers' Association favoring legislation to increase the power of the Interstate Commerce Commission.*

[Presented by Mr. Heitfeld March 19, 1902.]

SPOKANE, Wash., *March 10, 1902.*

Hon. HENRY HEITFELD, Hon. FRED C. DUBOIS, Hon. THOS. L. GLENN,
*Washington, D. C.*

GENTLEMEN: At a meeting of this association, representing an annual output of 250,000,000 feet of lumber and 500,000,000 shingles, held in this city March 8, the following resolutions were adopted by unanimous vote:

"*Resolved,* That the interests of the entire country and particularly the States of Washington and Idaho, and the lumber and shingle industries, will be materially advanced by the passage of the bill now before Congress enlarging the powers of the Interstate Commerce Commission.

"That the Eastern Washington and Northern Idaho Lumber Manufacturers' Association heartily indorse the pending measure known as House bill No. 8337.

"That the secretary is hereby directed to submit a copy of this resolution to each of the Senators and Congressmen from the States of Washington and Idaho, and request that their influence be exerted in support of the measure."

Regarding the above instructions, I beg of you to give the measure your unqualified support. The present interstate-commerce law, as it now stands, is a dead letter as far as its enforcement is concerned, and shippers of lumber products from our States have and are suffering from the effects of the inability of the Commission to enforce the law, and the flagrant abuses consequent upon its nonenforcement.

Yours, truly,

GEO. W. HOAG, *Secretary.*

---

21.

*Petitions of Coppes Brothers & Zook, of Nappanee; of Manitau Flouring Mills, of Rochester; of Winter Wheat Millers' League, of Indianapolis, all in the State of Indiana, praying for certain amendments to the interstate-commerce law.*

[Presented by Mr. Fairbanks, March 21, 1902.]

NAPPANEE, IND., *March 14, 1902.*

Hon. CHAS. W. FAIRBANKS,
*Washington, D. C.*

DEAR SIR: For the last several years the millers of our vicinity have experienced a great deal of trouble to hold our export flour trade, and in spite of our utmost endeavor our own trade has almost entirely ceased, excepting at an actual loss.

We have been convinced this comes almost entirely out of freight discrimination in rates on flour for export. We are advised by the Winter Wheat Millers' League that House bill No. 8337 and Senate bill No. 3575 will correct this evil if adopted. If so, it will be worth a great deal of money to the mills of this State, and especially to Goshen and our own mill, who do considerable exporting. If after a study of these bills you find them otherwise unobjectionable, we will be very thankful indeed to know that you support the same.

Yours, respectfully,

COPPES BROS. & ZOOK.

---

ROCHESTER, IND., *March 14, 1902.*

Hon. C. W. FAIRBANKS, *Washington, D. C.*

DEAR SIR: There has been introduced in the Senate a bill designated as Senate bill 3575, known as the Nelson-Corliss bill, which I would be pleased to have you support if you can see your way clear so to do. The serious effect of the discrimination in freight rates against flour for export is about to wipe out of existence the small mills of this country. There is no business that represents the capital of the mills of this country that pays so small a profit. Kindly give this matter your careful consideration, and, if possible, assist in giving us the help we pray for.

Yours, most truly,

R. C. WALLACE.

WINTER WHEAT MILLERS' LEAGUE,
*Indianapolis, Ind., March 15, 1902.*

Hon. C. W. FAIRBANKS, *Washington, D. C.*

DEAR SIR: In the name of the millers of the United States, I beg to call your attention to Senate bill 3575.

Newspaper dispatches announce that a very strong railroad lobby is now in Washington, and that one of the representatives of that interest has announced that they did not purpose that any legislation along the lines proposed in bill No. 3575 should pass.

As secretary of the Winter Wheat Millers' League, I am constrained to write you frankly as to the situation the miller is in, and to say that politically the Republican party, if relief is not afforded our industry, will feel its effect.

The millers of this country have sufficient capacity to grind into flour every bushel of wheat grown in this country and with proper treatment at the hands of the transportation companies could export all of any surplus in the form of the manufactured product. By this I mean the same rate as is accorded to wheat. At present the shippers of wheat are receiving a discriminating rate which means a difference of 5 cents to 10 cents a barrel against flour. Any of our large mills would be glad to run night and day on a margin of 10 cents a barrel or less. As it is they are not able to export any at a profit. Further, if this wheat was ground by our own mills, instead of sending it abroad to be ground, it would mean from $8,000,000 to $10,000,000 additional wages for our own laborers. Again, under such conditions the farmer would get his mill feed much cheaper, and it would yield them a saving of several million dollars per annum. The present unfavorable condition of our flour mills is the result of this discrimination, and the transportation companies have gone the limit, in my judgment, and unless relief is given by this Congress the second largest industry in our country will be practically ruined.

Politically fully 90 per cent of our millers are Republicans; but there will be formed an organization among the millers, who number over 16,000, who will act independent in politics. Every mill, nearly, in the country is a political headquarters, and their influence on their own and with the farmers will mean enough votes to hold the balance of power in a large number of Western States.

I am writing you frankly, for I am certain that you are not fully informed as to the situation, and it is, in my judgment, to your interest to know it. ·

I shall ask that you give these points the consideration they deserve, and that you aid us in getting a hearing from the committee having the bill in charge, and that you also give it your unqualified support.

Thanking you in advance for your support and trusting to be honored with a reply,

I am, sir, yours, respectfully,

E. E. PERRY, *Secretary.*

---

. 22.

*Petition of the Merchants and Manufacturers' Association of Milwaukee, Wis., and others, praying for the passage of the so-called Nelson-Corliss bill to amend the interstate-commerce law.*

[Presented by Mr. Quarles, March 25, 1902.]

MILWAUKEE, WIS., *March 17, 1902.*

Hon. J. V. QUARLES, *Washington, D. C.:*

DEAR SIR: At a meeting of the board of directors of the Merchants and Manufacturers' Association held on Friday, the 14th instant, the following preamble and resolution were unanimously adopted:

" Whereas recent decisions of the Federal courts have rendered the interstate-commerce law ineffective in the protection of the public from unreasonable and discriminative rates imposed by the common carriers of the country, which was the purpose of its enactment; and

" Whereas a bill has been introduced in Congress, prepared under the direction of the executive committee of the interstate-commerce law convention, known as the Nelson-Corliss bill, designated as House bill 8337 and Senate bill 3575, intended to remedy the defects found to exist in the present law: Therefore,

*Resolved,* That the Merchants and Manufacturers' Association of Milwaukee hereby indorses said bill and respectfully requests the Senators and Representatives in Congress from this State to exert their influence in every proper way to secure its enactment into law, and to obtain such precedence for its consideration over other pending measures as its great importance demands.

Kindly give this matter your careful consideration, and oblige,
Yours, very sincerely,

L. C. WHITNEY, *Secretary.*

---

23.

*Petition of the Wisconsin Retail Lumber Dealers' Association, praying for the passage of the so-called Nelson-Corliss bill to amend the interstate-commerce law.*

[Presented by Mr. Quarles, March 25, 1902.]

SAUK CITY, WIS., *March 13, 1902.*

Senator JOSEPH V. QUARLES,
        *Washington, D. C.*

DEAR SIR: At the annual meeting of the Wisconsin Retail Lumber Dealers' Association, held in the city of Milwaukee February 19, 1902, the following preamble and resolution was unanimously adopted:

"Whereas a bill, prepared under the direction of the executive committee of the interstate-commerce law convention held in St. Louis November 20, 1900, has been introduced in both Houses of the Congress of the United States, designated as House bill 8337 and Senate bill 3575, and known as the Nelson-Corliss bill, to so amend the interstate-commerce act as to give it the effectiveness which characterized its operation until the Commission was divested of the authority which it was understood to possess by recent decisions of the Federal courts: Therefore,

"*Resolved*, That the Wisconsin Retail Lumber Dealers' Association, in convention assembled at the city of Milwaukee, February 19, 1902, does hereby indorse the said bill and respectfully request the honorable Senators and Representatives in Congress from this State to give it their support and exert their influence to the utmost, in every proper way, to insure its early enactment."

Hoping that your personal views are in accord with the above resolution and request of your constituents, I remain,
Yours, respectfully,

PAUL LACHMUND, *Secretary.*

---

24.

*Memorial of the legislature of the State of Minnesota, urging the passage of S. 3575.*

[Presented by Mr. Nelson, April 1, 1902; also by Mr. Clapp.]

Whereas the power and right to "regulate commerce among the several States," given by the Constitution to Congress, has, by repeated decisions of the Supreme Court, been held to include the right to fix reasonable maximum rates for common carriers engaged in the transportation of such commerce; and

Whereas the Congress attempted to delegate its power in this regard to the Interstate Commerce Commission, and attempted to give said Commission the necessary authority for that purpose; and

Whereas the Supreme Court of the United States has recently decided that the act creating the said Interstate Commerce Commission is seriously defective and incomplete, and that while said act confers on said Commission the power to declare existing rates unreasonable, it does not give said Commission the power to prescribe a tariff of reasonable rates to replace those found to be unreasonable; and

Whereas since said decision there is no tribunal having the power to correct any unreasonable rates or classifications of freights in the domain of interstate commerce; and

Whereas one of the most important functions of the Government is thus suspended, and immediate legislation is imperatively necessary to clothe said Interstate Commerce Commission with adequate power to regulate interstate commerce and to prescribe reasonable maximum rates for the transportation thereof, and the State of

Minnesota as well as the entire Northwest is vitally interested in the enactment of such a law; and

Whereas the bill (S. 3575) introduced February 5, 1902, in the Senate of the United States by Senator Knute Nelson, contains all of the provisions necessary to invest said Interstate Commerce Commission with the powers needed for the purposes aforesaid, and said bill is therefore one of the most important bills now before Congress; Therefore, be it

*Resolved by the legislature of the State of Minnesota,* That we heartily indorse said bill (S. 3575) and respectfully urge the early passage of the same by the Congress of the United States; and be it

*Further resolved,* That we indorse and approve the action of Senator Nelson in introducing and advocating said bill.

*Resolved further,* That a copy of this memorial be sent by the secretary of state to each member of Congress from Minnesota and to the President of the Senate of the United States.

Approved March 10, 1902.

STATE OF MINNESOTA, *Department of State:*

I, P. E. Hanson, secretary of state of the State of Minnesota, do hereby certify that the above and foregoing is a true and correct copy of S. F. No. 54, adopted at the extra session of the legislature, 1902.

In witness whereof I have hereunto set my hand and caused the great seal of the State to be affixed, at the capitol in St. Paul, this 27th day of March, A. D. 1902.

[SEAL.]              P. E. HANSON, *Secretary of State.*

---

25.

*Petitions of the National Hay Association, of Winchester; of Hydraulic Roller Mills, of Milton; of W. H. Small & Co., of Evansville; of City Roller Mills, of Jeffersonville, praying for certain amendments to the interstate-commerce law.*

[Presented by Mr. Fairbanks, April 4, 1902.]

WINCHESTER, IND., *March 22, 1902.*

*To the Members of Congress:*

I am directed by the board of directors of the National Hay Association, an organization composed of about seven hundred shippers and receivers, doing business in various parts of the country, to direct your attention to the present ineffectiveness of the decrees of the Interstate Commerce Commission; and also, the chaotic state of the railroad situation, by reason of the judicial interpretation which has been placed upon the interstate-commerce act of 1887.

There is now pending in the House a bill which was introduced by Representative Corliss, and a like bill in the Senate, introduced by Senator Nelson, the provisions of which appear to the directors of this association to be fair and reasonable, not prejudicial to the interests of the carriers, but advantageous to shippers and receivers.

As an association we indorse this act, and desire to urge upon you the necessity of a prompt amendment, either by means of the bill referred to or in some other manner of the interstate-commerce act.

I have the honor to remain,

Very respectfully, yours,

P. E. GOODRICH, *Secretary-Treasurer.*

---

EVANSVILLE, IND., *March 25, 1902.*

Hon. CHAS. M. FAIRBANKS, *Washington, D. C.*

DEAR SIR: We wish to earnestly request you to give your full support to the Corliss bill, recently introduced into the House of Representatives by Representative Corliss, of Michigan.

Yours, truly,             W. H. SMALL & Co.

JEFFERSONVILLE, IND., *March 15, 1902.*

Hon. C. W. FAIRBANKS, *Washington, D. C.*

DEAR SIR: There has been introduced in the Senate a bill designated as Senate bill 3575. We ask you to kindly support this bill, as it is of the highest importance to millers in the way of again securing fair profits on flour.

The discrimination of freight rates has been a very hard proposition for millers to overcome, and we therefore ask you to kindly support bill.

Thanking you in advance, we are,

Yours, truly,  ·                                   EBERTS & BRO.

———

MILTON, IND., *March 27, 1902.*

Senator FAIRBANKS, *Washington, D. C.*

DEAR SIR: All millers operating in the State of Indiana are aware of the serious effect of discrimination in freight rates against flour offered for export; therefore the milling has suffered greatly in the past. We note that a bill has been introduced in the Senate as S. 3575 which we believe will correct the evil of discriminating against flour offered as export. We believe it is a question of life and death to the milling interest if the above is not passed. We trust, therefore, that you can and will give the bill your hearty support.

We remain, yours, very truly,                 J. NORTH & SON,
                                               D. B. N.

———

26.

*Papers pertaining to S. 3575, being an act to amend an act entitled "An act to regulate commerce."*

[All presented by Mr. Burrows, April 7, 1902.]

GRAND RAPIDS, MICH., *February 25, 1902.*

Mr. JULIUS C. BURROWS, *Washington, D. C.*

DEAR SIR: There is a bill before Congress to amend the interstate-commerce act so as to enable the commissioners to enforce their decisions. It is House bill No. 8337.

The purpose of said bill is to confer upon the Commission such authority as it actually exercised in enforcing its decisions, until the Supreme Court held that no such authority was conferred by the interstate-commerce act. The bill does not impose any hardship upon the carrier nor enlarge the powers of the Commission with respect to rate changing, but simply gives the Commission power to enforce decisions, which, although generally respected by the railway companies, may in certain cases under the present provisions of the act be disregarded.

We believe this bill is worthy of your support and should be passed.

Yours, very truly,

FULLER & RICE LUMBER AND MANUFACTURING COMPANY,
A. P. IRISH, *Vice-President.*

———

DETROIT, MICH., *March 27, 1902.*

Hon. J. C. BURROWS, *Washington, D. C.*

MY DEAR SIR: As large shippers of hay, we are very much interested in the bill of Representative Corliss to amend the interstate-commerce act, so that the decrees of the Commission may be made effective, and we earnestly hope you will use your efforts favorably toward this act.

Yours, truly,                                   JOHN L. DEXTER & Co.

———

HOLLY, MICH., *March 13, 1902.*

Hon. J. C. BURROWS,
    *United States Senate,. Washington D. C.*

DEAR SIR: We write to request that you lend your aid in the support of bill (S. 3575) to correct the evil of discrimination in freight rates against flour for export.

This is such a serious question to all small mills in the country that we hope you will take it upon yourself to help in every way to have this bill enacted into a law. Unless this happens it will be necessary very soon for all small millers to get out of the business.

We feel sure that you are interested and that we may depend upon you in this hour for final action. Trusting that this bill will have your careful personal attention, we are.

Yours, truly,
HOLLY MILLING COMPANY,
CHAS. H. S. POOLE.

---

GREENVILLE, MICH., *March 13, 1902.*

Hon. J. C. BURROWS, *Washington, D. C.*

DEAR SIR: We write to ask you if you can not, in the interest of the milling business in the United States, especially in Michigan, give your earnest support to the bill known as the Nelson-Corliss bill (S. 3575), which is proposed to amend the interstate-commerce law.

At the present time there is a great discrimination in the freight rates between wheat and flour for export, in favor of the wheat and detrimental to the flour and the milling interest. The milling interest in this country has been badly handicapped for the last few years by reason of the great difference in the rates of freight between wheat and flour, and it has nearly killed the milling business in Michigan, as well as in the other States, and if the present condition continues it will be a great loss to the country at large, as now the advantage is all in favor of the foreign millers and against the American millers.

The bill mentioned above is to correct this evil, and we wish you would do all you can to get it enacted, and greatly oblige,

Yours, truly,
E. MIDDLETON & SONS.

---

HARBOR BEACH, MICH., *March 18, 1902.*

Hon. JULIUS C. BURROWS,
*Senate Chamber, Washington.*

DEAR SIR: We are very much interested in the bill S. 3575, and would be very much pleased to have you vote for it and do what you can for its passage.

Yours, truly,
THE HURON MILLING COMPANY,
BELA W. JENKS, *Secretary.*

---

GRAND RAPIDS, MICH., *March 15, 1902.*

Mr. J. C. BURROWS,
*Senate Chamber, Washington, D. C.*

DEAR SIR: I have previously written you as regards to the dullness in the milling trade all over the United States, especially in Michigan. In this regard I would call your attention to a bill which has been introduced as Senate bill No. 3575, and House bill 8337, also known as the Nelson-Corliss bill. It is certainly of the greatest importance that this bill be enacted into a law, and see if the milling interest can not be benefited. It is a bill to amend the interstate-commerce law, giving the Commission power to enforce its findings.

Hope that you will not only see your way clear to vote for this bill, but that you will give it your moral influence. We know if you and Senator McMillan will put your shoulders to the wheel the bill will pass.

Kindly do the best you can for it, and oblige,

Very respectfully,
C. G. A. VOIGT.

---

ALMA, MICH., *March 22, 1902.*

Hon. JULIUS C. BURROWS,
*Washington, D. C.*

DEAR SIR: I wish to call your attention to a bill which I understand is now before the Senate, known as S. 3575, which, if passed, will enlarge the powers of the Interstate Commerce Commission. It is a well-known fact that the railroads are discriminating in their freight rates against mill products and against products in the line of agriculture—that this condition of affairs tends to restrict the trade of milling institutions, both large and small.·

I hope that you will work and vote for this bill, as its passage will materially help the milling interests in this State.

I remain, respectfully, yours,

ALMA ROLLING MILLS.
F. G. SCOTT.

---

ALBION, *March 14, 1902.*

Hon. JULIUS C. BURROWS:

At the meeting of the Albion Farmers' Club on the above-mentioned date the following resolution was passed:

"*Resolved,* That as a club we approve the Nelson–Corliss bill and desire you, as our Representative in Congress, to use all proper means to secure its passage to the end that it shall become the law of the land."

JACOB WARTMAN, *President.*
MRS. S. A. BASCOM, *Secretary.*

---

WHITE PIGEON, MICH., *March 13, 1902.*

Hon. J. C. BURROWS, *Washington, D. C.*

DEAR SIR: It is generally supposed, and undoubtedly a fact, the manufacturing industries of our country never were' as prosperous and making the money they are at present. All are prosperous with one great exception. This one exception mentioned, "the flour-milling industry," with the greatest investment in plants and working capital, giving employment to more labor than any single manufacturing industry in the United States, does not share in the general prosperity. It has made no money for some years past, matters are growing worse, and it is now nearing the point where it is a struggle for existence.

It is hardly necessary to call your attention to this fact. Your knowledge of the industries of the country and their condition will tell you this, but with a slight investigation of the condition of the mills in your own State, nay, not necessary to go beyond the limits of your own town, to have this assertion verified.

There is a cause for all this, and it rests in the discrimination in freight rates against flour for export. Wheat, our raw material, is carried on the same trains for the same vessels for export, always for less and often for less than one-half the amount which mills are compelled to pay on the manufactured product.

For the purposes of correcting this evil it is proposed to amend the interstate-commerce law, giving the Commission power to enforce its findings. To this end there has been introduced in the Senate a bill designated as S. 3575, which I trust you will find consistent to give your earnest support and best efforts to become a law.

Very respectfully, yours,

R. J. HAMILTON.

---

THE MERCHANTS AND MANUFACTURERS' EXCHANGE,
*Detroit, April 5, 1902.*

Whereas there is an extensive demand on the part of the public for some legislation which shall regulate the rates of freight and classification of merchandise charged by the transportation companies of the country, and which shall clothe the Interstate Commerce Commission with the power to enforce its decisions and to make such regulations as shall protect the shippers from extortion at any time; and

Whereas we believe that competition among the railroads of the United States has practically ceased, by reason of consolidations and agreements among themselves, and so destroyed the hope of relief by that means; Therefore, be it

*Resolved,* By the board of directors of the Merchants' aud Manufacturers' Exchange of Detroit, Mich., representing nearly 200 of the largest shippers in our city, that we indorse the bill introduced by the Hon. John B. Corliss, member of Congress of this district, known as H. R. 8337, and the one introduced by Senator Nelson, known as S. 3675, and respectfully request all the Senators and Representatives from Michigan to support the passage of same at the proper time.

JAS. INGLIS, *President.*
WALTER S. CAMPBELL, *Secretary.*

27.

*Resolution adopted by the Commercial Club of Belleville, Ill., favoring the enactment of legislation to regulate interstate commerce.*

[Presented by Mr. Cullom, April 23, 1902.]

BELLEVILLE, ILL., *April 9, 1902.*

Hon. S. H. CULLOM, *Washington, D. C.*

DEAR SIR: The following resolution will explain itself:

"*Resolved by the Belleville Commercial Club, of the city of Belleville, Ill.*, That in our judgment the present interstate commerce law, as interpreted by the Supreme Court, is insufficient and practically inoperative for the purpose for which it was framed. We therefore urge upon our Senators and Representatives the importance of doing everything in their power to further the passage of H. R. 8337, S. 3575, to amend the act to regulate commerce. Belleville, Ill., April 7, 1902."

Please give this a part of your valuable time and attention.

Very respectfully,

W. F. KIRCHER, *Secretary.*

—

28.

*Resolution of Business Men's Association of Davenport, Iowa, favoring passage of S. 3575.*

[Presented by Mr. Dolliver, April 9, 1902.]

DAVENPORT, IOWA, *March 18, 1902.*

Hon. J. P. DOLLIVER, *Washington, D. C.*

SIR: The following resolution, passed at our last meeting, is explanatory of itself:

*Resolved*, That the Davenport Business Men's Association heartily indorse the bill known as S. 3575 and H. R. 8337, an act to regulate commerce; and request our representatives to use their best endeavors to have the bill passed. Any consideration you may give the matter will greatly oblige,

Yours, respectfully,

DAVENPORT BUSINESS MEN'S ASSOCIATION,
M. BUNKER, *Secretary.*

—

29.

*Petition by the Boston Fruit and Produce Exchange, of Boston, Mass., praying that Congress shall enact such legislation as will enable the Interstate Commerce Commission to enforce their findings.*

[Presented by Senator Hoar, April 10, 1902.]

At a meeting of the board of directors of the Boston Fruit and Produce Exchange held Tuesday, April 8, 1902, it was voted:

"That the board respectfully petition the Congress of the United States to enact such legislation as will enable the Interstate Commerce Commission to enforce their findings, and that a copy of this resolution be sent to each of our Senators and Representatives in Congress."

A true copy.

Attest:

B. F. SOUTHWICK, *Secretary.*

Hon. GEORGE FRISBIE HOAR,
*Washington, D. C.*

30.

*Petitions of Puritan Bed Spring Company et al., praying for certain amendments to the interstate commerce law.*

[Presented by Mr. Fairbanks, April 10, 1902.]

INDIANAPOLIS, IND., *March 28, 1902.*

The Furniture Manufacturers' Association of Indianapolis, Ind., at its last regular meeting, held March 10, 1902, adopted the following resolution:

"*Resolved,* That we, the Furniture Manufacturers' Association of Indianapolis, Ind., do heartily indorse the provisions of House bill 8337 and Senate bill 3575, known as the "Nelson-Corliss bill," and we do hereby urge our representatives in Congress to use their best endeavors to promote this bill and to secure its passage."

PURITAN BED SPRING COMPANY,
Per M. F. SHAW, *Treasurer,*
BASS & WOODWORTH,
Per W. H. BASS.
WESTERN FURNITURE COMPANY,
W. L. HAGEDON, *President,*
                                        *Committee.*

Hon. JESSE OVERSTREET, *Representative Seventh District.*
Hon. C. W. FAIRBANKS, *Senator from Indiana.*
Hon. A. J. BEVERIDGE, *Senator from Indiana.*

---

31.

*Memorial of the Board of Trade of Grand Rapids, Mich., and Merchants and Manufacturers' Exchange of Detroit, Mich., praying for the passage of the so-called Nelson-Corliss interstate-commerce bill.*

[Presented by Mr. McMillan, April 14, 1902.]

DETROIT, *April 5, 1902.*

Whereas there is an extensive demand on the part of the public for some legislation which shall regulate the rates of the freight and classification of merchandise charged by the transportation companies of the country and which shall clothe the Interstate Commerce Commission with the power to enforce its decisions and to make such regulations as shall protect the shippers from extortion at any time; and

Whereas we believe that competition among the railroads of the United States has practically ceased by reason of consolidations and agreements among themselves and so destroyed the hope of relief by that means: Therefore, be it

*Resolved by the board of directors of the Merchants and Manufacturers' Exchange of Detroit, Mich.* (representing nearly 200 of the largest shippers in our city), That we indorse the bill introduced by the Hon. John B. Corliss, M. C., of this district, known as H. R. No. 8337, and the one introduced by Senator Nelson, known as S. No. 3575, and respectfully request all the Senators and Representatives from Michigan to support the passage of same at the proper time.

JAS. INGLIS, *President.*
WALTER S. CAMPBELL, *Secretary.*

---

Whereas it is believed the interests of all shippers and of all communities, except perhaps a favored few, will be promoted by equal freight charges and privileges to all; and

Whereas the Interstate Commerce Commission has been deprived, by judicial interpretations, of the authority to regulate rates and to enforce its decisions which it originally exercised as intended by the framers of the act creating it: Therefore,

*Resolved by the Grand Rapids Board of Trade,* That we hereby indorse and approve the so-called Corliss-Nelson bill, now pending in Congress, the purpose of which is to restore to the Commission such authority as it actually exercised from the time of its organization until the Supreme Court denied that such authority was conferred upon it. Particularly do we indorse these sections of the bill intended to make the orders of the Commission immediately operative and to provide for the enforcement of obedience to the orders of the Commissioners.

*Resolved further,* That copies of this resolution be forwarded to Senators James McMillan and J. C. Burrows and to each Representative from Michigan in the National Congress.

I hereby certify that the foregoing is a true and correct copy of preamble and resolutions duly adopted by the board of directors of the Grand Rapids Board of Trade this 8th day of April, 1902.

[SEAL.] H. D. C. VAN ASMUS, *Secretary.*

---

32.

*Resolution of the Merchants' Exchange of the city of Buffalo, State of New York, favoring the passage of Senate bill No. 3575 and House bill No. 8337.*

[Presented by Mr. Platt, of New York, April 14, 1902.]

The original interstate-commerce act has been interpreted by the Untied States Supreme Court in various cases, so as to greatly restrict the powers of the Commission to effectively accomplish the results intended by such act. Bills have been introduced in the Senate and House, known as Senate bill No. 3575 and House bill No. 8337, which are identical, and having for their object to confer upon the Interstate Commerce Commission authority to make effective its administrative orders and giving to the defendants the right of appeal to the United States courts, and which continue to limit the authority of the Commission to the correction of rates when it appears after investigation that such rates are unreasonable and discriminative; and these bills also repeal the provision of the present interstate-commerce act relating to imprisonment for violation of said act, and in place thereof providing for fines to be imposed for violations thereof; these amendments we believe to be essential for the proper administration of the duties and purposes of the Interstate Commerce Commission: Now, therefore,

The Buffalo Merchants' Exchange urges upon the Interstate Commerce Committee of the Senate favorable consideration of Senate bill No. 3575, and upon the Interstate and Foreign Commerce Committee of the House favorable consideration of House bill No. 8337, having for their purpose the amendment of the interstate-commerce act, to the end that favorable action may be taken thereon at this session of Congress; and that the Secretary be directed to transmit a copy of this resolution to the respective committees of the Senate and House of Representatives, the Senators from the State of New York and the Representatives in Congress from the county of Erie, requesting their cooperation in securing such legislation.

A true copy.

F. HOWARD MASON, *Secretary.*

---

33.

*Resolution adopted by the Utah Wool Growers' Association, indorsing amendment to the interstate-commerce act proposed by Congressman J. B. Corliss.*

[Presented by Senator Rawlins April 15, 1902.]

Whereas the operations of the Interstate Commerce Commission under the present law are absolutely worthless, for the reason that they have no power to enforce their decisions; and

Whereas there has been introduced in the House of Representatives of the Fifty-seventh Congress by Congressman J. B. Corliss, of Michigan, a bill amending the interstate-commerce act, correcting the evils, and giving the Commission power to enforce its rulings, which has the unqualified indorsement of the Interstate Commerce Commission and shippers at large throughout the country; and

Whereas the live-stock interests of the United States are heavy shippers and therefore interested in anything pertaining to or governing transportation: Therefore, be it

*Resolved,* That the Utah Wool Growers' Association in convention assembled urge the members of Congress to vote for the passage of this amendment to the interstate-commerce act: And be it further

*Resolved,* That the secretary of this association is hereby instructed to send copies of this resolution to the Committee on Interstate Commerce of the House, and also to write personal letters to the members of Congress and Senators from this State urging that they work for the passage of this measure.

E. H. CALLESTER, Secretary.<br>JESSE M. SMITH.

## 34.

*Resolution adopted by the Utah Cattle Growers' Association, indorsing the amendment to the interstate-commerce act proposed by Congressman J. B. Corliss.*

[Presented by Senator Rawlins, of Utah, April 15, 1902.]

Whereas the operations of the Interstate Commerce Commission under the present law are absolutely worthless, for the reason that they have no power to enforce their decisions; and

Whereas there has been introduced in the House of Representatives of the Fifty-seventh Congress by Congressman J. B. Corliss, of Michigan, a bill amending the interstate-commerce act, correcting the evils, and giving the Commission power to enforce its rulings, which has the unqualified indorsement of the Interstate-Commerce Commission and shippers at large throughout the country; and

Whereas the live stock-interests of the United States are heavy shippers and therefore interested in anything pertaining to or governing transportation: Therefore, be it

*Resolved,* That the Utah Cattle Growers' Association in convention assembled urge the members of Congress to vote for the passage of this amendment to the interstate-commerce act; and, be it further

*Resolved,* That the secretary of this association is hereby instructed to send copies of this resolution to the Committee on Interstate Commerce of the House, and also to write personal letters to the members of Congress and Senators from this State urging that they work for the passage of this measure.

_____ _____,<br>President Utah Cattle Growers' Association.<br>WESLEY K. WALTON,<br>Secretary.

## ·35.

*Petition of lumber manufacturers for the enlargement of the power of the Interstate Commerce Commission.*

[Presented by Mr. Clapp April 28, 1902, also by Mr. Elkins, also by Mr. Cockrell.]

*Resolution to members of Congress from board of directors of the Missouri, Kansas, and Oklahoma Association of Lumber Dealers:*

At the fourteenth annual convention of the Missouri, Kansas, and Oklahoma Association of Lumber Dealers, held at Kansas City, Mo., January 28–29, 1902, the following resolution was unanimously adopted:

*Resolved,* That the Missouri, Kansas, and Oklahoma Association of Lumber Dealers hereby invokes the aid of Senators and Representatives in Congress in securing the passage of laws enlarging the powers of the Interstate Commerce Commission so as to give that body increased powers.

The Missouri, Kansas, and Oklahoma Association of Lumber Dealers has a membership of 1,500, and represents in this matter the interests of the legitimate lumber trade of the Southwest. The lumber dealers of this territory have suffered from unjust discriminations on the part of the railroad companies at various times, and have been unable to secure any redress through the Interstate Commerce Commission owing to its present limited powers to enforce its rulings.

They, the lumber dealers represented by this association, feel that in justice to the business interests of the country in general, and to the interests of the lumber trade in particular, action should be taken at the present session of Congress to give the Interstate Commerce Commission increased powers, and, further, that H. R. 8337 and

S. 3575, known as the "Nelson-Corliss bill," will, if passed, give the Interstate Commerce Commission the necessary power to enforce its rulings.

Therefore the board of directors of this association, acting for and in behalf of the lumber trade of the Southwest, does hereby earnestly and heartily indorse the "Nelson-Corliss bill," and requests that the Senators and Representatives representing the Southwest will use their best endeavors and influence in assisting in the passage at the present session of Congress of the bill above referred to.

The president and secretary of the Missouri, Kansas, and Oklahoma Association of Lumber Dealers are hereby authorized and instructed to affix their signatures to this document, and the secretary is hereby instructed to forward a copy of same to each Senator and Representative from Missouri and Kansas, and to such other Senators and Representatives as the executive committee of this association may deem advisable.

E. S. MINER,
A. A. WHITE,
E. C. ROBINSON,
ROBERT PIERCE,
J. E. EVANS,
J. R. MOOREHEAD,
E. R. BURKHOLDER,
F. L. ADAMS,
GEO. D. HOPE,
JAMES COSTELLO,
JESS R. LASSWELL,
H. B. BULLEN,
L. F. MILLER,
A. L. TAYLOR,
PAUL KLEIN,
*Board of Directors.*

E. S. MINER, *President.*
By HARRY A. GORSUCH, *Secretary.*

---

38.

*Petitions for Nelson-Corliss bill by Grand Rapids Board of Trade et al.*

[Presented by Mr. Burrows, April 29, 1902.]

Whereas it is believed the interests of all shippers and of all communities, except perhaps a favored few, will be promoted by equal freight charges and privileges to all; and,

Whereas the Interstate Commerce Commission has been deprived by judicial interpretations of the authority to regulate rates and to enforce its decisions which it originally exercised, as intended by the framers of the act creating it: Therefore,

*Resolved by the Grand Rapids Board of Trade,* That we hereby indorse and approve the so-called Corliss-Nelson bill, now pending in Congress, the purpose of which is to restore to the Commission such authority as it actually exercised from the time of its organization until the Supreme Court denied that such authority was conferred upon it. Particularly do we indorse these sections of the bill intended to make the orders of the Commission immediately operative, and to provide for the inforcement of obedience to the orders of the Commissioners.

*Resolved further,* That copies of this resolution be forwarded to Senators James McMillan and J. C. Burrows and to each Representative from Michigan in the National Congress.

I hereby certify that the foregoing is a true and correct copy of preamble and resolutions duly adopted by the board of directors of the Grand Rapids Board of Trade this 8th day of April, 1902.

[SEAL.]

H. D. C. VAN ARMUS, *Secretary.*

---

SAGINAW, MICH., *February 24, 1902.*

Hon. J. C. BURROWS, *Washington, D. C.*

DEAR SIR: At a recent meeting of the trustees of the National Wholesale Lumber Dealers' Association, held in New York City, the trustees of this association were unanimous in their opinion that some legislation tending to amend the interstate-commerce act so as to enable the Commissioners to enforce their decisions was most desirable, and that some legislation looking toward the above end should be passed.

A committee was appointed at that meeting, of which the Hon. Charles M. Betts, of Philadelphia, was chairman, and the committee has made a report that after a careful examination of House bill No. 8337 they believe that said bill is entitled to the active support of every member of the National Wholesale Lumber Dealers' Association. We accordingly write you to use your influence in favor of the passage of this act.

A recent decision of the Interstate Commerce Commission in favor of the National Wholesale Lumber Dealers' Association, in a matter brought before the Commission by the association on behalf of members interested, brings home to the lumbermen the importance to their business of the interstate-commerce law, and we are anxious to impress upon you gentlemen representing us in Congress the necessity to encourage such legislation as will enable the provisions of the law to be more effectively carried out. It is of vital importance to our business interests that some such legislation should be enacted.

We therefore call the matter to your attention and earnestly request that you give this matter due consideration, advising us of any suggestions you may have in regard to the best method of our cooperating with you in this important matter.

Very truly, yours,

MERSHON, SCHUETTE, PARKER & Co.,
By F. E. PARKER, *Treasurer.*

---

37.

*Letter from Hon. Martin A. Knapp, chairman of Interstate Commerce Commission.*

WASHINGTON, D. C., *May 9, 1902.*

Hon. STEPHEN B. ELKINS,
   *Chairman Committee on Interstate Commerce, Washington, D. C.*

DEAR SIR: The Interstate Commerce Commission responds as follows to your request for a report on Senate bill 3521 and Senate bill 3575, which were referred to the Commission for that purpose.

The bill No. 3575, known as the Nelson bill, contains substantially some of the specific recommendations of the Commission in its report to the Congress for 1898. As to subjects covered by this bill, it is identical in scope, and nearly identical in phraseology, with the measures then proposed. This bill is approved by the Commission for the reasons stated in said report and other reports to the Congress.

This does not imply that the Commission would insist upon everything contained in this measure or object to its modification in some particulars. For example, the Commission is not strenuous about the minimum fine provided in the first section, which amends section 10 of the present law, or the number of days within which certain things are required to be done by section 2, which amends section 15 of the act, or the limitation upon the suspension by the court of the operation of an order made by the Commission during the pendency of proceedings in review, as provided in another part of said second section. What is meant is that the Commission approves the substantial provisions of this bill and would not favor changing them in important respects.

Nor is this bill recommended as a complete and sufficient measure. It would not cover the changes that ought to be made nor fully adapt the law to existing conditions. It would, however, in the judgment of the Commission, be a great improvement upon the present statute and distinctly aid the purposes for which the law was enacted.

The bill, No. 3521, though differing materially in form and excepting the second section, appears to have substantially the same purpose and to accomplish substantially the same changes in the present law as the Nelson bill. If this assumption is correct, the bill 3521, with some modifications, which would doubtless be acceptable to its author, would meet the approval of the Commission, except the second section, though the form of the Nelson bill is preferred. That is to say, it seems on the whole better to amend specifically certain sections of the present law than to enact an independent measure, although the same results were contemplated in one case as in the other.

As to the second section, which confers rights of contract between competing roads not now allowed, the Commission is not agreed. A majority of its members believe that amendments of this kind, with proper restrictions and connected with other needed legislation and not otherwise, should be adopted and would aid the success of public regulation. One member of the Commission, however, is unwilling to recommend any legislation which would legalize the combination of competing carriers.

Those who favor the general principle and purpose of this second section are not satisfied that the restrictions and safeguards now contained in that section are adequate to prevent an abuse of the privileges proposed to be granted. ·

This statement is designed to show the general attitude of the Commission as nearly as may be to the bills in question. Individual members may supplement this with the expression of their personal views either in written communications or in oral statements before the committee, if the latter course is preferred.

Very respectfully,

MARTIN A. KNAPP, *Chairman.*

*Concurrent resolution of the twenty-ninth general assembly of Iowa relative to the Nelson-Corliss bill.*

[Presented by Mr. Allison, May, 10, 1902.]

I, W. B. Martin, secretary of state of the State of Iowa, do hereby certify that the attached instrument of writing is a true and correct copy of a concurrent resolution passed by the legislature of the State of Iowa in relation to the Nelson-Corliss bill as the same appears of record in this office.

In testimony whereof I have hereunto set my hand and affixed the seal of the secretary of state of the State of Iowa.

Done at Des Moines, the capital of the State, April 30, 1902.

[SEAL.]                                                W. B. MARTIN, *Secretary of State,*

By D. A. HITES, *Deputy.*

No. —.

PREAMBLE AND CONCURRENT RESOLUTION IN RELATION TO THE INTERSTATE-COMMERCE LAW.

Whereas it is generally believed that the effectiveness of the interstate-commerce law has been seriously impaired by certain decisions of the Federal courts, and that the law in its present state is practically inoperative in remedying the evils of the transportation service of the country, which was the purpose of its enactment; and

Whereas a bill designated as H. R. 8337 and S. 3575, known as the Nelson-Corliss bill, is now pending in the two Houses of Congress to amend the interstate-commerce act by conferring upon the Commission created thereby additional powers for the purpose of enabling it to enforce the provisions of the act and giving its rulings immediate effect pending review by the courts: Therefore, be it

*Resolved by the senate (the house concurring),* That the Senators and Representatives in Congress from this State be, and are hereby, respectfully requested to give said measure careful consideration and to use their efforts in every proper way to secure its early enactment or the enactment of some other measure which will afford the relief sought.

[Adopted April 9, 1902.]

39.

*Resolution of the Chamber of Commerce of New Haven, Conn., favoring S. 3575, an act to regulate commerce.*

[Presented by Mr. Platt, of Connecticut, May 23, 1902.]

NEW HAVEN, CONN., *May 15, 1902.*

Hon. O. H. PLATT,

*United States Senate, Washington, D. C.*

DEAR SIR: At the meeting of the chamber last evening the following preambles and resolutions, upon the recommendation of the committee on railroads and transportation, to whom the subject had been referred, were unanimously adopted:

"Whereas there is now pending before the United States Senate and House of

Representatives an act to regulate commerce, generally known as the interstate-commerce act, as more fully set forth in Senate bill No. 3575 and House of Representatives bill No. 8337; and

"Whereas a careful investigation of these bills prove to the satisfaction of the members of this chamber that their passage would result in great benefit to the entire community at large: It is therefore

"*Resolved,* That the Senators and Representatives from this State be earnestly requested to give the above-mentioned bill their active support and to exert their influence in every proper way to secure its enactment; and be it further

"*Resolved,* That copies of these resolutions be forwarded to our Senators and Representatives immediately upon their adoption."

  Yours, very truly,        JOHN CURRIN GALLAGHER,
                          *Secretary.*

---

## 40.

*Resolution of the Commercial Exchange of Philadelphia, Pa., favoring legislation providing for uniform inland rates of transportation.*

[Presented by Mr. Quay May 31, 1902.]

                      PHILADELPHIA, *April 29, 1902.*

Hon. MATTHEW STANLEY QUAY,
   *Washington, D. C.*

SIR: At a meeting of the transportation committee of the Commercial Exchange of Philadelphia held Tuesday, April 29, 1902, the following preambles and resolution were unanimously adopted:

"The COMMITTEE ON INTERSTATE AND FOREIGN COMMERCE,
        "*House of Representatives, Washington, D. C.:*

" Whereas the necessity for such legislation as will give uniform inland freight rates to all shippers of like commodities, and provide such penalty as will insure a full observance of the interstate-commerce laws, has long been apparent to every commercial locality; and

" Whereas there are now pending before the Congress several bills of amendments, each possessing its respective merits: Therefore,

" *Resolved,* that we hereby respectfully petition the present Congress to pass such legislation as will bring to the commercial interests of this country the much needed uniform inland rates and provide effective penalties against all violations of the laws, thus guaranteeing stability of rates to those whose business is dependent upon inland transportation."

  Respectfully, yours,          ARMON. D. ACHESON, *Secretary.*

---

*Resolution adopted by board of directors of Illinois Manufacturers' Association of Chicago, praying for the passage of House bill 8337.*

[Presented by Mr. Mason, June 4, 1902.]

Whereas it is almost the unanimous opinion of men competent to judge, as expressed in private conversation, in public speeches, in carefully prepared newspaper and magazine articles, and in testimony given before Congressional and other committees of inquiry, that no combination of capital, whether in the hands of individuals, firms, or corporations, is dangerous to the public welfare unless the parties controlling such capital are given an undue advantage over others by means of railroad rates or special transportation facilities which are denied to their competitors and the general public; and

Whereas this opinion finds voice and echo in the heart of the average American citizen, since he asks for nothing in the conflicts of business life but " a fair field and no favor;" and

Whereas the Constitution of the United States, as interpreted by the decisions of the Supreme Court, gives Congress complete control over interstate commerce, to the extent, if need be, of passing upon their tariffs for the railroad corporations, subject only to the limitation that such tariffs shall be just and reasonable; and

Whereas it is competent for Congress to exercise this power; it is competent for them to delegate it to a body established by themselves for the express purpose and charged with the sole duty of exercising it; and

Whereas when the interstate commerce law was enacted it was supposed to be stringent enough to remedy the abuses in transportation matters which had even then grown unbearable, but this opinion has been shown by the experience of the past fourteen years to have not been well founded; and

Whereas there is now pending in Congress a bill known as H. R. 8337, introduced in the House of Representatives January 9, 1902, by the Hon. John B. Corliss, of Michigan, amending the interstate-commerce law, and which has been so carefully drawn, under the light of the decisions of the United States courts, that if enacted into law it is confidently expected will so strengthen the interstate-commerce law that it will fulfill the purposes for which it was originally intended, and that the Interstate Commerce Commission, acting under it, will be able to protect the honest railroad corporations from the cut-throat rates of unscrupulous competitors, as well as from the rapacity and greed of hitherto "favored shippers," and at the same time will be able to secure to the general public the same fair and equal treatment at the railroad ticket and freight offices of the country which they now receive at its post-offices and custom-houses, and to which by law they are entitled: Therefore, be it

*Resolved by the board of directors of the Illinois Manufacturers' Association,* That the speedy enactment into law of H. R. 8337 is demanded by every consideration of the public welfare; and we do therefore respectfully and earnestly urge the Congress of the United States to enact this bill into law during the present session of Congress.

*And be it further resolved,* That copies of the foregoing preamble and resolutions be forwarded to the Senators and Representatives of the United States Congress from the State of Illinois.

---

### 42.

*Memorial to the Senate of the United States, by the Commercial Club of Duluth, Minn., in favor of the Nelson-Corliss bill.*

[Presented by Mr. Clapp, June 6, 1902.]

DULUTH, *May 31, 1902.*

Hon. MOSES E. CLAPP,
 *United States Senator, Washington, D. C.*

DEAR SIR: At a regular meeting of the members of the Commercial Club of Duluth, held in the clubrooms Wednesday evening, May 21, 1902, the following resolution was adopted:

"*Resolved,* That the Commercial Club of Duluth, Duluth, Minn., hereby approves of the bill introduced in Congress known as the Nelson-Corliss bill, and requests the Representatives of the State of Minnesota in the Senate and the House of Representatives to give said bill their active support, and exert their influence in every proper way to secure its enactment.

"*Resolved further,* That a copy of this resolution be sent by the secretary of the club to the Representatives of the State of Minnesota in the Senate and the House of Representatives."

Yours, very truly, ALBERT L. PRESTON, *Secretary.*

---

### 43.

*Memorial opposing the passage of the Elkins bill, legalizing pooling, by the Atlanta Freight Bureau.*

[Presented by Mr. Clay, June 16, 1902.]

Whereas our attention having been called to a bill now pending in the United States Senate, known as the Elkins bill, the purpose of which being to legalize pooling of freight by the railroads of this country, which we believe would be greatly to the disadvantage of both shippers and producers: Therefore, be it

*Resolved,* That the Atlanta Freight Bureau is opposed to the passage of said bill, and that its traffic manager is hereby instructed to write Senators A. O. Bacon and A. S. Clay and Congressman L. F. Livingston, requesting them to use their best efforts toward the defeat of said bill.

44.

*Memorial against the passage of the Elkins bill, by the directors of the Atlanta Chamber of Commerce.*

[Presented by Mr. Clay, June 16, 1902.]

Whereas Senator Elkins has introduced in the United States Senate a bill which legalizes pooling of freight by the railroads of this country, which we believe would be greatly to the disadvantage of both shippers and producers: Therefore, be it

*Resolved,* That the directors of the Atlanta Chamber of Commerce are opposed to the passage of said bill, and the secretary is instructed to write our Senators and Representatives in Congress, asking them to use their best efforts for the defeat of the measure.

*Resolved further,* That the secretary be instructed to communicate this action of the directors to other boards of trade and commercial bodies in this section, and request them to take the same action.

---

45.

*Resolution of Buffalo Merchants' Exchange, praying for favorable action on Senate bill 3575.*

[Presented by Mr. Elkins.]

BUFFALO, N. Y., *April 12, 1902.*

Hon. STEPHEN B. ELKINS,
    *Chairman Committee on Interstate Commerce, Washington, D. C.*

MY DEAR SIR: I inclose herewith copy of resolutions adopted by the Buffalo Merchants' Exchange relating to bill which has been referred to your committee.

On behalf of the Buffalo Merchants' Exchange I beg to express the wish that the bill referred to in these resolutions may receive the careful and favorable consideration of your committee.

I am, very respectfully, yours,          F. HOWARD MASON,
                                               *Secretary.*

---

The original interstate-commerce act has been interpreted by the United States Supreme Court in various cases so as to greatly restrict the powers of the Commission to effectively accomplish the results intended by such act. Bills have been introduced in the Senate and House—known as Senate bill No. 3575 and House bill No. 8337—which are identical, and having for their object to confer upon the Interstate Commerce Commission authority to make effective its administrative orders, and giving to the defendants the right of appeal to the United States courts, and which continue to limit the authority of the Commission to the correction of rates when it appears, after investigation, that such rates are unreasonable and discriminative; and these bills also repeal the provision of the present interstate-commerce act relating to imprisonment for violation of said act, and in place thereof providing for fines to be imposed for violations thereof. These amendments we believe to be essential for the proper administration of the duties and purposes of the Interstate Commerce Commission: Now, therefore,

The Buffalo Merchants' Exchange urges upon the Interstate Commerce Committee of the Senate favorable consideration of Senate bill No. 3575, and upon the Interstate and Foreign Commerce Committee of the House favorable consideration of House bill No. 8337, having for their purpose the amendment of the interstate-commerce act, to the end that favorable action may be taken thereon at this session of Congress, and that the secretary be directed to transmit a copy of this resolution to the respective committees of the Senate and House of Representatives, the Senators from the State of New York, and the Representatives in Congress from the county of Erie, requesting the cooperation in securing such legislation.

A true copy.

F. HUVAN MASON, *Secretary.*

46.

*Resolution of the Atlanta (Ga.) Freight Bureau favoring passage of S. 3575.*

[Presented by Mr. Nelson, June 19, 1902.]

Whereas our attention having been called to a bill now pending before Congress known as the Nelson-Corliss bill, the purpose of which is to enlarge the jurisdiction and powers of the Interstate Commerce Commission; and

Whereas we believe that the public interests would be better subserved by granting the Interstate Commerce Commission full power to adjudicate all rate differences, to name just and reasonable rates, and to enforce its decrees: Therefore, be it

*Resolved,* That the Atlanta Freight Bureau indorses the Nelson-Corliss bill, and the traffic manager is instructed to forward copies of this resolution to Senators A. S. Clay and A. O. Bacon and Congressman L. F. Livingston with the request that they use their best efforts toward the passage of said bill.

---

47.

*Resolution of the Atlanta (Ga.) Freight Bureau opposing passage of S. 3521.*

[Presented by Mr. Nelson, June 19, 1902.]

Whereas our attention having been called to a bill now pending in the United States Senate known as the Elkins bill, the purpose of which being to legalize pooling of freight by the railroads of this country, which we believe would be greatly to the disadvantage of both shippers and producers: Therefore, be it

*Resolved,* That the Atlanta Freight Bureau is opposed to the passage of said bill, and its traffic manager is hereby instructed to write Senators A. O. Bacon and A. S. Clay and Congressman L. F. Livingston requesting them to use their best efforts toward the defeat of said bill.

---

48.

*Resolution directing the Interstate Commerce Commission to investigate rates filed with said Commission by common carriers, etc.*

Mr. Carmack submitted the following resolution:

"*Resolved,* That the Interstate Commerce Commission be, and is hereby, directed to investigate and report to the Senate during the month of December next, in such form and to such extent as may be practicable—

1. The rates filed with said Commission by common carriers subject to the act to regulate commerce and now in force on import and domestic traffic of like kind carried from ports of entry in the United States to interior points of destination which show material differences, in favor of through shipments of imported articles and against shipments of imported articles and against shipments of like articles originating at such ports of entry.

2. What, if any, kinds or classes of imported articles have actually been transported at any time between January 1 and July 1 of the present year by common carriers subject to the act to regulate commerce at rates from ports of entry in the United States to interior points of destination materially less than the rates contemporaneously charged by such carriers upon the same kinds or classes of articles as domestic shipments from such ports of entry to the same interior points of destination; and whether, if it can be ascertained, the rates actually charged upon both the import and domestic traffic were in conformity with the rates in effect thereon as shown in rate schedules filed with said Commission.

3. Show in said report in connection with any such differences in schedule rates in favor of import and against domestic shipments the tariff or customs duties in force under the laws of Congress upon such import traffic carried at any time during the six months' period above specified; and to enable compliance with this requirement

F R P——14

the Secretary of the Treasury is hereby directed to furnish the said Commission, upon its application, a statement showing the tariff or customs duties applicable to such import traffic.

4. Whether in the opinion of said Commission any such differences in rates in favor of import and against domestic shipments operate to produce discriminations and preferences in favor of foreign manufacturers and shippers and against American manufacturers and shippers which ought to be removed, but which can not be remedied by proceedings under the act to regulate commerce; and if so, in what manner that statute should be amended to prevent such discriminations and preferences.

# APPENDIX.

# THE ACT

## TO

# REGULATE COMMERCE

## AS AMENDED,

### TOGETHER

## WITH ACTS SUPPLEMENTARY THERETO.

---

WASHINGTON:
GOVERNMENT PRINTING OFFICE.
1895.

F R P——15

# ORIGINAL AND AMENDING ACTS.

Public No. 41, approved February 4, 1887, and in effect April 5, 1887 (U. S. Stat. at Large, Vol. 24, p. 379; Sup. to Rev. Stat., Vol. 1, p. 529). Public No. 125, approved and in effect March 2, 1889 (U. S. Stat. at Large, Vol. 25, p. 855; Sup. to Rev. Stat., Vol. 1, p. 684). Public No. 72, approved and in effect February 10, 1891 (U. S. Stat. at Large, Vol. 26, p. 743; Sup. to Rev. Stat., Vol. 1, p. 891). Public No. 38, approved and in effect February 8, 1895 (U. S. Stat. at Large, Vol. 28, p. —).

# SUPPLEMENTARY ACTS.

Public No. 54, approved and in effect February 11, 1893 (U. S. Stat. at Large, Vol. 27, p. 443). Public No. 113, approved and in effect March 2, 1893 (U. S. Stat. at Large, Vol. 27, p. 531). Public No. 237, approved and in effect August 7, 1888 (U. S. Stat. at Large, Vol. 25, p. 382; Sup. to Rev. Stat., Vol. 1, p. 602).

# THE ACT TO REGULATE COMMERCE.

*Be it enacted by the Senate and House of Representatives of the United States of America in Congress assembled,* That the provisions of this act shall apply to any common carrier or carriers engaged in the transportation of passengers or property wholly by railroad, or partly by railroad and partly by water when both are used, under a common control, management, or arrangement, for a continuous carriage or shipment, from one State or Territory of the United States, or the District of Columbia, to any other State or Territory of the United States, or the District of Columbia, or from any place in the United States to an adjacent foreign country, or from any place in the United States *Carriers and transportation subject to the act.* through a foreign country to any other place in the United States, and also to the transportation in like manner of property shipped from any place in the United States to a foreign country and carried from such place to a port of transshipment, or shipped from a foreign country to any place in the United States and carried to such place from a port of entry either in the United States or an adjacent foreign country: *Provided, however,* That the provisions of this act shall not apply to the transportation of passengers or *Act does not apply to transportation wholly within one State.* property, or to the receiving, delivering, storage, or handling of property, wholly within one State, and not shipped to or from a foreign country from or to any State or Territory as aforesaid.

The term "railroad" as used in this act shall include all bridges and ferries used or operated in connection with any railroad, and also all the road in use by any corporation operating a railroad, whether owned or operated under a contract, agreement, or lease; and the term "transportation" *What the terms "railroad" and "transportation" include.* shall include all instrumentalities of shipment or carriage.

All charges made for any service rendered or to be rendered in the transportation of passengers or property as aforesaid, or in connection therewith, or for the receiving, delivering, storage, or handling of such property, shall be reasonable and just; and every unjust and unreasonable *Charges must be reasonable and just.* charge for such service is prohibited and declared to be unlawful.

**4**

SEC. 2. That if any common carrier subject to the provisions of this act shall, directly or indirectly, by any special rate, rebate, drawback, or other device, charge, demand, collect, or receive from any person or persons a greater or less compensation for any service rendered, or to be rendered, in the transportation of passengers or property, subject to the provisions of this act, than it charges, demands, collects, or receives from any other person or persons for doing for him or them a like and contemporaneous service in the transportation of a like kind of traffic under substantially similar circumstances and conditions, such common carrier shall be deemed guilty of unjust discrimination, which is hereby prohibited and declared to be unlawful.

Unjust discrimination defined and forbidden.

SEC. 3. That it shall be unlawful for any common carrier subject to the provisions of this act to make or give any undue or unreasonable preference or advantage to any particular person, company, firm, corporation, or locality, or any particular description of traffic, in any respect whatsoever, or to subject any particular person, company, firm, corporation, or locality, or any particular description of traffic, to any undue or unreasonable prejudice or disadvantage in any respect whatsoever.

Undue or unreasonable preference or advantage forbidden.

Every common carrier subject to the provisions of this act shall, according to their respective powers, afford all reasonable, proper, and equal facilities for the interchange of traffic between their respective lines, and for the receiving, forwarding, and delivering of passengers and property to and from their several lines and those connecting therewith, and shall not discriminate in their rates and charges between such connecting lines; but this shall not be construed as requiring any such common carrier to give the use of its tracks or terminal facilities to another carrier engaged in like business.

Facilities for interchange of traffic.

Discrimination between connecting lines forbidden.

SEC. 4. That it shall be unlawful for any common carrier subject to the provisions of this act to charge or receive any greater compensation in the aggregate for the transportation of passengers or of like kind of property, under substantially similar circumstances and conditions, for a shorter than for a longer distance over the same line, in the same direction, the shorter being included within the longer distance; but this shall not be construed as authorizing any common carrier within the terms of this act to charge and receive as great compensation for a shorter as for a longer distance: *Provided, however,* That upon application to the Commission appointed under the provisions of this act, such common carrier may, in special cases, after investigation by the Commission, be authorized to charge less for longer than

Long and short haul provision.

Commission has authority to relieve carriers from the operation of this section.

for shorter distances for the transportation of passengers or property; and the Commission may from time to time prescribe the extent to which such designated common carrier may be relieved from the operation of this section of this act.

SEC. 5. That it shall be unlawful for any common carrier subject to the provisions of this act to enter into any contract, agreement, or combination with any other common carrier or carriers for the pooling of freights of different and competing railroads, or to divide between them the aggregate or net proceeds of the earnings of such railroads, or any portion thereof; and in any case of an agreement for the pooling of freights as aforesaid, each day of its continuance shall be deemed a separate offense. *Pooling of freights and division of earnings forbidden.*

SEC. 6. (*As amended March 2, 1889.*) That every common carrier subject to the provisions of this act shall print and keep open to public inspection schedules showing the rates and fares and charges for the transportation of passengers and property which any such common carrier has established and which are in force at the time upon its route. The schedules printed as aforesaid by any such common carrier shall plainly state the places upon its railroad between which property and passengers will be carried, and shall contain the classification of freight in force, and shall also state separately the terminal charges and any rules or regulations which in any wise change, affect, or determine any part or the aggregate of such aforesaid rates and fares and charges. Such schedules shall be plainly printed in large type, and copies for the use of the public shall be posted in two public and conspicuous places, in every depot, station, or office of such carrier where passengers or freight, respectively, are received for transportation, in such form that they shall be accessible to the public and can be conveniently inspected. *Printing and posting of schedules of rates fares, and charges including rules and regulations affecting the same, terminal charges and freight classifications.*

Any common carrier subject to the provisions of this act receiving freight in the United States to be carried through a foreign country to any place in the United States shall also in like manner print and keep open to public inspection, at every depot or office where such freight is received for shipment, schedules showing the through rates established and charged by such common carrier to all points in the United States beyond the foreign country to which it accepts freight for shipment; and any freight shipped from the United States through a foreign country into the United States, the through rate on which shall not have been made public as required by this act, shall, before it is admitted into the United States from said foreign country, be subject to cus- *Printing and posting of schedules of rates on freight carried through a foreign country.*

*Freight subject to customs duties in case of failure to publish through rates.*

toms duties as if said freight were of foreign production; and any law in conflict with this section is hereby repealed.

No advance shall be made in the rates, fares, and charges which have been established and published as aforesaid by any common carrier in compliance with the requirements of this section, except after ten days' public notice, which shall plainly state the changes proposed to be made in the schedule then in force, and the time when the increased rates, fares, or charges will go into effect; and the proposed changes shall be shown by printing new schedules, or shall be plainly indicated upon the schedules in force at the time and kept open to public inspection. Reductions in such published rates, fares, or charges shall only be made after three days' previous public notice, to be given in the same manner that notice of an advance in rates must be given.

*Ten days' public notice of advances in rates must be given.*

*Three days' public notice of reduction in rates must be given.*

And when any such common carrier shall have established and published its rates, fares, and charges in compliance with the provisions of this section, it shall be unlawful for such common carrier to charge, demand, collect, or receive from any person or persons a greater or less compensation for the transportation of passengers or property, or for any services in connection therewith, than is specified in such published schedule of rates, fares, and charges as may at the time be in force.

*Published rates not to be deviated from.*

Every common carrier subject to the provisions of this act shall file with the Commission hereinafter provided for copies of its schedules of rates, fares, and charges which have been established and published in compliance with the requirements of this section, and shall promptly notify said Commission of all changes made in the same. Every such common carrier shall also file with said Commission copies of all contracts, agreements, or arrangements with other common carriers in relation to any traffic affected by the provisions of this act to which it may be a party. And in cases where passengers and freight pass over continuous lines or routes operated by more than one common carrier, and the several common carriers operating such lines or routes establish joint tariffs of rates or fares or charges for such continuous lines or routes, copies of such joint tariffs shall also, in like manner, be filed with said Commission. Such joint rates, fares, and charges on such continuous lines so filed as aforesaid shall be made public by such common carriers when directed by said Commission, in so far as may, in the judgment of the Commission, be deemed practicable; and said Commission shall from time to time prescribe the measure of publicity which shall be given to

*Copies of schedules of rates, fares, and charges must be filed with Commission.*

*Copies of contracts, agreements, and arrangements must be filed with Commission.*

*Joint tariffs must be filed with Commission.*

*Power of Commission to prescribe publicity.*

such rates, fares, and charges, or to such part of them as it may deem it practicable for such common carriers to publish, and the places in which they shall be published.

No advance shall be made in joint rates, fares, and charges, shown upon joint tariffs, except after ten days' notice to the Commission, which shall plainly state the changes proposed to be made in the schedule then in force, and the time when the increased rates, fares, or charges will go into effect. No reduction shall be made in joint rates, fares, and charges, except after three days' notice, to be given to the Commission as is above provided in the case of an advance of joint rates. The Commission may make public such proposed advances, or such reductions, in such manner as may, in its judgment, be deemed practicable, and may prescribe from time to time the measure of publicity which common carriers shall give to advances or reductions in joint tariffs. *Ten days' notice to Commission of advance in joint rates, fares, and charges. Three days' notice to Commission of reduction in joint rates, fares, and charges. Power of Commission to make advances or reductions public.*

It shall be unlawful for any common carrier, party to any joint tariff, to charge, demand, collect, or receive from any person or persons a greater or less compensation for the transportation of persons or property, or for any services in connection therewith, between any points as to which a joint rate, fare, or charge is named thereon than is specified in the schedule filed with the Commission in force at the time. *Joint rates, fares, and charges must not be deviated from.*

The Commission may determine and prescribe the form in which the schedules required by this section to be kept open to public inspection shall be prepared and arranged, and may change the form from time to time as shall be found expedient. *Commission may prescribe forms of schedules of rates, fares, and charges.*

If any such common carrier shall neglect or refuse to file or publish its schedules or tariffs of rates, fares, and charges as provided in this section, or any part of the same, such common carrier shall, in addition to other penalties herein prescribed, be subject to a writ of mandamus, to be issued by any circuit court of the United States in the judicial district wherein the principal office of said common carrier is situated, or wherein such offense may be committed, and if such common carrier be a foreign corporation in the judicial circuit wherein such common carrier accepts traffic and has an agent to perform such service, to compel compliance with the aforesaid provisions of this section; and such writ shall issue in the name of the people of the United States, at the relation of the Commissioners appointed under the provisions of this act; and the failure to comply with its requirements shall be punishable as and for a con- *Penalties for neglect or refusal to file or publish rates, fares, and charges.*

fully assist, or shall willingly suffer or permit, any person or persons to obtain transportation for property at less than the regular rates then established and in force on the line of transportation of such common carrier, shall be deemed guilty of a misdemeanor, and shall, upon conviction thereof in any court of the United States of competent jurisdiction within the district in which such offense was committed, be subject to a fine of not exceeding five thousand dollars, or imprisonment in the penitentiary for a term of not exceeding two years, or both, in the discretion of the court, for each offense.

Penalties for false billing, etc., by shippers and other persons: Fine and imprisonment.

Any person and any officer or agent of any corporation or company who shall deliver property for transportation to any common carrier, subject to the provisions of this act, or for whom as consignor or consignee any such carrier shall transport property, who shall knowingly and willfully, by false billing, false classification, false weighing, false representation of the contents of the package, or false report of weight, or by any other device or means, whether with or without the consent or connivance of the carrier, its agent or agents, obtain transportation for such property at less than the regular rates then established and in force on the line of transportation, shall be deemed guilty of fraud, which is hereby declared to be a misdemeanor, and shall, upon conviction thereof in any court of the United States of competent jurisdiction within the district in which such offense was committed, be subject for each offense to a fine of not exceeding five thousand dollars or imprisonment in the penitentiary for a term of not exceeding two years, or both, in the discretion of the court.

Penalties for inducing common carriers to discriminate unjustly: Fine and imprisonment. Joint liability with carrier for damages.

If any such person, or any officer or agent of any such corporation or company, shall, by payment of money or other thing of value, solicitation, or otherwise, induce any common carrier subject to the provisions of this act, or any of its officers or agents, to discriminate unjustly in his, its, or their favor as against any other consignor or consignee in the transportation of property, or shall aid or abet any common carrier in any such unjust discrimination, such person or such officer or agent of such corporation or company shall be deemed guilty of a misdemeanor, and shall, upon conviction thereof in any court of the United States of competent jurisdiction within the district in which such offense was committed, be subject to a fine of not exceeding five thousand dollars, or imprisonment in the penitentiary for a term of not exceeding two years, or both, in the discretion of the court, for each offense; and such person, corporation, or company shall also, together with said common carrier, be liable, jointly or severally, in an action on the case to be brought by any consignor or consignee discriminated against in any court of the United States of competent jurisdiction for all damages caused by or resulting therefrom.

SEC. 11. That a Commission is hereby created and established to be known as the Inter-State Commerce Commission, which shall be composed of five Commissioners, who shall be appointed by the President, by and with the advice and consent of the Senate. The Commissioners first appointed under this act shall continue in office for the term of two, three, four, five, and six years, respectively, from the first day of January, anno Domini eighteen hundred and eighty-seven, the term of each to be designated by the President; but their successors shall be appointed for terms of six years, except that any person chosen to fill a vacancy shall be appointed only for the unexpired time of the Commissioner whom he shall succeed. Any Commissioner may be removed by the President for inefficiency, neglect of duty, or malfeasance in office. Not more than three of the Commissioners shall be appointed from the same political party. No person in the employ of or holding any official relation to any common carrier subject to the provisions of this act, or owning stock or bonds thereof, or who is in any manner pecuniarily interested therein, shall enter upon the duties of or hold such office. Said Commissioners shall not engage in any other business, vocation, or employment. No vacancy in the Commission shall impair the right of the remaining Commissioners to exercise all the powers of the Commission.

*Interstate Commerce Commissioners—how appointed.*

*Terms of Commissioners.*

" SEC. 12. (*As amended March 2, 1889, and February 10, 1891.*) That the Commission hereby created shall have authority to inquire into the management of the business of all common carriers subject to the provisions of this act, and shall keep itself informed as to the manner and method in which the same is conducted, and shall have the right to obtain from such common carriers full and complete information necessary to enable the Commission to perform the duties and carry out the objects for which it was created; and the Commission is hereby authorized and required to execute and enforce the provisions of this act; and, upon the request of the Commission, it shall be the duty of any district attorney of the United States to whom the Commission may apply to institute in the proper court and to prosecute

*Power and duty of Commission to inquire into business of carriers and keep itself informed in regard thereto.*

*Commission required to execute and enforce provisions of this act.*

*Duty of district attorney to prosecute under direction of Attorney-General.*

under the direction of the Attorney-General of the United States all necessary proceedings for the enforcement of the provisions of this act and for the punishment of all viola-

tions thereof, and the costs and expenses of such prosecution shall be paid out of the appropriation for the expenses of the courts of the United States; and for the purposes of this act the Commission shall have power to require, by subpœna, the attendance and testimony of witnesses and the production of all books, papers, tariffs, contracts, agreements, and documents relating to any matter under investigation.

"Such attendance of witnesses, and the production of such documentary evidence, may be required from any place in the United States, at any designated place of hearing. And in case of disobedience to a subpœna the Commission, or any party to a proceeding before the Commission, may invoke the aid of any court of the United States in requiring the attendance and testimony of witnesses and the production of books, papers, and documents under the provisions of this section.

"And any of the circuit courts of the United States within the jurisdiction of which such inquiry is carried on may, in case of contumacy or refusal to obey a subpœna issued to any common carrier subject to the provisions of this act, or other person, issue an order requiring such common carrier or other person to appear before said Commission (and produce books and papers if so ordered) and give evidence touching the matter in question; and any failure to obey such order of the court may be punished by such court as a contempt thereof. The claim that any such testimony or evidence may tend to criminate the person giving such evidence shall not excuse such witness from testifying; but such evidence or testimony shall not be used against such person on the trial of any criminal proceeding.

"The testimony of any witness may be taken, at the instance of a party in any proceeding or investigation depending before the Commission, by deposition, at any time after a cause or proceeding is at issue on petition and answer. The Commission may also order testimony to be taken by deposition in any proceeding or investigation pending before it, at any stage of such proceeding or investigation. Such depositions may be taken before any judge of any court of the United States, or any commissioner of a circuit, or any clerk of a district or circuit court, or any chancellor, justice, or judge of a supreme or superior court, mayor or chief magistrate of a city, judge of a county court, or court of common pleas of any of the United States, or any notary public, not being of counsel or attorney to either of the parties, nor interested in the event of the proceeding or investigation. Reasonable notice must first be given in writing by the party or his attorney proposing to take such deposition to the opposite party or his attorney of record, as either may be nearest, which notice shall state the name of the witness and the time and place of the taking of his deposition. Any person may be compelled to appear and depose, and to produce documentary evidence, in the same manner as witnesses may be compelled to appear and testify and produce documentary evidence before the Commission as hereinbefore provided. *Reasonable notice must be given.* *Testimony by deposition may be compelled in the same manner as above specified.*

"Every person deposing as herein provided shall be cautioned and sworn (or affirm, if he so request) to testify the whole truth, and shall be carefully examined. His testimony shall be reduced to writing by the magistrate taking the deposition, or under his direction, and shall, after it has been reduced to writing, be subscribed by the deponent. *Manner of taking depositions.*

"If a witness whose testimony may be desired to be taken by deposition be in a foreign country, the deposition may be taken before an officer or person designated by the Commission, or agreed upon by the parties by stipulation in writing to be filed with the Commission. All depositions must be promptly filed with the Commission." *When witness is in a foreign country.* *Depositions must be filed with the Commission.*

Witnesses whose depositions are taken pursuant to this act, and the magistrate or other officer taking the same, shall severally be entitled to the same fees as are paid for like services in the courts of the United States. *Fees of witnesses and magistrates.*

SEC. 13. That any person, firm, corporation, or association, or any mercantile, agricultural, or manufacturing society, or any body politic or municipal organization complaining of anything done or omitted to be done by any common carrier subject to the provisions of this act in contravention of the provisions thereof, may apply to said Commission by petition, which shall briefly state the facts; whereupon a statement of the charges thus made shall be forwarded by the Commission to such common carrier, who shall be called upon to satisfy the complaint or to answer the same in writing within a reasonable time, to be specified by the Commission. If such common carrier, within the time specified, shall make reparation for the injury alleged to have been done, said carrier shall be relieved of liability to the complainant only for the particular violation of law thus complained of. If such carrier shall not satisfy the complaint within the time specified, or there shall *Complaints to Commission. How and by whom made. How served upon carriers.* *Reparation by carriers before investigation.* *Investigations of complaints by the Commission.*

appear to be any reasonable ground for investigating said complaint, it shall be the duty of the Commission to investigate the matters complained of in such manner and by such means as it shall deem proper.

Complaints forwarded by State Railroad Commissions.

Said Commission shall in like manner investigate any complaint forwarded by the railroad commissioner or railroad commission of any State or Territory, at the request of such commissioner or commission, and may institute any inquiry on its own motion in the same manner and to the same effect as though complaint had been made.

Institution of inquiries by the Commission on its own motion.

Complainant need not be directly damaged.

No complaint shall at any time be dismissed because of the absence of direct damage to the complainant.

Commission must make report of investigations.

SEC. 14. (*As amended March 2, 1889.*) That whenever an investigation shall be made by said Commission, it shall be its duty to make a report in writing in respect thereto, which shall include the findings of fact upon which the conclusions of the Commission are based, together with its recommendation as to what reparation, if any, should be made by the common carrier to any party or parties who may be found to have been injured; and such findings so made shall thereafter, in all judicial proceedings, be deemed prima facie evidence as to each and every fact found.

Reparation.

Findings of Commission prima facie evidence in judicial proceedings.

Reports of investigations must be entered of record.

All reports of investigations made by the Commission shall be entered of record, and a copy thereof shall be furnished to the party who may have complained, and to any common carrier that may have been complained of.

Service of copies on parties.

Reports and decisions. Authorized publication to be competent evidence.

The Commission may provide for the publication of its reports and decisions in such form and manner as may be best adapted for public information and use, and such authorized publications shall be competent evidence of the reports and decisions of the Commission therein contained, in all courts of the United States, and of the several States, without any further proof or authentication thereof. The Commission may also cause to be printed for early distribution its annual reports.

Publication and distribution of annual reports of Commission.

SEC. 15. That if in any case in which an investigation shall be made by said Commission it shall be made to appear to the satisfaction of the Commission, either by the testimony of witnesses or other evidence, that anything has been done or omitted to be done in violation of the provisions of this act, or of any law cognizable by said Commission, by any common carrier, or that any injury or damage has been sustained by the party or parties complaining, or by other parties aggrieved in consequence of any such violation, it shall be the duty of the Commission to forthwith cause a copy of its report in respect thereto to be delivered to such common carrier, together with a notice to said common carrier to cease and desist from such violation, or to make reparation for the injury so found to have been done, or both, within a reasonable time, to be specified by the Commission; and if, within the time specified, it shall be made to appear to the Commission that such common carrrier has ceased from such violation of law, and has made reparation for the injury found to have been done, in compliance with the report and notice of the Commission, or to the satisfaction of the party complaining, a statement to that effect shall be entered of record by the Commission, and the said common carrier shall thereupon be relieved from further liability or penalty for such particular violation of law.

SEC. 16. (*As amended March 2, 1889.*) That whenever any common carrier, as defined in and subject to the provisions of this act, shall violate, or refuse or neglect to obey or perform any lawful order or requirement of the Commission created by this act, not founded upon a controversy requiring a trial by jury, as provided by the seventh amendment to the Constitution of the United States, it shall be lawful for the Commission or for any company or person interested in such order or requirement, to apply in a summary way, by petition, to the circuit court of the United States sitting in equity in the judicial district in which the common carrier complained of has its principal office, or in which the violation or disobedience of such order or requirement shall happen, alleging such violation or disobedience, as the case may be; and the said court shall have power to hear and determine the matter, on such short notice to the common carrier complained of as the court shall deem reasonable; and such notice may be served on such common carrier, his or its officers, agents, or servants in such manner as the court shall direct; and said court shall proceed to hear and determine the matter speedily as a court of equity, and without the formal pleadings and proceedings applicable to ordinary suits in equity, but in such manner as to do justice in the premises; and to this end such court shall have power, if it think fit, to direct and prosecute in such mode and by such persons as it may appoint, all such inquiries as the court may think needful to enable it to form a just judgment in the matter of such petition; and on such hearing the findings of fact in the report of said Commission shall be prima facie evidence of the matters therein stated; and if it be made to appear to such court, on such hearing or on report of any such person or persons, that the lawful order or requirement of said Commission drawn in question

has been violated or disobeyed, it shall be lawful for
such court to issue a writ of injunction or other proper
process, mandatory or otherwise, to restrain such common carrier from further continuing such violation or disobedience of such order or requirement of said Commission, and enjoining obedience to the same; and in case of any disobedience of any such writ of injunction or other proper process, mandatory or otherwise, it shall be lawful for such court to issue writs of attachment, or any other process of said court incident or applicable to writs of injunction or other proper process, mandatory or otherwise, against such common carrier, and if a corporation, against one or more of the directors, officers, or agents of the same, or against any owner, lessee, trustee, receiver, or other person failing to obey such writ of injunction, or other proper process, mandatory or otherwise; and said court may, if it shall think fit, make an order directing such common carrier or other
person so disobeying such writ of injunction or other proper process, mandatory or otherwise, to pay such sum of money, not exceeding for each carrier or person in default the sum of five hundred dollars for every day, after a day to be named in the order, that such carrier or other person shall fail to obey such injunction or other proper process, mandatory or otherwise; and such moneys shall be payable as the court shall direct, either to the party complaining or into court, to abide the ultimate decision of the court, or into the Treasury; and payment thereof may, without prejudice to any other mode of recovering the same, be enforced by attachment or order in the nature of a writ of execution, in like manner as if the same had been recovered by a final decree in personam in such court. When the subject in dispute shall be of the value of two thousand dollars or more, either party to such proceeding before said
court may appeal to the Supreme Court of the United States, under the same regulations now provided by law in respect of security for such appeal; but such appeal shall
not operate to stay or supersede the order of the court or the execution of any writ or process thereon; and such court may, in every such matter, order the payment of such
costs and counsel fees as shall be deemed reasonable. Whenever any such petition shall be filed or presented by
the Commission it shall be the duty of the district attorney, under the direction of the Attorney-General of the United States, to prosecute the same; and the costs and expenses
of such prosecution shall be paid out of the appropriation for the expenses of the courts of the United States.

If the matters involved in any such order or requirement of said Commission are founded upon a controversy requiring a trial by jury, as provided by the seventh amendment to the Constitution of the United States, and any such common carrier shall violate or refuse or neglect to obey or perform the same, after notice given by said Commission as provided in the fifteenth section of this act, it shall be lawful for any company or person interested in such order or requirement to apply in a summary way by petition to the circuit court of the United States sitting as a court of law in the judicial district in which the carrier complained of has its principal office, or in which the violation or disobedience of such order or requirement shall happen, alleging such violation or disobedience as the case may be; and said court shall by its order then fix a time and place for the trial of said cause, which shall not be less than twenty nor more than forty days from the time said order is made, and it shall be the duty of the marshal of the district in which said proceeding is pending to forthwith serve a copy of said petition, and of said order, upon each of the defendants, and it shall be the duty of the defendants to file their answers to said petition within ten days after the service of the same upon them as aforesaid. At the trial the findings of fact of said Commission as set forth in its report shall be prima facie evidence of the matters therein stated, and if either party shall demand a jury or shall omit to waive a jury the court shall, by its order, direct the marshal forthwith to summon a jury to try the cause; but if all the parties shall waive a jury in writing then the court shall try the issues in said cause and render its judgment thereon. If the subject in dispute shall be of the value of two thousand dollars or more either party may appeal to the Supreme Court of the United States under the same regulations now provided by law in respect to security for such appeal; but such appeal must be taken within twenty days from the day of the rendition of the judgment of said circuit court. If the judgment of the circuit court shall be in favor of the party complaining he or they shall be entitled to recover a reasonable counsel or attorney's fee, to be fixed by the court, which shall be collected as part of the costs in the case. For the purposes of this act, excepting its penal provisions, the circuit courts of the United States shall be deemed to be always in session.

*Petition to United States courts in cases of disobedience when trial by jury is necessary.*

*Findings of fact of the Commission shall be prima facie evidence.*

*Trial by jury.*

*Trial by court.*

*Appeals to Supreme Court of United States.*

*Counsel or attorney's fees.*

SEC. 17. (*As amended March 2, 1889.*) That the Commission may conduct its proceedings in such manner as will best conduce to the proper dispatch of business and to the

*Interstate Commerce Commission. Form of procedure.* ends of justice. A majority of the Commission shall constitute a quorum for the transaction of business, but no Commissioner shall participate in any hearing or proceeding in which he has any pecuniary interest. Said Commission may, from time to time, make or amend such general rules or orders as may be requisite for the order and regulation of proceedings before it, including forms of notices and the service thereof, which shall conform, as nearly as may be, to those in use in the courts of the United States.

*Parties may appear before the Commission in person or by attorney.* Any party may appear before said Commission and be heard, in person or by attorney. Every vote and official act of the Commission shall be entered of record, and its proceedings shall be public upon the request of either party interested. *Official seal.* Said Commission shall have an official seal, which shall be judicially noticed. Either of the members of the Commission may administer oaths and affirmations and sign subpœnas.

SEC. 18. (*As amended.*) That each Commissioner shall *Salaries of Commissioners.* receive an annual salary of seven thousand five hundred dollars, payable in the same manner as the judges of the courts of the United States. The Commission shall appoint a secretary, who shall receive an annual salary of *Secretary—how appointed; salary.* three thousand five hundred dollars, payable in like manner. The Commission shall have authority to employ and fix the *Employees.* compensation of such other employees as it may find necessary to the proper performance of its duties. Until *Offices and supplies.* otherwise provided by law, the Commission may hire suitable offices for its use, and shall have authority to procure all necessary office supplies. *Witnesses' fees.* Witnesses summoned before the Commission shall be paid the same fees and mileage that are paid witnesses in the courts of the United States. *Expenses of the Commission—how paid.* All of the expenses of the Commission, including all necessary expenses for transportation incurred by the Commissioners, or by their employees under their orders, in making any investigation, or upon official business in any other places than in the city of Washington, shall be allowed and paid on the presentation of itemized vouchers therefor approved by the chairman of the Commission.

*Principal office of the Commission.* SEC. 19. That the principal office of the Commission shall be in the city of Washington, where its general sessions shall be held; but whenever the convenience of the public or the parties may be promoted or delay or expense prevented thereby, the Commission may hold special sessions *Sessions of the Commission.* in any part of the United States. *Commission may prosecute inquiries by one or more of its members in any* It may, by one or more of the Commissioners, prosecute any inquiry necessary to its duties, in any part of the United States, into any matter or question of fact pertaining to the business of any *part of the United States.* common carrier subject to the provisions of this act.

SEC. 20. That the Commission is hereby authorized to re- *Carriers subject to the act must render full annual reports to Commission.* quire annual reports from all common carriers subject to the provisions of this act, to fix the time and prescribe the manner in which such reports shall be made, and to require from such carriers specific answers to all questions upon which the Commission may need information. Such annual reports shall show in detail the amount of capital stock issued, the amounts paid therefor, and the manner of payment for the same; the dividends paid, the surplus fund, if any, and the *What reports of carriers shall contain.* number of stockholders; the funded and floating debts and the interest paid thereon; the cost and value of the carrier's property, franchises, and equipments; the number of employees and the salaries paid each class; the amounts expended for improvements each year, how expended, and the character of such improvements; the earnings and receipts from each branch of business and from all sources; the operating and other expenses; the balances of profit and loss; and a complete exhibit of the financial operations of the carrier each year, including an annual balance-sheet. Such reports shall also contain such information in relation to rates or regulations concerning fares or freights, or agreements, arrangements, or contracts with other common carriers, as the Commission may require; and the said Commission may, within its discretion, for the purpose of enabling *Commission may prescribe methods of keeping accounts.* it the better to carry out the purposes of this act, prescribe (if in the opinion of the Commission it is practicable to prescribe such uniformity and methods of keeping accounts) a period of time within which all common carriers subject to the provisions of this act shall have, as near as may be, a uniform system of accounts, and the manner in which such accounts shall be kept.

SEC. 21. (*As amended March 2, 1889.*) That the Commis- *Annual reports of the Commission to Congress* sion shall, on or before the first day of December in each year, make a report, which shall be transmitted to Congress, and copies of which shall be distributed as are the other reports transmitted to Congress. This report shall contain such information and data collected by the Commission as may be considered of value in the determination of questions connected with the regulation of commerce, together with such recommendations as to additional legislation relating thereto as the Commission may deem necessary; and the names and compensation of the persons employed by said Commission.

**SEC. 22.** (*As amended March 2, 1889, and February 8, 1895.*)

That nothing in this act shall prevent the carriage, storage,

*Persons and property that may be carried free or at reduced rates.* or handling of property free or at reduced rates for the United States, State, or municipal governments, or for charitable purposes, or to or from fairs and expositions for exhibition thereat, or the free carriage of destitute and homeless persons transported by charitable societies, and

*Mileage, excursion, or commutation passenger tickets.* the necessary agents employed in such transportation, or the issuance of mileage, excursion, or commutation passenger tickets; nothing in this act shall be construed to prohibit any common carrier from giving reduced rates to ministers of religion, or to municipal governments for the transportation of indigent persons, or to inmates of the National Homes or State Homes for Disabled Volunteer Soldiers, and of Soldiers' and Sailors' Orphan Homes, including those about to enter and those returning home after discharge, under arrangements with the boards of managers of said homes; nothing in this act shall be con-

*Passes and free transportation to officers and employees of railroad companies.* strued to prevent railroads from giving free carriage to their own officers and employees, or to prevent the principal officers of any railroad company or companies from exchanging passes or tickets with other railroad companies for their officers and employees; and nothing in this act

*Provisions of act are in addition to remedies existing at common law. Pending litigation not affected by act.* contained shall in any way abridge or alter the remedies now existing at common law or by statute, but the provisions of this act are in addition to such remedies: *Provided,* That no pending litigation shall in any way be affected by this act: *Provided further,* That nothing in

*Joint interchangeable five-thousand-mile tickets. Amount of free baggage.* this act shall prevent the issuance of joint interchangeable five-thousand mile tickets, with special privileges as to the amount of free baggage that may be carried under mileage tickets of one thousand or more miles. But before any common carrier, subject to the provisions of this act, shall issue any such joint interchangeable mileage tickets with special privileges, as aforesaid, it shall file with the Interstate Commerce Commission copies of the joint tariffs of rates, fares, or charges on which such joint interchangeable mileage tickets are to be based, together with specifications of the amount of free baggage permitted to be carried under such tickets, in the same manner as common carriers are required to do with regard to other joint rates by section six of this act; and all the provisions of said section

*Publication of rates.* six relating to joint rates, fares, and charges shall be observed by said common carriers and enforced by the Interstate Commerce Commission as fully with regard to such joint interchangeable mileage tickets as with regard to other joint rates, fares, and charges referred to in said section six. It shall be unlawful for any common carrier that has issued or authorized to be issued any such joint interchangeable mileage tickets to demand, collect, or receive from any person or persons a greater or less compensation for transportation of persons or baggage under such joint interchangeable mileage tickets than that required by the rate, fare, or charge specified in the copies of the joint tariff of rates, fares, or charges filed with the Commission in force at the time. The provisions of section ten of this act shall apply to any violation of the requirements of this proviso. Sale of tickets. Penalties.

NEW SECTION (*Added March 2, 1889*). That the circuit and district courts of the United States shall have jurisdiction upon the relation of any person or persons, firm, or corporation, alleging such violation by a common carrier, of any of the provisions of the act to which this is a supplement and all acts amendatory thereof, as prevents the relator from having interstate traffic moved by said common carrier at the same rates as are charged, or upon terms or conditions as favorable as those given by said common carrier for like traffic under similar conditions to any other shipper, to issue a writ or writs of mandamus against said common carrier, commanding such common carrier to move and transport the traffic, or to furnish cars or other facilities for transportation for the party applying for the writ: *Provided*, That if any question of fact as to the proper compensation to the common carrier for the service to be enforced by the writ is raised by the pleadings, the writ of peremptory mandamus may issue, notwithstanding such question of fact is undetermined, upon such terms as to security, payment of money into the court, or otherwise, as the court may think proper, pending the determination of the question of fact: *Provided*, That the remedy hereby given by writ of mandamus shall be cumulative, and shall not be held to exclude or interfere with other remedies provided by this act or the act to which it is a supplement. *Jurisdiction of United States courts to issue writs of peremptory mandamus commanding the movement of interstate traffic or the furnishing of cars or other transportation facilities. Peremptory mandamus may issue notwithstanding proper compensation of carrier may be undetermined. Remedy cumulative, and shall not interfere with other remedies provided by the act.*

Public No. 41, approved February 4, 1887, as amended by Public No. 125, approved March 2, 1889, and Public No. 72, approved February 10, 1891. Public No. 38, approved February 8, 1895.

An act in relation to testimony before the Interstate Commerce Commission, and in cases or proceedings under or connected with an act entitled "An act to regulate commerce," approved February fourth, eighteen hundred and eighty-seven, and amendments thereto.

*Be it enacted by the Senate and House of Representatives of the United States of America in Congress assembled*, That Attendance and testimony of witnesses and production of documentary evidence compulsory before the Commission, and in any case, criminal or otherwise, in the courts. no person shall be excused from attending and testifying or from producing books, papers, tariffs, contracts, agreements and documents before the Interstate Commerce Commission, or in obedience to the subpœna of the Commission, whether such subpœna be signed or issued by one or more Commissioners, or in any cause or proceeding, criminal or otherwise, based upon or growing out of any alleged violation of the act of Congress, entitled "An act to regulate commerce," approved February fourth, eighteen hundred and eighty-seven, or of any amendment thereof on the ground or for the reason that the testimony or evidence, documentary or otherwise, required of him, may tend to criminate him or subject him to a penalty or forfeiture. But no person shall be prosecuted or subjected to any penalty or forfeiture for or on account of any transaction, matter or thing, concerning which he may testify, or produce evidence, documentary or otherwise, before said Commission, or in obedience to its subpœna, or the subpœna of either of them, or in any such case or proceeding: *Provided*, That no person so testifying shall be exempt from prosecution and punishment for perjury committed in so testifying.

Penalties: fine or imprisonment, or both. Any person who shall neglect or refuse to attend and testify, or to answer any lawful inquiry, or to produce books, papers, tariffs, contracts, agreements and documents, if in his power to do so, in obedience to the subpœna or lawful requirement of the Commission shall be guilty of an offense and upon conviction thereof by a court of competent jurisdiction shall be punished by fine not less than one hundred dollars nor more than five thousand dollars, or by imprisonment for not more than one year or by both such fine and imprisonment.

Public No. 54, approved, February 11, 1893.

An act to promote the safety of employees and travelers upon railroads by compelling common carriers engaged in interstate commerce to equip their cars with automatic couplers and continuous brakes and their locomotives with driving-wheel brakes, and for other purposes.

*Be it enacted by the Senate and House of Representatives of the United States of America in Congress assembled,* That from and after the first day of January, eighteen hundred and ninety-eight, it shall be unlawful for any common carrier engaged in interstate commerce by railroad to use on its line any locomotive engine in moving interstate traffic not equipped with a power driving-wheel brake and appliances for operating the train-brake system, or to run any train in such traffic after said date that has not a sufficient number of cars in it so equipped with power or train brakes that the engineer on the locomotive drawing such train can control its speed without requiring brakemen to use the common hand brake for that purpose. *Driving-wheel and train brakes.*

Sec. 2. That on and after the first day of January, eighteen hundred and ninety-eight, it shall be unlawful for any such common carrier to haul or permit to be hauled or used on its line any car used in moving interstate traffic not equipped with couplers coupling automatically by impact, and which can be uncoupled without the necessity of men going between the ends of the cars. *Automatic couplers.*

Sec. 3. That when any person, firm, company, or corporation engaged in interstate commerce by railroad shall have equipped a sufficient number of its cars so as to comply with the provisions of section one of this act, it may lawfully refuse to receive from connecting lines of road or shippers any cars not equipped sufficiently, in accordance with the first section of this act, with such power or train brakes as will work and readily interchange with the brakes in use on its own cars, as required by this act. *When carriers may lawfully refuse to receive cars from connecting lines or shippers.*

Sec. 4. That from and after the first day of July, eighteen hundred any ninety-five, until otherwise ordered by the Interstate Commerce Commission, it shall be unlawful for any railroad company to use any car in interstate commerce that is not provided with secure grab irons or handholds in the ends and sides of each car for greater security to men in coupling and uncoupling cars. *Grab irons and handholds.*

Sec. 5. That within ninety days from the passage of this act the American Railway Association is authorized hereby to designate to the Interstate Commerce Commission the standard height of drawbars for freight cars, measured perpendicular from the level of the tops of the rails to the centers of the drawbars, for each of the several gauges of rail- *Standard height of drawbars for freight cars.*

roads in use in the United States, and shall fix a maximum variation from such standard height to be allowed between the drawbars of empty and loaded cars. Upon their determination being certified to the Interstate Commerce Commission, said Commission shall at once give notice of the standard fixed upon to all common carriers, owners, or lessees engaged in interstate commerce in the United States by such means as the Commission may deem proper. But should said association fail to determine a standard as above provided, it shall be the duty of the Interstate Commerce Commission to do so, before July first, eighteen hundred and ninety-four, and immediately to give notice thereof as aforesaid. And after July first, eighteen hundred and ninety-five, no cars, either loaded or unloaded, shall be used in interstate traffic which do not comply with the standard above provided for.

**Penalty for violation of the provisions of this act.** SEC. 6. That any such common carrier using any locomotive engine, running any train, or hauling or permitting to be hauled or used on its line any car in violation of any of the provisions of this act, shall be liable to a penalty of one hundred dollars for each and every such violation, to be recovered in a suit or suits to be brought by the United States district attorney in the district court of the United States having jurisdiction in the locality where such violation shall **Duty of United States district attorney.** have been committed, and it shall be the duty of such district attorney to bring such suits upon duly verified information being lodged with him of such violation having oc- **Duty of Interstate Commerce Commission.** curred. And it shall also be the duty of the Interstate Commerce Commission to lodge with the proper district attorneys information of any such violations as may come **Exceptions to the act.** to its knowledge: *Provided,* That nothing in this act contained shall apply to trains composed of four-wheel cars or to locomotives used in hauling such trains.

**Power of Interstate Commerce Commission to extend time of carriers to comply with this act.** SEC. 7. That the Interstate Commerce Commission may from time to time upon full hearing and for good cause extend the period within which any common carrier shall comply with the provisions of this act.

SEC. 8. That any employee of any such common carrier who may be injured by any locomotive, car, or train in use **Employee not deemed to assume risk of employment.** contrary to the provision of this act shall not be deemed thereby to have assumed the risk thereby occasioned, although continuing in the employment of such carrier after the unlawful use of such locomotive, car, or train had been brought to his knowledge.

Public No. 113, approved, March 2, 1893.

An act supplementary to the act of July first, eighteen hundred and sixty-two, entitled "An act to aid in the construction of a railroad and telegraph line from the Missouri River to the Pacific Ocean, and to secure to the Government the use of the same for postal, military, and other purposes," and also of the act of July second, eighteen hundred and sixty-four, and other acts amendatory of said first-named act.

*Be it enacted by the Senate and House of Representatives of the United States of America in Congress assembled*, That all railroad and telegraph companies to which the United States has granted any subsidy in lands or bonds or loan of credit for the construction of either railroad or telegraph lines, which, by the acts incorporating them, or by any act amendatory or supplementary thereto, are required to construct, maintain, or operate telegraph lines, and all companies engaged in operating said railroad or telegraph lines shall forthwith and henceforward, by and through their own respective corporate officers and employees, maintain, and operate, for railroad, Governmental, commercial, and all other purposes, telegraph lines, and exercise by themselves alone all the telegraph franchises conferred upon them and obligations assumed by them under the acts making the grants as aforesaid.

*Government aided railroad and telegraph lines must themselves maintain and operate*

SEC. 2. That whenever any telegraph company which shall have accepted the provisions of title sixty-five of the Revised Statutes shall extend its line to any station or office of a telegraph line belonging to any one of said railroad or telegraph companies, referred to in the first section of this act, said telegraph company so extending its line shall have the right and said railroad or telegraph company shall allow the line of said telegraph company so extending its line to connect with the telegraph line of said railroad or telegraph company to which it is extended at the place where their lines may meet, for the prompt and convenient interchange of telegraph business between said companies; and such railroad and telegraph companies, referred to in the first section of this act, shall so operate their respective telegraph lines as to afford equal facilities to all, without discrimination in favor of or against any person, company, or corporation whatever, and shall receive, deliver, and exchange business with connecting telegraph lines on equal terms, and affording equal facilities, and without discrimination for or against any one of such connecting lines; and such exchange of business shall be on terms just and equitable.

*Connecting telegraph lines.*

*Equal facilities required.*

SEC. 3. That if any such railroad or telegraph company referred to in the first section of this act, or company operating such railroad or telegraph line shall refuse or fail, in whole or in part, to maintain, and operate a telegraph line as provided in this act and acts to which this is supplementary, for the use of the Government or the public, for commercial and other purposes, without discrimination, or shall refuse or fail to make or continue such arrangements for the interchange of business with any connecting telegraph company, then any person, company, corporation, or connecting telegraph company may apply for relief to the Interstate Commerce Commission, whose duty it shall thereupon be, under such rules and regulations as said Commission may prescribe, to ascertain the facts, and determine and order what arrangement is proper to be made in the particular case, and the railroad or telegraph company concerned shall abide by and perform such order; and it shall be the duty of the Interstate Commerce Commission, when such determination and order are made, to notify the parties concerned, and, if necessary, enforce the same by writ of mandamus in the courts of the United States, in the name of the United States, at the relation of either of said Interstate Commerce Commissioners: *Provided*, That the said Commissioners may institute any inquiry, upon their own motion, in the same manner and to the same effect as though complaint had been made.

SEC. 4. That in order to secure and preserve to the United States the full value and benefit of its liens upon all the telegraph lines required to be constructed by and lawfully belonging to said railroad and telegraph companies referred to in the first section of this act, and to have the same possessed, used, and operated in conformity with the provisions of this act and of the several acts to which this act is supplementary, it is hereby made the duty of the Attorney-General of the United States, by proper proceedings, to prevent any unlawful interference with the rights and equities of the United States under this act, and under the acts hereinbefore mentioned, and under all acts of Congress relating to such railroads and telegraph lines, and to have legally ascertained and finally adjudicated all alleged rights of all persons and corporations whatever claiming in any manner any control or interest of any kind in any telegraph lines or property, or exclusive rights of way upon the lands of said railroad companies, or any of them, and to have all contracts and provisions of contracts set aside and annulled which have been unlawfully and beyond their powers entered into by said railroad or telegraph companies, or any of them, with any other person, company, or corporation.

Sec. 5. That any officer or agent of said railroad or tele- Penalties for failure to comply with the provisions of this act or the orders of the Interstate Commerce Commission. graph companies, or of any company operating the railroads and telegraph lines of said companies, who shall refuse or fail to operate the telegraph lines of said railroad or telegraph companies under his control, or which he is engaged in operating, in the manner directed in this act and by the acts to which it is supplementary, or who shall refuse or fail, in such operation and use, to afford and secure to the Government and the public equal facilities, or to secure to each of said connecting telegraph lines equal advantages and facilities in the interchange of business, as herein provided for, without any discrimination whatever for or adverse to the telegraph line of any or either of said connecting companies, or shall refuse to abide by, or perform and carry out within a reasonable time the order or orders of the Interstate Commerce Commission, shall in every such case of refusal or failure be guilty of a misdemeanor, and, on conviction thereof, shall in every such case be fined in a sum not exceeding one thousand dollars, and may be imprisoned not less than six months; and in every such case of refusal or failure the party aggrieved may not only cause the officer or agent guilty thereof to be prosecuted under the provisions of this section, but may also bring an action for the damages sustained Actions for damages may also be brought. thereby against the company whose officer or agent may be guilty thereof, in the circuit or district court of the United States in any State or Territory in which any portion of the road or telegraph line of said company may be situated; and in case of suit process may be served upon any agent of the company found in such State or Territory, and such service shall be held by the court good and sufficient.

Sec. 6. That it shall be the duty of each and every one Duty of railroad and telegraph lines subject to this act to file copies of contracts and a report with the Commission. of the aforesaid railroad and telegraph companies, within sixty days from and after the passage of this act, to file with the Interstate Commerce Commission copies of all contracts and agreements of every description existing between it and every other person or corporation whatsoever in reference to the ownership, possession, maintenance, control, use, or operation of any telegraph lines, or property over or upon its rights of way, and also a report describing with sufficient certainty the telegraph lines and property belonging to it, and the manner in which the same are being then used and operated by it, and the telegraph lines and property upon its right of way in which any other person or corporation claims to have a title or interest, and setting forth the grounds of such claim, and the manner in which the same are being then used and operated; and it shall be the duty of each and every one of said railroad and telegraph companies annually hereafter to report to the Interstate Commerce Commission, with reasonable fullness and certainty, the nature, extent, value, and condition of the telegraph lines and property then belonging to it, the gross earnings, and all expenses of maintenance, use, and operation thereof, and its relation and business with all connecting telegraph companies during the preceding year, at such time and in such manner as may be required by a system of reports which said Commission shall prescribe; and if any of said railroad or telegraph companies shall refuse or fail to make such reports or any report as may be called for by said Commission, or refuse to submit its books and records for inspection, such neglect or refusal shall operate as a for- feiture, in each case of such neglect or refusal, of a sum not less than one thousand dollars nor more than five thousand dollars, to be recovered by the Attorney-General of the United States, in the name and for the use and benefit of the United States; and it shall be the duty of the Interstate Commerce Commission to inform the Attorney-General of all such cases of neglect or refusal, whose duty it shall be to proceed at once to judicially enforce the forfeitures hereinbefore provided.

SEC. 7. That nothing in this act shall be construed to affect or impair the right of Congress, at any time hereafter, to alter, amend, or repeal the said acts hereinbefore mentioned; and this act shall be subject to alteration, amendment, or repeal as, in the opinion of Congress, justice or the public welfare may require; and nothing herein contained shall be held to deny, exclude, or impair any right or remedy in the premises now existing in the United States, or any authority that the Postmaster-General now has under title sixty-five of the Revised Statutes to fix rates, or, of the Government, to purchase lines as provided under said title, or to have its messages given precedence in transmission.

Public No. 237, approved, August 7, 1888.

○

CPSIA information can be obtained
at www.ICGtesting.com
Printed in the USA
BVHW04*1057170918
527708BV00014B/1359/P